MARY IN THE NEW TESTAMENT

Mary in
the New Testament

A Collaborative Assessment by Protestant and
Roman Catholic Scholars

Edited by

**Raymond E. Brown, Karl P. Donfried,
Joseph A. Fitzmyer, and John Reumann**

From discussions by

PAUL J. ACHTEMEIER	KARLFRIED FROEHLICH
MYLES M. BOURKE	REGINALD H. FULLER
RAYMOND E. BROWN	GERHARD KRODEL
SCHUYLER BROWN	J. LOUIS MARTYN
KARL P. DONFRIED	ELAINE H. PAGELS
JOSEPH A. FITZMYER	JOHN REUMANN

Sponsored by
the United States Lutheran—Roman Catholic Dialogue

PAULIST PRESS
New York/Mahwah

Library of Congress Cataloging in Publication Data
Main entry under title:

Mary in the New Testament.

Includes bibliographies and indexes.
1. Mary, Virgin—biblical teaching. 2. Bible. N.T.—Criticism, interpretation,
etc. I. Brown, Raymond Edward. II. Achtemeier, Paul J. III. United States
Lutheran-Roman Catholic Dialogue (Group).
BT611.M37   232.91   78-8797
ISBN   0-8091-2168-9

Published by

Fortress Press
Philadelphia, Pennsylvania

        and

Paulist Press
Mahwah, New Jersey

Manufactured in the United States of America

PREFACE

In 1973 a task force of NT scholars produced a collaborative study entitled *Peter in the New Testament*. They did this work at the request of the participants in the National Dialogue between Lutheran and Roman Catholic theologians who were then preparing a study on *Papal Primacy and the Universal Church*, the fifth volume in the series *Lutherans and Catholics in Dialogue* (Minneapolis: Augsburg, 1974).

The whole tone of that National Dialogue and its series of volumes had been governed by an effort to see in a *new* light the old problems that had been separating the churches. Certainly one of those problems was the claim of the papacy to authority over the church in terms of a succession to Peter. While discussing those claims, the theologians of the National Dialogue thought it would be helpful to see what modern biblical scholars with various church backgrounds could say in common about Peter's role in NT times. *Peter in the New Testament* was well received in scholarly circles, not only for the expertise of the contributors, but also because the ecumenical dimension of their work brought new insights. Perhaps the best testimony to the value of its contribution is the fact that it has been translated into German, French, Spanish, Dutch, and Japanese, along with a separate British edition. It has also been cited in the various ecumenical and interchurch dialogues about authority in the church, with respect to the papacy.

The scholars who took part in the discussions which produced *Peter in the New Testament* reported that working together was a learning experience that they wished to continue, and they proposed one more study on a very divisive topic in Christianity, namely, the role of Mary in Christian thought. As previously, they did not hope to settle all the ecumenical aspects of this question but only to ascertain what modern scholars could say in common about the picture of Mary in the various NT books. They approached the theologians of the National Lutheran/Roman Catholic Dialogue to inquire if such a biblical work could be useful to their discussions, as *Peter* had been. By this time the theologians had begun their discussion of papal infallibility and teaching authority. This was not a Marian subject; yet the definitions of the dogmas of the immaculate conception and the assumption of Mary were the most obvious exercises of the claim of papal infallibility, and therefore a Marian study would not be unrelated to the purposes of the Dialogue. Consequently the same sponsorship was given to the study of *Mary in the New Testament* as to the previous work on Peter.

We repeat here what we affirmed before. We know that some voices in Christendom have questioned both the propriety and the reliability of the critical approach to biblical research of which both the *Peter* and *Mary* volumes are examples. We ourselves recognize its limitations in reaching final theological conclusions. Nevertheless, it is our belief that responsible inquiry into original source material is a necessary task and should further our mutual understanding of issues that have vexed Christian relationships over the centuries. We rejoice that the task force, with four Lutheran and four Roman Catholic members, had the added participation of two Episcopalian members and two members of the Reformed tradition. This Marian biblical study is to the best of our knowledge a first on the subject in current ecumenical discussions and should be of service to many inter-Christian dialogues.

While this work has been carried on with all the techniques of scholarship, the editors have sought to phrase the results with an eye toward general intelligibility and pedagogical principles. The contributing scholars have understood that they are speaking not only to other scholars but also to the parish clergy and knowledgeable laity of the churches. We hope that that wide aim will make *Mary in the New Testament* useful for college, university, and seminary classrooms, as well as for more general discussion groups and adult education classes. Ample documentation and footnotes have been provided, for the experience with the previous volume on Peter has shown that such an ecumenical biblical study can serve as a resource in college religion classes and in seminars at theological schools.

All those who profit from this work will share our debt to the twelve scholars who worked without remuneration or royalty. Their generosity testifies to the importance they attribute to a study which is virtually unique as an ecumenical contribution. On behalf of the National Dialogue we express our appreciation to the Catholic Biblical Association of America and the Lutheran World Ministries for their financial contributions, and to the Auburn Program of Union Theological Seminary (N.Y.C.) for having placed its library reading room at the disposal of the task force for its meetings.

Paul C. Empie
Former General Secretary
U.S.A. National Committee
Lutheran World Federation

✠ T. Austin Murphy
Auxiliary Bishop of Baltimore
Bishops' Committee for Ecumenical and Interreligious Affairs

CONTENTS

CHAPTER ONE: ORIGINS OF THE STUDY*

Like the earlier work on Peter,[1] this study on Mary in the NT and other early Christian sources grows out of the National Lutheran-Catholic Dialogue, sponsored officially by the U.S.A. National Committee of the Lutheran World Federation (now Lutheran World Ministries) and the National Conference of Catholic Bishops. Since 1965 theologians from these two traditions have engaged in dialogue, producing joint statements on the creed, baptism, the eucharist, the ministry, and papal primacy, pub-

*The first draft of this chapter was composed by John Reumann.

[1]*Peter in the New Testament: A Collaborative Assessment by Protestant and Roman Catholic Scholars* (ed. R. E. Brown, K. P. Donfried, and J. Reumann; Minneapolis: Augsburg; New York: Paulist, 1973). British edition, London: Chapman, 1974. French translation by J. Winandy, *Saint Pierre dans le Nouveau Testament* (LD 79; Paris: Cerf, 1974). Spanish translation by J. Garcia-Abril Pérez, *Pedro en el Nuevo Testamento* (Palabra inspirada, 15; Santander: Sal Terrae, 1976). Dutch translation (without inclusion of footnotes) by E. de Bekker, *Petrus in het Geloof van de Jonge Kerk* (Boxtel: Katholieke Bijbelstiching, 1976), introduction by F. Haarsma. German translation by R. Mohr, *Der Petrus der Bibel: Eine ökumenische Untersuchung* (Stuttgart: Calwer-V. and Katholisches Bibelwerk, 1976), introduction by F. Hahn and R. Schnackenburg. Japanese translation by Y. Magaki (Tokyo: Seibunsha, 1977), introduction by J. Reumann.

lished in a series of five volumes which frequently reflect agreements on issues that have been divisive since the Reformation.[2] These findings have been discussed and appreciated far beyond Lutheran and Roman Catholic circles, and are sometimes cited in other bilateral dialogues as well as ecumenically in world Christian conversations.

The study of Peter was deliberately designed to include scholars other than Lutherans and Roman Catholics, not only in order to draw upon their knowledge and viewpoints, but also to make the resulting assessment even more widely useful. Even though *Peter in the New Testament* was important for Lutheran-Catholic dialogue on papal primacy,[3] the decision to publish it in a separate volume stemmed chiefly from a desire to make it more readily available to students of the NT, historians, and others not specifically engaged in a dialogue on the papacy. These facts, as well as their experience in the Petrine task force, were in the thinking of participants in that study when they expressed a willingness to continue their cooperative work by taking up the question of Mary in the NT, as the Preface has noted.

The National U.S. Dialogue divided its approach to the papacy into two parts, dealing first with "primacy" (1970-73), and then with the even more controverted topic of "infallibility" (1973-78), an immense subject with ramifications for the teaching office of the church, and "the truth of the gospel" itself (Gal 2:14). The National Dialogue will issue its own full report on infallibility and teaching authority in the church as *Lutherans and Catholics in Dialogue, Volume VI*. Related to this question and particularly neuralgic for those outside Roman Catholicism are the definitions

---

[2]*Lutherans and Catholics in Dialogue*, published jointly by representatives of the U.S.A. National Committee of the Lutheran World Federation (New York) and the Bishops' Committee for Ecumenical and Interreligious Affairs (Washington, D.C.): *I. The Status of the Nicene Creed as Dogma of the Church* (1965); *II. One Baptism for the Remission of Sins* (1966); *III. The Eucharist as Sacrifice* (1967); *IV. Eucharist and Ministry* (1970). The fifth volume, *Papal Primacy and the Universal Church*, was published by Augsburg (Minneapolis, 1974) which has also reprinted Volumes I, II, and III in one volume.

[3]See *Papal Primacy and the Universal Church*, 11, 13-16, 29, 34, and 38-42.

of the immaculate conception of the Blessed Virgin Mary by Pius IX (1854) and of her assumption by Pius XII (1950). These have become examples of that infallibility which Vatican I (1870) set forth, even if the Second Vatican Council has moved further ecclesiologically in the matter of the church and Mary. The National Dialogue devoted some attention to the Marian definitions, but only as case studies in the exercise of papal infallibility rather than as a separate topic.

Nevertheless, recognizing that mariology is an important and controversial subject in interconfessional discussion, the National Dialogue in 1975 authorized a study on Mary in the NT.[4] The present volume results from that authorization. However, while the study group on Mary has kept the National Dialogue informed of its procedures and progress, *Mary in the New Testament* is an independent project.[5] It will be helpful, we hope, to the U.S. Lutheran-Catholic Dialogue, but also to other Christians in ecumenical discussion and to students of the NT and of Christian origins.

Four persons were nominated by the National Dialogue and authorized to serve as both a steering committee and editors for this study on Mary. Beginning with participants in the Petrine project, the study group was expanded to include a larger number of Christian scholars of other than Lutheran and Roman Catholic affiliation, with deliberate attention to securing balance and representation in various areas of specialization. The study group consisted of the following persons:

---

[4]The action was taken at the twentieth meeting of the National Dialogue in St. Louis, on Jan. 31, 1975, authorizing "a study on Mary in the New Testament with Professors R. E. Brown, K. P. Donfried, J. A. Fitzmyer, and J. Reumann to draw up a proposal for procedure, with report back to the National Dialogue." Discussion at the twenty-first meeting at Washington, D.C. on Sept. 18, 1975, reiterated the formal sponsorship by the National Dialogue but with awareness that findings might not be tied as closely to the National Dialogue as in the case of *Peter* and *Papal Primacy*.

[5]Reports have been made through those who are participants in both the National Dialogue and the Marian study group, Professors Fitzmyer, Froehlich, and Reumann, but no attempt has been made to build the results of the Mary study into Volume VI of the National Dialogue.

1. Rev. Dr. Paul J. Achtemeier, Union Theological Seminary, Richmond, Virginia.
2. Rev. Msgr. Myles M. Bourke, Rector of Corpus Christi Church and Adjunct Professor at Fordham University, New York, New York.
3. Rev. Dr. Raymond E. Brown, S.S. (steering committee), Union Theological Seminary, New York, New York.
4. Rev. Dr. Schuyler Brown, S.J., General Theological Seminary, New York, New York.[6]
5. Rev. Dr. Karl P. Donfried (steering committee), Smith College, Northampton, Massachusetts.
6. Rev. Dr. Joseph A. Fitzmyer, S.J. (steering committee), The Catholic University of America, Washington, D.C.[7]
7. Dr. (Theol.) Karlfried Froehlich, Princeton Theological Seminary, Princeton, New Jersey.
8. Rev. Dr. Reginald H. Fuller, Protestant Episcopal Seminary, Alexandria, Virginia.
9. Rev. Dr. Gerhard Krodel, Lutheran Theological Seminary, Philadelphia, Pennsylvania.[8]
10. Dr. J. Louis Martyn, Union Theological Seminary, New York, New York.
11. Dr. Elaine H. Pagels, Barnard College, New York, New York.
12. Rev. Dr. John Reumann (steering committee), Lutheran Theological Seminary, Philadelphia, Pennsylvania.

In the spring and summer of 1975 plans were made and assignments agreed upon for the cooperative study. Between September 1975 and December 1976, the study group held ten sessions (including one double session), regularly three and a half hours in duration. The meetings took place in New York City in the Auburn Library of Union Theological Seminary.[9] As back-

---

[6]After Sept. 1, 1977, on the staff of the American Bible Society, New York City.

[7]Until August 1976, Weston School of Theology, Cambridge, Massachusetts.

[8]After Sept. 1, 1977, Lutheran Theological Seminary, Gettysburg, Pennsylvania.

[9]We are indebted to Union and Auburn Seminaries for this hospitality.

ground, the group had the pattern for research initiated by the steering committee; and for each segment of the topic there was a set of questions, a study guide, or a more extensive presentation laid out by the member assigned to lead that session.[10] On particularly difficult problems there were sometimes written memoranda submitted by participants. Passages which mention Mary directly or have been related to her were examined first from the Gospels, in the sequence Mark, Matthew, Luke/Acts, and John;[11] then from Paul, Revelation, and non-canonical, patristic, and Gnostic sources. OT passages and themes which have been applied to Mary were taken up where pertinent in connection with NT passages (when the latter have direct quotations from the Hebrew scriptures or their Greek translations) but also as a separate topic at the meeting of January 1976, led by Schuyler Brown. One or more sessions were devoted to each segment of the NT, as reflected in the chapters of this book. Detailed minutes were usually kept, sometimes based on tapes with a verbatim recording of the discussions. These minutes were circulated to test points of agreement or disagreement in written form.

The actual drafting and composition of the book, chapter by chapter, began in 1976 and continued into 1978. In each instance a first draft of the chapter was prepared and circulated to all twelve participants.[12] Reactions to this draft were sent by the respondents to R. E. Brown who prepared a second draft of the chapter on the basis of those reactions. The second draft was also circulated and corrected in light of the reactions of the respondents. When it was deemed useful, drafts in process were discussed at plenary sessions; and matters of substantial revision were often treated at meetings of the four editors (May, Dec. 1977; March 1978), to which other participants able to attend were invited. There was a final plenary meeting of the entire study group in April 1978 to insure ample consultation before going to press. The bibliographies (sometimes drawn from bibliographies already

---

[10]The first footnote in each chapter will report who led the session(s) on that topic, and when the session(s) occurred.

[11]For the rationale behind the sequence, see Chap. 2, B3-6.

[12]The first footnote in each chapter will also identify the author of the initial draft.

submitted with the individual chapters) were composed by K. P. Donfried and Schuyler Brown.

The group which previously worked on *Peter in the New Testament* made a self-reflective comment worth repeating here, for the study group on Mary had much the same experience: "It is significant that all those engaged in the task force enjoyed this form of collaborative study and learned immensely from it. The interchange opened new horizons for all, so that the end product was achieved, not so much by way of compromise and concession, but by way of mutual and creative discovery."[13] Again we have found that we profited in ways which do not always emerge at the seminars of professional biblical meetings. Each of us learned by making suggestions and by seeing them meet with opposition and even defeat in group discussion, without embarrassment to anyone. We learned how others think about Mary, looking at her from different traditions. Yet we found we shared a common regard for "the mother of Jesus," as the Fourth Gospel consistently entitles her. From the NT pictures of her we have learned afresh something of what faith and discipleship ought to mean within the family of God.

As in the work on Peter, we conclude with the observation that the assessment of Mary which follows has emerged as *a collective study*, one truly representative of discussions by a group of scholars. The end product is often not what anyone of us would have written individually; yet each member of the group contributed to it in various ways. "In the publication of our collaborative effort, individuals have at times agreed to the serious consideration of views that they would not choose to make their own. The norm was not total agreement, but a consensus about reasonable limits of plausibility. The editing, which consisted largely in giving intelligible expression and order to this variety of views, has also respected the collaborative nature of the project."[14]

---

[13]*Peter in the New Testament*, 4-5.
[14]*Ibid.*, 5.

CHAPTER TWO:
PRESUPPOSITIONS OF
THE STUDY*

In our study of the place of Mary in the NT writings, we shall
follow the methods and approaches ordinarily used in the contemporary study of these Scriptures. It may be useful at the outset to indicate them, so the reader will be prepared for the later
chapters.

A. The Nature of the New Testament Writings

In facing any issue in Christianity that has roots in the NT,
one must take into account both the evidence supplied by the NT
writings themselves, composed 1900 years ago, and the subsequent cultural and ecclesiastical traditions which have influenced Christian interpretations of those writings. The problem of
intervening traditions is particularly acute in the instance of
Mary, the mother of Jesus, for mariological attitudes in the post-
Reformation West have been sharply divergent. Rather than to
impose anachronistically on the NT questions raised by these
subsequent traditions, it has been our intention to follow a
method which would best allow the NT writings to speak for
themselves and to teach us afresh. It is our judgment that the

---

*The first draft of this chapter was composed by P. J. Achtemeier,
using as a guide the similar chapter in *Peter in the New Testament*.

historical-critical method,[15] carefully and intelligently used, provides us with the best tool for achieving such a goal. We hope that the attempt to hear the voice of the earliest Christians on Mary's place in God's plan of salvation will be useful to others who seek to understand and evaluate the later church traditions. Indeed, by treating briefly some of the second-century developments in Christian attitudes toward Mary (see 4, under C below), we shall seek to erect a bridge for the careful study of the relationship between NT Marian references and later mariology. Our concern for careful historical research, however, cautions us not to confuse these two areas.

While giving primary attention to the NT witness, we are not suggesting that the NT constitutes simple history or disinterested reporting. It was composed by believing Christians, with the result that the history contained therein is consistently perceived "in faith." We shall want to say things about the "Mary of history" in the following pages, but we do so with the full knowledge that such comments are being derived from writings that intend to communicate the faith of the primitive churches. One of our tasks will be to trace the way in which historical facts have been molded by Christians in their attempt to understand Mary's role in what God has wrought in Jesus Christ, and that investigation leads us to the problem of NT composition.

B. The Composition of the New Testament Books and Their Marian Content

We have decided to investigate in a roughly chronological sequence those NT writings that make reference to Mary. Such

---

[15]This method, while implying in itself no denial of divine inspiration, insists that in interpreting the Scriptures, scholars must apply to them the ordinary rules applicable to other bodies of literature. See E. Krentz, *The Historical-Critical Method* (Philadelphia: Fortress, 1975). The recognition of the implications of historical criticism was first achieved by Protestant scholars. More recently such criticism has been accepted by Roman Catholic scholars, particularly under the rubric of acknowledging the different literary forms present in the Bible (a principle advocated by Pope Pius XII in his 1943 encyclical *Divino Afflante Spiritu*). See *JBC*, arts. 41 and 71.

an approach implies judgments about when and how the writings were composed. Because it is important to ask what the first hearers/readers understood, as well as what an author intended, attention must always be paid to the circumstances, character, and interests of the community addressed.

1. The Letters of Paul

While the apostle Paul does not mention Mary by name in any of his letters, he does on occasion refer to the birth of Jesus (Rom 1:3-4; Gal 4:4-5), as well as make more general references to modes of birth (Gal 4:28-29). We shall investigate those passages to see if they cast any light on Jesus' birth from Mary. In the letters of concern to us,[16] generally dated to the fifties, Paul wants to make certain theological points with his readers or hearers; and a consideration of specific Pauline passages by a group of scholars interested in Mary must not overlook the larger intention with which those passages were written—an intention that may be quite different from that of our inquiry.

2. The Gospels

The mother of Jesus appears in all four Gospels, and as a group these writings constitute the major witness to Mary in the NT. While there may be common features or memories in their picture of Mary, each Gospel will be discussed separately. This is necessitated by our understanding of how the Gospels were composed.

(a) The Three Stages of Gospel Formation

The earliest and most basic level is represented by *Stage One*; it consists of the historic deeds and sayings on which the

---

[16]Namely, Philippians, Romans, and Galatians. For the purpose of this discussion it matters little whether one considers the authentic Pauline letters to be seven (1 Thessalonians, Galatians, Philippians, 1-2 Corinthians, Romans, Philemon) or ten (including also 2 Thessalonians, Colossians, Ephesians). Nor does the Deutero-Pauline character of the Pastorals (1-2 Timothy, Titus) affect our treatment.

Gospel narrative was based. *Stage Two* is marked by the formation of traditions about those events as they were interpreted
through the eyes of faith. Early Christians, according to their
different situations and concerns, selected deeds and sayings,
narrated them, and reflected on them theologically. This was the
work both of communities and individuals, especially the apostolic preachers. *Stage Three* is that of the four written Gospels,
where an individual evangelist entered the process of selecting,
combining, and rethinking the pre-Gospel traditions in order to
shape a narrative that represented his own theological view of
Jesus (and, presumably, to a large degree that of his community).

In order to answer questions about Mary we must work
backwards through these three stages. We possess the final Gospels and so we are better informed about *Stage Three* than about
the earlier stages. Our primary task, as we conceive it, is to report
how each evangelist understands Mary and her place in the salvation accomplished in and through Jesus. The last phrase in the
preceding sentence is extremely important, for we would not do
justice to the evangelist if we did not recognize that his primary
interest is Jesus. Despite Mary's prominence in the Lucan infancy
narrative, for example, that narrative tells us far more about
Luke's view of Jesus than about Mary's psychological attitudes.
Moreover, because we respect the theology of each evangelist,
we must be cautious when the same scene appears in two or three
Gospels—it may have a different nuance in each. Also, in the
process of determining the Gospel meaning of passages, the final
court of appeal must be the text as we have it before us, not a
reconstruction for which we have no evidence in the ancient texts
and versions. This is particularly important in the case of John,
where elaborate rearrangements of material to determine the
evangelist's "original gospel" have been proposed.

Where possible, it is also useful for us to attempt to press
back to *Stage Two* by seeing if we can discover the pre-Gospel
traditions about Mary. We shall be cautious here, but in some
instances we think we can recognize what represents tradition
(i.e., pre-Gospel tradition) as distinct from what represents redaction (the work of the evangelist). Often the tradition had its own
theological outlook, and the really important question in relation

to *Stage Two* is whether or not the theological outlook of this pre-Gospel tradition about Mary was preserved by the respective evangelists or changed by them.

It is when we press back to *Stage One* that we come to the "Mary of history." The classical quest in Gospel scholarship has been for the "Jesus of history"; and it is well-known that, despite the centrality of Jesus in the Gospel material, the quest for the historical Jesus is difficult indeed. In *Peter in the New Testament*, we were careful not to neglect the quest for the historical Simon (Cephas, Peter). But there is less Gospel material referring to Mary than to Peter, and so our quest will be even more difficult here. With the exception of the four chapters of infancy narrative in Matthew and Luke, the Gospel accounts concern the *ministry* of Jesus; and there are indications that Mary did not follow Jesus about during the ministry but remained at home with the family.[17] Consequently, she is mentioned only a few times, and we are thus given little chance to determine her historical attitudes and actions during the ministry. The real issue pertaining to *Stage One* may be that of keeping it distinct from Stages Two and Three. In a pre-critical period of biblical interpretation it was often presumed that the evangelists were narrating uninterpreted history, so that the detection of the Gospel-meaning was the detection of history. For the most part, both scholarship and the churches have moved beyond this simplistic understanding. But even with the advent of criticism, there is a tendency to confuse Stage Two with Stage One and to think that if one can get behind the Gospel to earlier sources, one has history. Our insistence that the three stages must be kept distinct arises not from a negative spirit or skepticism but from a desire to respect the nature of the Gospels as works of faith, written to bring out the religious meaning of what

---

[17]In Mark 3:31 and Luke 8:19 Mary *comes* with Jesus' brothers to where Jesus is, and Mark 3:21 implies that they had set out from another place on this journey. In Mark 6:1-3 and Matt 13:53-55, when Jesus goes from the Sea of Galilee and comes to "his own country," the people of that region mention the presence among them of Jesus' mother, and brothers, and sisters. Mary is portrayed at Cana in Galilee (and thus near Nazareth) in John 2:1-11; and afterwards (2:12) she and his brothers go down with Jesus to Capernaum but stay there only a few days.

they narrate, rather than as works designed to answer our historical curiosity.

(b) The Infancy Narratives

By way of exception to the above comments about general
Gospel formation, some remarks are appropriate concerning the
"infancy narratives" which introduce the Gospels of Matthew
and Luke. Each narrative has its peculiarities which will be better
discussed when we treat Mary's role in Matthew and in Luke.
Here our concern is centered on how the infancy material in
general differs from the rest of the Gospel material.

Intrinsic to *Stage One* described above, centered on the historic words and deeds of Jesus, is the fact that some of those who
were followers of Jesus during the ministry became members of
the post-resurrectional church; and so there is a high probability,
and even moral certitude, that eyewitnesses brought over into
Christian tradition historical reminiscences of what Jesus did and
said. In Acts 1:21-22 Luke calls attention to "the men who have
accompanied us during all the time the Lord Jesus went in and out
among us, beginning from the baptism by John until the day when
he was taken up from us." For information about the events surrounding Jesus' birth, however, we have no possibility of such
direct apostolic eyewitness—no one would seriously suggest that
Peter, or Andrew, or the sons of Zebedee were present at
Bethlehem. Therefore, we have no way of knowing that the infancy narratives are rooted in the kind of eyewitness reminis-
cence that stands at the font of the Gospel tradition about the
public ministry of Jesus.

Because Joseph features prominently in Matthew's infancy
narrative and Mary features prominently in Luke's infancy narrative, it has been suggested (at least in the pre-critical age of biblical scholarship) that Joseph and Mary supplied the eyewitness
verification for the infancy material. It must be emphasized that
this is a sheer guess, supported by nothing in the subsequent
information in the NT about Mary or, *a fortiori*, about Joseph
(who never appears in the public ministry of Jesus and was probably dead by that time). Moreover, this theory of family eyewitness tradition faces two serious objections.

First, not a single item of peculiarly infancy narrative information is clearly verified anywhere else in the NT,[18] e.g., that John the Baptist was of priestly descent and was related to Jesus; that Jesus was virginally conceived and born at Bethlehem; that people like the magi, King Herod the Great, the chief priests, and the shepherds heard that the Messiah had been born; that Jesus had been in Egypt. In fact some of these items of information in the infancy narrative information are extremely difficult to reconcile with information in the Gospel accounts of Jesus' ministry. If the Baptist was a relative of Jesus (Luke 1:36), how awkward is the portrait in the Fourth Gospel (1:33) where he says of Jesus, "I myself did not know him." If so many people knew about Jesus' birth in the Davidic city of Bethlehem and the claim that he was the Messiah, how is it that those who knew him well at Nazareth are dumbfounded when he shows marks of greatness and a religious calling (Matt 13:53-58)? If Herod the Great knew of Jesus' birth and persecuted him, why does the son of Herod the Great not know Jesus, and why does he confuse him with the Baptist (14:1-2)? If it was known from Jesus' infancy that he was the Messiah, the Son of God, why is this such a startling discovery and revelation later on (Matt 16:16-17)?

The *second* objection against positing a detailed eyewitness tradition behind the infancy narratives is that Matthew 1-2 and Luke 1-2 agree between themselves on very few points.[19] The annunciation of the forthcoming conception of Jesus is given to Mary in Luke; yet long after Mary is pregnant Joseph knows nothing of this, according to Matthew. Matthew makes no men-

---

[18]An exception to this rule is Luke 3:2 which calls John "the son of Zechariah," the only reference outside the Lucan infancy narrative to the parentage of John the Baptist. But coming immediately after chaps. 1-2, this exception is not significant, since it is obviously a Lucan harmonization of the Baptist material in chap. 3 with what has gone before.

[19]Brown (*Birth*, 34-35) lists eleven points of agreement, the most important of which are: a chronological reference to the reign of Herod the Great; the parents are Mary and Joseph who are married but have not yet come to live together; Joseph is of Davidic descent; an angel announces the conception of the child through the Holy Spirit and directs that the child be named Jesus; the birth takes place at Bethlehem; ultimately the family goes to Nazareth.

tion of the (Lucan) census that is supposed to have brought
Joseph and Mary from Nazareth to Bethlehem; rather he seems
to indicate that Mary and Joseph were natives of Bethlehem
where they lived in a house (2:11). Luke mentions nothing of magi
or of persecution of Jesus by Herod. In fact, the peaceful pilgrim-
age of Mary and Joseph from Bethlehem to Jerusalem (Luke
2:23-40) and their uneventful return to Nazareth stand in stark
contrast, even contradiction, to Matthew's story of a flight for
their lives from Bethlehem to Egypt.

These two obstacles to positing family traditions behind the
infancy narratives are supplemented by the uniqueness of the OT
coloring in these narratives. Matthew's Joseph echoes the
Genesis picture of Joseph who received revelation in dreams
(37:19: "the dreamer" [literally, "the master of dreams"]) and
who went to Egypt. Matthew's description of King Herod's
slaughter of the male children of Bethlehem, while the infant
Jesus was spared, echoes the Pharaoh's execution of the male
children of the Hebrews, from which the infant Moses was
spared. (Matt 2:20b virtually quotes Exod 4:19.) Luke's description of Zechariah and Elizabeth echoes the Genesis description of
Abraham and Sarah (cf. Luke 1:18 and Gen 15:8; 17:17). Luke's
description of the parents' presentation of Jesus in the Temple,
where he was greeted by Simeon, echoes the presentation of
Samuel by his parents in the central shrine, where he was received
by Eli (1 Sam 1:24; 2:20)—even as the Magnificat of Jesus' mother
echoes the canticle of Hannah, Samuel's mother (1 Sam 2:1-10).
Such echoes raise the possibility that much of the story of Jesus'
infancy was not based on eyewitness memory but was shaped by
OT models, on the principle that the infancy of Jesus served as a
transition from the history of Israel to the Gospel story of Jesus'
ministry. These observations should make us very cautious when
we seek to press back to historical events from the evangelists'
portraits of Mary in the infancy narratives.

3. The Gospel of Mark

We have proceeded on the theory that Mark is the earliest of
the written Gospels, and that it was a source upon which Matthew

and Luke relied for a large portion of their material.[20] Of course, this is not the only possible solution to the problem of how the Synoptic Gospels are interrelated. For instance, a small number of scholars, Protestant and Roman Catholic, think that Mark was written after Matthew and Luke, and that Mark drew upon what those Gospels had in common.[21] No one of us, however, accepts that hypothesis; and to base a study of Mary on a hypothesis that has such minority acceptance would vitiate our goal of presenting results acceptable to most scholars. Nevertheless, in footnotes, from time to time, we shall point out how the various minority solutions of the Synoptic problem would affect the conclusions we have reached. Moreover, we stress that an acceptance of the general priority of Mark over Matthew and Luke does not commit us to the thesis that in every instance the Marcan version of a scene is the most primitive.[22]

It has been recognized from antiquity that the author whom we call Mark was himself not an eyewitness of the ministry of Jesus. But in the second-century (according to the tradition reported by Papias) it was suggested that Mark was "Peter's interpreter" who incorporated into the Gospel that apostle's

---

[20]See B. H. Streeter, *The Four Gospels: A Study of Origins Treating of the Manuscript Tradition, Sources, Authorship, & Dates* (London: Macmillan, 1927); B. de Solages, *A Greek Synopsis of the Gospels: A New Way of Solving the Synoptic Problem* (Leiden: Brill, 1959); Kümmel, *Introduction*, 56-80; J. A. Fitzmyer, "The Priority of Mark and the 'Q' Source in Luke," *Jesus and Man's Hope* (Perspective Books, 1; ed. D. G. Miller; Pittsburgh Theological Seminary, 1970), 1. 131-70; F. Neirynck, "La matière marcienne dans l'évangile de Luc," *L'Evangile de Luc: Problèmes littéraires et théologiques: Mémorial Lucien Cerfaux* (BETL 32; Gembloux: Duculot, 1973), 158-201. Further literature can be found in the notes in these writings.

[21]B. Orchard, *Matthew, Luke & Mark: The Griesbach Solution to the Synoptic Question* (Manchester: Koinonia, 1976).

[22]J. A. T. Robinson (*Redating,* 94) states: "Rather I believe that there was written (as well as oral) tradition underlying each of them [the Synoptic Gospels], which is sometimes preserved in its most original form by Matthew, sometimes by Luke, though most often, I would judge, by Mark." This affirmation of general Marcan priority by Robinson is interesting in light of his extraordinary (and virtually solitary) position that all the NT books are to be dated before A.D. 70.

eyewitness testimony. This theory of authorship was of greater concern to us in the book *Peter in the New Testament* than it is in a discussion of Mark's evidence about Mary. There we were not inclined to accept the Papias tradition at face value for a number of reasons,[23] and we have found no cause to change our mind. While we continue to use the traditional name "Mark," we recognize that we have no reliable knowledge about the identity of the author or about the identity of those who composed the traditions upon which the author drew; and what Mark gives us has to be evaluated upon its own merits, not upon the merits of ancient identifications of author or source.

Written in the late sixties (?), Mark supplies our earliest NT references to Mary by name.[24] These are found in 3:20-35 and in 6:1-6a. Fortunately, in both instances a knowledge of form criticism and of Marcan redactional (editing) technique enables us to detect the possibility of pre-Marcan traditions and sayings. Indeed, this very first material will enable us to exemplify for the reader the likelihood of differing views of Mary in *Stages Two* and *Three* of the Gospel tradition mentioned above. Although Mark makes no specific statement about Mary's virginal conception, we shall look carefully at passages where a few scholars have thought to find evidence for it, e.g., Mark 6:3. It is only in the post-NT period that we have evidence for a debate about whether, after Jesus (Mary's first-born — Matt 1:25; Luke 2:7), she and Joseph had other children. Nevertheless, we shall study Mark's attitude toward the "brothers" and "sisters" of Jesus and the possibility of determining the exact degrees of relationship involved.[25] We shall have to ask whether Mark had a negative view toward the family of Jesus (including Mary); and if so, whether he originated this view, or shared the attitude of his source.

---

[23] See *Peter in the New Testament* 12, n. 24.

[24] It is disputed whether or not there were references to Mary in "Q," the hypothetical written source (of an antiquity comparable to Mark) used by Matthew and Luke. In any case this tradition would be extant in written form only in Matthew and Luke.

[25] Matthew's information is not substantially different from Mark's on this point, so the treatment of the issue in Mark need not be repeated in the chapter on Matthew.

4. The Gospel of Matthew

As we have indicated above, we accept the common scholarly opinion that this Gospel drew upon Mark and upon "Q" (a collection of sayings-material known also to Luke). That is harmonious with the even more widespread thesis[26] that the evangelist was not Matthew (or Levi), one of the Twelve who followed Jesus, and was not an eyewitness of the ministry; rather he was an unknown "second-generation" Christian who wrote in the last third of the first century (the eighties?). Despite the later date, we do not rule out a priori the possibility or even likelihood that occasionally Matthew may have had access to traditions earlier than those contained in Mark; but in each instance the material under investigation will have to support such a claim.

In narrating the ministry of Jesus, Matthew has parallels (12:46-50; 13:53-58) to the two scenes in Mark where Mary appears or is mentioned, although there are variances in Matthew's accounts. As we shall see, these variances are to be related to the fact that Matthew, unlike Mark, has an "infancy narrative," in which Mary's conception of Jesus is described. This narrative, consisting of the first two chapters of Matthew, has a canonical parallel only in Luke; and so our main key to its meaning will be its conformity or lack of conformity with the style and theology of the rest of Matthew. We shall have to determine what Matthew himself conveys about Mary through the genealogy (1:2-17), the

---

[26]Many of those who think that Matthew was written prior to Mark reject any theory that Matthew was composed by an eyewitness. Although in 1911 the Roman Catholic Pontifical Biblical Commission taught both Matthean priority and substantial eyewitness origin for Matthew, in 1955 Catholics were given complete freedom with regard to such decrees (*JBC* art. 72, §§5, 6, 25, 28). There is the ancient claim of Papias (Eusebius, *History*, 3.39,16) that Matthew "compiled the sayings [*logia*] in the Hebrew language"; but the evaluation of this claim involves many difficulties: (a) we do not have any such collection in Hebrew or Aramaic; (b) we do not know whether it was a gospel similar to our canonical Gospels; (c) we have no idea how this collection of sayings is related to the Greek Gospel of Matthew; (d) we are uncertain of Papias' accuracy, since Eusebius (3.39,13) describes him as "a man of exceedingly little intelligence"; (e) Papias' corresponding information about Mark does not seem accurate (see above, n. 23).

annunciation (1:18-25), the formula citations of Scripture (e.g., of Isa 7:14 in Matt 1:23), and a passage such as 2:11 (where the magi find the child with "Mary his mother"). Yet, as emphasized earlier, we must keep in mind that both the placing of this material at the beginning of the Gospel and the story-line of the rest of the infancy narrative suggest that Matthew's main interest here is centered on Jesus, not on Mary. In his own words, Matthew is telling us about the birth of Jesus Christ (1:18); and in 2:11, 13, 14, 20, 21 ("the child and his mother"), the primary attention is directed to the child. After determining the Matthean intention in the infancy material, we shall also have to ask whether the narrative is entirely a Matthean composition, or whether there is some underlying pre-Matthean tradition pertinent to Mary and/or Jesus' birth.

5. *The Gospel of Luke*

We assume that, like the Gospel of Matthew, this Gospel was composed late in the first century and that the evangelist drew upon the Gospel of Mark, upon "Q," and upon some special material.[27] There is no ancient claim that the author was an eyewitness of the ministry. While we shall continue to use the traditional designation "Luke," there is no need for us to enter into the debate whether he was in fact Luke, the companion of Paul. The same author composed Acts after the Gospel;[28] but since there is only one mention of Mary in Acts (1:14) and that occurs before the main narrative opens, we shall weave the information in Acts into the Lucan Gospel picture of Mary.

---

[27]The question of Luke's special source(s) is a complicated one in the light of the "proto-Luke" hypothesis advanced by B. H. Streeter (1924). Streeter maintained that Luke drew upon an ancient narrative source, independent of Mark, into which the "Q" material had already been fused. He regarded Proto-Luke and Mark as of approximately equal historical value. Without committing ourselves to such a theory, we have recognized the possibility of material independently available to Luke ("L"). For a recent discussion of Luke's sources, see Fitzmyer, "The Priority of Mark" (see above, n. 20).

[28]Acts 1:1 mentions a *first* book; for a discussion of the sequence of the Lucan writings, see Kümmel, *Introduction*, 150-51.

In narrating the ministry, Luke (8:19-21; 4:16-30) has parallels to the two scenes in Mark where Mary appears or is mentioned, but with even greater variances than appear in Matthew's Gospel—indeed, there is a possibility that in 4:16-30 Luke may be drawing on a tradition other than Mark 6:1-6a. Moreover, Luke has an additional reference to Mary in 11:27-28; it resembles the motif of 8:19-21, so that some would speak of a duplicate tradition.

Looming larger in the popular imagination than the additional references to Mary in Acts and in the ministry account is the Lucan treatment of Mary in the infancy narrative. Even as did the author of Matthew, Luke has prefaced his Gospel with two chapters pertaining to the events that surrounded Jesus' conception, birth, and youth. The Lucan account is much longer than the Matthean account and gives a prominent place to John the Baptist, who is never mentioned in the Matthean infancy narrative. For our purposes, however, the most interesting aspect of the Lucan infancy narrative is the prominence given to Mary. The annunciation of Jesus' conception, which in Matthew was directed to Joseph, is addressed by the angel to the virgin Mary (Luke 1:26-38); she visits her relative Elizabeth who greets her as "the mother of my Lord" (1:43); according to most textual witnesses she recites a hymn of praise, the Magnificat (1:46-55); she gives birth to Jesus at Bethlehem (2:1-20); she presents him in the Temple and is greeted by Simeon (2:22-40); and she features prominently in the scene of the finding of Jesus in the Temple at age twelve (2:41-52). Since Luke twice tells us that Mary *kept* all these things pondering them in her heart (2:19, 52), we shall be interested primarily in whether there is a unity between the portrait of Mary in the infancy narrative and the Lucan portrait of her in the ministry after Jesus has begun to speak publicly. But we shall also be interested in the possibility of pre-Lucan traditions—the plural being used advisedly—since the hymnic material (e.g., the Magnificat) may well be of different origin from the rest of the material. And if we press beyond *Stage Two* to *Stage One*, the question of the "Mary of history" is particularly acute here; for some have read Luke's reference to eyewitnesses (1:2) to include Mary who would have pondered over the infancy events in her heart (2:19, 51). On the other hand, historical difficulties about Luke's information on the census (2:1-4) and on the customs of presentation and purification (2:22-24) will have to be considered.[29]

We have already cautioned that in discussing Mary in the Gospels we must not let our inquiry obscure the fact that the evangelist's primary interest is in Jesus, not in Mary. This caution needs re-emphasis in the instance of Luke whose work is so carefully orchestrated in the service of an overarching theology and christology. Luke's interest in the parents of Jesus in the infancy narrative, for example, is partially determined by the parallelism that he sets up between them and the parents of John the Baptist. His interest in the presentation of the infant Jesus in Jerusalem at the beginning of the Gospel is partially determined by the parallelism that he sets up in having Jesus in Jerusalem at the end of the Gospel.

6. The Gospel of John

Despite the ancient attribution of the Fourth Gospel to John, son of Zebedee and companion of Jesus, we accept the common scholarly view that it was composed by an anonymous "second-generation" Christian.[30] The Fourth Gospel was probably the last of the Gospels to be written (nineties?). The disputed question of the Johannine relation to the Synoptic Gospels[31] is not of concern to us here, for none of the scenes in which Mary appears in the Synoptic Gospels is duplicated in John. Without ever being iden-

---

[29]The great difficulty of reconciling the Lucan infancy narrative with the Matthean infancy narrative would also have to be kept in mind, although some who would defend Lucan historicity regard Matthew's account as basically an imaginative retelling of OT stories (e.g., the birth of Moses).

[30]We do *not* identify the evangelist with "the disciple whom Jesus loved" (mentioned in John 19:35 and 21:24 as a source for the Gospel's testimony). It is not necessary for our purposes here to take a position on whether or not that beloved disciple was John, son of Zebedee, or on whether the evangelist was a follower of the beloved disciple, a theory that might establish a chain of eyewitness tradition.

[31]The thesis of a basic Johannine independence of the Synoptics has

tified by name, the mother of Jesus appears at the beginning of the ministry in John as the one whose petition leads to the changing of water to wine at Cana, the first of Jesus' signs. She reappears in the company of "the disciple whom Jesus loved" at the end of the ministry, as they stand at the foot of the cross, where Jesus addresses them and establishes a new family relationship between them. These scenes are not found in the Synoptic tradition, although the possibility has been raised that they are the Johannine equivalents of Synoptic motifs. Because the scenes are peculiarly Johannine, the task of pressing back to pre-Johannine traditions (*Stage Two*) and even to history (*Stage One*) is peculiarly difficult. However, they offer abundant material for *Stage Three* study: the symbolism that the mother of Jesus has for the evangelist; the question of her role in reference to Jesus and the Johannine community; and the possible OT motifs that may be echoed in the Johannine description and dialogue.

7. *The Book of Revelation or the Apocalypse*

We rejected the theory (debated even in antiquity) that this apocalypse was the work of the author of the Fourth Gospel. However, we saw no reason to deny its attribution to an otherwise unknown[32] Christian prophet named John (Rev 1:1), who probably wrote at the end of the first century (nineties?) in order to strengthen the faithful in Asia Minor at a time of persecution by the Roman authorities. We regarded as fanciful and contrary to the apocalyptic literary genre any attempt to find in the book a systematic prediction of events of the distant future, even of the end of the world. In part, it must be interpreted through its similarities to Jewish works with strains of apocalyptic (Ezekiel,

---

become the majority opinion in Fourth Gospel research. Especially influential on this point were the works of P. Gardner-Smith, *Saint John and the Synoptic Gospels* (Cambridge: University Press, 1938) and of C. H. Dodd, *Historical Tradition in the Fourth Gospel* (Cambridge: University Press, 1963).

[32]Theories identifying him with other men named John in the first century (John the Presbyter mentioned by Papias; John the Baptist) have little to recommend them.

Daniel, *4 Ezra, 2-3 Baruch*), which were also written with abundant (and re-used) symbolism in times of persecution.

There is no specific mention of Mary in Revelation. In 12:1-17, however, there is a highly symbolic portrait of a woman who gives birth to a child "who is to rule over all the nations with a rod of iron"—a description taken from Psalm 2 which indicates that the child is the Davidic Messiah. In later mariology this woman was identified as Mary; and we shall have to test whether this identification is consonant with the intentions of the prophet John, either on a primary or on a secondary level. The reference to "the rest of her offspring" in 12:17 (seemingly Christians) and the description of the woman as appearing in the heaven surrounded by the sun, the moon, and the stars (12:1), as well as the close connection of the birth with being snatched off to God (12:5), complicates any identification of Mary with the woman who gives birth to the messianic child.

C. Theological Method in Evaluating New Testament Evidence

It is not too difficult to reach a considerable degree of scholarly agreement on the authorship and date of the pertinent NT writings and to recognize the passages that must be studied. But the principal and more difficult task of this book will be the exegesis of those passages. Inevitably there will be a certain amount of disagreement in that interpretation, and we shall report differences of opinion (and whether or not they cut across confessional lines), so that the work will be truly useful to those who wish to know "what scholars are saying." However, the import of our relatively large amount of *agreement* is missed unless the reader sees that there is also an agreement on some theological implications of NT exegesis. Therefore, it seems wise to spell out these agreed-upon attitudes at the beginning of our study.

1. New Testament Pluralism

We have accepted the fact that there is clear diversity of knowledge and judgment among the NT writers. This recognition does not deny that the Scriptures are the word of God who is One; rather it affirms that this word has been expressed through the insight and writing of human authors, no one of whom has more than a partial glimpse of "the breadth and length and height and depth" of the revelation in Jesus Christ. A recognition of this diversity or pluralism is ancient, for the church resisted attempts to give greater uniformity to the Christian Scriptures, e.g., that of Marcion who would have had a short canon of NT books[33] which could be interpreted as rejecting the OT heritage; and that of Tatian who in his *Diatessaron* harmonized the four Gospels into a single life of Christ. Today, with a more critical exegesis, however, we are aware of many diversities that our forefathers harmonized; and we have tried to respect that greater awareness.

First, on an exegetical level we have resisted interpreting one author through information or theological outlook supplied by another. For instance, Simeon's prophecy in Luke 2:35 that a sword would pierce through Mary's soul is admittedly obscure, but we have insisted that it must be explained through information supplied by Luke/Acts itself. Thus, we have rejected attempts to interpret it in the light of the scene in John 19:25-27 where the mother of Jesus stands at the foot of the cross. Luke shows no knowledge of that scene: in the Lucan crucifixion the women from Galilee stand at a distance (23:49); and the mother of Jesus is never mentioned among the women present in the scenario of crucifixion and empty tomb (24:10). Or to mention another example, the only explicit references to Mary's conceiving as a virgin occur in the Matthean and Lucan infancy narratives. While we have been willing to discuss the *possibility* that Paul, Mark, and John knew of such a tradition, we have firmly rejected the argument that *surely* they knew what Matthew and Luke reported. In our judgment the burden of proof lies in the opposite direction, namely, on those who wish to show an implicit knowledge of the virginal conception in works which have

---

[33]Marcion's canon consisted of the Gospel of Luke (minus the infancy narrative) and ten of the Pauline letters (without the Pastorals)—he read Paul's opposition to the Law as a rejection of the OT. His attitude served as a catalyst in the Church's acceptance of a wider canon which showed a proper appreciation of the OT.

no explicit reference to it.[34] Furthermore, we have felt no compulsion to reconcile diverse information.[35] The Matthean infancy narrative seems to assume that Mary and Joseph lived in Bethlehem before the flight into Egypt: it pictures them as living in a house there when the magi came (2:11), and it takes great pains to explain why they did not return to Judea from Egypt but went instead to Galilee. Luke, on the other hand, is quite specific that for Mary and Joseph Nazareth was "their own city" (2:39; 1:26-27); and he introduces the motif of the census to explain how they happened to be in Bethlehem when Jesus was born (2:1-6). His description of the circumstances of birth makes it clear that they had no house of their own at Bethlehem (2:7).

Second, and more important, we have allowed for quite different outlooks on Mary among the NT authors. Paul places no emphasis on Mary, although the fact that his letters are problem-oriented cautions us against sweeping conclusions from silence. The Marcan references, at least in the interpretation that seemed most plausible to us, do not present Mary during the ministry as belonging to the new family of Jesus constituted by the proclamation of the kingdom and characterized by discipleship and doing God's will (3:31-35). Indeed, the Marcan Jesus seems to receive neither understanding nor honor from his own relatives (3:21; 6:4). Luke, on the other hand, presents Mary as the first to hear and accept the will of God about Jesus (1:38); and during the

---

[34]For example, Miguens, *Virgin Birth*.

[35]To some this may seem a rejection of biblical inerrancy. Yet "inerrancy" has had a varied acceptance in the traditions of the different Christian churches, and some would even reject it as unbiblical. A Lutheran scholar's reflections are presented by A. C. Piepkorn, "What Does 'Inerrancy' Mean?" *CTM* 36 (1965), 577-93. Roman Catholic readers of this book may note the limitations which Vatican Council II put on the range of biblical inerrancy: "The Books of Scripture must be acknowledged as teaching firmly, faithfully, and without error that truth which God wanted put into the Sacred Writings for the sake of our salvation" (*Dei Verbum* III, 11). In the example cited in the text above, confusion on the part of one or both NT authors as to Mary's original place of residence could be tolerated by Catholics loyal to Vatican II, since that piece of geographical information is scarcely a truth intended by God "for the sake of our salvation."

ministry Luke seems to include the mother and brothers of Jesus as examples of the seed that falls on good soil by hearing the word of God and holding it fast (8:15, 21). An older generation of interpreters would have tended either to read Mark through Luke's eyes or to interpret Luke 8:19-21 through the more negative Marcan parallel (3:31-35). We respect differences in the accounts.

Moreover, besides accepting such diversities, we have insisted that they form a part of "the NT picture of Mary," which now ceases to be a uniform picture. In the previous discussions on *Peter in the New Testament* we spoke of tracing a "trajectory" of NT views of Peter. Perhaps the term trajectory, borrowed from missile plotting, is too mechanical to describe what we mean; for it may imply that the direction is always forward and is determined from the beginning or launching.[36] However, we do wish to keep the idea that the NT picture is neither static nor uniform, that there is change from one period to another, and that there is diversity even within roughly contemporary Christian communities. Moreover, as we shall see below, we wish to indicate that the picture does not close with the NT and that lines of development in the biblical picture continue in the second century.

2. The Canonical Status of a Pluralistic New Testament

All the scholars participating in this study (and the confessions to which they adhere) agree on a canon of 27 NT books. The very notion of a canon or norm implies a responsibility of the churches to these NT writings and the word they proclaim. Obviously, this question of responsibility becomes more difficult when we recognize a diversity of views among the NT authors. If Christians today wish to be responsible to the biblical view of Mary, how is that done if there are several biblical views? In point of

---

[36]For objections to the term "trajectory," see J. Reumann, "Exegetes, Honesty, and the Faith," *CurTM* 5 (1978), 16-32. Perhaps a better term is "line of development," a translation of *Entwicklungslinie*; but all these terms, it should be remembered, are being used in an analogous way.

fact, we suspect that Christians of the past implicitly recognized that there were diverse views in the NT, and that in being faithful to the NT they were, knowingly or unknowingly, being faithful to certain sections of the NT, while benignly neglecting others. But if we leave aside judgments about the past, the formal recognition of diversity makes implicit or unknowing preferences more difficult. In the desire for a more open recognition of the problem, modern scholarship has called attention to the issue of a "canon within the canon"[37] — a recognition that within the large canon of 27 books, there is often a select group of NT writings which (for historical and/or theological reasons) are regarded as more central or normative than others, and hence in a certain sense as more canonical. Thus, in the present instance, one group might argue that, if there is a difference between the Marcan and Lucan views of Mary, Mark is the earlier Gospel and hence the one to be favored. Another group might contend that under the guidance of the Spirit Luke found Mark's view inadequate, and the Lucan view is the more mature and better balanced. However, such selectivity may be an inadequate response to the diversity.

As scholars belonging to different confessions, we recognize that in many theological issues our churches have in fact (and again perhaps unknowingly) given preference to what today would be recognized as one NT position when in fact there were others. We are not necessarily denigrating that preference since we may believe that God guided our confessions or traditions in making their choices. But in describing the diversity of the NT picture, we are seeing for ourselves that the emphasis of other Christian confessions may also have biblical warrant or basis. Thus the real challenge may be to invite the various confessions, which have recognized a diversified NT as canonical, to respect diversity within their own views of a topic like mariology, and to give more attention to NT attitudes hitherto underplayed. So

---

[37]For discussions in English of this complicated problem, see E. Käsemann, "The Canon of the New Testament and the Unity of the Church," *Essays on New Testament Themes* (SBT 41; London: SCM, 1964); R. E. Brown, *JBC* art. 67, §§92-97; W. Marxsen, *The New Testament as the Church's Book* (Philadelphia: Fortress, 1972).

conceived, diversity does not challenge canonicity but reinforces it against unconscious selectivity; it does not destroy the peculiar genius of individual confessions but calls attention to a wealth that might otherwise be overlooked.

3. *The Relation between History and Tradition*

When we discussed above (B2a) the three stages of Gospel formation, we insisted that often biblical scholarship is most competent in reference to *Stage Three*: the meaning intended by the evangelist and his theological view of Mary. As scholarship pushes back to *Stage Two*, i.e., the existence of pre-Gospel traditions and the view of Mary in those hypothetical traditions, it enters a more speculative realm. And we recognized the severe limitations the material puts upon scholarship in its attempt to reach *Stage One* and determine the historical events constituting Mary's role. Thus an investigation such as ours is far more certain about theology than it can ever be about history. This limitation must be taken seriously and yet evaluated properly.

First, we must resist the tendency to jump in either direction from our limited control of historicity. On the left, there is a tendency to judge that, because historicity cannot be proved, the events described were not historical. On the right, because of traditional Christian respect for the veracity of the Scriptures, there is an even stronger tendency to judge that, while historicity cannot be proved, it is likely that the events described were historical. In point of fact, one cannot state an a priori likelihood in this question. When historicity cannot be established with overwhelming probability, the likelihood of historicity or nonhistoricity must be judged on the basis of the evidence pertinent to *each* event or saying transmitted in the NT or the Gospels. Thus, for instance, the historicity of the census described by Luke cannot be presupposed on the basis of a general credence in Lucan reliability. It must be discussed on the basis of such evidence as is offered in Roman history and Jewish history. If the probabilities are strongly against historicity, the rebuttal that one still does not have 100% certitude that there was no census such as Luke describes really becomes an evasion based on the false supposition that historicity is to be presupposed unless disproved. Such a presupposition is invalid in writings that do not have history as their primary goal.

Second, uncertainties about the historicity of some NT events or sayings in which Mary figures does not render our investigation fruitless. Precisely since the NT writings were documents of faith, our greater ability to determine the theology of the author and his community corresponds to their nature. Whether based on history or not, the mariology of Mark, Matthew, Luke, and John emerges; and thus we learn how our Christian ancestors looked upon Mary. For some modern readers only history is important; but in Christian theology a succession to the *faith* of the apostolic era has been more important. Whether or not Mary was the first Christian disciple may be theologically less important than the conclusion that Luke presents her thus.[38] After all, those Christians who in any form believe in the inspiration of Scripture must recognize that the Holy Spirit chose to give us Luke's theological account of Jesus rather than an eyewitness and verbatim record, written on the spot.

4. The Relation of the Biblical Evidence to Post-biblical Mariology

In the course of centuries mariology has had an enormous development,[39] and most of it lies outside the focus of our study. However, one area of this later mariology is so close to our NT study that we have devoted a chapter of our book to it, namely, the second-century evidence pertinent to Mary in the apocryphal gospels and in the patristic writers. We detected a variety of views about Mary in the NT itself and some possible lines of development from one view to the other; therefore second-century developments were important to us since they might stand in continuity with the first-century views and help to confirm our diagnosis. Moreover, we thought that an investigation of the second century would serve as a useful bridge for scholars who might

---

[38]See the perceptive study of P. Minear, "The Interpreter and the Birth Narratives," *SymBU* 13 (1950), 1-22.

[39]A very readable account is offered by Graef, *Mary*.

wish to study the relationship of later Marian theology to the NT.

The formal study of other mariological questions, even though they have some relation to the Bible, would lie beyond the chosen scope of our work. For instance, in some Roman Catholic mariology, there is a study of how Mary's role was foreshadowed in certain OT passages, on the principle that, just as God prepared the way for His Son in the history of Israel, so too He prepared the way for the mother of His Son. Among the more prominent passages in such a discussion are: (a) Gen 3:15, where God says to the serpent, "I will put enmity between you and the woman, and between your seed and her seed; it [the seed] shall bruise your head, and you shall bruise its heel";[40] (b) Isa 7:14, where the prophet says to King Ahaz, "Behold, the young girl is (or shall be) with child and shall give birth to a son, and she will call his name Emmanuel";[41] (c) the female portrait of "Wisdom" in Prov 8; Sir 24; Wis 7:24ff.;[42] (d) the female personification of Israel or Zion, and the figure of the Daughter of Zion, especially when she is pregnant and is promised joy after the birth of her child (Isa 66:7-14; Zeph 3:14-20).

Some of these passages are cited explicitly or perhaps im-

---

[40]In the Hebrew text of Gen 3:15 the word for "seed" is the masculine noun *zera'*, used in the collective sense of "offspring." In the second part of the verse it is resumed by the masc. pronoun *hû'*, which is properly translated "it," as a reference to the collective offspring. Yet Christian tradition has usually understood the singular masculine pronoun to refer to Christ, sometimes translating it as "he," an individual offspring. Since the consonants *hw'* were sometimes pointed in the Masoretic tradition as feminine (*hî'* — see Gen 3:20; 23:15), a basis was offered for the reading *ipsa*, "she," in Latin Vulgate manuscripts. This reading, which has the woman crushing the head of the serpent, reinforced the mariological understanding of Gen 3:15 in the Western church.

[41]This passage was cited by Christians according to the LXX as quoted in Matt 1:22-23: "Behold the *virgin* will be with child" (see below, Chap. 5, nn. 192-195).

[42]The NT already begins to describe Jesus as divine Wisdom (compare Luke 11:49 with Matt 23:34; also see Heb 1:2-3; 1 Cor 1:24; Col 1:15). However, the fact that both in Hebrew and Greek "Wisdom" is feminine in gender and that in some passages (Prov 8:22) she is created by God led ultimately to a shift of reference from Jesus to Mary, especially in the liturgy.

plicity in the NT, and we shall discuss them in appropriate places in the book;[43] but some general remarks on the Christian use of the OT are in order here. A theory of the foreshadowing of the NT in the OT reflects, at times, a naïve or precritical understanding of prophecy, as if the Israelite prophets foresaw in detail the career of Jesus. Most modern scholars would maintain that the OT prophets dealt with their own time and the immediate future, and not with far distant Christian history. A somewhat more subtle form of the theory of foreshadowing sees the intention of God reflected in passages of the OT without the human author's knowledge, whence the claim for a "fuller sense" (*sensus plenior*)[44] which God has placed in the Scriptures to be discovered at a later period. Still other scholars refuse to speculate about what God intended by way of Christian reference when He inspired an OT passage and prefer to concentrate on what the NT author read out of the OT. Yet even then it is difficult to decide when a Christian interpretation of the OT is legitimate exegesis, drawing out potentialities that were there, and when it is imaginative to the point of eisegesis. The criteria for evaluating a more-than-literal exegesis of the OT are not clear, although in many traditions the consensus of the Church Fathers has been given great weight.

A related problem is the evaluation of the added possibilities of meaning gained by once-separate books when they are joined in the one canonical collection which we call the Bible. As far as a study of Mary is concerned, this question, sometimes called "canonical criticism," affects not only the relationship between the Testaments, but also internal relationships within the NT. For example, we shall see how difficult it is to determine whether a Mary/Eve parallelism was in the mind of the Fourth Evangelist when he described the mother of Jesus at Cana (2:1-11) and at the foot of the cross (19:25-27), or in the mind of the author of the Book of Revelation when he described the struggle between the mother of the messianic child and the dragon who was the ancient serpent (Revelation 12). But when John and Revelation are put in

---

[43]See below, pp. 91-92, 122-24, 128-34, 189-90, 217, 237-39, 280-81.
[44]*JBC*, art. 71, §§56-70.

the same canon, a catalytic action may occur so that the two women are brought together and the parallelism to Eve becomes more probable. While we cannot settle such hermeneutical questions or devote much time to them, we have kept them in mind when they have seemed to be pertinent.

After this general chapter on the method, content, and presuppositions of our study, we are now prepared to turn to the investigation of the role of Mary in the NT.

CHAPTER THREE:
THE BIRTH OF JESUS
IN THE PAULINE WRITINGS*

Mary is not mentioned in the Pauline corpus. At times, however, some Pauline verses have been thought to refer to her or to bear on the broader question of Mary in the NT because they pertain in some way to the birth of Jesus. These passages are Gal 1:19; 4:4-5; 4:28-29; Rom 1:3-4; and Phil 2:6-7. The greater part of this chapter will be devoted to the texts in Galatians; but first Rom 1:3-4 and Phil 2:6-7 deserve our attention since they may involve pre-Pauline formulations or ideas and thus are possible witnesses to earlier Christian tradition.

A. Possible Pre-Pauline Formulations in Philippians and Romans

Since the passage in Rom 1:3-4 will require detailed discussion, we shall begin with a Philippians passage which, for our purposes, needs but a few words.

1. Pre-existence in Phil 2:6-11

Most scholars recognize that Phil 2:6-11 is an early Christian hymn, perhaps derived from a pre-Pauline liturgical setting and

---

*The discussion for this chapter was led by J. A. Fitzmyer, who also composed the first draft. One half-session of the task force (Sept. 1976) was devoted to the evidence of Paul.

incorporated by the apostle into his letter. The first two verses speak of Christ Jesus who, "though he was in the form of God, . . . emptied himself, taking the form of a servant, being born [*genomenos*, from *ginesthai*] in the likeness of men." These verses would be relevant to our discussion only if they contained an implication of pre-existence.[45] If Paul intended that implication, he would then have seen no contradiction between pre-existence and Jesus' Davidic descent (which Paul mentions in Rom 1:3). Be that as it may, there is no suggestion here of a virginal conception of Jesus. Indeed, it is significant that pre-existence and virginal conception are nowhere brought together in the NT, and nowhere is there an indication that one demands the other. Thus Paul's possible reference to pre-existence still leaves open the question about the mode of Jesus' conception.

2. *Davidic Descent and Divine Sonship in Rom 1:3-4*

The address or *praescriptio* of Paul's letter to the Romans (1:1-7) is a lengthy one, expanded by the use of ideas that are discussed in the letter itself and by what many interpreters have considered to be a fragment of early pre-Pauline kerygmatic preaching.[46] The latter is found in vv. 3-4:

> [3] . . . (*the gospel*) *concerning His Son, who was born of the seed of David according to the flesh:* [4]*designated Son of God in power according to a spirit of holiness as of the resurrection from the dead, Jesus Christ our Lord.*

---

[45]Pre-existence is affirmed by Hengel, *Son of God*, 1-2, 76, 87; see further R. P. Martin, *Carmen Christi: Philippians ii.5-11 in Recent Interpretation and in the Setting of Early Christian Worship* (SNTSMS 4; Cambridge: University Press, 1967), chap. V, "The Pre-Existent Being." For other scholars who deny that vv. 6-7 refer to pre-existence, see H.-W. Bartsch, *Die konkrete Wahrheit und die Lüge der Spekulation* (Frankfurt/Bern: Lang, 1974); P. Grelot, *Bib* 53 (1972), 495-507; J. Murphy-O'Connor, *RB* 83 (1976), 25-50; C. H. Talbert, *JBL* 86 (1967), 141-53.

[46]See C. H. Dodd, *The Apostolic Preaching and Its Developments* (London: Hodder & Stoughton, 1936), 14; Fuller, *Foundations*, 165-66, 187-89; Käsemann, *Römer*, 8-11; Kuss, *Römerbrief*, 1. 4.

As the text now stands, the parallelism involved has been seen in the following way:

a. born
b. of the seed of David
c. according to the flesh

a. designated
b. Son of God in power
c. according to a spirit of holiness
d. as of the resurrection from the dead.[47]

The parallelism, taken together with other grammatical features,[48] is the basis for the conviction of many interpreters that vv. 3-4 are derived from a pre-Pauline formula. Some interpreters think that Paul has himself modified the kerygmatic fragment by the addition of the introductory phrase mentioning "His Son" and the final phrase identifying Jesus as "our Lord"—using well-known Pauline christological titles.[49] Still others would identify as Pauline such phrases as *kata sarka* (according to the flesh) and *kata pneuma* (*hagiōsynēs*—according to a spirit of holiness). For example, R. Bultmann[50] thinks the original pre-Pauline formula was constructed as follows (adapted to the wording of our translation):

(Jesus Christ) the Son of God,
Born of the seed of David,
Designated Son of God in power as of the resurrection from the dead.

Part of the problem here is the sense of the flesh/Spirit contrast in *kata sarka* and *kata pneuma hagiōsynēs*. Clearly Paul is not using

---

[47]Michel, *Brief*, 38. It may be questioned whether this analysis is wholly adequate because it neglects the contrast between *tou huiou autou*, "His Son" (v. 3), and *huiou theou en dynamei*, "Son of God in power" (v. 4). See further below. The translation "as of the resurrection from the dead" for *ex anastaseōs nekrōn* really cloaks several problems: e.g., whether *ex* means "by, through" or "from the time of," and whether *nekrōn* should be translated "from the dead" or "of the dead." See below, n. 65.

[48]See further Käsemann, *Römer*, 8.

[49]See Michel, *Brief*, 38.

[50]*Theology*, 1. 49.

these phrases with the connotation that the contrast between *kata sarka* and *kata pneuma* often has elsewhere in his writings (Rom 8:4-9; Gal 3:2-3; 5:16-25; 6:8; Phil 3:3).[51] But it is precisely this difference in connotation, together with the fact that the phrase *pneuma hagiōsynēs* is found only here in the Pauline corpus[52] (over against the more frequent [*to*] *pneuma hagion*, 1 Thess 4:8; Rom 15:13, 16, 19), which suggests pre-Pauline formulation. However, no matter what one wants to say about the meaning of the second of these phrases, the first, *kata sarka*, is not unrelated to Paul's usage in Rom 9:3, 5,[53] where the phrase expresses relationship by human descent or kinship.

In using an earlier Christian formula in Rom 1:3-4, Paul raises two issues that concern us at least indirectly in a treatment of Mary, namely, the Davidic descent of Jesus, and his status as Son of God.

THE DAVIDIC DESCENT OF JESUS. In Rom 1:3 Paul assumes this descent and bears witness to it,[54] as do other NT passages including the infancy narratives of Luke and Matthew; 2 Tim 2:8 (*ek spermatos Dauid*[55]); Mark 12:35-37 and parallels. Paul's major

---

[51]In these other passages *sarx*, "flesh," and *pneuma*, "spirit," are in conflict with each other rather than complementary as in Rom 1:3-4. The conflict between *sarx* and *pneuma*, although frequent in Paul, is found elsewhere in the NT (John 6:63) and may not be of Pauline origin.

[52]*Pneuma hagiōsynēs* is found in Greek in *T. Levi* 18:11. The expression is Semitic, being an exact translation of *rûaḥ qōdeš*, found in Palestinian Hebrew texts from Qumran (1QS 4:21; 9:3). The Hebrew form with a possessive suffix, "his holy spirit" is attested in the OT (Isa 63:10-11; Ps 51:13) as well as in Qumran literature (1QS 8:16; CD 2:12; 1QH 7:6-7; 9:32)—a phrase rendered in the LXX as *to pneuma to hagion sou / autou*. Although the LXX employs *hagiōsynē* (Ps 30:4), it does not use this noun in a phrase with *pneuma*. Paul's unmodified use of *pneuma hagiōsynēs* may, then, reflect a Palestinian formulation.

[53]See Moule, *IBNTG*, 59. Perhaps one should also compare the use in Gal 4:28-29; see below.

[54]Indeed, the fact that Jesus' Davidic descent occurs only here in the undisputed Pauline writings (see above, Chap. 2, n. 16) may be a sign of its pre-Pauline origin.

[55]The phrase thus occurs also in a later Pastoral Epistle, even though it has little connection with the immediate context in which it is used. Bultmann (*Theology*, 1. 49 n.) regards it as derived from an earlier Christian tradition.

affirmation in these verses, however, bears on what is said about *the risen Jesus* in contrast to his status "according to the flesh." It is not of great importance to him that Jesus had David in his ancestral lineage, even though that might be the basis of his being recognized as *Christos*.

The Greek verb used in v. 3 in the phrase "*born* of the seed of David" has been the subject of speculation relevant to a study of Mary. The best Greek MSS have *tou genomenou,* the middle participle of *ginesthai,* "become," "come into being," "be born."[56] A few minuscule MSS, however, read the passive participle, *gennōmenou,* from *gennan,* "beget," "bear" (in the passive: "be born").[57] The same textual fluctuation will be found below, when we discuss Gal 4:4. Because *genomenou* is the best reading both here and in Gal 4:4 and because another form of the verb *ginesthai* is also used in Phil 2:7 (see above), some commentators have tried to argue that Paul used this verb in all three passages precisely because he was aware of the virginal conception of Jesus,[58] who was not "begotten" (verb *gennan,* i.e., by a human father), but simply "came into being" (verb *ginesthai*). It is, however, far from certain that the preferred reading *genomenou* meant for Paul "come into being" rather than "be born," since *ginesthai* was often used in the sense of "to be born" (see Tob 8:6; Wis 7:3; Sir 44:9).[59] We may doubt that such a fine distinction between "being born" and "coming into existence" was intended by Paul, especially on the grounds that he was aware of the virginal conception of Jesus. (It should be noted that those NT writers who know of the virginal conception of Jesus use of him the verb *gennan* [Matt 2:1, 4; Luke 1:35], which in this hypothesis Paul avoids in order to hint at the virginal conception!) As O. Michel has recognized,

---

[56] See BAG, 157-59.

[57] MSS 51, 61*, 441; *gennōmenou* is also reflected in some ancient versions (Syr^h) and patristic quotations (Augustine). However, this variant is not even mentioned in the *apparatus criticus* of the *UBSGNT* nor considered important enough for comment by Metzger, *TCGNT,* 505. The further variant *gennōmenon* is found in some minuscle MSS of Gal 4:4 (917, 88, 919, 436, 206, etc.).

[58] See McHugh, *Mother,* 274-77; Edwards, *Virgin Birth,* 68-78.

[59] Yet McHugh, *Mother,* 274, questions whether it ever has this meaning in the NT, even in John 8:58.

ginesthai ek can designate either birth or origin.[60] Paul's real goal in the parallelism of Rom 1:3-4 is not so much to connect Jesus with the Davidic line as to affirm that Jesus, the Davidic Messiah, is *risen*. To read more into the use of the verb *ginesthai* in Rom 1:3 (or for that matter in Gal 4:4 or in Phil 2:7) is over-interpretation and is close to eisegesis.

As for the reference to "the seed [*sperma*] of David" in Rom 1:3, it should be obvious that Paul is using *sperma* in a figurative sense, well-known in the OT (e.g., Gen 12:7; Ps 89:4). It is scarcely intended to refer specifically to male semen; it refers to progeny. Thus, if this phrase does not constitute an argument for the virginal conception, neither does it constitute an argument against it.

THE DIVINE SONSHIP OF JESUS. In contrast to Jesus' Davidic descent "according to the flesh" stands Paul's affirmation that Jesus was "designated Son of God in power according to a spirit of holiness as of the resurrection from the dead" (vs. 4). Though some commentators have tried to interpret the prepositional phrase *en dynamei*, "in power," as a modifier of the participle *horisthentos*, "designated,"[61] it is more commonly taken as the modifier of the phrase *huiou theou*, which it follows, "Son of God in power."[62] This is what Jesus became "as of the resurrection." Such status is contrasted not only with his origin, "of the seed of David," but also indirectly with his condition as "His Son" (i.e., God's Son). The latter phrase, at the beginning of v. 3, refers at least to the earthly Jesus, whether or not it implies his status as pre-existent Son.

The risen Jesus became the "Son of God in power," *kata pneuma hagiōsynēs*. Whatever the origin of this phrase "spirit of holiness" in Rom 1:4 (see above), clearly it does not differ in

---

[60]Michel, *Brief*, 39.

[61]See Sanday and Headlam, *Romans*, 9. The Goodspeed translation has "decisively declared"; *NEB*, "by a mighty act."

[62]For a discussion of reasons for taking *en dynamei* with *huiou theou*, see Cranfield, *Romans*, 1.62. It should further be noted that *huiou theou* functions in v. 4 as a predicate noun with *horisthentos* and as such is without the article. Cf. *ho dikaios ek pisteōs*, "righteous through faith," Gal 3:11 (as defended by some interpreters).

Paul's theology from *pneuma hagion*, "Holy Spirit." (We understand, of course, that neither phrase has the full-blown trinitarian
sense of later theology.) However, the contrast of *kata pneuma
hagiōsynēs*, "according to a spirit of holiness," and *kata sarka*,
"according to the flesh," shows that the former cannot be understood as something distinct from Jesus, but rather designates
something inherent in him or constitutive of him. The *kata*-con-
trast seems to refer to spheres or modes of consideration of him
who is Son: according to the flesh, he is one thing; according to
the spirit of holiness, another.[63] What is affirmed here by *kata
pneuma hagiōsynēs* has to be understood in the light of what Paul
writes in 1 Cor 15:45: "the last Adam became a life-giving spirit."
In other words, as of the resurrection Jesus became a life-giving
principle, productive of new life for Christians; and this in virtue
of the Spirit: *pneuma, pneuma hagion*, or—in pre-Pauline
formulation—*pneuma hagiōsynēs*.[64]

It is clear that in speaking thus of Jesus, Paul puts emphasis
on "as of the resurrection from the dead."[65] He is not speaking of
the Jesus of the public ministry and *a fortiori* not of his birth.[66]

---

[63]Can one translate *kata pneuma hagiōsynēs* as "by the Spirit of
Holiness"? If "by" were meant here to denote agency, it would be a
peculiar use of *kata*. Is it otherwise attested? On the other hand, *kata*
with the accusative can express "goal, purpose" (BAG, 407) and could
be related to the use of *eis* in 1 Cor 15:45. But *kata* is undoubtedly used
here in the sense of either "relationship" (BAG 408, §6), or possibly
"norm" (BAG, 408, §5). See further D. C. Duling, *NTS* 20 (1973-74), 73,
who distinguishes between the "temporal and spatial" use of *kata* and
the "instrumental" use.

[64]Part of the problem that is involved in such a Pauline statement is
the apostle's mode of relating *kyrios* to *pneuma*. There are times when he
speaks of the *kyrios* without clearly distinguishing him from the *pneuma*,
and times when he lines up triadic texts that became the springboard for
the later trinitarian formulations. See Fitzmyer, *Pauline Theology*, 41-43;
J. S. Vos, *Traditionsgeschichtliche Untersuchungen zur paulinischen
Pneumatologie* (Assen: Van Gorcum, 1973).

[65]We have preferred above the temporal sense of *ex anastaseōs
nekrōn* (with Cranfield, *Romans*, 62; Käsemann, *Römer*, 9). But a causal
meaning, "on the ground of," "by," cannot be certainly excluded (Murray, *Romans*, 10-11).

[66]However, commentators who would regard *en dynamei* and *ex*

Paul never speaks (and so far as we can tell, knows nothing) about the activity of the Spirit as a generative principle in the birth of Jesus, such as is attested in the infancy narratives (Matt 1:20; Luke 1:35). It is, of course, possible that the sort of pre-Pauline tradition which is embedded in Rom 1:3-4, mentioning *Dauid*, *dynamis*, and *pneuma*, could have been inherited also by Luke, who then related these terms to his treatment of the virginal conception and used them in his own formulation (Luke 1:32, 35).[67] This Lucan use of the material would represent a linking of the (originally post-resurrectional) activity of the Spirit with the conception of Jesus and would represent a development of NT christology different from the christology which one finds in Paul's writings.

B. Passages of Possible Marian Import in Galatians

When we turn from the pre-Pauline material to passages which are clearly of Pauline origin, those that concern us are all in Galatians, a letter generally thought to have been written in the 50s and thus before the Gospels.

1. James, the Brother of the Lord (Gal 1:19)

Indirectly related to our quest about Mary is a Galatian reference to a very important figure of the Jerusalem church whom Paul went up to greet shortly after his conversion. Paul visited

---

anastaseōs nekrōn as (Pauline?) additions to the original formula might find in that hypothetical earlier formula a parallelism that could be referred to the birth of Jesus: "born of the seed of David according to the flesh" // "designated Son of God according to a spirit of holiness." If such were the original formula, then Luke's formulation in 1:32, 35 would be still closer to it. But—aside from the speculative character of determining such "additions"—the form of Rom 1:3-4 is such that the parallelism clearly involves the risen Jesus, and the sphere of influence of the Spirit has to do with that status.

[67]As he seems to have used other formulas that existed before him, such as "called Son of the Most High," "called Son of God," etc. (see J. A. Fitzmyer, *NTS* 20 [1973-74], 393-94).

Jerusalem three years after his return to Damascus from Arabia
(1:17-18); and in Jerusalem he met with Cephas, but saw "none of
the other apostles except James, the brother of the Lord"
(1:19).[68] The mention here of *ton adelphon tou Kyriou*, "the
brother of the Lord," bears on the discussion of Mary in the NT,
for it may be asked in what sense we are to understand *ton adelphon*. Is "the brother" of Jesus a child of Mary? Since this is an
identifying title which has to be related in the long run to the
phrase in Mark 6:3 identifying Jesus as "brother of James" (*adelphos Iakōbou*), we shall defer to the later discussion of the meaning of *adelphos* in the Marcan passage.[69] It is impossible to tell
from this isolated reference in what sense Paul would have understood what is obviously an already established Christian identification of this James of Jerusalem.

2. Born of a Woman (Gal 4:4)

Chapters 3 and 4 of Galatians present Paul's arguments in
defense of the thesis propounded in 2:15-21 about justification by
faith and not by the Law. His arguments appeal to an experience
of the reception of the Spirit by the Galatian Christians (3:1-5) and
to an understanding of various elements of the Abraham story in
Genesis (3:6-4:31). Into his interpretation of that story he introduces an argument from one of the institutions of his own day—
inheritance as related to a will or testament. All of this he compares with the influence of the Mosaic Law. Under that Law men
and women were in an inferior condition and not really "the offspring of Abraham" (3:29). A person in such a condition was like
a child, a minor, subject to a "custodian" (3:25) and to "guardians
and trustees" (4:2). By contrast, when the time came for the child
to attain to its majority and to be freed of such supervisors, Christ
Jesus was sent by the Father to redeem those who would put faith

---

[68]Various aspects of this verse have already been discussed in *Peter
in the New Testament*, 30-32.

[69]See pp. 65-72 below. One should recall here the excursus by
J. B. Lightfoot, "The Brethren of the Lord," who held the Epiphanian
view that the brothers were children of Joseph by a previous marriage.
See below, Chap. 9, C2.

in him and to insure their status as real adoptive sons and heirs, as the offspring of Abraham.

As part of this figurative development of the effect of the Christ-event, Paul wrote (4:4-5):[70]

> [4]*But when the time had fully come, God sent forth His Son, born of a woman, born under the Law,* [5]*in order to redeem those who were under the Law, so that we might receive adoption as sons.*

In these verses Paul is concerned above all to relate redemption and adoptive sonship (and heirship) to a certain point in salvation, namely, to the moment when Jesus became a member of humanity and of the Jewish race. As part of that concern, he speaks of God's sending "His Son, born of a woman, born under the Law."[71] One may debate whether "His Son" implies preexistence or not, but in any case Paul is certainly stressing Jesus' humanity ("one born of a woman") and his relation to Israel ("one born under the Law").

The phrase, *genomenon ek gynaikos*, "born of a woman," is a frequently-used Jewish expression to designate a person's human condition. It reflects *'ādām yělûd 'iššāh* of Job 14:1, "a human being (that is) born of a woman . . ."[72] (cf. Job 15:14;

---

[70]J. C. O'Neill (*The Recovery of Paul's Letter to the Galatians* [London: S.P.C.K., 1972]) would regard vv. 4-5 as "not originally written by Paul, but . . . cited from Jewish Christian liturgy" (p. 58) and as "a short credal affirmation in poetic form" (p. 59). These verses would be a gloss added to Paul's own argument as a "first addition, which helped prompt verses 1-3, 8-10 the second addition (*ibid.*). The highly speculative character of O'Neill's argument, based mainly on what he considers "strictly incompatible" images (p. 56) in vv. 1-3 and 4-7, renders his argument quite unconvincing. See the reviews of the book by J. Drury, *JTS* ns 24 (1973), 551-52; J. A. Fitzmyer, *TS* 34 (1973), 150-52; J. Murphy-O'Connor, *RB* 82 (1975), 143-44.

[71]As in Rom 1:3, the preferred reading here is again *genomenon*, which we have translated "born"; see above, n. 56. Many patristic writers read *gennōmenon*, and it was common with either reading to see in Gal 4:4-5 a reference to Mary's virginal conception of Jesus. Such an interpretation reached far beyond the patristic period, as E. de Roover ("La maternité") makes clear.

[72]The LXX translates this Hebrew phrase as *brotos gar gennētos gynaikos* in 14:1; in 15:15 and 25:4 *brotos* is put in parallelism with *gennētos gynaikos*.

25:4). The phrase is found in the same sense in the NT, applied to John the Baptist, *en gennētois gynaikōn*, "among those born of women" (Matt 11:11; Luke 7:28). As a Semitic expression it is further found in Qumran literature from Palestine.[73] Such a description simply stresses the human condition of Jesus. Thus no convincing argument for Paul's awareness of the virginal conception can be drawn from this phrase—nor from Paul's use of *genomenon* (*ginesthai*) instead of *gennōmenon* (*gennan*, as seen on pp. 37-38 above), nor from Paul's omission here of any mention of a father.[74] (The implication that Paul should have said "begotten of a man" is unfounded since there is no evidence that such an idiom existed as a ready alternative to *yělûd 'iššāh*.) Seemingly the apostle was simply making use of a stereotyped literary expression and not attempting to supply detail on *how* the Son became man.

If one were to ask how Paul could write that Jesus was "born of a woman," or even that he "came into being from a woman," without implying some reference to Mary, one would have to answer that Paul does thus indirectly refer to her. But it is a reference to her simply as mother, in her maternal role of bearing Jesus and bringing him into the world. There is not the slightest hint here that Jesus was her "first born" (see Luke 2:7) or that she was a virgin. Paul simply does not mention the virginal conception,[75] and there is no reason to think that he knew of it. On the other hand, a christological affirmation such as Paul makes here is not at all incompatible with the christology of other and later NT writers who maintain the virginal conception.

---

[73]1QH 13:14, *wmh ylwd 'šh bkwl* [*m'śykh*], "and what is a human being [lit., one born of woman] among all [your works]"; 1QS 11:21, *wylwd 'šh mh yšb* [? to be read perhaps as *yḥšb*] *lpnyk*, "and (for) what is a human being [to be regarded?] before you?" Cf. 1QH 18:12-13, 16, 23-24.

[74]Some commentators, both Protestant and Roman Catholic, have, of course, so argued; see Cranfield, *Romans*, 59; H. E. W. Turner, "Expository Problems: The Virgin Birth," *ExpTim* 68 (1956-57), 12; McHugh, *Mother*, 175-76; Miguens, *Virgin Birth*, 46-53. But is their argument really cogent?

[75]Cf. Legault, "Saint Paul," as contrasted with the views of R. J. Cooke, G. A. Danell, and W. C. Robinson.

How unimportant the phrase "born of a woman" really was for Paul may be shown by the fact that, of the three things asserted about Jesus in v. 4 (Son, born of a woman, born under the Law), only the first and third are taken up in the parallel description of Christians in v. 5 (he redeemed those *under the law*; he brought it about that we receive adoptive *sonship*).[76]

Finally, we may cite a Christian author who is fully aware of the virginal conception, in order to show how he can use phrases akin to Gal 4:4 and Rom 1:3 and yet leave no doubt about his intention. His phraseology stands in sharp contrast to these Pauline passages. Ignatius of Antioch once wrote to the Smyrnaeans (1.1), with obvious dependence on Rom 1:3:

> I give glory to Jesus Christ, the God who has given you such wisdom. For I have observed that you are established in immovable faith, as if nailed to the cross of the Lord Jesus Christ, both in flesh and spirit, and that you are confirmed in love by the blood of Christ, and that you are fully persuaded concerning our Lord, that he is in truth of the family of David according to the flesh [*ek genous*

---

[76]Possibly a chiastic arrangement is involved here: (a) "born of a woman," (b) "born under the Law"; (b') "in order (*hina*) to redeem those who were under the Law," (a') "so that (*hina*) we might receive adoption as sons." And it has been argued that this arrangement suggests that Jesus was born under the Law in order to free those who live under the domination of the law, and that he was born of a woman in order that those who are born of a woman might receive adoptive sonship (of God). Indeed, M. Dibelius ("Jungfrauensohn," p. 29, n. 47) not only so argues but also concludes: "The passage clearly presupposes that Christ was born of a woman in the same sense and in the same manner as all human beings. If it read: *genomenon ek parthenou*, the words would be stripped of their meaning." But it can be debated whether this chiastic arrangement expresses the full intent of the Pauline passage. Is the contrast between Jesus who was born of a woman and "us" who are born of a woman (so that we might receive adoptive sonship), or rather between "His Son" sent by God and our receiving "sonship"? Do not *huion* ("Son") and *huiothesian* ("adoption as sons") stand in contrast? If so, an attempt to view these verses in chiastic arrangement becomes doubtful. In any case, much more important for Paul is the double "sending" of the Son and "sending" of the Spirit of the Son (v. 6), whereby the adoptive sonship is either constituted (see Rom 8:14-16) or at least manifested. Cf. E. Schweizer, *ZNW* 57 (1966), 199-210; TDNT 8, 375-76.

Daueid kata sarka], Son of God by the will and power of God, truly born of a Virgin [*gegennēmenon alēthōs ek parthenou*], and baptised by John that "all righteousness might be fulfilled by him."

This passage shows clearly what happens to such traditional phrases used by one who is aware of the virginal conception.

3. Born according to the Spirit (Gal 4:28-29)

The last Pauline passage that may have some bearing on the birth of Jesus is only indirectly of interest. At one point in his allegorical interpretation of the Hagar.and Sarah story of Gen 16:15 and 21:1-14, Paul introduces an element that is not found in the Genesis account itself, viz., the birth of Isaac "according to the Spirit." The Pauline text runs as follows:

> [27]*For it is written,*
> *"Rejoice, O barren one who does not bear;*
> *break forth and shout, you who are not in travail;*
> *for the children of the desolate one are many more*
> *than the children of her that is married"* [Isa 54:1].
> [28]*Now we, brethren, like Isaac, are children of promise.* [29]*But just as at that time he who was born according to the flesh persecuted him who was born according to the Spirit, so it is now.* [30]*But what does the Scripture say? "Cast out the slave and her son; for the son of the slave shall not inherit with the son of the free woman"* [Gen 21:10]. [31]*So, brethren, we are not children of the slave woman but of the free woman.*

The Genesis story makes it clear that Isaac was born as a child of promise (see Gen 21:1-2; cf. 18:10, 14). Earlier in this chapter of Galatians (4:23), Paul contrasted *dia tēs epangelias*, "through promise" with *kata sarka*, "according to the flesh." In that contrast, *kata sarka* can only mean something like "in the natural way" or "in the common course of nature." But here Paul uses the same phrase to make the contrast *kata sarka / kata pneuma* (v. 29), so that Isaac becomes a child "born according to the Spirit" (Gal 4:29).

The thrust of Paul's argument is clear: Just as Ishmael, born *kata sarka*, persecuted[77] Isaac, born *kata pneuma*, so now those whose interest is *kata sarka*, i.e., the opponents of Paul, are troubling and disturbing those who have been born anew *kata pneuma* (in the Pauline sense of the Christian experience). Paul sums up his advice by quoting Gen 21:10, "Cast out the slave girl and her son"; and he urges the Galatians to have nothing more to do with the opponents, for the Galatians are free—"children of the free woman."

What Paul is doing here is making a category of Christian experience (*kata sarka* / *kata pneuma*) flow back over the biblical reality which in the allegory prefigures it. The *pneuma* is introduced into the retelling of the Genesis story, but only to insure the Christian message that where the Spirit is, there is freedom (see 2 Cor 3:17). The Spirit is introduced by Paul to emphasize the condition of the child born to Sarah, namely, free.[78]

But is it possible that Paul intends more by the contrast between *ho kata sarka gennētheis* and *ton kata pneuma*? Does he imply that Isaac was conceived through the activity of the Spirit without the intervention of a father? Such an interpretation of this Pauline passage has been proposed by, among others, C. Clemen[79] and M. Dibelius.[80] And if Paul were alluding to such an understanding of the birth of Isaac, would it possibly further

---

[77]Paul introduces here an idea that is not in Genesis, that Ishmael "persecuted" Isaac. See R. Le Déaut, *Bib* 42 (1961), 28-48, esp. 37-43.

[78]Another example of this flow-back is found in the use of *pneumatikos* in 1 Cor 10:1-11. For a fuller explanation of this mode of interpretation, see P. Grelot, "La naissance," 475-77. Cf. A. Sand, *Der Begriff "Fleisch" in den paulinischen Hauptbriefen* (Biblische Untersuchungen, 2; Regensburg: Pustet, 1967), 154-55, no. 2: "The principal idea of the whole presentation is obviously the element of the 'miraculous,' not however in relation to physical impotency, but in relation to deliverance from slavery." Sand's comment is a clear—but implicit—correction of what Dibelius ("Jungfrauensohn," 28, n. 45) considered the miraculous or Spirit-created aspect of the passage: "The miraculous aspect of the birth certainly lies in the begetting."

[79]*Religionsgeschichtliche Erklärung des Neuen Testaments: Die Abhängigkeit des ältesten Christentums von nichtjüdischen Religionen und philosophischen Systemen* (2d ed.; Giessen: Töpelmann, 1924), 119-21.

[80]"Jungfrauensohn," 1-78.

imply an awareness of the virginal conception of Jesus?[81] If so, the Pauline passage would represent a stage in the development intermediary between a miraculous interpretation of Isaac's birth as a virginal conception and the Lucan (or Matthean) narrative of the Spirit's activity in the conception of Jesus.

Dibelius argued that in Judaism of Paul's time there existed two traditions about the birth of Isaac. One tradition, found in conservative rabbinic Judaism of Palestine, explained the birth in terms of a miraculous assistance of God which facilitated the course of nature, so that Abraham as husband was not excluded.[82] The other tradition, found in Hellenistic Judaism, which had been influenced by Greek mythology and allegory, explained the birth as the result of a conception by the Holy Spirit with no involvement of Abraham. Dibelius traced to Philo of Alexandria such an understanding of the conception of Isaac through God's creative Spirit. In his treatise *De Cherubim* (13:45), Philo alludes to Gen 21:1, "The Lord visited Sarah as he had said, and the Lord did to Sarah as he had promised." Apropos of this verse, he says, "He [Moses, regarded as the author of Genesis] shows us Sarah conceiving at the time when God visited her in her solitude." Dibelius maintains that Philo's description of Sarah as *monōtheisa*, "in her solitude" (i.e., with a detail that goes beyond the OT description itself), reveals that he thought of Isaac as

---

[81] Dibelius (*ibid.*, 29) denies any application of this notion by Paul to the conception of Jesus: "Paul nowhere speaks of the miraculous birth of Jesus and clearly manifests the diametrically opposed direction of this interest: He lays decisive stress on the fact that Christ began his earthly existence like that of any other human being, through a natural birth."

[82] See *Genesis Rabbah*, 47 and 53 (on Gen 17:16 and 21:1). Dibelius refers to a third-century teacher, Resh Laqish, who is said to have explained that God supplied Sarah with an ovary. Aside from the problem of connecting this late Jewish tradition with first-century Palestinian Judaism, it should be noted that nothing in these passages says anything very explicit about Abraham's involvement in the birth of Isaac. See J. Theodor and C. Albeck, *Bereschit Rabba mit kritischem Apparat und Kommentar* (2 vols.; Berlin: Poppelauer, 1912, 1927), 1. 472 (§47:2), 534-60 (§53:1-5); cf. H. Freedman and M. Simon, *Midrash Rabbah: Translated into English with Notes, Glossary and Indices* (10 vols.; London: Soncino, 1939), 1. 400, 461-65.

conceived in her through "the activity of the creative 'holy Spirit' " with "the exclusion of her husband."[83]

Now this understanding of Isaac's birth which Dibelius postulates for Hellenistic Judaism was also hypothetically what "Paul learned and taught."[84] Dibelius' interpretation of the Pauline passage in Galatians does not depend solely on the use of the phrase *kata pneuma*; he rather makes much of Paul's use of Isa 54:1 in the allegory and of the contrast between Sarah, "the desolate one" (*hē erēmos*), and "her who has a husband." The contrast suggests that Sarah was "desolate," because she equivalently had no husband. Thus Paul would be saying about her what Philo does by using *monōtheisa*, "in her solitude"; and Paul would have thought that Isaac was born to Abraham, through the activity of God's creative spirit and without the physical involvement of Abraham himself.

Dibelius' interpretation of Philo's *De Cherubim,* however, has not gone unchallenged. It has been seriously called in question by P. Grelot, who has thoroughly analyzed the allegorical character of the writing and concluded there was no current theologoumenon such as Dibelius claimed.[85] He has shown that the Philonic text deals rather with the divine origin of virtue and of the fruits that it bears and with the conditions necessary in the soul for the production of these fruits — the soul being regarded as a virgin when it produces them. Hence the extent to which Philo's text says anything about an interpretation of Gen 21:1 in terms of a Spirit-caused conception of Isaac is quite questionable.[86]

Moreover, an understanding of the birth of Isaac is reflected

---

[83]"Jungfrauensohn," 30.

[84]*Ibid.* Dibelius' interpretation of Paul is defended by R. H. Fuller, *CBQ* 40 (1978), 119-20 (against Brown, *Birth*, 524).

[85]"La naissance," 469-71, 561-70. Cf. Boslooper, *Virgin Birth*, 194: "What is incorrect is the idea that Philo is speaking about 'virgin birth' and in doing so supplies us with a parallel to the Gospels in Hellenistic Judaism."

[86]Dibelius ("Jungfrauensohn," 30) makes much of the distinct way in which the Spirit was understood in Palestinian rabbinic interpretation ("as an organ of inspiration, but generally not as a creative principle of life") over against the Hellenistic Jewish, and especially Philonic, understanding of it as "life-giving power." Hence he often refers to the creative

in another of Paul's letters, which seems to show that he thought of Abraham as a father in a true sense. In Rom 4:19 he says, "He [Abraham] did not weaken in faith when he considered his own body, which was as good as dead because he was about a hundred years old, or when he considered the barrenness of Sarah's womb."[87] The question raised by this passage is: Why would Abraham be made to speak of "his own body," if it were not somehow involved in the act of begetting Isaac? Moreover, in Rom 8:9-10 Paul seems to take it for granted that the children of the patriarchs were conceived by intercourse.

Hence it remains problematic whether Paul, in constructing his allegory of Sarah and Hagar, was referring to the birth of Isaac by divine impregnation and whether his use of Isa 54:1 was meant to suggest this precise nuance.[88] And it is still more questionable whether this birth "according to the Spirit" sheds any light on the problem of the virginal conception of Jesus in the NT.[89]

We have discussed the Pauline passages that deal directly or indirectly with the birth of Jesus. What is said about that birth is formulated in the course of other developments of Pauline theological concern. We have tried to emphasize in each case what is the main concern of Paul in these passages and to relate to it what is otherwise and only incidentally pertinent to the birth of Jesus.

---

activity of the Spirit in the conception of Isaac. But in *De Cherubim* 12-13 (§§40-53), where the story of Sarah is developed, Philo usually speaks of "God" (*theos*) and never once uses "Spirit" (*pneuma*). It is Dibelius himself who has introduced the Spirit into the Philonic version of the Isaac story. Cf. Grelot, "La naissance," 472.

[87] Dibelius ("Jungfrauensohn," 29) mentions Rom 4:18-21, but only to give it short shrift.

[88]The use of Isa 54:1 in the allegory is otherwise quite intelligible without the exploitation of the description of Sarah as "desolate" in the sense that Dibelius understands it.

[89]If one agrees that Paul does not exclude Abraham's involvement in the birth of Isaac in Galatians, then he can speak of the birth of a child "according to the Spirit" without any connotation of virginal conception.

CHAPTER FOUR:
MARY IN THE
GOSPEL OF MARK*

In the Marcan Gospel there is only one scene in which Mary appears (3:31-35); there is another in which she is clearly mentioned (6:1-6), and still another scene or series of incidents in which some scholars think she is mentioned (15:40, 47; 16:1). These three scenes constitute the subdivisions of our treatment.

A. Who Constitute the Family of Jesus? (3:31-35)

The passage reads as follows:[90]

> [31]*And his mother and brothers came; and standing around outside, they sent to him and called him.* [32]*And a crowd was sitting about him; and they said to him, "Your mother and your brothers are*

---

*The discussion for this chapter was led by P. J. Achtemeier, and the first draft was composed by K. P. Donfried. One and a half sessions of the task force (Sept. and Oct., 1975) were devoted to the evidence of Mark.

[90]We have made the same choice as did the committees for the *RSV* and *UBSGNT* in favoring the shorter reading of v. 32, as found in the Alexandrian and Caesarean textual families of MSS. A longer reading, "Your mother and your brothers *and your sisters* are outside" is found in Codex Bezae and the later Byzantine tradition. See Metzger *TCGNT*, 82. Much depends on the relationship between v. 32 (as part of 31-34) and v.

outside, asking for you." [33]*And he replied, "Who are my mother and my brothers?"* [34]*And looking around on those who sat about him, he said, "Behold my mother and my brothers!* [35]*Whoever does the will of God is my brother, and sister, and mother."*

Let us first consider the passage in itself, then in its Marcan context.

1. The Passage in Itself

In the terminology of form criticism (i.e., the classification of scriptural units according to their literary genre), this passage has been regarded as almost a classical example of the biographical apophthegm—a short unit consisting of a saying of Jesus set in a brief narrative context.[91] According to this analysis, v. 35 would represent the saying of Jesus about doing God's will, with vv. 31-34 constituting the immediate narrative context for that saying. (For some scholars this narrative context would have been invented and is fictional; for others it would have been derived from tradition and adapted as a setting—in either case it is secondary in importance to the saying.) There are several arguments for the thesis that the saying in 35 originally circulated independently of the present context. First, a somewhat similar saying is found in

35, which mentions "my brother, and sister, and mother." Those who favor the shorter reading in 32 argue that the reference to "sisters" was read back by a scribe from 35 in order to harmonize the two verses—but note the different word order, the plural vs. the singular, and the lack of a similar "reading back" in 31 (where one might have most expected it) and 33. Supporters of the shorter reading also point out that there is no reference to "sisters" in the parallel passages in Matt 12:47 and Luke 8:30—but that could be the very reason why a scribe who was interested in harmonizing omitted the "sisters" from Mark. We note that Mary and the brothers are mentioned without the sisters in Acts 1:14, *Gospel of Thomas*, Logion 99; *2 Clement* 1:11, while sisters are mentioned when Jesus discusses family relationship in Mark 10:29. A decision on the original reading is difficult and is of no particular significance for the NT picture of Mary.

[91]This is the terminology preferred by Bultmann, *History*, 11, 29-31, 143. Terms used by others to describe this genre include "paradigm" by M. Dibelius, *From Tradition to Gospel* (New York: Scribners, 1935), 43; and "pronouncement story" by V. Taylor, *The Formation of the Gospel Tradition* (London: Macmillan, 1935), 71-72.

quite a different context in Luke 11:28: "Happy [*makarioi*], rather, those who hear the word of God and keep it"—a blessing that is Jesus' response to the woman who blessed his mother (11:27). Second, there is a lack of consistency between 32 and 35 in the order, number, and description of family members.

When v. 35 is considered in itself, it tells us who constitute Jesus' family—a family that for want of a better term we may call his "eschatological family," i.e., the family called into being by Jesus' proclamation of the kingdom. This eschatological family (brother, sister, and mother[92]) consists of those who do God's will. The context in 31-34 highlights the demand involved in being a member of the eschatological family: the eschatological family constituted by doing the will of God is not identical with the biological, physical, or natural family (mother, brothers) constituted by human relationship. How sharp is this contrast? What does 3:31-35 taken in itself tell us about Jesus' attitude toward his physical family? The physical family is outside asking for him; the eschatological family is inside already seated around him. Does this mean that Jesus has rejected his physical family or replaced them by the eschatological family? The least it seems to mean is that the physical family has no real importance in the new standard of values established by the proclamation of the kingdom; the family that really matters to Jesus is the eschatological family. Although the "outside" vs. "inside" staging indicates that the physical family members are not among those whom Jesus currently regards as his eschatological family, the passage in itself does not exclude the physical family members from *eventual* participation in the eschatological family.[93] Yet they can participate

---

[92]Observe that Jesus does not mention father. The implication seems to be that no human being in the eschatological family is a father to Jesus, for God is Jesus' father (Mark 14:36; cf. Matt 23:9). Some would find an implication also about Jesus' physical family, i.e., that he had no human father; but this will be discussed below, pp. 61-64.

[93]Historically there is no evidence that the closest members of Jesus' natural family were active disciples during his ministry, i.e., joined his company and followed him. In John 2:12 "his mother and his brothers" are kept distinct from "his disciples"; see also the distinction between Jesus' brothers and his disciples in John 7:3. A post-resurrectional appearance of Jesus to his brother James is mentioned in 1 Cor 15:7.

only if they do the will of God. The point of the passage is to
define the eschatological family, not to exclude the physical family. Thus the passage is in harmony with the outlook expressed in
Mark 10:29-30: "Truly I say to you, there is no one who has left
house or brothers or sisters or mother or father or children or
lands, for my sake or for the Gospel, who now in this time will not
receive a hundredfold: houses and brothers and sisters and
mothers and children and lands, with persecutions; and who in
the age to come will not receive eternal life."

2. The Passage in the Marcan Context of 3:20-35

Mark has set the passage in a sequence of events that may
help us to determine Mark's own interpretation of the attitude of
Jesus toward his physical family (i.e., his redactional theology).
There are signs that Mark sees the events in 3:20-35 as a unit
which may be outlined as follows:[94]

Introduction (20)
(A)   Jesus' "own" set out to seize him (21)
        21a: "His own" hear of his activity and set out to
                seize him
        21b: Their charge: "He is beside himself."
(B)   The dialogue between Jesus and the Jerusalem scribes
        (22-30)
        22a: The first charge of the scribes: "He is possessed
                by Beelzebul."
        22b: The second charge of the scribes: "By the prince
                of demons he casts out demons."
        23-27: Jesus replies to the second charge of the scribes
        28-30: Jesus replies to the first charge of the scribes
(A') Jesus' mother and brothers come and ask for him, resulting
        in the definition of who are his family (31-35)

In considering this outline, there is a twofold question about
the relationship between A and A'. Does Mark intend to identify

---

[94]See Schweizer, Mark, 82-84. In regarding v. 20 as the introduction,
we are rejecting the suggestion of Crossan, "Mark," that 20 belongs to
the preceding pericope. Lambrecht, "Relatives," gives a detailed response to Crossan.

Jesus' own with Jesus' mother and brothers, and does he intend
that Jesus' definition of his eschatological family serve as a reply
to the charge of his "own" that he is beside himself? There is
another question about the relationship between A and B. Are his
"own" like the scribes in their hostility to Jesus?

With those questions in mind, we may begin with the meaning of "his own" (*hoi par' autou*) in v. 21. Various translations are
found, and it is noteworthy that the *RSV* has shifted from "his
friends" in the first edition to "his family" in the second edition
(1973). In itself the term *hoi par' autou* is ambiguous and could
mean simply those who were customarily around him.[95] And if
the unity of the present sequence is a Marcan creation, we would
be very hard pressed to determine who were "his own" when
what is now v. 21 was an isolated fragment of tradition.[96] But the
Marcan context inclines us strongly toward the conclusion that
Mark understood a reference to Jesus' relatives (and thus to agree
with the more recent *RSV* version).

As we fix our attention on that context, we find that Jesus
has begun a ministry at the Sea of Galilee (3:7), so that Mark can
now speak of Jesus as having a home in that area (3:19b [20a]).
The crowd attracted by Jesus has gathered together at the home,
"so that they could not even eat" (3:20b)—the "they" is not
identified. It is then that we are told that "his own" heard this and
went out. From where did they go out? Those who interpret "his
own" as those surrounding Jesus understand Mark to mean that
they went out from the house to the crowd. But this is very
unlikely, for then there is no sequence to the Marcan
statement—the "his own" never come to the crowd. Moreover,
in 3:31-35 Jesus' disciples are still inside the house with him. A
more likely interpretation is that "his own" refers to Jesus' relatives at Nazareth who have heard what was happening in Capernaum and have set out to seize him. That Mark pictures "his
own" as living at a distance is suggested by the fact that he uses

[95]See BAG, 614-15. The meaning "family, relatives" is found chiefly
in Koine Greek.

[96]If, even as an isolated tradition, v. 20 referred to the relatives of
Jesus, it may have meant only his "brothers." In John 7:4 the brothers of
Jesus are said not to have believed in him, but no NT verse ever says
specifically that Jesus' mother did not believe in him.

the dialogue between Jesus and the scribes (3:22-30) as a filler before the mother and the brothers arrive (3:31). This is an example of the Marcan *Schachteltechnik* ("Boxing in; Sandwiching"), similar to the sequence in 5:21-24, 25-34, 35-43. There Jesus sets out for Jairus' home; and the interval of his journey is filled in with the scene of the woman with the hemorrhage, before Jesus arrives in the vicinity of Jairus' home (5:35). The comparison of the two scenes makes it likely that for Mark the "mother and brothers" of 3:31 who arrive (at the house in Capernaum) asking for Jesus are the same as the "his own" of 3:21 who set out (from Nazareth) to seize him.[97]

Yet, even if it is probable that Mark understands the "his own" as Jesus' family, the description of their reactions as described in 21 is not without difficulty. We understand the verse to mean: "And when his family heard it, they went out to seize him; for they were saying, 'He is beside himself.' " But Mark's Greek allows other translations on three points, which have been exploited by those anxious to preserve a better view of Jesus' family. The first is *auton*, the object of the verb "to seize"; this *auton* could be the crowd, so that the implication would be that the family went out to prevent the crowd from harming Jesus. The second is the subject of the verb "were saying"; the translation "for people were saying" (*RSV* 1973) implies that the "they" who spoke were another group different from the family of Jesus. The third concerns the verb *existēmi* "to be beside oneself": some would propose a subject other than Jesus ("The crowd is beside itself [with enthusiasm]"); others would allow that Jesus is the subject but would soften the impact of the verb until it means little more than "overworked."[98] In the abstract these translations are

---

[97] An additional argument for this interpretation of Mark is offered by the fact that both Matthew and Luke omit Mark 3:20-21. One plausible reason for this omission is that they read these verses as a reference to Jesus' mother and brothers and found that offensive; this might reflect their incipient mariological concern and/or respect for James, the brother of the Lord, who had been the head of the Jerusalem church and was martyred.

[98] Among the more recent attempts to soften the apparently offensive character of Mark 3:21, one may cite the studies in the bibliography for

not impossible,[99] but the Marcan text militates against them.

We see this when we begin to compare A and B in our outline. It is probable that Mark intends a parallelism between 21 and 22. Verse 22 reads: "And the scribes who had come down from Jerusalem were saying, 'He is possessed by Beelzebul. And it is by the prince of demons that he casts out demons.' " In both 21 and 22 there is mention of a group ("his own" and the scribes); in each there is a participle which sets the scene ("when they had heard" and "who had come down from Jerusalem"), and each has the verb *elegon*, "were saying." Just as "the scribes" is the subject of "were saying" in 22, so the parallelism suggests that "his own" is the subject of "were saying" in 21. The statement of the scribes in 22 clearly refers to Jesus, and the parallelism suggests that the statement of "his own" in 21 refers to Jesus. The statement in 22 is a harsh double charge about Jesus, and so it is unlikely that 21 can be reduced to a mild worry that Jesus is overworked. Thus we emerge with the sequence:

His own were saying, "He is beside himself."
The scribes were saying, "He is possessed by Beelzebul.
It is by the prince of demons that he casts out demons."

Both groups have a negative outlook on Jesus. It has been suggest-

---

this chapter by Hartmann, Schroeder, and Wansbrough. In particular, Wansbrough translates 3:21 thus: "When they heard it, his followers went out to calm it down, for they said that it was out of control with enthusiasm." Wenham, "Meaning," effectively refutes this translation; yet he admits that Wansbrough may be correct in arguing that it is the crowd and not Jesus which is "out of its mind." In part this depends on the very difficult relationship between Mark and Q in reference to this pericope. We would be more inclined to admit that *on a pre-Marcan level* the crowd may have been the subject of the charge (note the emphasis on the "crowd's astonishment" in Q, as attested by Matt 12:23 and Luke 11:14c). But the parallelism that Mark has established between 21 and 22 means that for Mark Jesus is the subject of the charge.

[99]But there are difficulties as Best, "Mark III," points out. Mark generally uses a plural pronoun when he refers to a crowd; thus he would scarcely say "to seize *it*," referring to seizing or stopping the crowd. The verb *existēmi* is not easily understood to mean "beside oneself with enthusiasm." It is clumsy to posit a change of subject for the two verbs "they went out" and "they were saying."

ed that Mark found the statement of Jesus' own relatives so
shocking that he placed next to it an even harsher judgment by the
scribes, so that it would not seem so bad by comparison.[100] That
reasoning seems arbitrary, but it suggests that there may be an
intensification in Mark's description of the two groups, depending
on why "his own" wished to seize him—was it for his own
good?[101]

This leads us to the final point: the reaction of the natural
family in A (in the outline) as contrasted with that of the disciples
of Jesus in A', and the possibility that just as Jesus answered
systematically the charges of the scribes in B, so also his words in
A' are an implicit answer to the charge of his family in A. The
least one can conclude from the preceding discussion is that his
family misunderstood Jesus and thought he was beside himself.
The scribes' reaction to Jesus is even harsher in the charge that he
is demon-possessed. Now in contrast to rejection by misunderstanding on the part of his family and to open hostility on the part
of the scribes, we find the reaction on the part of those whom
Jesus has chosen to be with him (3:14). They form a crowd seated
around him (3:32), a crowd that clearly does not think that he is
beside himself or demon-possessed. Their very presence shows
openness to the will of God, and so Jesus designates them as his
true eschatological family, his brother, and sister, and mother.
Thus, the Marcan context considerably sharpens the meaning of
3:31-35, and for Mark the natural family seems to be replaced by
an eschatological family. And it is the eschatological family that is

---

[100]Haenchen, *Weg*, 139ff.

[101]Mark scarcely attributes to Jesus' family the same hostility that
he attributes to the Pharisees (and thus presumably to the scribes as well)
in 3:6, for the latter want to destroy him. Yet some would put Mark's
attitude toward Jesus' family on a par with Mark's attitude toward the
Twelve, who, in the view of some scholars, represent a theological position to which Mark is opposed, e.g., T. J. Weeden, *Mark—Traditions in
Conflict* (Philadelphia: Fortress, 1971), 23-51; W. Kelber, *The Kingdom
in Mark* (Philadelphia: Fortress, 1974), 25-27; E. Trocmé, *The Formation
of the Gospel according to Mark* (Philadelphia: Westminster, 1975), 130-
36. Mark's attitude toward the Twelve is susceptible to another interpretation, however, which is not so pessimistic, e.g., *Peter in the New
Testament*, 57-73; Achtemeier, *Mark*, 92-100; E. Best, "The Role of the
Disciples in Mark," *NTS* 23 (1976-77), 377-401.

inside "the house" with Jesus—a possible reference to the church.[102]

B. The Rejection of Jesus in His Own Country (6:1-6a)

This scene, which presumably takes place at Nazareth, is described as follows:[103]

> [1]*He went away from there and came to his own country, and his disciples followed him.* [2]*And on the sabbath he began to teach in the synagogue; and many who heard him were astonished, saying, "Where did this man get all this? What is the wisdom given to him? What mighty works are wrought by his hands?* [3]*Is not this the carpenter, the son of Mary, and brother of James and Joses and Judas and Simon? And are not his sisters here with us?" And they took offense at him.* [4]*And Jesus said to them, "A prophet is not without honor, except in his own country, and among his own relatives, and in his own house."* [5]*And he could do no mighty work there, except that he laid his hands on a few sick people and healed them.* [6]*And he marveled because of their unbelief.*

Let us first consider what Mark tells about Mary in this passage, and then turn to a corollary question about the brothers of Jesus.

1. The Carpenter, the Son of Mary

In the terminology of form criticism this passage too has been classified as an apophthegm or paradigm,[104] a saying of or

---

[102]However, we cannot say that Mark means to exclude the natural family permanently from the following of Jesus. Presumably family members could become disciples on the same basis as anyone else.

[103]The reading in 6:3, "the carpenter, the son of Mary," is supported by the overwhelming majority of the Greek textual witnesses and is adopted by the best-known recent translations. However, P[45] (the most ancient Greek textual witness to Mark) and minuscule MS 565, as well as some copies of the Old Latin (Itala) and Vulgate versions, read "the son of the carpenter and of Mary," a reading preferred by Taylor, *Mark*, 299-300. For a detailed discussion, see McArthur, "Son," 47-52. As we shall point out in the text, the other three Gospels refer to Jesus in a similar setting as "the carpenter's son" or "the son of Joseph," so that the variant reading may represent a scribal attempt to harmonize Mark with the other Gospels.

[104]See above, n. 91.

pertinent to Jesus set in a brief narrative context. Here the saying is the proverb in v. 4 (or more exactly, the first part of v. 4) which was traditionally associated with Jesus: "A prophet is not without honor except in his own country"[105]—the reference to relatives and house in the second part of v. 4 may be a Marcan expansion to provide a link with 3:20-35. In any case, the present form of v. 4 gives strong support to the interpretation in the preceding section that Mark believed that Jesus was not understood by his family.[106]

Once again scholars would disagree on whether the framework in 1-3 and 5-6 was created or derived from tradition and adapted, but most would agree that it is transmitted by the evangelist for the sake of the proverb. Indeed, one can see a certain tension between the narrative context and v. 4, which suggests that diverse elements have been brought together. The context concerns the villagers who are astonished at the distance between Jesus' teachings or works and his humble origins, with the result that they do not believe in him. The saying in v. 4 concerns not only a lack of honor in the prophet's own country (which would fit the context), but also a lack of honor among his own relatives and in his own house. In v. 4 Jesus is aware that a prophet does not receive honor in his own country; yet in v. 6 he marvels because of the unbelief he encounters in his own country. The end of v. 2 seems to presume that Jesus has done mighty works that the people have seen; yet in v. 5 we are told that he could do no mighty work there.

Granted the likelihood that we have a constructed scene, what does it tell us about Mary? The key phrase is that which the villagers use to describe Jesus as they have known him, "Is not

---

[105]In Papyrus Oxyrhynchus 1, lines 31-36, we read: "Jesus says, 'A prophet is not acceptable in his own country; nor does a physician perform healings on those who know him.' " In the *Gospel of Thomas*, Logion 31, it is phrased thus: "No prophet is acceptable in his own village; no physician heals those who know him."

[106]And once again (see above, n. 97), the two evangelists who know of the virginal conception do not allow the Marcan passage to stand without modification: in Matt 13:35 there is no reference to a lack of honor "among his own relatives"; and in Luke 4:23 both "among his own relatives" and "in his own house" are omitted.

this the carpenter, the son of Mary?" We may compare this to
parallel passages in the other Gospels:[107]

Matt 13:55:   "Is not this the son of the carpenter? Is not his
              mother called Mary?"
Luke 4:22:   "Is not this the son of Joseph?"
John 6:42:   "Is not this Jesus the son of Joseph? Do we not
              know his father and his mother?"

Two things are noteworthy: first, only Mark's version calls Jesus
a carpenter; second, only Mark's version makes no mention
whatsoever of Jesus' father. The first point is of less importance
for our interests. Whether it is Jesus or his father who was the
carpenter (or both), the question is meant to stress his humble
origins as contrasted with his current reputation as a teacher and
a worker of mighty deeds.

The second question is much more integral to our concerns.
Why does Mark make no mention of Joseph or of Jesus' father, as
do the other three Gospels? (We may note that there was no
mention of Joseph in 3:31 even when Mark made reference to
"his mother and brothers"; but in that instance Matthew and
Luke agreed with Mark.) And why does Mark use the designation
"son of Mary," which is found only here in the NT? We may
discuss four different explanations that have been offered:[108]

(a) Mark is trying to stress the human characteristics of
Jesus in order to refute the exaggerated supernatural claims of the
Marcan congregation—Jesus is human, a carpenter, and born of
woman. Thus, "son of Mary" conveys little more than Paul does
when he says Jesus is "born of woman" (Gal 4:4—see above,

---

[107]The scenes in Matt 13:53-58 and Luke 4:16-30 are clearly parallel
to Mark 6:1-6, although Luke is not necessarily drawing upon Mark in his
much larger Nazareth scene. John 6:42 has a different setting (the complaint of the Jews on the shore of the Lake of Galilee), but this verse
seems to be the Johannine equivalent of Mark 6:3.

[108]It has been suggested that "son of Mary" is just an informal
description used by the villagers, somewhat analogous to our colloquial
"O yes! That's Mary's boy from down the street." See McArthur, "Son,"
57. However, this does not explain Mark's general failure to mention the
father of Jesus in ministry scenes. Moreover, one may ask what would be
the purpose of informality in what is otherwise a dramatic scene.

Chap. 3, B2). This attitude is favored by some of the Marcan interpreters who see Mark's Gospel consistently stressing that Jesus is the crucified one, rather than a supernatural miracle worker.[109] Besides the debatable quality of this analysis of Marcan purpose, one must ask whether the scene as Mark presents it has any evident polemic against Jesus as a wonder worker. Moreover, the people in the scene who object that Jesus is a carpenter and the son of Mary are characterized as unbelievers, a designation which would scarcely lead the reader to sympathize with their evaluation of Jesus, or to regard it as the evaluation that Mark wishes to inculcate.

(b) Mark is hinting at the virginal conception of Jesus.[110] Since Mark never mentions the virginal conception, this is an interpretation of Mark that arises only because of information given in Matthew and Luke—a methodological difficulty. An attempt to avoid this difficulty is the suggestion that the Matthean and/or Lucan form of the villagers' question is closer to the original, pre-Marcan form of the question. That original form would then have been modified by Mark (with no dependence on Matthew and Luke[111]) by changing "the son of the carpenter and of Mary" to "the carpenter, the son of Mary," to avoid giving

---

[109]Such an approach to 6:1-6a finds support in Lathrop, *Who*, 35. By means of a comparison with 15:27-39b, he attempts to show that 6:1-6a is closely related to Mark's *theologia crucis*:

6:1-2a	15:22-27:	setting
6:2b-3a	15:29-32:	attitude of enemies
6:3c-5a	15:33-39a:	impotence of Jesus, interrupted by a word from him
6:5b	15:39b:	the breaking out of the revelation in this impotence

[110]For example, Miguens, *Virgin Birth*, 6-27, who argues for Marcan knowledge of the virginal conception against Brown, *Virginal Conception*, 57-59; and Fitzmyer, "Virginal Conception," 556-58. It is part of Miguens' general thesis that the virginal conception was known by most NT authors (Paul and John included) and not by only Matthew and Luke.

[111]Another theory which supposes Marcan knowledge of Matthew and Luke has been invoked to substantiate Mark's awareness of the virginal conception. In Chap. 2, n. 21, we mentioned the Griesbach solution to the Synoptic problem, a solution that we did not accept. According to W. R. Farmer, *The Synoptic Problem: A Critical Analysis* (New

Jesus a human father. This view faces formidable difficulties. First, the authors who do speak of a virginal conception (Matthew and Luke) saw no difficulty in referring to Jesus as "the son of the carpenter" and "the son of Joseph"; and so it is strange logic to argue that an author who does not mention the virginal conception conveyed that idea by changing the expression. Second, in 6:3 this implicit reference to the virginal conception would be on the lips of the villagers. One would have to explain how they knew of it, or why Mark would try to convey such a Christian perception by placing it on the lips of those whom Jesus designates as unbelievers. Third, if Mark knew of the virginal conception, why does he have a reference to Jesus' family (including his mother) as thinking that Jesus is beside himself (3:21); and why does he have Jesus say obliquely that he is not honored by his own relatives? Such a negative attitude of Mary toward Jesus seems irreconcilable with Mary's having known that this was a miraculous child conceived without a human father. At least, the two authors who speak of a virginal conception did not find such a negative attitude reconcilable with that tradition, for they omitted both the Marcan passages just cited. Thus, this interpretation of Mark has little to recommend it.

(c) The villagers are casting a slur on Jesus: he is a carpenter, an ordinary manual laborer; and he is the son of Mary, so called because there is doubt about his father. In other words, Jesus is implicitly referred to as illegitimate. There is some evidence that referring to a man as the son of his mother is an

---

York: Macmillan, 1964), 232, if Mark knew Matthew's Gospel, he may have changed "the son of the carpenter" to "the carpenter" because he was aware that "the Virgin Birth stories were known and understood in such a way as to preclude the idea of a human father for Jesus." However, if one wants to argue on the basis of the Griesbach hypothesis, and to posit Marcan knowledge of "a developing doctrine concerning the birth of Jesus to a virgin," then how does one explain Mark's addition to Matthew and Luke of passages relatively hostile to Mary, such as 3:21 (as an introduction to 3:31-35) and the last clauses of 6:4 ("and among his own relatives, and in his own house"). See below, Chap. 5, n. 207. Here, as elsewhere, the Griesbach hypothesis seems to raise more problems than it solves.

indication of illegitimacy;[112] however, there is no attestation of
this use in the Bible.[113] It is true that two other Gospel passages
can be cited as lending support to a charge of illegitimacy,[114] but
the Marcan allusion would be very subtle and scarcely intelligible
for a Gentile audience for whom elsewhere Mark has to explain
the most elementary Jewish customs (7:3). Moreover, if that were
Mark's understanding of "son of Mary," why would he go on to
mention the brothers and sisters. Were they too to be considered
illegitimate?

(d) Jesus' father is not mentioned because he is dead. This is
the simplest and most satisfactory explanation of the absence of
Joseph in 3:31-35 and also in 6:1-6. The villagers point to Jesus'
relatives who are living in Nazareth and who are visible evidence
that his beginnings were very ordinary. They do not point to
Joseph because he is not there, and Jesus is called "son of Mary"
because she is there. In favoring this theory, we are not arguing
that sons of widows were normally called by their mother's
name.[115] Nor are we contending that "son of Mary" was Jesus'
regular designation; he was usually known as the "son of Joseph."
The anomalous use here flows from the context in which the
villagers are naming Jesus' relatives. (Similarly the context makes
intelligible the usage of Luke 7:12 where the deceased is identified
as "the only son of his mother who was a widow.") Thus we see
no profound Marian significance in the fact that Jesus is called
"son of Mary."

---

[112]See Stauffer, "Jeschu," for a variety of arguments favoring this
position. He mentions specifically that in Samaritan and Mandaean usage
the designation "Jesus, son of Mary" would have a pejorative sense. In
his book *Jerusalem und Rom* (Bern: Francke, 1957), 118, Stauffer points
to a Jewish legal principle: A man is illegitimate when he is called by his
mother's name, for a bastard has no father.

[113]A strong argument against the illegitimacy interpretation is offered by McArthur, "Son."

[114]In Matt 1:18-19 the suspicion is relatively clear; in John 8:41 it is
at most implicit, in the Jews' answer to Jesus: "*We* were not born of
fornication," if the emphatic "we" implies "not we but you." See below,
Chap. 7, A7.

[115]In 1 Kings 17:17 a child of the widow of Zarephath is called "the
son of the woman," but that is scarcely probative, as McArthur, "Son,"
44-45, 52, points out.

2. The Brothers and Sisters of Jesus

Mark 6:3 names four brothers of Jesus and mentions his sisters. This reference to Jesus' family gained Marian significance only in later centuries as Christians debated whether Mary remained a virgin after the birth of Jesus.[116] If the brothers mentioned in Mark 3:31 and 6:3 and the sisters mentioned in 6:3 are Mary's children, obviously she did not remain a virgin; if they are not, her continued virginity is tenable.[117] The discussion centers first on the meaning of *adelphos*, "brother,"[118] and secondly on the conclusion that can be drawn from the names of the brothers.

The term *adelphos*, which is used in Mark 6:3, would normally denote a blood brother, "son of the same mother,"[119] *frater germanus*. It is well known that in the NT *adelphos* at times denotes other relationships:[120] e.g., "co-religionist" (Rom 9:3, where it is in the plural, and further specified as referring to kinsmen [*syngeneis*] according to the flesh); "neighbor" (Matt 5:22-24)—but these instances do not help with the problem at hand, for here Jesus' mother and sisters are mentioned also. More pertinent would be the use of *adelphos* for step-brother in Mark 6:17-18.[121] In the Greek OT *adelphos* is sometimes used in the

---

[116]The title "Ever Virgin" (*aeiparthenos, semper virgo*) arose early in Christianity; the first instance is a dubious passage in Peter of Alexandria (died 311—see *PG* 18. 517B). It was a stock phrase in the Middle Ages and continued to be used in Protestant confessional writings (Luther, Calvin, Zwingli, Andrewes; *Book of Concord*, Smalcald Articles). For the contrary views of Tertullian and Helvidius, see below, Chap. 9, C2.

[117]Some of the argument on this point does not recognize that more is needed to establish the continued virginity of Mary than the absence of further children.

[118]We shall concentrate on *adelphos* with the understanding that what is said applies to *adelphē*, "sister," as well. Jesus' "sisters" are mentioned only in Mark 6:3 and Matt 13:56.

[119]Liddell-Scott-Jones, *A Greek-English Lexicon* (Oxford: Clarendon, 1940), 1. 120.

[120]See BAG, 15-16; also J. J. Collins, *TS* 5 (1944), 484-94. As we saw in Mark 3:34-35, "brother(s)" applies to disciples as part of an eschatological family.

[121]Philip, called by Mark the *adelphos* of Herod, was his step-brother, although one might argue (with some risk) that Mark thought he was the blood brother.

broad sense of "kinsman, relative," e.g., in the LXX of Gen
29:12, Jacob tells Rebekah "that he is her father's *adelphos*
(kinsman)"; also Gen 24:48. The Greek usage here obviously reflects the underlying Hebrew in which *'āḥ* means both "(blood)
brother" and "kinsman." The same range of meaning seems to be
attested for Aramaic *'ăḥā'*.[122]

Granted this broad Greek usage of *adelphos*, one may raise
the question whether Mark 6:3 could be using *adelphos* (and the
feminine *adelphē*) in the broad sense of "kin" or "relative," so
that the men and women mentioned would not be blood brothers
or sisters of Jesus.[123] In this case the Greek would reflect an
underlying Hebrew/Aramaic usage; but such an interpretation
would be methodologically valid only if there were reason to
suspect a Semitic background. Now it is not implausible that
Jesus' relatives would have been remembered according to the
way they were designated in Aramaic or Hebrew. Moreover this
scene is set in Nazareth and the question about Jesus' family is
being asked by villagers who presumably would have spoken
Aramaic. But, as mentioned above, there is no scholarly agreement on whether the context is a creation or is derived from
tradition. (If there is preserved tradition in the setting, one would
have to distinguish between what the meaning may have been in
the pre-Marcan situation [perhaps "kin, relatives"] and how
Mark may have understood it ["brothers"].) Further, since the
"brothers" are mentioned twice with Mary[124] and since the nor-

---

[122]See J. A. Fitzmyer, *JNES* 21 (1962), 16-17 for a father writing to
his son: "To my son from your brother." There is a problem in the
Aramaic usage, however, since it may be a stylized mode of addressing
an "equal" in social standing. See also the *Genesis Apocryphon* from
Qumran Cave 1 (2:9) for an example of a wife calling her husband
"brother" and an instance of the same in Greek papyri in U. Wilcken,
Urkunden der Ptolemäerzeit (Berlin: De Gruyter, 1927), 1. 300, no. 59.

[123]The most complete defense of this can be found in Blinzler,
Die Brüder.

[124]The association of the *adelphoi* with Mary means that those who
deny that they are her children must find an explanation why they are
several times pictured with her. If they are Jesus' cousins, are they
Mary's nephews who are taking care of their widowed aunt? If they are
Jesus' half-brothers, now that Joseph is dead, is Mary responsible for
these, his children by a former marriage?

mal meaning of *adelphos* is "blood brother," the suspicion of a Semitic background would not be enough in itself to warrant the broader translation. Clearly it is the later church tradition that has led many to argue for the broad translation; for already by mid-second century, in the *Protevangelium of James*, 9:2, Christians were being told that the "brothers" were children of Joseph by a previous marriage.[125]

The Marcan reference to *adelphoi* and *adelphai* is not the only NT evidence as to whether Mary had other children. There are texts in the Matthean and Lucan infancy narratives that some have thought to point to her having children after Jesus was born (Matt 1:25; Luke 2:7), but we may postpone our discussion of those until Chap. 5, A2; Chap. 6, A4. Here we must discuss the further evidence supplied by Mark's list of the names of the brothers of Jesus in 6:3: "James and Joses and Judas and Simon." But to discuss these names, one has to consider Mary, the mother of James and Joses, whom Mark mentions in describing the death and burial of Jesus.

---

[125]The *Protevangelium* shows itself unhistorical on most other details it reports about Mary's youth, e.g., her being reared at the Temple. Consequently its witness to Joseph's previous children (Jesus' half-brothers) does not inspire much confidence, although it was widely accepted as late as Epiphanius of Salamis in the fourth century. Another thesis, stemming from Jerome in the fourth century, is that the *adelphoi* were cousins of Jesus, either through Mary's sister or through Joseph's sister or brother. John 19:25 mentions a sister of Mary; and we shall discuss below the problem of Mary of Clopas, whom Jerome identified as daughter of Clopas and sister of Mary the virgin—he thought that she was the wife of Alphaeus (see James son of Alphaeus in the apostolic list; n. 135 below). It is important to realize that while Epiphanius and Jerome were arguing that the brothers were half-brothers or cousins, Helvidius and others were arguing that they were blood brothers. McHugh, *Mother*, 200-54 discusses all this at length and opts for the thesis that they were sons of Joseph's brother-in-law brought up by Joseph after his brother-in-law's death. Today most who deny the blood-brother relationship make no attempt to specify the relationship and suspect that all that was remembered in antiquity was that they were relatives or kin. If a specific relationship were remembered, e.g., cousin, some Greek speaker should have begun to use the available specific Greek term, e.g., *anepsios*, which appears in the NT at Col 4:10.

C. Mary, James, and Joses (15:40, 47; 16:1)

According to Mark 6:3 Jesus is "the son of Mary, and brother of James and Joses and Judas and Simon";[126] according to Matt 13:55 his mother is called Mary and his brothers are "James and Joseph and Simon and Judas." Thus, the first two brothers are James and Joses or Joseph. In the Marcan list of the women who look on the cross from afar (15:40), besides Mary Magdalene and Salome, there is a "Mary the mother of James the younger [*tou mikrou*] and of Joses"; in Matt 27:56 she appears as "Mary the mother of James and Joseph." If this Mary is the same as Mary the mother of Jesus, then we would have conclusive evidence that the brothers of Jesus (specifically James and Joses/Joseph) are her children. If this Mary is not the mother of Jesus, then we can ask whether the James and Joses/Joseph are the same as the James and Joses/Joseph who are called *adelphoi* of Jesus. If they are, we would have conclusive evidence that the *adelphoi* (which would then mean "relatives") are not the children of Jesus' mother.

Let us begin by seeking to clarify the identity of this Mary who appears in Mark and Matthew in the crucifixion scene. John also has a group of women in that scene, but they are standing next to the cross whereas in the Marcan/Matthean account the women are at a distance. The difference of locales probably represents thematic interests of the evangelists;[127] and so it is worthwhile to make a comparison of the respective traditions of the names. If we read the description in John 19:25 to mean that there are four women,[128] we emerge with the following schema:

---

[126]Minor variants in some MSS affect the name Joses, e.g., Jose or Joseph—the latter form probably being due to harmonization with Matt 13:55.

[127]The Synoptic evangelists could have in mind Ps 38:12(11): "My kinsmen stand at a distance from me" (also Ps 88:9[8]); John needs to have the mother of Jesus and the beloved disciple close so that Jesus can speak to them. Harmonization has also been attempted: at first they stood at a distance, but in the darkness that covered the earth they slipped closer.

[128]John can be read to involve *two* women (his mother and his mother's sister, i.e., Mary of Clopas and Mary Magdalene); but it is odd that the mother of Jesus would be identified as "Mary of Clopas." (Cer-

Mark 15:40	Matt 27:56	John 19:25
		Jesus' mother
Mary Magdalene	Mary Magdalene	His mother's sister
Mary mother of	Mary mother of	Mary the wife of
James the younger	James and of	Clopas
and of Joses	Joseph	
Salome	The mother of the	Mary Magdalene
	sons of Zebedee	

In the Johannine scene constituted by 19:25-27 the only woman that receives attention is the mother of Jesus who is associated with the beloved disciple. This leads to the suggestion that John added her name to a traditional list of three women[129] and moved the whole scene to the foot of the cross in order that Jesus might speak to his mother and the beloved disciple. If that suggestion has merit, our comparison should be between the three women in Mark/Matthew and the three women John mentions after Jesus' mother. Mary Magdalene is obviously the same in all three lists. As for the Salome mentioned by Mark, one could propose that she is the mother of the sons of Zebedee (Matthew's list) and the sister of Mary, the mother of Jesus (John's list). Such an identification might explain the tradition that the mother of the sons of Zebedee asked Jesus for special consideration for them (Matt 20:20); i.e., it was another instance of family claims being made on Jesus which he rejected. Finally one could identify Mary the mother of James the younger and of Joses/Joseph (Mark's list and Matthew's) with Mary the wife of Clopas (John's list).[130] There are an excessive number of "ifs" in this hypothesis, but it does

---

tainly, then, Mary would be either the daughter or the mother of Clopas, not his wife; for Mary the mother of Jesus was the wife of Joseph.) John can also be read to involve *three* women (his mother, and his mother's sister[Mary of Clopas], and Mary Magdalene); but it is unlikely that two sisters would each be named Mary.

[129]However, R. T. Fortna, *The Gospel of Signs* (SNTSMS 11; Cambridge: University Press, 1970), 130, thinks that all four women were in the pre-Johannine source, and that only the beloved disciple was added by John.

[130]If James and Joses/Joseph are the *adelphoi* (kinsmen) of Jesus—see below—then their mother is a relative of Jesus as well, so that most of the women who had come to the crucifixion would have been relatives of Jesus!

offer a reason for thinking that the Mary who is designated as the mother of James and Joses/Joseph is not the Mary who is the mother of Jesus. Furthermore, it is unlikely that Mark would knowingly describe the mother of the crucified Jesus (called "his mother" in 3:31) simply as the mother of James and Joses.[131]

But if it seems likely that Mary the mother of James and Joses/Joseph is *not* the mother of Jesus, who are the James and Joses/Joseph named in Mark 15:40 and Matt 27:56? Are they identical with the James and Joses/Joseph listed first among the four *adelphoi* of Jesus in Mark 6:3 and Matt 13:55?[132] If so, those *adelphoi* would not be sons of Jesus' mother. Some argue against identity, pointing out that it is inconsistent to distinguish between the two Marys and yet to identify the two sets of sons, especially since four sons are named in the first Marcan/Matthean passage while only two are recalled in the second. Moreover, James is called "the younger" in 15:40 but not in 6:3. Others argue for identity on the basis of the same variant Joses/Joseph which appear in the two Marcan/Matthean sets of names. In evaluating these arguments, let us look at the three references to the sons of Mary in the crucifixion and post-crucifixion setting. The woman with Mary Magdalene is described as follows:[133]

Mark 15:40:	Mary mother of James the younger and of Joses
Matt 27:56:	Mary mother of James and of Joseph
Mark 15:47:	Mary (mother) of Joses
Matt 27:61:	the other Mary
Mark 16:1:	Mary (mother) of James
Matt 28:1:	the other Mary

---

[131]See Blinzler, *Die Brüder*, 73-82. Of course, Mark may not have known that the mother of James and Joses was also the mother of Jesus. Or is it possible that Mark chose to identify the mother of Jesus by the names of her other sons (James and Joses) because Jesus has been identified as "Son of God" at 15:39?

[132]The frequency of such patriarchal names as James (*Iakōbos*) and Joseph in the first century warns us against too easily assuming identity.

[133]Of the three Marcan texts, the Greek word for "mother" occurs only in the first.

Two questions must be asked. First, why is James called *ho mikros*, "the younger" or "the less"? The traditional explanation has been that it was to distinguish him from James the son of Zebedee, called in later tradition "the greater." But that has usually involved the assumption that James "the younger" was James the brother of the Lord (Gal 1:19; cf. 2:9,12; I Cor 15:7), who in turn was often (and erroneously[134]) identified with "James (the son) of Alphaeus," mentioned in all four lists of the Twelve.[135] Other explanations have been that he was called "the younger" or "the less" in comparison with his older and greater brother Jesus. Since the NT does not have a James called *ho makros*, "the greater," we have no certainty that a comparison is intended. The designation *ho mikros* might have meant no more than that this particular James was small in stature.[136]

The second question concerns the order of composition of the three Marcan texts under discussion. If 15:40 was the original designation ("Mary mother of James the younger and of Joses"), the designations using the name of only one son in 15:47 and 16:1 may be a type of shorthand. However, it has been suggested[137] that the sequence was just the opposite and that 15:40 is a Marcan joining of the single-name designations in 16:1 and 15:47, so that "Mary mother of James" and "Mary mother of Joses" were joined to produce "Mary mother of James the younger and of

---

[134]We say erroneously because Acts 1:13 and 1:14 keep clearly distinct "James of Alphaeus" (in the list of the Eleven) and the brothers of Jesus. A distinction between "the other apostles" and "the brothers of the Lord" is found in 1 Cor 9:5. See above, n. 93.

[135]Similarly (and also erroneously) Judas, one of the last two of the brothers mentioned in Mark 6:3 and Matt 13:55, has been identified with "Judas of James" (understood as "Judas the brother of James"; see Jude 1) in the Lucan lists of the Twelve (Luke 6:16 and Acts 1:13).

[136]See BAG 523a, and the parallels in the Greek usage of *mikros* cited there.

[137]See L. Schenke, *Auferstehungsverkündigung und leeres Grab: Eine traditionsgeschichtliche Untersuchung von Mk 16, 1-8.* (SBS 33; Stuttgart: Katholisches Bibelwerk, 1968), 25-37. He understands Mark 15:42-47 and 16:1-8 to contain originally independent tradition, and 15:40-41 to be a Marcan composition designed to set the stage for those later two passages. See further Blinzler, *Die Brüder*, 82-86.

Joses."[138] There are difficulties in either approach and the possibility of a confusion of names is evident. The members of the task force agreed that there was no way to be certain whether the evidence of Mark 15:40 (and 15:47; 16:1) solves the problem of the nature of the relationship between Jesus and those called his brothers and sisters in Mark 6:3. We were not even agreed on which solution might be called the more likely. But we did agree on these points:

(1) The continued virginity of Mary after the birth of Jesus is not a question directly raised by the NT.

(2) Once it was raised in subsequent church history, it was that question which focused attention on the exact relationship of the "brothers" (and "sisters") to Jesus.

(3) Once that attention has been focused, it cannot be said that the NT identifies them *without doubt* as blood brothers and sisters and hence as children of Mary.

(4) The solution favored by scholars will in part depend on the authority they allot to later church insights.[139]

---

[138]The addition of "the younger" in this theory would have served as a distinguishing epithet because Mark knew of other men named James in the Christian movement, e.g., in the list of the Twelve.

[139]A recent commentary by a Roman Catholic, R. Pesch, *Das Markusevangelium* (HTKNT II/1; Freiburg: Herder, 1976), 322-25, identifies these relatives as blood brothers and sisters of Jesus and children of Mary. It has been stated in Roman Catholic theological works that the perpetual virginity of Mary is a matter of faith (a dogma attested in the constant teaching of the Church); see for instance, K. Rahner, *Mary Mother of the Lord* (New York: Herder & Herder, 1963), 15, 63, 65. And so it remains to be seen if Church authorities will tolerate Pesch's theory.

CHAPTER FIVE:
MARY IN THE
GOSPEL OF MATTHEW*

In this Gospel we may distinguish two kinds of passages in which Mary appears: first, a group of uniquely Matthean references to Mary in the infancy narrative of chaps. 1-2; second, Matthean texts that have a parallel to passages already discussed in Mark. The latter include Matt 12:46-50, parallel to Mark 3:31-35 (the question of who constitute the family of Jesus); and Matt 13:53-58, parallel to Mark 6:1-6a (the rejection of Jesus in his own country).[140] In discussing this second group of texts we shall be interested in the extent to which Matthew differs from Mark, so that we can detect his own interests (i.e., his redactional theology). It seems wiser to begin with the treatment of Mary in the first group of texts which come at the very beginning of the Gospel. Since we may assume a certain homogeneity in Matthew's outlook upon Mary, the insight gained from the first group of

---

*The discussion for this chapter was led by K. P. Donfried and M. M. Bourke, and the first draft was composed by K. P. Donfried. One session of the task force (Nov. 1975) was devoted to the evidence of Matthew (as well as discussion during the sessions on Mark).

[140]There is also Matt 27:56, 61; 28:1, which constitute a parallel to Mark 15:40, 47; 16:1, dealing with Mary, James, and Joseph/Joses and the problem of the identity of Jesus' "brothers." However, we have already discussed these texts in detail in Chap. 4C, and there is no need to mention them again here.

texts may enable us better to understand why Matthew varies
from Mark in the common scenes.

A. Mary in the Birth Narrative (Chaps. 1-2)

Unlike Mark, Matthew begins the Gospel narrative with two
chapters that pertain to Jesus' conception, birth, and infancy;
only then (chap. 3) does he join the Marcan outline with the story
of Jesus' baptism. Scholars do not agree whether these chapters
in themselves served as a preliminary unit in Matthew's Gospel
plan (as we would suspect from studying the parallelism with
Mark), or whether the preliminary unit continued to Matt 4:17.[141]
Nevertheless, partisans of both divisions agree that the infancy
narrative is very much part of Matthew's Gospel and of his
theological outlook. Therefore, before discussing the Marian passages a few general remarks about Matthean theology and about
the theology of the infancy narratives would be in order.

First, Matthean theology in general. Like the other
evangelists, Matthew shaped his theology and christology against
the background of the life of his community. The frequent OT
citations and the length of Matthew's collection of sayings
directed against scribes and Pharisees (chap. 23) have made virtually all commentators recognize that at some period in the
community's history there was intense dialogue with and polemic
against Jewish authorities or against the positions which they
represented. Indeed, it has been specified by some that the
Judaism in question was the Pharisaism which survived the de-
struction of the Temple in A.D. 70 and which found its spokesmen
in the teachers at Jamnia.[142] What we cannot tell for certain is
whether this polemic was of the recent past or was still going on

---

[141]Kingsbury, *Matthew*, 1-17.

[142]See especially Davies, *Setting*, 256-315. It was through the instigation of the teachers at Jamnia that the twelfth of the Eighteen Bene-
dictions *(Shemoneh Esreh)* was introduced—the *Birkat ha-Mînîm*—
calling down a curse on the *mînîm*, i.e., on the deviants or heretics,
including the Christians. From that time on (ca. A.D. 85) it became increasingly difficult for believers in Jesus to remain affiliated with Jewish
synagogues.

and thus contemporary with the writing of the Gospel.[143] And the Jewish interest is not the only optic in the Gospel, for perhaps more than any other evangelist Matthew puts a stress on the mission to the Gentiles (Matt 28:19).[144] The kingdom of God will be taken away from the chief priests and the Pharisees and given to a nation that produces fruit (21:43, 45). A plausible conclusion is that Matthew's was a mixed community with a Jewish base but with an increasing number of Gentile converts.[145] In that case, Matthew would be presenting a Jesus who would be convincing to both sides. On the one hand, he would be reinforcing the Jewish Christians against an anti-Jesus polemic on the part of their non-Christian Jewish confreres guided by the authorities at Jamnia. To these Christians Matthew would be giving an arsenal of Scripture citations which proved the place of Jesus in God's plan of salvation. On the other hand, Matthew would be seeking to justify the increasing presence of Gentiles in the community by showing that a sense of exclusivism was not justified (3:7-10) and that God had planned from the beginning an inclusion of Gentiles.

Second, the theology of the infancy narrative. Just as for the Gospel, so also for the infancy narratives, several plans of organization have been detected.[146] One theory places the emphasis on

---

[143]Is a saying such as Matt 23:2, "The scribes and Pharisees sit on the chair of Moses; so practice and observe whatever they tell you," an echo of a past situation in the history of the Matthean community, or is it representative of the evangelist's attitude when he is writing the Gospel? Is the evangelist a Jew, and perhaps even a converted scribe (13:52), or is he a Gentile (Strecker, *Weg*, 34; also K. W. Clark, *JBL* 66 [1947], 165-72)?

[144]This holds true whether the *panta ta ethnē* of 28:19 means "all the nations (including Israel)" or "all the Gentiles"; see D. R. A. Hare and D. J. Harrington, *CBQ* 37 (1975), 359-69.

[145]See Kümmel, *Introduction*, 114-18. This is probably the view accepted by most scholars; yet there are others who stress almost entirely the Jewish side or the Gentile side. See respectively R. Hummel, *Die Auseinandersetzung zwischen Kirche und Judentum im Matthäusevangelium (BEvT* 33; Munich: Kaiser, 1961), and P. Nepper-Christensen, *Das Matthäusevangelium—ein judenchristliches Evangelium?* (Aarhus University Press, 1958).

[146]If one accepts the thesis of pre-Matthean sources, the difference in these analyses may result from whether preference is given to the pattern of the sources (lying just below the surface) or to that of the final redaction.

the five fulfillment citations interspersed in the narrative that follows the genealogy of 1:1-17[147]—both by way of precisely balanced generations (1:17) and by way of prophecies Matthew would be showing that God had prepared for the coming of His Messiah. Another theory acknowledges the wisdom of the division of the infancy narrative into two chapters, one terminating with the child being called Jesus (1:25), the second terminating with his being called a Nazorean (2:23). In either case the theme of the identity of Jesus as Son of David and Emmanuel, as well as how he possessed those identities seems to dominate 1:1-25. A type of geographical theology, with birth at Bethlehem, flight to Egypt, and return to Nazareth seems to dominate 2:1-23.[148] It is interesting to note that 1:1, which may be the title not only of the genealogy but also of the whole infancy narrative, refers to Jesus both as "son of David" and "son of Abraham." Clearly, the annunciation takes up the "son of David" motif by having Joseph, son of David (1:20), acknowledge Jesus as his son by naming him. Correspondingly, the coming of the magi who are clearly Gentile may be meant to take up the "son of Abraham" motif.[149] In that case Matthew would be speaking through the two titles to the respective groups within his community. But even without a dou-

---

[147]Isa 7:14 in Matt 1:22-23; Mic 5:1[2] and 2 Sam 5:2 in Matt 2:5b-6; Hos 11:1 in Matt 2:15b; Jer 31:15 [LXX 38:15] in Matt 2:17-18; an unknown citation (Isa 4:3? Judg 16:17?) in Matt 2:23b. Those who base the plan of the infancy narrative on these citations are clearly giving preference to Matthew's redaction over any possible sources.

[148]The key to this analysis is given in the title of Stendahl's article "Quis et Unde?" ("Who?" refers to chap. 1; "Whence?" refers to chap. 2). However, Paul, L'Evangile, 96, is perceptive in suggesting that Stendahl's "Qui et d'où" needs a "Comment?" and a "Quand?"—in this case chap. 1 deals with Quis et Quomodo? (Who and How?), while chap. 2 deals with Ubi et Unde? (Where and Whence?). See Brown, Birth, 52-54.

[149]Some scholars suppose that Paul's view of the Gentile Christians as heirs of the promises to Abraham (Gal 3:6-9) was widespread and known to Matthew. Yet while Matt 3:7-10 stresses the possibility that the Pharisees and Sadducees would be replaced by new children to Abraham, it is not clear that Gentiles are meant. Perhaps the OT promise of a universal blessing through Abraham (Gen 22:18) would be enough to make the association.

ble thrust of the titles, the heroes of Matthew's narrative are *Joseph*, a just Jew obedient to the Law (1:19), and *the magi*, Gentiles responsive to God's revelation through the star; the villains are the Jewish king, the chief priests, the scribes, and all Jerusalem (2:3-4).[150] Thus there is little doubt that throughout the infancy narrative Matthew was conscious of alignments within and without the Christian community of his own time.

With those general remarks we are now ready to proceed to an analysis of Mary's role in the various parts of the infancy narrative.

1. Mary in the Genealogy (1:1-17)

Matthew divides his genealogy into three subsections of fourteen generations each (1:17). There are many problems about his mathematics, about the names in the genealogy, about omissions and about its historicity; but it is not our purpose to enter into those problems here.[151] We are concerned only with the light that the genealogy throws upon Matthew's view of Mary whom he mentions at the very end of the list of ancestors in 1:16. That he does have a special interest in Mary is suggested by three observations: (a) When Matthew reaches the birth of Jesus, he breaks the "A begot [or was the father of] B" pattern that he has used for every other birth in the list. In 1:16 he speaks rather of "Mary of whom was begotten Jesus."[152] (b) In 1:18-25 he proceeds to give

---

[150]Herod is the greatest villain; but Matt 2:20 associates others with Herod, most logically those in 2:4 who enabled him to find where the Messiah would be born.

[151]See the long discussion in Brown, *Birth*, 57-95.

[152]It is impossible to be certain whether the *egennēthē* of 1:16 should be translated "was begotten" or "was born." The former is suggested by the fact that in the rest of the genealogy this verb *gennan* means "beget," and that in 1:20 the related form *to gennēthen* clearly refers to the child begotten in Mary. We are presuming the correctness of the reading "Jacob was the father of Joseph, the husband of Mary of whom was begotten Jesus, who is called the Christ," supported by the overwhelming weight of MS evidence. In particular we have not accepted the reading supported only by the Old Syriac (Sinaiticus): "Jacob was the father of Joseph; and *Joseph*, to whom the virgin Mary was betrothed, *was the*

further light on why he did not say in 1:16: "Joseph begot [was the father of] Jesus by Mary." Stendahl[153] may exaggerate when he calls 1:18-25 "the enlarged footnote to the crucial point in the genealogy," but his instinct is quite right in underlining the continuity of thought. (c) Mary is not the only woman in the genealogy and through the inclusion of a group of four OT women (Tamar, Rahab, Ruth, Uriah's wife) Matthew may be calling attention to Mary's role.

We must devote more attention to the last point, for it was unusual in first-century Judaism to list a woman's name in a genealogy, let alone the five women that Matthew lists.[154] The seeming biblical exceptions (e.g., the mention of David's wives in 1 Chr 3:1-10) are not real parallels; and the OT lists that are closest to the first and second parts of Matthew's genealogy (from Abraham to the Babylonian captivity), namely those in Ruth 4:18-22 and 1 Chr 2:5-15; 3:10-19, offer no adequate explanation for Matthew's inclusion of four women of biblical fame, since in none of the OT genealogies do women occur with this frequency. Thus it is a reasonable supposition that, whether Matthew composed the list of Jesus' ancestors entirely by his own research and reflection or whether he drew upon popular forms of royal and messianic genealogies, it is he who was responsible for the presence of women in the genealogy. Their presence must have served his purposes. Accordingly, we must ask two questions: What do the four OT women have in common among themselves? How do they prepare for the birth of Jesus and for the fifth woman, Mary? Many hypotheses have been proposed in response to these questions, of which the following are the most important:

---

father of Jesus, who is called the Christ." This reading probably resulted from a scribe's attempt to make the last entry in the genealogy match the other entries. Despite the claim of some scholars that the Syriac Sinaiticus reading denies the virginal conception, it may well be that the scribe thought that the introduction of "virgin" before "Mary" protected the non-physical character of the begetting. See Metzger, *TCGNT*, 2-7.

[153]Stendahl, "Quis," 102.

[154]Johnson, *Purpose*, 153ff.

Theory I:	The Four OT Women Were Gentiles or Foreigners.
Theory II:	They Were Subjects of Controversy in the Jewish Debate about the Davidic Messiah
Theory III:	They Were Sinners.
Theory IV:	Although Marked by Irregular Marital Unions, They Were Vehicles of God's Messianic Plan.

Below we shall discuss these one by one; but before we begin, it is wise to mention a general difficulty. In seeking what is common among the women, we cannot depend solely on the OT narrative; we must also seek to know how the women were considered in the Judaism of Jesus' time. The theological outlook of the first century, through which Jews read the Scriptures, was often quite different from the outlook of the original authors. In seeking to know Jewish attitudes toward these women in Jesus' time, scholars have limited resources: late intertestamental literature, the Dead Sea Scrolls, Philo and Josephus, and indications in the NT. In proposing one or the other of the above theories, modern scholars have sought to fill in the lacunae of our first-century knowledge by citing later Jewish positions attested in the rabbinical literature (Talmud and midrashim). But these writings, composed between a century and a millennium after the NT, are uncertain guides to the Judaism of Jesus' time; for they represent a chronological development of one strain of that Judaism (Pharisaism). We shall mention attitudes about the four OT women that scholars have found in the later rabbinical writings, but always with a caution about the extent to which these attitudes help us to detect Matthew's mind.

THEORY I: *The Four OT Women Were Gentiles or Foreigners*.[155] According to the biblical narrative, three of the women were non-Israelites (Tamar, Rahab, and Ruth); and the fourth woman (Bathsheba), although an Israelite, is identified by Matthew not under her own name but as the wife of Uriah, who was a Hittite. Their inclusion could be seen as God's preparation

---

[155]A theory that had the support of Martin Luther, this is strongly defended by Stegemann, "Uria."

of the birth of a Messiah for the Gentiles and perhaps even for "the son of Abraham."[156] However, there are a number of difficulties: (a) Matthew calls no attention to the fact that Uriah was a Hittite; (b) Later Jewish writings (see caution above) present these women not primarily as Gentiles but as proselytes or converts;[157] (c) In such a theory the women have nothing in common with Mary (although in the Third Reich this theory was used to argue that Mary was not a Jew). It is a bit too subtle to argue that the four women represent the Gentile side of Jesus' distaff inheritance, and Mary represents the Jewish side. In general, this theory, *taken alone*, does not seem sufficient to us.

THEORY II: *The Four OT Women Were Subjects of Controversy in the Jewish Debate about the Davidic Messiah*.[158] This is in harmony with the general theory that Matthew had an apologetic motif in the infancy narrative and in the genealogy: he was trying to prove Jesus was the Messiah against contrary claims (the existence of which we can only suspect) that Jesus was illegitimate,[159] that he was not born in Bethlehem,[160] that he was not of true Davidic ancestry,[161] etc. Later Jewish writings (see caution above) show debates among rabbis about the dubious character of some women in the ancestry of David.[162] While this theory may have some points to be considered, the lateness and uncertainty of the evidence pertinent to Jewish attitudes makes it unsatisfactory in our judgment.

---

[156]See the difficulty in n. 149 above.

[157]Paul, *L'Evangile*, 32-33; Str-B, 1. 22.

[158]This theory is defended by Johnson, *Purpose*, who contends that otherwise it is difficult to find something shared by the four women.

[159]The charge of illegitimacy (Brown, *Birth*, 534-42) appears in the second century in the *Acts of Pilate* 2:3; and in the work of Celsus (Origen, *Against Celsus*, 1.28,32,69). It is echoed in the later rabbinic legends about Ben Stada. See the discussion of John 8:41 in Chap. 7, A7, below for possible first-century evidence about the charge.

[160]This objection against Jesus appears in John 7:40-43.

[161]Except as part of the illegitimacy charge, we have no evidence of an ancient denial of Jesus' Davidic origins.

[162]In the medieval *Midrash Rabbah* VIII 1 on Ruth 4:18-21, David is portrayed as protesting the charge that his descent is tainted because of Ruth the Moabitess; he countercharges that the tribe of Judah as a whole is descended from Tamar whose union with Judah was reprehensible.

THEORY III: *The Four OT Women Were Sinners.*[163] In the Bible, Tamar posed as a harlot to seduce her father-in-law (Gen 38:24); Rahab was a prostitute (Josh 2:1); Ruth can be read to have seduced Boaz;[164] Uriah's wife committed adultery with David (2 Samuel 11). Matthew's reason for introducing such sinners might be for theological purposes: Jesus is to save his people from their sins (Matt 1:23). Or as an apologetic against Jews who accuse Mary of sinful behavior, Matthew may be pointing to sinful women in the genealogy of the Messiah according to Jewish tradition. Once again there are many difficulties: (a) The righteousness of Tamar was recognized in Gen 38:26;[165] there is no clear evidence that the author of Ruth thought of his heroine as sinful; and first-century evidence holds up Rahab as a good model (Heb 11:1; Jas 2:25; *1 Clement* 12:1); even Bathsheba's adultery was not always condemned in later rabbinic literature (see caution above) because she ultimately gave birth to Solomon.[166] Thus it is far from certain that Matthew's readers would have thought of all these women as sinners. (b) The suggestion as to how Matthew might have used theologically the reference to sinful women is a bit far-fetched, for already there were enough sinful men in the genealogy to show Jesus' unity with a sinful race. (c) Similarly dubious is an apologetics which answers (assumed) Jewish charges of Mary's sinfulness by pointing to other sinful women—Would that make Jesus' suspected origins less objectionable?

THEORY IV: *The Four OT Women, Marked by Irregular Marital Unions, Were Vehicles of God's Messianic Plan.*[167] According

---

[163]Already proposed by Jerome, *In Matt.* 9; *PL* 26. 22. For a thorough refutation, see Spitta, "Die Frauen."

[164]See the treatment of Ruth 3:1-18 in E. F. Campbell, *Ruth* (AB 7; Garden City: Doubleday, 1975), 131.

[165]So also Philo, *On the Virtues*, 220-22.

[166]Str-B, 1. 28.

[167]See especially R. Bloch, " 'Juda engendra Pharès et Zara, de Thamar' (*Matt* 1, 3)," in *Mélanges bibliques rédigés en l'honneur de André Robert* (Paris: Bloud & Gay, 1957), 381-89; also Paul, *L'Evangile*, 30-37. These authors point out that in the later rabbinic works the term "Holy Spirit" was used to describe how God made use of these women, even as it appears (in a different way) in Matt 1:20; but see the caution above on the applicability of rabbinic references.

to this suggestion, what the four women had in common with each other was not a sinful union (which was true only in Bathsheba's case) but an irregular or an extraordinary union which might be despised by outsiders.[168] Yet through these unions, in which the woman was often the heroic figure, God carried out His promises and plan. Tamar was the instrument of God's grace by getting Judah to propagate the messianic line; it was through Rahab's courage that Israel entered the Promised Land; it was through Ruth's initiative that she and Boaz became great-grandparents of King David; and it was through Bathsheba's intervention that the Davidic throne passed to Solomon. The advantage of this theory is that it does not go beyond the biblical evidence and that it gives the women something in common with Mary as she will be described in Matt 1:18-25. It also explains why such unexpected women were chosen by Matthew—the better known wives of the men in Matthew's genealogy (e.g., Sarah, Rebekah, and Rachel) would not have shared with Mary the irregular or extraordinary marital union.[169] The women as instances of divine providence would also be harmonious with the theme of the other instances in which Matthew departs from his "A begot [was the father of] B" pattern, e.g., Judah *and his brothers*, Perez *and Zerah*; Jeconiah *and his brothers*.[170] In each of those cases there is a selectivity and providence exercised by God in the choice of which person propagates the messianic line.

While there may be elements of truth in the first three theories, the last mentioned theory seems to be the most probable. If it is accepted, it means that even before Matthew tells the story in 1:18-25, he calls attention to Mary as an instrument of

---

[168]This is clear from the biblical stories themselves in the cases of Tamar and Juda, of Ruth and Boaz, and of Bathsheba and David. We know nothing of Rahab's marriage with Salmon which has no other biblical support, but marriage with a former prostitute must have had a certain irregularity.

[169]The fact that these four forerunners who had irregular unions were also non-Israelites or married to a non-Israelite (Theory I) may have been a plus value in Matthew's mind.

[170]Davis, "Fulfillment," 523 joins together five places where the rhythmic formula of the genealogy is broken and regards them as testing-moments of the fulfillment of God's promise.

God's providence in the messianic plan. With this purpose he reports in 1:16: it was "Mary of whom was begotten Jesus, who is called the Christ."

2. Mary and the Conception of Jesus (1:18-25)

With v. 18 we begin the actual narrative of Jesus' conception and birth. This is a narrative that Matthew may well have drawn from earlier sources; but first we shall discuss Mary's role in the story as it now stands, and only then turn to pre-Matthean levels (*Stage Two*, as described above in Chap. 2, B2).

(a) Matthew's View of Mary's Role

The opening verse (18), "Now as for [Jesus] Christ, his birth took place in this way," connects the ensuing narrative with the genealogy in general and the description of Jesus' birth in v. 16 in particular.[171] Although in the genealogy Matthew has traced Jesus' Davidic descent through Joseph, he did *not* describe Joseph as begetting Jesus. His peculiar way of describing the birth now has to be explained. Matthew's introduction to the scene presupposes Jewish marriage customs, as known to us from rabbinic documents but with sufficient confirmation in the NT.[172] There were two steps: (a) a formal exchange of consent before witnesses (Mal 2:14), called *'ērûsîn*, which is usually translated as "betrothal," even though it was a legally ratified marriage, since it gave the young man rights over the girl.[173] She was henceforth his wife (notice the term *gynē*, "wife," in Matt 1:20, 24), and any infringe-

---

[171]The word for "birth" in 1:18, *genesis* (according to the best textual witnesses) is the same word used in the title of the genealogy in 1:1; and the opening phrase in 1:18, "Now, as for [Jesus] Christ," picks up on the last words of 1:16: "Mary of whom was begotten Jesus, who is called the Christ."

[172]Jeremias, *Jerusalem*, 365-68; Str-B, 1. 45-47; 2. 393.

[173]Matthew seems to presume that virginity was expected of Mary before Joseph took her to his home. According to later Jewish commentary (*m. Ketubot* 1:5; *b. Ketubot* 9b, 12a) in parts of Judea it was not unusual for the husband to be alone with the wife on at least one occasion in the interval between the exchange of consent and the move to the home (and so interim marital relations were not absolutely condemned).

ment of his marital rights could be punished as adultery. Yet the
wife continued to live at her own family home for about a year. (b)
The subsequent taking of the bride to the husband's home (Matt
25:1-31). This transferral was the *nîśû'în*, and marked the moment
when the husband assumed the wife's support. According to
Matthew, Joseph and Mary were between the two steps; and so
Mary's pregnancy, which was not by Joseph, has the appearances
of adulterous behavior. The Christian reader is informed that this
pregnancy was through or of the Holy Spirit—Matthew is anxious that there be no scandalous misunderstanding of Mary
among his audience. But Joseph does not possess this knowledge,
and as a just man he is about to divorce Mary because of suspected adultery.[174]

It is then that the angel of the Lord appears to him in a dream
to change the course of his action. There are two basic points of
importance in the angel's message: the first concerns the origin of
Mary's pregnancy, i.e., "the child begotten in her is through [or
"of"—*ek*] the Holy Spirit"; the second concerns Joseph's duty
toward the mother and the child, i.e., he is to go ahead with the
second step in the marriage by taking his wife to his home; and
when the child is born, he is to call his name Jesus. These two
points explain why in 1:16, although Matthew traced Jesus'
Davidic ancestry through Joseph, he did not say that Joseph
begot the child. The child was begotten through the Holy Spirit;

But in Galilee no such leniency was tolerated, and the wife had to be
taken to the husband's home as a virgin. This difference between Judean
and Galilean sensibilities has often been applied to Matthew's account to
show that it is a historical account in which Joseph acts as a Galilean.
However, in Matthew 1-2 Joseph is not a Galilean but has a house in
Bethlehem of Judea (2:1, 11). Moreover, the permission for the husband
to visit the wife may have arisen in Judea especially *after* A.D. 70 when,
under Roman occupation, the troops might rape a virgin.

[174]This seems to us the best understanding of 1:19; it interprets
dikaios, "just," to mean observant of the Law (cf. Luke 1:6) and understands the clause which follows as exceptive: "but unwilling to expose
her to public disgrace." The particular law may have been Deut 22:20-21
which required the stoning of a young woman who, on being first brought
to her husband, was found not to be a virgin. Presumably, in a less severe
legal system, the command to "purge this evil" could have been met by

yet he is a true Davidid, for Joseph, "son of David" (1:20), acknowledged him by naming him. To the angel's message about the conception of the child Matthew adds a formula citation (1:22-23) showing that this conception fulfilled Isaiah's prophecy of a virgin conceiving and bearing a son. He then continues briefly to assure us that Joseph carried out the angel's command—indeed, carried it out so exactly that Mary who had conceived as a virgin remained a virgin till she bore Jesus.

Thus, on the level of Matthean intention, the narrative reinforces and specifies what was already hinted at when Mary was mentioned in the genealogy after the references to the four OT women. The marriage situation is irregular: Joseph had a right that his betrothed wife be brought to his home as a virgin—in point of fact she was a virgin, but pregnant, and already the possible source of scandal.[175] This irregularity and hint of scandal gives Mary's marital situation something in common with that of Tamar, Rahab, Ruth, and Bathsheba. Furthermore, God used those women's situations to accomplish His messianic purpose;

---

divorce instead of by stoning. Or else, Joseph as a "just" observer of the Law may have wished to break his union with someone whom he suspected to be an adulteress, not because a specific law commanded him to do so, but because of his repugnance toward marrying a woman who had violated the Law. See M. M. Bourke, *CBQ* 40 (1978), 121-22.

Two other explanations of *dikaios* have been offered: (a) "*kind* [merciful], *and so* unwilling . . ."; thus C. Spicq, *RB* 71 (1964), 206-14; (b) "*respectful* [in fear of God]"; this theory assumes that Joseph knew the child was of the Holy Spirit; and since he could not take as spouse the woman whom God had chosen as His sacred vessel, he was going to divorce her quietly. Often called the "fear" hypothesis, as distinct from the "suspicion" hypothesis which we have accepted, this theory would have the angel tell Joseph in v. 20: "Do not be afraid to take Mary your wife into your home; true [*gar*] the child begotten in her is through the Holy Spirit, but she will give birth. . . . " See X. Léon-Dufour, "L'Annonce." A major objection is that in the stereotyped pattern of the heavenly annunciation of birth in the Old Testament, the revelation to the visionary tells what was *not* already known; and the more obvious meaning here is that Joseph did not know the origins of Mary's pregnancy.

[175]It is difficult to be certain whether "she was found to be with child" in 1:18 simply means that she was with child or has the implication that people knew of the pregnancy. Who was the agent of *heurethē* ("she was found")?

and now in a more startling way than in any of the preceding
instances, by means of the Holy Spirit, He causes Mary to conceive the Messiah himself. Through naming by the Davidid Joseph,
this Messiah is the son of David; but through conception by the
Holy Spirit, the Messiah is Emmanuel, "God with us." The child
conceived in Mary's womb is the Son of God (2:15).

Clearly then, Mary plays a role in God's plan of saving His
people, and indeed she was foreseen from the time of Isaiah[176] as
the virgin who would give birth to Emmanuel. Yet in the Matthean infancy narrative she remains an instrument of God's action
and her personal attitudes are never mentioned. Once she has
given birth to Jesus, she and the child become the object of
Joseph's care (2:13-14, 20-21); and it is Joseph who is given the
center stage of the drama. In this, Matthew's birth story is a sharp
contrast to Luke's.

Before we leave the level of Matthew's intention, we should
look further at the assurance in 1:25 that Joseph had no sexual
relations with Mary before ("did not know her until") she gave
birth to Jesus. There is no doubt that Matthew's primary interest
is in what preceded the birth of Jesus and in the fulfillment of Isa
7:14 which gives "the virgin" the double role of conceiving and
bearing a son. Verses 18-22 tell us that Mary was a virgin when
she conceived through the power of the Holy Spirit; v. 25 tells us
that she remained a virgin even until Jesus was born. Thus, *in
itself* the verse tells us nothing about what happened by way of
marital relations after Jesus was born.[177] It is only when this
verse is combined with Matthew's reference to Mary and the

---

[176]See above, Chap. 2, C4, for a discussion of prophetic foreshadowing. Although, as we shall explain below, we do not think that Isaiah was
writing with foresight about the birth of Jesus, that was Matthew's interpretation of Isaiah's mind. This is not surprising in the midst of a
Judaism which thought that prophets of old spoke of the distant future, as
instanced in the Qumran commentary (pesher) on Habakkuk: "God told
Habakkuk to write down what would happen to the final generation, but
God did not make known to him when time would come to an end"
(1QpHab 7:1).

[177]In English when something is negated *until* a particular time,
occurrence after that time is usually assumed. However, in discussing
the Greek *heōs hou* after a negative ("not . . . until," "not . . . before"),

brothers of Jesus (12:46), along with the sisters (13:55-56) that a likelihood arises that (according to Matthew's understanding) Joseph did come to know Mary after Jesus' birth and that they begot children. It is impossible to be certain whether Matthew would have had independent knowledge on this point, or was simply following the surface indications of Mark.[178] See the discussion above on the historical identity of these "brothers" at the end of Chap. 4.

(b) Possible Pre-Matthean Attitudes toward Mary

While the narrative in 1:18-25 (and in chap. 2 as well) bears clear marks of Matthean thought and style, many scholars have detected pre-Matthean sources or items of tradition.[179] The most frequently mentioned include:

—A narrative centered around the three angelic dream appearances to Joseph in 1:20-21, 24-25; 2:13-15a; 2:19-21.[180] In this narrative, through a flight to Egypt and a return, God protected the child savior from the wicked King Herod who slaughtered male children in seeking to destroy him. It is generally proposed that this story echoed the OT narratives of Joseph ("the master of dreams" in Gen 37:19) who went down to Egypt, of the infant Moses who escaped the wicked Pharaoh, and of

---

K. Beyer, *Semitische Syntax im Neuen Testament* (Göttingen: Vandenhoeck & Ruprecht, 1962), 1. 132, n. 1, points out that in Greek and in Semitic (Aramaic, Hebrew) this type of negation often has no implication at all about what happened after the limit of the "until" was reached.

[178]Christians who accept Mary's continued virginity after the birth of Jesus (*semper virgo*; *virginitas post partum*) have generally contended that Matthew makes no clear assertion on this point (which is true). In a more subtle understanding of biblical "inerrancy" (see above, Chap. 2, n. 35), theoretically it could be admitted by such Christians that Matthew thought (without real information) that Mary had other children.

[179]C. T. Davis, "Tradition"; Soares Prabhu, *Formula*; and Brown, *Birth*, 109-19, all reconstruct pre-Matthean sources with about seventy-five percent agreement on the nature of those sources.

[180]Scholars are indebted for this observation to W. Knox, *The Sources of the Synoptic Gospels* (Cambridge: University Press, 1953, 1957), 2. 122, although his suggestions have been made more precise in the course of research.

Moses who returned after the Pharaoh's death (Exod 4:19) to lead Israel out of Egypt.[181]

—A narrative (woven into 2:1-12) of the magi from the East who, having come when they saw the star of the Messiah, foiled the wicked King Herod, and then returned. Some have seen here an echo of the story of Balaam, whom Philo[182] calls a *magos*, who, having come "from the East" (Num 23:7, LXX), envisioned the future greatness of Israel in terms of a star which would rise from Jacob (Num 24:17, LXX), much to the displeasure of the wicked King Balak, and then returned home.

—An angelic annunciation of the birth of the Messiah woven together with the dream vision to Joseph in 1:18-25.

—A theme of the begetting of God's Son through the Holy Spirit (1:20-21).

—A theme of Mary's virginal conception of Jesus.

Only the last two really concern us in this book. With the possible exception of 2:11, Mary has no real role in Matthew 2, the passage which would contain the substance of the first two proposed sources. (Nor are we really concerned here with the question of whether those first two proposed sources are historical, although the OT parallels clearly open the possibility of imaginative Christian constructions.) The third proposed pre-Matthean source, an annunciation of birth, is in its technical aspect also outside our concern. The chief argument for such a source is that there is also an annunciation of birth in Luke, so that one could imagine a general tradition of annunciation which each evangelist adapted according to the interests of his narrative, Matthew directing the annunciation to Joseph, and Luke directing it to Mary. However, the annunciation of birth is so stereotyped in the OT[183] that either evangelist could have composed his annunciation directly without pre-Gospel Christian

---

[181]Another possible OT source is the story of Jacob/Israel, who was persecuted by Laban, and who eventually went down to Egypt. See M. Bourke, "Literary Genus."

[182]*Life of Moses*, 1.50 (§276).

[183]See below p. 113; also the birth annunciations of Ishmael (Gen 16:7-12), Isaac (17:1-21; 18:1-12), and Samson (Judg 13:3-23), and the table of parallel features in Brown, *Birth*, 156; Léon-Dufour, "L'Annonce," 77.

sources. In any case, what would pertain to Mary in the proposed pre-Gospel annunciation would be the begetting through the Holy Spirit and the virginal conception—the last two points above. Let us discuss in detail the possibility of the pre-Matthean status for those points.

BEGETTING THROUGH OR OF THE HOLY SPIRIT. The idea of God's begetting or acknowledging Jesus as His Son, and the role of the Holy Spirit in that sonship are found elsewhere in the NT. Modern study of NT christology stresses the antiquity of the resurrection as the crucial moment in Christians' understanding Jesus, and so it is not surprising to find the resurrection referred to as the begetting of Jesus in Acts 13:32-33: "What God promised to the fathers, He has fulfilled for us their children by raising Jesus, as it is written in Psalm Two: 'You are my Son; today I have begotten you.' "[184] The Spirit of Holiness (Holy Spirit?) enters the picture of resurrection sonship in Rom 1:3-4: "Born of the seed of David according to the flesh; designated Son of God in power according to a spirit of holiness as of resurrection from the dead."[185] Now, the Gospels were written at a stage of christology when it was understood that the resurrection revealed what Jesus *had already been* during the ministry. Thus, the beginning of the public ministry in all the Gospels has Jesus coming to John the Baptist and a revelation by God that Jesus is His Son, as the Holy Spirit descends on Jesus.[186] The first part of the verse from Psalm 2, cited above in reference to the resurrection, is echoed by a heavenly voice at the baptism of Jesus in the Synoptic Gospels; indeed in Codex Bezae and the Old Latin tradition of Luke 2:22 the whole verse is cited at the baptism: "You are my Son; today I have begotten you."

In the OT the begetting of the king as God's son, referred to

---

[184]This is reported in a speech by Paul. While these speeches in Acts are generally recognized as Lucan compositions, they may contain nuggets of early Christian theology. See E. Schweizer, "Concerning the Speeches in Acts," in *Studies in Luke-Acts*, ed. L. E. Keck and J. L. Martyn (New York: Abingdon, 1966), 208-16, esp. 212.

[185]See the discussion of this text above, Chap. 3, esp. nn. 52, 63.

[186]Mark 1:11; Matt 3:17; Luke 3:22. The majority of textual witnesses read "Son of God" in John 1:34.

in the psalm, was a figurative begetting through coronation and adoption. When the psalm was referred to the resurrection and/or the baptism, there was also a sense in which the begetting was figurative, even though the Christians who used it saw Jesus as God's Son in a way that went beyond the OT usage (as witnessed by the role of the Holy Spirit—the Spirit of God was in and upon Jesus in a unique way). However, when christological reflection moved back farther[187] to the beginning of Jesus' life, there would have been a tendency for the begetting to be thought of more literally (although a begetting by divine power or through the Holy Spirit always remains *analogous* to human begetting). Thus, in the heavenly revealed message of Matt 1:20, "the child begotten in her is through [or 'of'] the Holy Spirit," many scholars would see a christological terminology, previously used of the resurrection and of the beginning of the public ministry, now being applied to the conception of Jesus. Like the other evangelists, Matthew is clear that Jesus did not *become* the Son of God through the resurrection; Jesus was God's Son during the ministry (3:17; 14:33; 16:16). But Matthew is clearer than Mark[188] that Jesus did not *become* the Son of God at the baptism; Jesus was God's Son from his conception.[189] In this approach there was

---

[187]In part one may detect a chronological sequence in which a moment of christological understanding was moved back from the resurrection (early preaching) to the baptism and ministry (Mark) and finally to the conception (Matthew, Luke). However, we must not think that the thought of all Christians moved in this direction: some may have still been asserting that Jesus was "adopted" by God at the baptism, when Matthew and Luke were denying this. Moreover, there were other lines of development: traces of a pre-existence christology (which never mentions conception or birth) may be found in the Pauline letters (Phil 2:5-7; 1 Cor 8:6; Col 1:15-17) and in John (1:1, 14; 17:5). See above, Chap. 3, n. 45.

[188]We say "clearer than Mark" without judging whether Mark held the view that Jesus *became* God's Son at his baptism. In any case Mark's christological views should not be interpreted in the ontological categories of the later Adoptionist controversy.

[189]There is no indication of pre-existence in Matthew (see n. 187). Matthew does not use the term "Son of God" in 1:18-25, probably because he wanted to respect the attention which the Isaian prophecy gives to "Emmanuel, i.e., God with us." That this designation is equivalent to "Son of God" can be deduced from 2:15.

a pre-Matthean tradition behind the message of the angel (and this is fortified by the fact that the Lucan angel, using somewhat different vocabulary, will have the same christological message—Luke 1:35); but this tradition has no special mariological content, other than that Mary's conception of Jesus had become a "christological moment," even as the baptism and the resurrection.

VIRGINAL CONCEPTION. The tradition of the virginal conception is a more likely vehicle for a pre-Matthean mariology (even though the conception is primarily reported for its christological content). Granted the possibility that "begetting the Son of God," with an accompanying reference to the Holy Spirit, may represent early Christian theology which is now being applied to the conception of Jesus, why was that conception described by Matthew in terms of a *virginal* conception? Is the idea of a virginal conception Matthew's own addition, or was it pre-Matthean?

It is not unthinkable that it was Matthew who personally introduced the theme of a virginal conception. In the whole of 1:18-25 "virgin" is mentioned only in 1:23, the fulfillment citation from Isaiah; and it is the majority opinion of scholars that it was Matthew himself who added such fulfillment citations.[190] However, it should be noted that the likelihood that Matthew himself added Isa 7:14 to the scene does not necessarily mean that the idea of the virginal conception came from Matthew.[191] If one studies Matthew's technique with fulfillment citations, one notes that he can use them to illustrate a theme that was already in his

---

[190]For a general discussion of fulfillment citations in Matthew, see K. Stendahl, *The School of St. Matthew* (Philadelphia: Fortress, 2d ed., 1968; orig. 1954); R. H. Gundry, *The Use of the Old Testament in St. Matthew's Gospel* (Theologische Dissertationen 2; Basel: University Press, 1969) and the summary analysis of views by F. van Segbroeck in Didier, *L'Evangile*, 107-30. For arguments that Matthew added the five formula citations (see above, n. 147) to the infancy narrative, see Davis, "Tradition"; Soares Prabhu, *Formula*; and Brown, *Birth*, 96-104.

[191]In part this discussion depends on whether Luke's description of Jesus' conception has been influenced by Isa 7:14. Those who think so would give a more formative role to Isa 7:14 in shaping both Matthew and Luke's thought, perhaps even on a pre-Gospel level.

source. (For instance, the idea that shortly after his baptism Jesus went to Galilee was found by Matthew in his source [Mark 1:14]; he introduced a citation of Isa 9:1-2 [Matt 4:12-16] because he saw that this journey to Galilee fulfilled the words of the prophet.) Moreover, a knowledge of the Hebrew and the LXX of Isa 7:14[192] gives no indication of a reference to a virginal conception. The Hebrew of Isa 7:14 speaks only of the conception of a child by a young girl.[193] The LXX does use the Greek word that normally designates a virgin (*parthenos*),[194] but the conception is future— the girl now a virgin will in the future conceive a child, presumably in a natural way. The whole context of the Isaian passage indicates that the prophet was speaking of a girl who lived in his own time and certainly not of the birth of a child to take place 700 years later. And so it is unlikely that Matthew first came to the idea of the virginal conception of Jesus by reflecting on Isa 7:14, a text that, as far as we know, no Jew had previously seen as indicative of the virginal conception of the Messiah. However, if there was already an idea that Jesus had been virginally conceived, this may have reminded Matthew of Isa 7:14 which he would *then* have reinterpreted as foretelling this conception.[195]

---

[192]The literature on this verse is enormous, but the details are conveniently summarized by R. G. Bratcher, *BT* 9 (1958), 97-126.

[193]The Hebrew word *'almâ*, used nine times in the OT, describes a young woman who has reached the age of puberty and is thus marriageable. (It never describes a married woman, although in the Ugaritic *Keret* text, II, 21-22, the cognate word *ǵlmt* is in poetic parallelism and thus rough equivalence with *'att*, "wife.") The word puts no stress on virginity even if, because of Israelite ethical and social standards, most young girls covered by the range of this term would in fact be virgins. Yet in Cant 6:8 it refers to women of the king's harem; see also Prov 30:19.

[194]The Jewish opponent of Justin in the *Dialogue with Trypho*, 43.8; 67.1, etc., correctly points out that *neanis*, "young girl," would be a better translation of *'almâ* than is *parthenos* (but note he never denies Justin's explicit claim that *parthenos* is the LXX reading). The Liddell and Scott Greek Lexicon gives several instances of a secular Greek use of *parthenos* for women who were not virgins. But the word seems to have become more specialized in later Greek (Bratcher [n. 192 above] 112), and most of the 65 LXX usages are clear references to virgins.

[195]Of course, he would have understood that he was discovering the real meaning of the text. The Qumran sectarians, who saw in the proph-

Independently of the Isaian passage, are there other ways in which Matthew himself may have come to the idea of a virginal conception without our supposing a pre-Matthean tradition? Some scholars have proposed that it was purely *a deduction from Christian theology*. We have seen above that "begetting through the Holy Spirit" was a theological way of describing divine sonship, which in the infancy narrative was being associated with the conception of Jesus. Would a Christian like "Matthew" have concluded that since Jesus was God's Son, he had no human father? There would have been no background for this type of conclusion in the OT: God could call the king His son (Ps 2:7) even when all the people in the country knew who the king's earthly father was—paternal lineage was what entitled him to be king. Some would seek background in Greco-Roman or other pagan religions where male gods begot sons of earthly women.[196] But to accept this suggestion we would need evidence that Matthew tended to draw upon such Gentile religious background and that he would find pagan sexual myths suitable for adaptation. We would need to explain why his own description of the conception of Jesus is quite asexual (God is not the male partner—the conception is discreetly "of the Holy Spirit"), and why such a putative pagan borrowing has been set in a story that has a Jewish background (patriarch Joseph; birth of Moses, mentioned above) and supposes Jewish marriage customs. A more serious possibility of background may be found in a combination of Greco-Roman and Jewish influences, chiefly in the religious thought of those Jews brought up outside Palestine. We have discussed above (Chap. 3, B3) Philo's description of the generation of virtues in the human soul[197] in which he employs allegorically the stories of the births

---

ets like Habbakuk references to their own community, argued that their Righteous Teacher had been given by God to understand the mysteries of the prophets' words (1QpHab 7:3-5). Also, see above, Chap. 2, C4.

[196]These were not really virginal conceptions; they were conceptions by divine impregnation without a *human* male parent. Parallels have also been suggested in the area of world religions, e.g., the conception of the Buddha and of Zoraster's son. Boslooper, *Virgin Birth*, has detailed discussion of these proposed parallels.

[197]Philo, *On the Cherubim*, 12-15.

of the patriarchs who were begotten through the instrumentality of God, e.g., "Rebekah, who is perseverance, became pregnant from God." We saw there the suggestion that underlying the Philonic allegory was a Hellenistic Jewish theory wherein the real patriarchs were begotten directly by God without male intervention. Yet we also saw that this interpretation has been challenged, and so we remain without *sure* proof of the existence in Judaism of an idea of virginal conception that might have caused Matthew (or the pre-Gospel tradition) to introduce that motif into Jesus' birth story.

Another suggestion of a derivation of the virginal conception through logic is more complicated since it involves *a combination of history and theology*. It supposes that the situation described in Matthew is historically correct, i.e., that Mary conceived in the interim between the exchange of consent ('*ērûsîn*) and the transferal to Joseph's home (*nîśû'în*). This supposition gains support from the fact that Luke's account where Mary is still a virgin and yet betrothed (1:27) seems to imply the same interim situation. Were this interim situation purely fictional, it is not clear why Christian invention would have located the moment of conception so awkwardly—for instance, if Mary were imagined to have conceived through the Holy Spirit on the night in which her husband took her to his home, just before marital relations would normally have begun, Jesus would have been born at the proper interval without hint of scandal. But as it is, the Matthean story necessitates that Jesus will be born noticeably early after his parents came to live together. Thus, there may have been an irregularity about the birth of Jesus which his opponents would interpret in terms of illegitimacy and of sin on Mary's part.[198] A Christian like Matthew, convinced of the sinlessness of Jesus,[199] may have believed that freedom from sin had to reach to his origins as well,

---

[198]See above, n. 159; and below, Chap. 9, B1, for second-century evidence pertaining to the Jewish charge that Jesus was illegitimate.

[199]As evidence for the wide acceptance of the sinlessness of Jesus, see: 2 Cor 5:21; 1 Pet 2:22; Heb 4:15; 1 John 3:5. In Matthew a possible allusion to sinlessness is 3:14; but cf. G. Bornkamm, *Jesus of Nazareth* (New York: Harper, 1960), 48-49.

and thus have emerged with the idea of a virginal conception.[200] On the principle that similar ideas do arise independently in different places, it might be argued that Luke came to the same conclusion. But if one accepts this (clearly tenuous) explanation of the derivation of the idea of a virginal conception, it is easier to presume that both Matthew and Luke derived their knowledge of it from an earlier theological interpretation of the facts surrounding Jesus' birth.

We have not exhausted all the possible explanations of the origin of Christian belief in a virginal conception; yet we have concentrated sufficiently on those explanations which would make it possible to argue that it was the evangelist who first got the idea and introduced it into the birth narrative. We have seen that such explanations contain many difficulties. And thus, with some differences of emphasis among us, we recognize the possibility or even the probability of a pre-Gospel acceptance of the virginal conception.[201]

For those inquirers who wish to press beyond *Stage Two* of Gospel formation to *Stage One* (above, Chap. 2, B2) and to ask about the *factual historicity* of the virginal conception, the evidence available for critical study is even more limited. The idea that a memory of a virginal conception was transmitted in family circles (from Joseph and/or Mary) and then made public in a pre-Gospel period faces two major objections.[202] First, why is there no clear reference to it (and often seemingly no knowledge of it) in any other NT witness beside Matthew and Luke? Igno-

---

[200]In this theory the virginal conception is not purely a derivation from a theological principle; there is a historical catalyst. Another catalyst, especially for the Matthean formulation, could have been Isa 7:14.

[201]If there was a pre-Matthean narrative of the magi, as many scholars suggest (see above, n. 179), does the indication in 2:11 that "they saw the child with Mary his mother" (with no mention of Joseph) indicate that the magi story presupposed a virginal conception? The reference is too fleeting to constitute a real argument.

[202]The arguments against a family tradition have been strongly advocated by A. Vögtle, *BibLeb* 11 (1970), 51-67, a Roman Catholic scholar.

rance of the virginal conception on the part of many early Christians becomes all the more peculiar if there was a widespread calumny charging illegitimacy on the basis of the irregularity of Jesus' birth chronology. How did Christians who had no knowledge of the virginal conception answer that charge? Second, would not a knowledge of the circumstances surrounding Jesus' birth, as well as the simple fact of the virginal conception, have been transmitted; and if so, how do the Matthean and Lucan stories come out so differently?

In summation, we see no way in which a modern scientific approach to the Gospels can establish the historicity of the virginal conception (or, for that matter, disprove it). This is in no way a negation of the position of the many Christians who accept the historicity of the virginal conception[203] because of their appreciation of the authority of the evangelists or their sources, or because of their belief in biblical inerrancy on such an important matter,[204] or because of the teachings of their church about the virgin birth.[205] And, of course, the limited possibilities of an investigation into historicity does not detract from the clear christological purpose of the evangelists that has shaped the creedal affirmation known from early centuries: "born of the Virgin Mary."[206]

---

[203]We say "many" Christians because even in official church statements qualifications appear, e.g., *Doctrine in the Church of England: The Report of the Commission on Christian Doctrine Appointed by the Archbishops of Canterbury and York in 1922* (London: SPCK, 1938), 82: "Many of us hold . . . that belief in the Word made flesh is integrally bound up with belief in the Virgin Birth. . . . There are, however, some among us who hold that a full belief in the historical Incarnation is more consistent with the supposition that our Lord's birth took place under the normal conditions of human generation."

[204]The use of the term "inerrancy" need not imply a fundamentalist attitude toward Scripture; see above, Chap. 2, n. 35, for a more subtle understanding of inerrancy.

[205]Brown, *Virginal Conception*, 66, who argues that "the totality of the *scientifically controllable* evidence leaves an unresolved problem," also contends (p. 35) that "the virginal conception would be classified as a doctrine infallibly taught by the ordinary magisterium" of the Roman Catholic Church.

[206]J. N. D. Kelly, *Early Christian Creeds* (2d ed.; London: Longmans, 1960), 145-46, comments on the introduction of this motif

Reminding ourselves once again that our chief interest and capability has been in detecting *Matthew's attitude* toward Mary in the infancy narrative (*Stage Three* of Gospel formation), what does it add to that attitude if we have discovered the possibility and even the likelihood of a pre-Matthean acceptance of the virginal conception? It would mean, at least, an earlier date for the favorable outlook upon Mary as specially and marvelously employed by God in His plan for the coming of the Messiah, His Son. Next we shall turn to discussing how Matthew's view of Mary's place in the infancy narrative caused him to modify the somewhat unfavorable portrait of Jesus' family, including Mary, which he found in Mark's account of the public ministry. If there was a favorable pre-Matthean view of Mary's place in the infancy of Jesus, the view may have existed contemporaneously with the writing of Mark's Gospel. Thus we would have an early instance of pluralism in Christian mariology, with very different views of Mary held at the same period of time in Mark and in the pre-Matthean tradition of Jesus' conception.

B. Mary in the Public Ministry

The reader of Matthew has gained first impressions about Mary from the infancy narrative. While she is mentioned only briefly in both the genealogy and the subsequent conception narrative, there can be no doubt that she has a positive place in the birth story of the messianic king. How does she fare when this Messiah begins to proclaim the kingdom? That this is not a primary interest of Matthew is suggested by the fact that he has no new ministry references to Mary beyond those of Mark. But the two pertinent Matthean passages concerning Mary which are parallel to Mark exhibit significant differences from the attitude of

---

into the Old Roman Creed ca. A.D. 175. *In part* it was to counter a heresy that questioned the reality of Jesus' humanity, although an anti-Gnostic motif should not be exaggerated. The greater emphasis in this phrase was on a fuller christological statement. Thus, "born of the Virgin Mary" was not primarily mariological; it presupposed that Mary had conceived as a virgin, but it had a different focus from the modern concern with the historicity of the virginal conception.

the earlier Gospel;[207] and so at least we can test the consistency
of Matthew's attitude toward Mary throughout the Gospel, even
if that is not a major theme.

1. The Disciples Constitute the Family of Jesus (12:46-50)

When we discussed the parallel passage in Mark 3:31-35 as a
unit by itself, we saw that it was meant to define the eschatological family of Jesus constituted by the proclamation of the kingdom. This definition was in terms of doing the will of God, as
contrasted with a biological relationship to Jesus. But if the passage itself indicated that the physical family (mother and brothers) had no real importance in Jesus' standard of values, Mark
hardened this impact by means of the scene with which he prefaced it (3:20-30). The Marcan context introduced Jesus' mother
and brothers as "his own" who had set out to seize him because
they were saying, "He is beside himself." Thus, for Mark the
physical or natural family which does not understand Jesus is
replaced by an eschatological family which follows him to hear
the word of God and do His will.

The Matthean form of the passage is not very different from
Mark's:

> [46]*While he was still speaking to the crowds, behold his mother and
> his brothers stood outside asking to speak to him.* [48]*But he replied
> to the man who told him, "Who is my mother, and who are my
> brothers?"* [49]*And stretching out his hand toward his disciples, he
> said, "Here are my mother and my brothers!* [50]*For whoever does
> the will of my Father in heaven is my brother, and sister, and
> mother."*

---

[207]As indicated in Chap. 2, B3, we accept the thesis that Matthew
was written after and in dependence upon Mark. If one were to argue the
contrary, then Mark's attitude toward Mary would be considerably hardened. A Mark who would have written after Matthew would have omitted the infancy narratives and all specific reference to a virginal conception. (See above, Chap. 4, n. 111.) In place of a Mary to whom God gave
a place in the coming of the Messiah, Mark would have introduced a
Mary who thought that her son was beside himself when he began his
ministry. The statement found only in Mark (6:4) that Jesus was a
prophet without honor "among his own relatives" would become a corrective of a Matthean picture where Mary witnessed the worship that the
magi gave to Jesus (Matt 2:11).

Without the textually dubious v. 47,[208] Matthew mentions only once that the physical mother and brothers are outside; moreover he mentions the "disciples" specifically in v. 49 (as contrasted with Mark's "those who sat about him").[208a] Even in the passage itself, then, the weight of Matthew's emphasis falls on the eschatological family of disciples, with the physical family serving more as a catalyst rather than a contrast in the remarks.

However, it is not so much in the passage itself that Matthew differs from Mark but in the context. The introductory scene in which "his own" think he is beside himself is completely absent. Presumably the omission was deliberate, and it can be understood if Matthew interpreted Mark's "his own" to include Jesus' mother. In the logic of Matthew's Gospel, Jesus' mother had virginally conceived her son; she knew of an angelic message that he would save his people from their sins; she had seen how God protected him from the wicked king and had planned geographically his destiny, bringing him to Nazareth. She could scarcely show such misunderstanding of his mission to think that he was beside himself. Thus the Matthean scene involving the true family of Jesus is much milder in its totality than is the Marcan scene and much less likely to be read as a replacement or a rejection of the physical family.

2. *The Rejection of Jesus in His Own Country (13:53-58)*

This scene comes in Matthew after the third teaching discourse of Jesus (13:1-52), a discourse in parables. And so when Jesus arrives in "his own country," presumably Nazareth, there

---

[208]Omitted in the best textual witnesses, this verse reads: "Someone told him, 'Your mother and your brothers are standing outside, asking to speak to you.' " Metzger, *TCGNT*, 32, thinks that it was accidentally omitted by scribes because of homeoteleuton. But one could argue that the passage makes sense without it, and that scribes added it to harmonize Matthew with Mark.

[208a]The Marcan description sets up a sharper dichotomy between those sitting inside and the mother and brothers standing outside. Another, minor difference between Matt 12:50 and Mark 3:35 is Matthew's preference for "my Father" over Mark's usage of "God."

has been a lengthier proclamation of the kingdom than in Mark, and the impact of the rejection is heightened. Once more the passage itself differs only in a few details from Mark's account:[209]

> [53]And when Jesus had finished these parables, he went away from there; [54]and coming to his own country, he taught them in their synagogue, so that they were astonished and said, "Where did this man get this wisdom and these mighty works? [55]Is not this the son of the carpenter? Is not his mother called Mary? Are not his brothers James and Joseph and Simon and Judas? [56]And are not all his sisters with us? Where did this man get all this?" [57]And they took offense at him. But Jesus said to them, "A prophet is not without honor, except in his own country, and in his own house." [58]And he did not do many mighty works there because of their unbelief.

There are two differences, however, that are significant for mariology. In 6:4 Mark wrote: "A prophet is not without honor, except in his own country, *and among his own relatives*, and in his own house." The idea that Jesus' own relatives did not honor him is consonant with Mark's report that "his own" thought he was beside himself (3:21). Since Matthew has omitted the earlier reference, it is not surprising to find him omitting Jesus' relatives from the list of those who do not honor him.[210] Once again it would be difficult to imagine that a mother who had conceived Jesus through the Holy Spirit would not honor him.

The second difference from Mark is more difficult and leads us to recall the parallel sayings from Luke, already mentioned in discussing Mark above (Chap. 4, B1):[211]

---

[209]Besides the main differences mentioned above, we may note these: (a) a created transition from the parable discourse; (b) a heightening of the directness of Jesus' message to the people of Nazareth: "he taught them in their synagogue," as compared to Mark's "he began to teach in the synagogue"; (c) a separation into two questions (end of vv. 54 and 56) of what Mark 6:2 had placed together; (d) an omission in the last verse of Mark's clause "except that he laid his hands on a few sick people and healed them."

[210]It is difficult to be certain how Matthew interpreted the lack of honor "in his own house (*oikia*)," read in sequence to "his own country." If it means "household," is it less personal than Mark's "among his own relatives"?

[211]There our primary interest was in determining the significance of Mark's failure to mention Jesus' father, and it seemed most plausible that

Mark 6:3:   "Is not this the carpenter, the son of Mary?"

Matt 13:55: "Is not this the son of the carpenter? Is not his mother called Mary?"

Luke 4:22: "Is not this the son of Joseph?"

John 6:42: "Is not this Jesus the son of Joseph? Do we not know his father and his mother?"

If Matthew is dependent upon Mark, why does he change "the carpenter" to "the son of the carpenter"? Did he consider the reference to Jesus demeaning?[212] In the last verse of this pericope Matthew's appreciation of Jesus' dignity caused him to change Mark's "he *could* do no mighty works there" to "he did not do many mighty works there." The same "higher" christology may have made Matthew prefer to think of Jesus as the son of a carpenter, rather than a carpenter (with or without the catalyst of some historical knowledge of Joseph's trade).

If one accepts that explanation as the most likely, how does one account for the fact that Matthew, Luke, and John all agree in designating Jesus as the son of his *father* over against Mark? Does this challenge the thesis that Matthew and Luke drew upon Mark, and make it possible that it was Mark who changed Matthew and Luke? (This suggestion is sometimes related to the thesis discussed in Chap. 4, B1, that Mark was trying to hint at the virginal conception by mentioning only Jesus' mother. We saw the im-

---

Joseph was dead. We presume here what was said on that occasion about the Marcan passage as apophthegm or paradigm, with the central attention on: "A prophet is not without honor except in his own country."

[212]As we see from Origen, *Against Celsus*, 6.36, the charge that Jesus was a workman was being used by Jewish opponents in post-NT times; Origen replies that "Jesus himself is not described as a carpenter anywhere in the Gospels accepted by the churches" (a reply which indicates that he did not read "the carpenter" in Mark 6:3). On the range of *tektōn* covering artisans in stone, wood, and metal, see P. H. Furfey, "Christ as *Tektōn*," *CBQ* 17 (1955), 324-35. Arguing that the word means "architect, builder," Albright and Mann, *Matthew*, 172-73, connect *tektōn* with the Aramaic word *naggārā'*. They think of Joseph and Jesus as *builders* on call to travel to other cities, and thus in the ranks of master craftsmen. On the slimmer evidence of much later Talmudic sayings involving *naggārā'*, G. Vermes, *Jesus the Jew* (London: Collins, 1973), 21-22, argues very dubiously for the meaning of "scholar, learned man"!

plausibility of that thesis on several grounds. Since Matthew and Luke, the two authors who are commonly acknowledged as accepting the virginal conception, do not hesitate to call Jesus "the son of the carpenter" and "the son of Joseph," the problem of the virginal conception is almost certainly extraneous to this whole discussion.) There is an easier solution than that of Marcan editing of Matthew and Luke. The Lucan scene (4:16-30) differs in many ways from that of Mark/Matthew; and it is far from certain that Luke's "Is not this the son of Joseph?" is an adaptation of the much longer Mark 6:3 with its reference to Mary, the brothers and the sisters.[213] John's scene in Chap. 6, at the Sea of Galilee, is very different from the Synoptic scene in "his own country" or Nazareth; and his saying in 6:42 may be totally independent of the Synoptic tradition. (If it is not, the fact that John is closer to Luke is not surprising, for many scholars posit a contact between Lucan and Johannine tradition on a pre-Gospel level.) In other words, the Lucan and Johannine "Is not this (Jesus) the Son of Joseph?"[214] may be quite unrelated to Matthew's "Is not this the son of the carpenter?" This would mean that we do not have three redactions of Mark accidentally emerging with roughly the same reading—something that would be hard to believe. Rather only Matthew's account would have come from editing Mark, an editing for which we have already seen a plausible explanation in the previous paragraph.

It is worth noting, too, that Matthew's identification of Jesus by both father and mother is reminiscent of the initial picture of the parents of Jesus given in chap. 1. It was important for Matthew's argument there that Jesus was truly the son of Joseph (because Joseph acknowledged him), for that proved that Jesus was a Davidid. The mention of Mary immediately after Joseph in 13:55 would remind the reader of the fact that she was Jesus' mother through the Holy Spirit, as Matthew described in 1:18-25.

---

[213]Schürmann, *Lukasevangelium*, 235-36, gives four arguments for why Luke 4:22 is not to be considered a rewriting of Mark 6:3.

[214]The last of Schürmann's arguments (n. 213) is that the Lucan and Johannine expression "son of Joseph" is probably an old tradition, and that one cannot claim that Mark's "son of Mary" is necessarily more original.

Thus, it would seem that Matthew's adaptation of the two Marian scenes that he borrowed from Mark's account of the ministry is in harmony with the view of Mary he presented in chaps. 1-2. The negative aspect of the Marcan picture has been toned down to at least neutrality, but a neutrality that would probably pick up coloring from the initial positive impression given the reader at the beginning of the Gospel.

CHAPTER SIX:
MARY IN THE
GOSPEL OF LUKE
AND THE
ACTS OF THE APOSTLES*

As in Matthew's Gospel, so also in Luke's Gospel we may distinguish two kinds of passages pertinent to a study of Mary: *first*, an extensive set of references to Mary in the infancy narrative[215] of chaps. 1-2, where she has an important role in the annunciation, the visitation, the birth at Bethlehem, the presentation in the Temple, and the finding of Jesus in the Temple; *second*, four relatively brief passages in the narrative of Jesus' public ministry. Like Matthew, Luke offers a genealogy of Jesus, and the first of the four ministry passages is a line in that genealogy (3:23) which indicates that Jesus is only the "supposed" son of Joseph. The second and third Lucan ministry passages have

---

*The discussion for this chapter was led by R. E. Brown, and the first draft was composed by J. Reumann. Three sessions of the task force (Jan., Feb., March, 1976) were devoted in whole or in part to the evidence of Luke/Acts.

[215]"Infancy" or "birth" narrative is not a fully appropriate term for the first two chapters of either Matthew or Luke: in each Gospel chap. 1 antedates the birth. Luke has the added complication of a story of Jesus at age twelve (2:41-51).

Synoptic parallels, namely, Luke 4:16-30 narrating the rejection of Jesus at Nazareth (cf. Mark 6:1-6a; Matt 13:53-58); and Luke 8:19-21 pertaining to who constitute the family of Jesus (cf. Mark 3:31-35; Matt 12:46-50). The fourth ministry passage (11:27-28), where a woman from the crowd proclaims the blessedness of Jesus' mother, is peculiar to Luke. Mary is mentioned only once in the Acts of the Apostles (1:14), in a listing of those who had gathered together to pray in Jerusalem after the ascension and before Pentecost. Chronologically, this is the last specific reference to Mary and her fate in the NT narrative of the Christian movement.

The Lucan Marian material is more abundant than that of any other NT writer; and in order to keep our Lucan chapter proportionate to the style and content of the other chapters of this book, we shall have to resist detailed discussion of many uncertainties about Luke's purpose, procedure, sources, etc., simply referring the more inquisitive reader to existing studies of such questions. Thus, we intend to treat the passages of Marian import in the sequence in which they now appear in Luke/Acts, even though we are aware that the existing order may not reflect the original order of composition. This decision benignly neglects the possibility that Luke wrote chaps. 3-24 of the Gospel and the Book of Acts before writing the infancy narrative (1:5-2:51) which he ultimately prefixed to the Gospel,[216] or that Luke composed a first edition, Proto-Luke, and then later added material from Mark and elsewhere.[217] Such theories will concern us only when they seriously affect our working back through the three stages of Gospel formation (see above, Chap. 2, B2), from the evangelist's narrative through his pre-Gospel sources to the historical situation of Jesus. Our choice of emphasis reflects our conviction that primacy should be given to the portrait of Mary in the final form of Luke/Acts preserved for the Christian community—the only form about which we can be certain.[218]

---

[216]Variations of this position are advocated by Conzelmann and Oliver, and challenged (diversely) by Tatum and Minear (see Bibliography).

[217]See above, Chap. 2, n. 27; also Taylor, "Luke," 184-85.

[218]We shall be conscious that in the existing NT canon, Acts follows all four Gospels and is separated from Luke by John. This makes the

Theologically, Luke/Acts reflects a definite plan or program, best described as a salvation-history approach.[219] More than the other evangelists, Luke betrays a consciousness of world history (Luke 3:1). His stated purpose in 1:1-4 has historical overtones, and Luke/Acts bears a resemblance to the style of some of the Greek and Jewish histories in circulation in the first century A.D. This historical mindset shaped his presentation of the theme of salvation, so that the centrality of what God has done in Jesus is seen in relation to God's past mercies to His people and to His continued action through the Spirit in the church.[220] We shall be inquiring about the role that Luke gives to Mary in this overall plan of salvation history.[221] Other commonly recognized Lucan theological emphases that are of interest to us include the universality of God's salvific plan, a special place for women, the unique blessedness of the poor, the atmosphere of prayer and Temple piety, and the joy of lives lived in obedience to God.[222] As we shall see, all these interests provide color for the Lucan portrait of Mary.

A. Mary in the Birth Narrative (Chaps. 1-2)

After a preface (1:1-4) which stresses Luke's concern to write an "orderly" narrative on the basis of accounts delivered ("handed down") from "eyewitnesses and ministers of the word,"[223] the evangelist presents us with two chapters of narra-

---

reference to Mary in Acts 1:14 even more final and climactic in terms of the "canonical hermeneutic" of the passage.

[219]The peculiar Lucan combination of theology and history has been expounded in the full-scale works of Conzelmann, Flender, and Marshall.

[220]A general Lucan tripartite view of salvation history involving Israel, Jesus, and the church is widely accepted, without any necessary commitment on our part to Conzelmann's understanding of those divisions, e.g., in attributing John the Baptist to the period of Israel.

[221]Räisänen, *Mutter*, entitles one section of his Lucan treatment: "Maria in der Heilsgeschichte."

[222]See Kümmel, *Introduction*, 139-47; Taylor, "Luke," 183-84; J. Navone, *Themes of St. Luke* (Rome: Gregorian, 1970).

[223]This may represent a sequence of initial "eyewitnesses," followed by "ministers of the word," culminating in Luke himself and second- or

tive consisting of an alternating sequence of blocks of material about John the Baptist and Jesus:

John the Baptist	Jesus
Annunciation of birth (1:5-25)	Annunciation of birth (1:26-38)

Visitation of Mary to Elizabeth (1:39-56)
("Magnificat," vv. 46-55)

John the Baptist	Jesus
Birth of John (1:57-58)	Birth of Jesus (2:1-20) ("Gloria in Excelsis," vv. 13-14)
Circumcision (1:59-79) ("Benedictus," vv. 67-79)	Circumcision (2:21)
	Purification at the Temple and blessings by Simeon, Anna (2:22-38) ("Nunc Dimittis," vv. 28-32)
	Return to Nazareth (2:39)
Growth of the child (1:80)	Growth of the child (2:40)
	Finding Jesus at age twelve in the Temple (2:41-51)
	Growth of the child (2:52)

Although in this parallelism what is said about the Baptist is generally matched by what is said about Jesus, clearly Jesus is presented as a superior who will outstrip John in significance (1:41-44; also contrast 1:80 with 2:40, 52). The four hymns of praise indicated above, the poetic promises (1:14-17, 32-33, 35, 41-44; 2:33-35), and the stress on the role of the Spirit (1:15, 17, 35, 41, 47, 67, 80; 2:25-27) create an atmosphere not unlike that surrounding Pentecost as described in Acts 2.[224] In this atmosphere Luke gives real prominence to Mary on the Jesus-side of the parallel sequence, and in the visitation which links the two sides.

Considerable scholarly debate has been devoted to these chapters. Does their remarkably Semitized Greek style indicate

---

third-generation Christians. See G. Klein, "Lukas 1,1-4 als theologischer Programm," in *Zeit und Geschichte: Dankesgabe an Rudolf Bultmann* (ed. E. Dinkler; Tübingen: Mohr, 1964), 192-216, esp. 208-9. As to whether Mary is to be included among these "eyewitnesses," see below.
[224]See P. Minear, "Luke's Use," 128-29.

that Luke used Hebrew or Aramaic sources in composing them, or is he simply imitating the Semitized Greek of the LXX, perhaps because this narrative is so redolent of the OT? Did he draw upon an existing collection (Christian or Jewish, Semitic or Greek) for the Magnificat, Benedictus, Gloria, and Nunc Dimittis which have certain resemblances one to the other? Was the Baptist material derived by Luke from a source composed by the Baptist's followers about their master? Scholars are so divided on these questions[225] that little could ever be based with certainty on the way we might choose to answer them. Fortunately answers to them are not crucial to our study.

What *is* crucial is our evaluation of the ancient hypothesis that Mary was one of Luke's sources, so that much of chaps. 1-2 reflects an eyewitness account.[226] This hypothesis does not rest on a specific testimony of a church writer in the early centuries but is an inference flowing from two observations: *first*, Luke speaks of eyewitnesses in 1:2, just before he begins the infancy narrative; *second*, Mary is the only human being who could have had personal knowledge of what is narrated in 1:26-38.

The first observation must be qualified by certain limitations. Luke's reference to "those who were eyewitnesses *from the beginning* [*ap' archēs*]," in 1:2 evokes primarily the group Peter describes in Acts 1:21-22: "the men who have accompanied us during all the time that the Lord Jesus went in and out among us, *beginning* [*arxamenos*] from the baptism of John." Luke is speaking chiefly of apostolic eyewitnesses of the ministry, i.e., "of the things that have been accomplished *among us*" (1:1). One cannot exclude the possibility of eyewitnesses for the period before the baptism (narrated in 3:1-21),[227] but neither can a reference to that

---

[225]For the various positions, see McHugh, *Mother*, 435-37; Brown, *Birth*, 239-50; Turner, "Relation"; W. Wink, *John the Baptist in the Gospel Tradition* (SNTSMS 7; Cambridge: University Press, 1968), 56-86; J. R. Wilkinson, *A Johannine Document in the First Chapters of St. Luke's Gospel* (London: Luzac, 1902).

[226]Often this hypothesis is developed into a romantic narrative involving John, son of Zebedee (see below, Chap. 7, n. 465).

[227]In 1:3 Luke speaks of having followed all things closely *anōthen* ("for some time past," "from the start"); the same word is used in Acts 26:4 for the beginning of Paul's *life*.

period be assumed.[228] Moreover, one should be cautious about
the general import of Luke's reference to eyewitnesses. He is
modeling his introduction (1:1-4) on a pattern known in Hellenistic historians whose appeal to eyewitnesses is not always to be
taken literally—it may amount to no more than a claim to credi-
bility.[229] Finally, Luke's desire to write an "accurate" (*akribōs*)
account does not necessarily imply historicity, as we can see from
a study of those sections of Luke/Acts for which we have comparative material.[230]

The second observation, which concerns Mary's personal
testimony to the annunciation, has validity only if the scene containing her dialogue with the angel is historical narrative—if it is
historical, she must be the ultimate source of it. Historical intent
was assumed when the Gospels were thought to be biographies,
and virtually the whole Bible was classified as history. Today
interpreters recognize that the Bible is a library consisting of
books or parts of books classifiable under many different literary
categories, including didactic fiction, parable, and imaginative
retelling. The intention (and the ability) of an author to write a
historical narrative must be proved. The majority of scholars
today would have serious questions about the overall historicity
of the Lucan infancy narrative, for they point to inaccuracies in
the reference to the census of Quirinius as a setting for the birth of

---

[228]See above Chap. 2, B2b, for differences between the infancy narratives and the rest of the Gospels.

[229]The role of eyewitnesses in Acts has at times been exaggerated
because ancient parallels to Lucan style have been neglected; e.g., V. K.
Robbins, *BR* 20 (1975), 5-18, points out that "we-passages" are characteristic of ancient sea-voyage narratives, and need not indicate that the
author was an eyewitness of events described.

[230]The Lucan sense of order allows Luke to transpose the Marcan
sequence of the call of Peter and the healing of his mother-in-law (Mark
1:16-31; Luke 4:38-39; 5:1-11). The chronology of Acts where Gamaliel's
speech is placed before the conversion of Paul would mean that in the
mid-30s Gamaliel refers to the revolt of Theudas which took place under
Fadus (A.D. 44-46; see Josephus, *Ant.* 20:5,1; §§97-99) and seemingly
places it before the revolt of Judas the Galilean which took place in A.D. 7
(Acts 5:37; Josephus, *Ant.* 18:1,6; §23).

Jesus[231] and in the description of the customs of purification and presentation.[232] Mary is intimately involved in both these scenes of chap. 2, and such inaccuracies make it unlikely that she could have been an eyewitness-source for the basic narrative.[233] And so, while we do not exclude the possibility and even the likelihood that some items of historical information about Jesus' birth have come to Luke,[234] we are not working with the hypothesis that he is giving us substantially the memoirs of Mary. Rather, the possibility that he constructed his narrative in the light of OT themes and stories will be stressed.[235]

1. Mary and the Conception of Jesus (1:26-38)

The first reference to Mary in Luke occurs when the angel Gabriel is sent to Nazareth "to a virgin betrothed to a man of the

---

[231]J. Finegan, *Handbook of Biblical Chronology* (Princeton: University, 1964), 235-38; G. Ogg, *ExpTim* 79 (1967-68), 231-36; Brown, *Birth* 547-56.

[232]In Luke 2:22 he speaks of "*their* purification," seemingly thinking that both parents were purified, when the custom referred only to the mother. Also he seems to think (incorrectly) that the Law required the presentation of the firstborn at the Temple. In 2:24 Luke describes the doves or the pigeons as a gift on the occasion of the presentation, when according to Lev 12:6 they were the gift prescribed for the purification. See Räisänen, *Mutter*, 125-27; Brown, *Birth*, 447-51.

[233]When we treat chap. 2, we shall discuss the possibility that it draws upon sources different from those underlying chap. 1. Theoretically, that hypothesis could mean that Mary is the source for parts of chap. 1 but not for chap. 2. However, it is scarcely likely that Mary would be the source for information about the child's conception, without supplying information about the birth.

[234]The few substantial points in which Matthew and Luke agree (see above, Chap. 2, n. 19) deserve special consideration: Davidic descent of Joseph, the role of the Holy Spirit, virginal conception, birth at Bethlehem.

[235]The interpretation of the birth of Jesus against the background of OT texts is sometimes referred to as *midrash*, but both the definition and applicability of that term are questioned. See A. Wright, *The Literary Genre of Midrash* (Staten Island: Alba, 1967), 139-42; R. Le Déaut, *Int* 25 (1971), 259-82; Brown, *Birth*, 557-63.

house of David, whose name was Joseph; and the virgin's name
was Mary" (1:26-27). Gabriel's annunciation is concerned with
the future greatness of Jesus, and its primary emphasis is christological. We should not forget this christology even though there
has been more Marian reflection (and literature) based on this
scene than on any other in the NT.

(a) The Marian Implications of the Annunciation Pattern.

The angel Gabriel's annunciation to Mary has close
similarities to the preceding narrative of the same angel's annunciation to Zechariah, as part of the John the Baptist/Jesus parallelism discussed above.[236] So close are the similarities that some
scholars have argued that Luke constructed the annunciation to
Mary upon the model of an annunciation to Zechariah found in a
hypothetical John-the-Baptist source.[237] However, the question
of interdependence becomes more complicated when we note
that the two Lucan annunciations of birth resemble in detail other
angelic annunciations, e.g., the "third Lucan annunciation" to the
shepherds (2:9-12); Matthew's annunciation to Joseph (Matt
1:20-23); and OT annunciations to Abraham (of Isaac's birth,
Genesis 17), to Samson's parents (Judges 13), to Moses (Exodus
3), and to Gideon (Judges 6).[238] A description of the steps in the
almost fixed structure or pattern of the angelic annunciation is
important for an evaluation of how Mary reacts in Luke.[239]

---

[236]Luke even dates the annunciation to Mary "in the sixth month" of
the pregnancy of Elizabeth, the mother of John the Baptist (1:26, 36).

[237]See above, n. 225. A variant of this is the suggestion that originally the annunciation of 1:26-38 was addressed to Elizabeth and concerned John the Baptist: G. Erdmann, *Vorgeschichten*, 9-11; P. Winter,
"Proto-Source," 186.

[238]In the list of parallels we give in the adjacent table, the first line
under each step lists Lucan birth annunciations; the second line lists
other birth annunciations; the third line lists annunciations (to Moses, to
Gideon) that do not concern birth, for obviously features like 3b and 3c
do not apply to them. The Lucan annunciation to the shepherds, which
comes after birth, inevitably differs in some aspects from the annunciations before birth (3b and 4).

[239]For more detail on annunciation patterns, see X. Léon-Dufour,
"L'Annonce," 77; S. Muñoz Iglesias, "El evangelio de la infancia en san
Lucas y las infancias de los héroes bíblicas," *EstBib* 16 (1957), 329-82.

THE ANNUNCIATION PATTERN

1. The *appearance* of an angel (of the Lord or the Lord Himself):
   —Zechariah (Luke 1:11), Mary (1:26-27), shepherds (2:9)
   —Joseph (Matt 1:20), Abraham (Gen 17:1), Samson's parents (Judg 13:3, 9, 11)
   —Moses (Exod 3:2), Gideon (Judg 6:11-12)

2. A *reaction* of fear, met (sometimes) by a "Do not be afraid":
   —Zechariah (Luke 1:12-13), Mary (1:29-30), shepherds (2:9-10)
   —Joseph (Matt 1:20), Abraham (Gen 17:3); Samson's parents (Judg 13:6, 22)
   —Moses (Exod 3:6), Gideon (Judg 6:22-23)

3. An *announcement* about the birth of a son:
   a. Address by name or title:
      —Zechariah (Luke 1:13), Mary (1:28,30)
      —Joseph (Matt 1:20), Abraham (17:5)
      —Moses (Exod 3:4), Gideon (Judg 6:12)
   b. The woman will conceive (has conceived) and will bear a son:
      —Zechariah (Luke 1:13), Mary (1:31), shepherds (2:11)
      —Joseph (Matt 1:20-21), Abraham (Gen 17:16, 19), Samson's parents (Judg 13:3)
   c. The naming of the child, sometimes with an etymology:
      —Zechariah (Luke 1:13), Mary (1:31)
      —Joseph (Matt 1:21), Abraham (Gen 17:19)
   d. The future accomplishments of the child:
      —Zechariah (Luke 1:15-17), Mary (1:32, 33, 35), shepherds (2:11)
      —Joseph (Matt 1:21), Abraham (Gen 17:19), Samson's parents (Judg 13:5)
      —Moses' future (Exod 3:10), Gideon's future (Judg 6:14)

4. An *objection* from the person who receives the announcement, "How so?":
   —Zechariah (Luke 1:18), Mary (1:34)
   —Abraham (Gen 17:17), Samson's parents (Judg 13:17)
   —Moses (Exod 3:11), Gideon (Judg 6:15)

5. The giving of a *sign* to reassure the recipient:
   —Zechariah (Luke 1:20), Mary (1:36-37), shepherds (2:12)
   —Samson's parents (Judg 13:9, 18-21)
   —Moses (Exod 3:12), Gideon (Judg 6:19-22)

A close study of this stereotyped pattern suggests that no matter what the origin of the information about the Baptist and Jesus found in 1:5-25 and 26-38, the format imitates OT annunciations.[240] Such an annunciation was a standard biblical way of preparing the reader for the career of a person who was destined to play a significant role in salvation history, a role already known to the author. The annunciation of Jesus' birth relates his story to an OT history which had involved similar annunciations.

A knowledge of the annunciation pattern throws light on Mary's question in Luke 1:34, literally rendered, "How can this be since I do not know a man?"[241] Too often this question has been assumed to be a biographical statement of Mary's puzzlement. Wishing to avoid the banal explanation that Mary did not know how children were conceived, fourth-century church Fathers[242] argued that the question made sense if Mary had already made up her mind (and even taken a vow) to remain a virgin, so that her objection takes on the tone of a resolve: "How can this be since I shall not know a man?" This hypothetical vow was seen confirmed by the post-NT tradition that after the virginal conception Mary remained a virgin for the rest of her life.[243] Yet such an interpretation of 1:34 reads into the text later concerns;[244] and the idea that a Galilean village girl, who had

---

[240]For the use of the term "midrash," see above, n. 235. E. Burrows, *The Gospel of the Infancy and Other Biblical Essays* (London: Burns Oates and Washbourne, 1940), 1-58, speaks of "imitative historiography."

[241]"Know" refers to sexual relations as in Matt 1:25. The *RSV* translation of Luke 1:34, "since I have no husband," obscures the fact that Mary does have a husband, Joseph. By speaking of betrothal in 1:27, Luke *seems* to suppose the same two-step marital sequence that is explicit in Matthew 1:18-25. The *'ērûsîn* (legally ratified marriage) has taken place, but Mary has not yet come to share bed and board with her husband (*nîśû'în*—see above, pp. 83-84).

[242]The earliest attestations are Gregory of Nyssa, Ambrose, and Augustine. See Graystone, *Virgin*.

[243]See below, pp. 273-75. McHugh, *Mother*, 193-99, argues that Luke composed 1:34 in light of knowledge that Mary always remained a virgin.

[244]A "spiritual marriage" may be implied in the mid-second-century *Protevangelium of James* where Joseph, an aged widower, protests

already entered into marriage, did so intending to remain a virgin and childless is out of harmony with the Jewish mentality of Jesus' time.[245] If we do not presume that we are dealing with biography, however, and recognize that an objection is a standard feature of the annunciation pattern, the question in 1:34 is easily explicable as a literary device designed to advance the story and the dialogue. It offers the angel a chance to explain that the conception will be virginal and to give the sign involving Elizabeth's pregnancy, thus preparing for the visitation. Yet the observation that the "How" question is a standard literary device in the annunciation pattern does not free us from discussing why that question and the angel's answer involves conception *by a virgin*.

(b) The Marian Implications of 1:34-35, 38

The role of the virginal conception in the Lucan annunciation is more complicated and debated than its role in the Matthean annunciation. We shall have to confine ourselves to the most important aspects of the scholarly discussions.

INTERPOLATION? The difficulties discussed above about the logic of Mary's question have led some scholars to suggest that the narrative in 1:26-38 has been complicated by additions. If one suspects a contradiction between Mary's status of being "betrothed (married) to a man whose name was Joseph" and her status as a virgin, one might regard the reference to betrothal as a secondary feature,[246] so that the annunciation originally came to an unmarried girl. However, since that theory still supposes a

---

against the marriage: "I already have sons and am old, but she is a girl" (9:2), and Mary wonders whether she is to conceive as other women conceive (11:4). H. Graef, *Mary*, 1.50, points out that the movement of women to live lives of consecrated virginity in the Egyptian desert greatly shaped the fourth-century picture of Mary.

[245]The (uncertain) practice of celibacy at Qumran is to be related to the levitical and eschatological ideals of that community and offers no real parallel for a commitment to virginity in marriage. See *JBC*, art. 68, §95; and H. Hübner, "Zölibat in Qumran?" *NTS* 17 (1970-71), 153-67.

[246]The interpolation, then, may have to be extended from 1:27 to the other mention of Mary as "betrothed" in 2:5. Presumably the influence for these interpolations would have come from Matt 1:18.

virginal conception (with Mary's question now made easier), it is
not so challenging to the traditional understanding of the scene as
the suggestion that the interpolation is to be found in 1:34c ("since
I do not know a man"), or in Mary's whole question and the first
part of the angel's response in 1:34-35, or even in the entire
dialogue of 1:34-37.[247] Without these verses, it is maintained, the
annunciation concerns the birth of the Messiah by normal relations between Mary and Joseph.

When this latter theory of interpolation posits a post-Lucan
scribe who added the problematic verses to harmonize Luke with
Matthew (which clearly posits a virginal conception), it runs up
against a twofold objection. First, there is no serious MS evidence for a scene without Mary's question.[248] Second, the style of
these verses is just as Lucan as any other part of the annunciation.[249] These objections are obviated if the theory posits interpolation by Luke himself into an earlier edition or pre-Lucan form of
the scene.[250] But there are other difficulties to be faced by the
thesis of Lucan interpolation. First, the argumentation for it is
weak.[251] Sometimes it is claimed that the reference to Jesus as
"Son of God" in v. 35 is repetitive of the description of him as
"Son of the Most High" in v. 32. Or the opposite argument may
be invoked, that "Son of God" in the context of v. 35 reflects
Hellenistic christology, somewhat in conflict with the Davidic
portrait of the "Son of the Most High" in 32. However, as we saw
in discussing Rom 1:3-4 there is no conflict in progressing from a
Davidic portrait to the description of Jesus as Son of God.

---

[247]Those who hold some form of this theory include Bultmann,
Cheyne, Conybeare, Hillmann, Holtzmann, Loisy, Schmiedel, Usener,
J. Weiss, and Zimmermann. An influential article in this direction was
that of A. von Harnack, *ZNW* 2 (1901), 53-57.

[248]See B. Brinkmann, *Bib* 34 (1953), 327-32.

[249]Taylor, *Historical Evidence*, 40-87. (In 1:34 only the causal con-
junction *epei* is unusual for Luke.) However, Räisänen, *Mutter*, 95, argues on the basis of vocabulary for Luke's use of a source here.

[250]This is related to the thesis that Luke added "as was supposed" to
the genealogical notice that Jesus was the son of Joseph in 3:23.

[251]The basic arguments are articulated briefly by Bultmann, *History*,
295-96. For arguments favoring integrity, see Machen, *Virgin Birth*,
119-68.

Moreover, a Qumran fragment, written in Aramaic,[252] sets "Son of God" and "Son of the Most High" in parallelism, so that attribution of the title in Luke 1:35 to an imported Hellenistic christology becomes very dubious. Second, the annunciation pattern constitutes a good argument for the integrity of 1:26-38: the "How" question (1:34), the response (1:35), and the sign (1:36) are quite appropriate to an annunciation, and quite parallel to similar features in the annunciation to Zechariah (1:18-20). Indeed, granted the Lucan tendency to make Jesus greater than John the Baptist, the miraculous conception of the Baptist by parents who were past the age and barren almost demands a miraculous conception of Jesus of a higher sort, such as the one described in 1:34-35. For these reasons the task force found the interpolation theory unpersuasive.

ORIGINS OF THE CHRISTOLOGY. If one agrees that 1:34-35 is an integral part of the annunciation scene and not an interpolation, what are the origins of the theological message found therein, especially of the christology and the virginal conception? (This question is pertinent whether one thinks that Luke is the original composer of the scene or drew it from a source. The task force itself tended toward original Lucan composition.) If we begin with the christology, the description of Jesus as God's Son is common in the NT. Elsewhere in Luke/Acts it is associated both with the resurrection (Acts 13:32-33) and with the baptism of Jesus (Luke 3:22), in each case reflecting Ps 2:7 ("You are my Son; today I have begotten you").[253] The possibility that 1:35 applies to Jesus' conception a type of formula previously used for the resurrection and the baptism is increased when we reflect on our previous study of Rom 1:3-4: ". . . the gospel concerning His Son, who

---

[252]4Q246 or 4QpsDan A^a: "He shall be hailed (as) the Son of God, and they shall call him Son of the Most High." See J. A. Fitzmyer, *NTS* 20 (1973-74), 391-94. For caution against assuming that "Son of God" necessarily reflects Hellenistic christology, see Fuller, *Foundations*, 31-33; also G. Fohrer, *"huios,* TDNT, 8. 347-53; M. Hengel, *Son of God*.

[253]This verse of the psalm is specifically quoted in Acts 13:33 and in the Western tradition of Luke 3:22 (Codex Bezae, Old Latin Itala—also citations of that verse by Justin Martyr, Clement of Alexandria, Origen).

was born of the seed of David according to the flesh; designated Son of God in power according to a spirit of holiness as of resurrection from the dead, Jesus Christ our Lord." The key terms of Rom 1:4, "Son of God," "power," and "Spirit of Holiness" (understood as Holy Spirit—see above, Chap. 3, A2) appear in the account of the baptism of Jesus when the Holy Spirit descends upon Jesus and God's voice designates Jesus as His Son, so that he can return in the power of the Spirit to Galilee (Luke 3:22; 4:14). These same three terms appear in the message of conception in 1:35: "The *Holy Spirit* will *come upon* you, and the *power* of the Most High will overshadow you; therefore the child to be born will be *called* holy, *Son of God*."[254] There is no mention of overshadowing, *episkiazein*, at the baptism; but that term occurs in the transfiguration (9:34) where the divine voice repeats the message of the baptism. The overshadowing by the cloud at the transfiguration is parallel to the descent of the Spirit at the baptism, even as the two images are parallel in 1:35.[255]

The closeness of the Lucan annunciation message to Rom 1:3-4 becomes more obvious when we realize that the earlier part of the message in 1:32-33 stresses Jesus' Davidic role,[256] just as Rom 1:3 speaks of Jesus' being born of the seed of David. However, while the (pre-Pauline) formula in Romans contrasts the Davidic and the divine sonships as two stages (one according to the flesh, the other as of resurrection), in Luke 1:32-33, 35 both sonships come about through conception.

Our contention, then, is that the Lucan annunciation mes-

---

[254]"Holy Spirit" is without an article in the Greek, so that "the Holy Spirit" is an interpretation both of *pneuma hagion* (Luke 1:35) and *pneuma hagiosynēs* (Rom 1:4). For other possible translations of the last words of the verse ("the holy child will be called Son of God"; "the child will be holy, will be called Son of God"), see Brown, *Birth*, 291-92.

[255]The title "holy" (Holy One) of Luke 1:35 is not given Jesus at the baptism, but it appears shortly after the baptism in Luke 4:34.

[256]The key ideas of 1:32-33 (that Jesus will be great, called Son of the Most High, will be given David's throne, a king over a house, eternal kingdom) are all found in Nathan's promise to David in 2 Sam 7:9, 13, 14, 16. For the Davidic component in NT christology, see Fuller, *Foundations*, 111-14, 162-64, 188-91; E. Lohse, "*huios Dauid*," *TDNT*, 8. 484-87.

sage is a reflection of the christological language and formulas of the post-resurrectional church. To put it in another way, the angel's words to Mary dramatize vividly what the church has said about Jesus after the resurrection and about Jesus during his ministry after the baptism. Now this christology has been carried back to Jesus at the very moment of conception in his mother's womb.[257] We found a very similar situation in Matthew (pp. 89-91 above); for both evangelists Jesus is God's Son from the very inception of his life.

All of this means that 1:32-33, 35 are scarcely the explicit words of a divine revelation to Mary prior to Jesus' birth; and hence one ought not to assume that Mary had explicit knowledge of Jesus as "the Son of God" during his lifetime.[258] As we shall see, like other followers of Jesus, the Lucan Mary became part of the great eschatological family of Jesus (mother and brother and sister to him) through obedient response to God's word and will (Luke 8:21). Presumably after the resurrection (see Acts 1:14) she came to vocalize her faith in Jesus in the christological language we have been discussing. We do not deny the possibility of a revelation to Mary at the conception of her son,[259] but in the Lucan annunciation we are hearing a revelation phrased in post-resurrectional language.

ORIGINS OF THE VIRGINAL CONCEPTION. These observations

---

[257]When the language of divine begetting was applied to the resurrection and the baptism, that language was obviously symbolic. Greater realism is possible when the language of divine begetting is applied to a conception, especially to a conception without a human father. However, even conception christology is not yet a reference to ontological sonship.

[258]The work of R. Laurentin, *Jésus au Temple*, is written in relation to the thesis that Mary knew Jesus' divinity from the time of the annunciation. Unless one supposes that Mary hid this insight from Jesus' followers, such a foreknowledge of his divinity renders unintelligible the long struggle toward that truth even after the resurrection. The Marcan portrayal of the messianic secret and the Marcan portrayal of Mary as not understanding would then become great distortions.

[259]If one accepts the historicity of the virginal conception, that very event must have constituted some sort of revelation to Mary, even if it took a lifetime for her to find a christological language in which to express that revelation.

about the origin of the christology in 1:35 do not solve the question of why that christology of divine sonship has been attached to the conception of Jesus *by a virgin*. In seeking to answer that question, we begin by warning the reader that it is not obvious to all that Luke did intend to describe a virginal conception. Although Mary is clearly presented as a virgin at the time of the annunciation (*parthenos* twice in 1:27; see 1:34), she is told "You will conceive" (1:31).[260] This future conception could be understood to take place ". . . in the usual human way, of a child endowed with God's special favor, born at the intervention of the Spirit of God, and destined to be acknowledged as the heir to David's throne as God's Messiah and Son."[261] This interpretation is not to be refuted simply by pointing out that the future conception is through the Holy Spirit (1:35); for as we have seen (Chap. 3, B3), Paul's reference to Isaac as "born according to the Spirit" (Gal 4:29) need not imply that he had no human father.[262]

The majority of the task force was persuaded, however, that Luke really assumed and intended to describe a virginal conception, even though he did not make this point so clearly as did Matthew. In reaching this conclusion, we did not use Matthew to interpret Luke but drew upon the structure and pattern of the Lucan infancy narrative. The parallelism between John the Bap-

---

[260]The Greek word *syllēmpsē* is future. We have not accepted the thesis of those who, assuming a Semitic original, argue that the underlying Hebrew *hārāh*, having no exact time value, was meant to describe a present action: "You have at this instant conceived." So G. H. Box, "Virgin Birth," *A Dictionary of Christ and the Gospels* (ed. J. Hastings; New York: Scribners, 1912), 2. 806. Graystone, *Virgin*, 89-93, cites attempts to read the Greek future tense as a past reference. This thesis is refuted by the numerous future tenses of the other verbs in the context of 1:31-33, 35, and by the fact that Mary can scarcely have conceived before she gives an affirmative response in 1:38. See Taylor, *Historical Evidence*, 38-40; J. Gewiess, "Die Marienfrage, Lk 1,34," *BZ* 5 (1961), 221-54 (English summary in *TD* 11 [1963], 39-42).

[261]Fitzmyer, "Virginal Conception," 567—a view resisted by R. E. Brown, "Luke's Description of the Virginal Conception," *TS* 35 (1974), 360-62.

[262]W. E. Phipps, *Was Jesus Married?* (New York: Harper & Row, 1970), 39-46, postulates for Jesus a dual paternity: the Holy Spirit along with a human father.

tist and Jesus is meant to show that Jesus is greater. In the instance of the Baptist the age and barrenness of the parents were overcome by divine intervention; one would expect a greater intervention in the instance of Jesus, and that expectation is not fulfilled if he is conceived without divine help. It is admirably fulfilled if there is a virginal conception. Moreover, the description of the barrenness and age of the parents of John the Baptist in 1:7 constitutes the substance of the "How" question in 1:18, and the obstacle to be overcome by divine power in the angel's response in 1:19-20. Similarly, the virginity of Mary described in 1:27 constitutes the substance of her "How" question in 1:34, and therefore should constitute the obstacle to be overcome by divine power in the angel's response in 1:35. A final argument for Luke's acceptance of the virginal conception is that the reference to Jesus as the "supposed" son of Joseph in 3:23 would make little sense if he had been begotten by Joseph.

However, in accepting the thesis that Luke did intend a virginal conception in 1:34-35, we wish to eschew certain misinterpretations of that thesis. What is being described is not a *hieros gamos*, a "sacred marriage" or mating between a god and a mortal.[263] Luke does not mean that God or the Holy Spirit is a substitute male partner; the "overshadowing" of 1:35 has no sexual implication.[264] The agency of the Spirit and the term "overshadow" come, as we have seen, from NT christological formulations where no sexual import is possible.[265] God is not a sexual partner but a creative power in the begetting of Jesus.[266] The

---

[263]Of course, some Greek readers of pagan background may have interpreted the Lucan scene in this way.

[264]There have been attempts to interpret "overshadow" sexually, both from a rabbinic background (D. Daube, *ZNW* 48 [1957], 119-20) and a pagan mystery-religion background (H. Leisegang, *Pneuma Hagion* [Leipzig: Hinrichs, 1922], 25-33. See the refutation in Dibelius, "Jungfrauensohn," 19-22.

[265]See above, p. 118. The role of the Spirit in Jesus' conception is a preparation for the wisdom Jesus will demonstrate in 2:46-52, for his ability to baptize with the Spirit (3:16), and for his being full of the Spirit after his own baptism (4:1). For "overshadow," besides the transfiguration (9:34), see Exod. 40:35.

[266]See L. Legrand, "Fécondité virginale selon l'Esprit dans le Nouveau Testament," *NRT* 84 (1962), 785-805.

marvelous aspect of this creative power whereby a child is begotten of a virgin reflects no downgrading of human generation, which in Hebrew thought (Gen 1:28; 8:17) is a commanded continuation and participation in God's creative activity. The thesis of later theology that Jesus had to be conceived of a virgin because the transmission of original sin was related to the sexual nature of human propagation is not at all reflected in Luke (or in Matthew).[267] Finally, in interpreting the virginal conception of Jesus as the begetting of God's Son,[268] we recognize that Luke is not talking about the incarnation of a pre-existent divine being. The idea of pre-existence is found in other NT works (above, Chap. 5, n. 187), but it represents a different christology from that implied in the virginal conception. (It is noteworthy that both pre-existence christology and conception christology implicitly reject the thesis that Jesus was a man who during his lifetime or at his baptism was adopted by God as His Son.) Only in the period after Luke (and after Matthew) do we find attested a sequential joining of the two christologies whereby the pre-existent divine Word takes flesh (Johannine ideas) in the womb of the virgin Mary (Lucan and Matthean ideas).[269]

We turn now to the specific question of the origin of the Lucan idea of a virginal conception of Jesus. As we have already seen, Matt 1:22-23 quotes Isa 7:14 in reflection upon the angel's annunciation of the virginal conception. Although we concluded that Matthew had probably added the quotation to an existing narrative which contained the virginal conception, we have now to raise the issue of the possible influence of Isa 7:14 upon Luke. There is no specific Lucan citation of the Isaiah passage, but a number of commentators have argued for an influence of Isa

---

[267]Brown, *Virginal Conception*, 38-41.

[268]Note the logic in 1:35: because the Holy Spirit comes upon Mary, the child to be born will be called "holy"; because the power of the Most High overshadows her, the child to be born will be called "Son of God." It is a verse that describes the product of the divine begetting. The *dio*, "therefore," which introduces the last line of 1:35 catches this idea since probably it has a causal connotation (cf. Phil 2:9).

[269]Ignatius, *Magn.* 8.2 (Jesus as the Word); *Eph.* 19.1 (virginity of Mary); also Aristides, *Apology*, 15.1; Justin, *Apology*, 1.21 and 33.

7:10-14 upon the Lucan annunciation scene.[270] Let us list the points of contact that have been suggested and evaluate them:

—"virgin" (*parthenos*) in both Luke 1:27 (twice) and Isa 7:14. This is a significant parallel; but in the Matthean account we saw the possibility of influence from Deut 22:23, the law pertaining to "a betrothed virgin," and that may have been a factor in any pre-Gospel tradition of a virginal conception of Jesus.

—"house of David" in both Luke 1:27 and Isa 7:12. Again significant, although the usage is different: a vocative address to the king in Isaiah, and a genealogical qualification of Joseph in Luke, similar to the genealogical qualification of Zechariah in the John-the-Baptist annunciation (1:5). Since Luke 1:32-33 echoes 2 Samuel 7 (see above, n. 256), the idea of "*house* of David" may have come from 2 Sam 7:11, 13, 16.

—"the Lord" in Luke 1:28 and Isa 7:10.[271] This is too common a biblical expression to be a significant parallel.

—"you will conceive in your womb and bear a son, and you will call his name . . ." in Luke 1:31 and Isa 7:14.[272] This is not a really significant parallel since such a statement is part of the

---

[270] A. Vögtle, "Offene Frage," 46; H. Schürmann, *Lukasevangelium*, 62-63; J.-P. Audet, "L'annonce à Marie," *RB* 63 (1956), 364-74. To the contrary, Fitzmyer, "Virginal Conception," 568, n. 89: "There is not a shred of evidence that Luke has fashioned his annunciation in dependence on Isaiah."

[271] Although *kyrios*, used by Luke, appears in the LXX of Isa 7:14 known to us, we have no clear evidence that in the first century A.D. *kyrios* was being used in Greek translations of the Hebrew Bible to render *YHWH*. See J. A. Fitzmyer, "The Semitic Background for the New Testament *Kyrios* Title," *A Wandering Aramean: Collected Aramaic Essays* (Missoula: Scholars Press, 1978); cf. G. Howard, "The Tetragram and the New Testament," *JBL* 96 (1977), 63-83. However, even if *kyrios* was not written, it may have been pronounced when a Greek reader saw the transcribed Hebrew divine name in his Greek Bible.

[272] The Greek of Luke is quite close to that of Isaiah with the possible exception of the verb "you will conceive in your womb." Luke 1:31 has *syllēmpsē en gastri*; a closely similar reading in Isa 7:14, *en gastri lēmpsetai*, is attested in codices B and C, some minuscules, and in the Syrohexaplar, and is accepted by Swete. A dissimilar reading, *en gastri hexei*, "have in the womb," is attested in codices S (Sinaiticus) and

stereotyped annunciation of birth (see 3bc in our chart above). Granting the OT pattern, Luke could scarcely use any other language to phrase the message of a forthcoming birth.

Overall the points of contact between Luke and Isaiah 7 are not specific enough for us to posit Lucan dependence upon Isaiah. Luke is dependent upon an OT pattern of annunciation; and, as we shall see, the story of the birth of Samuel has left far more certain traces upon the Lucan narrative than Isaiah 7.

We are left then with the same problem we faced when we considered Matt 1:18-25. If the idea of a virginal conception did not come simply from meditation on Isa 7:14, from where did it come? On pp. 93-96 above, we discussed various solutions proposed by scholars: a *purely theological origin* (a theologoumenon[273]) as a dramatization of the idea that Jesus was God's Son through the Holy Spirit—a dramatization colored by a putative Hellenistic Jewish tradition that the patriarchs were virginally conceived; a *mixed historical and theological origin,* wherein the supposed fact that Jesus was born noticeably soon after Mary and Joseph had come to live together was interpreted, not in terms of sinful intercourse between the parents, but in terms of the sinlessness of Jesus and sanctity of his parents; a *purely historical origin* involving a family tradition passed down from Mary. As we saw, all the proposed theories have difficulties. What we did agree upon, with some difference of emphasis among us, was "the possibility and even probability of a pre-Gospel acceptance of the virginal conception." In other words, recalling the three stages of Gospel formation spoken of in Chap. 2 (B2a), we traced the virginal conception to *Stage Two* but recognized the inability of a modern scientific approach to trace it to

---

Alexandrinus and many minuscules, and is accepted by Rahlfs and Ziegler. The similar reading may represent an attempt by a Christian scribe to conform the Isaian text to Luke. All of these MSS are Christian copies of the OT.

[273]As McHugh, *Mother*, 309-21 points out, this technical term has been in use at least since Dibelius' "Jungfrauensohn." But in general we have avoided it because it carries various meanings; see Fitzmyer, "Virginal Conception," 548-49, esp. nn. 25, 26. Some use it to mean the translation of a purely theological concept into a seemingly historical narrative.

Stage One, the stage of historicity—an inability that in no way constitutes a negation of historicity.[274]

MARY'S RESPONSE. All that we have said thus far about 1:34-35 does not tell us much about Luke's view of Mary. We have seen that her question in 1:34 does not reveal her personal attitude toward virginity; rather it leads into the angel's christological statement of 1:35: Jesus is God's Son conceived through the coming of the Holy Spirit. This marvelous conception, without male parent, reveals the creative power of God at work but tells us no more about Mary than that she is God's instrument. The real Lucan evaluation of Mary becomes apparent only in 1:38 through her reaction to the angel's christological revelation: "Behold the handmaid of the Lord. Let it be to me according to your word." If, as we have seen, 1:32, 33, 35 contains a basic post-resurrectional proclamation of Christian faith, then Mary is being presented as the first one to hear the gospel.

Below (B3) we shall discuss Luke 8:19-21, the Lucan form of the scene in Mark 3:31-35 and Matt 12:46-50 involving those who constitute Jesus' eschatological family of disciples. While Luke will modify the thrust of the scene as regards Jesus' physical family, he will retain substantially the same principle of what constitutes ideal discipleship, namely, to hear the word of God and do it (8:21; see also 8:15: to hear the word and hold it fast). In light of this, Mary's reaction to the angel's inaugural proclamation of the gospel is significant. Her "Behold the handmaid of the Lord" echoes the biblical description of the pious mother of Samuel: "Let your handmaid find favor in your eyes" (1 Sam 1:18). But Mary is more than an OT saint;[275] for her hearing the

---

[274]E. C. Hoskyns and F. N. Davey, *The Riddle of the New Testament* (3d ed.; London: Faber and Faber, 1947), 98-99: "Concerning the origin of the belief in the virgin birth the critical historian can say nothing. . . . This single point of agreement [between the two infancy narratives] proves only that neither evangelist was responsible for originating the belief. . . . Matthew and Luke adopt the virgin birth into their narratives. . . . Whether they were historically justified in so doing no critic can say."

[275]The last statement of the angel in 1:37, "With God no word [or thing, *rēma*] will be impossible," echoes the LXX of Gen 18:14, "With God will any word [or thing, *rēma*] be impossible?" asked in reference to Sarah.

word of God and accepting it means that she meets the criterion
of the eschatological family which Jesus will call together. Although she has been given a sign (1:36-37), she is a believer for
whom God's word is enough.[276] For Luke she is the first Christian
disciple. Later in Acts Luke will show that the Holy Spirit is the
prime mover in the Christian community—the Spirit that is already at work in Mary (1:35).

(c) The Marian Implications of 1:28

The first words of the angel Gabriel to Mary are a well-
known salutation, the translation of which is not without problems:

chaire, kecharitōmenē, ho kyrios meta sou (Nestle, *UBSGNT*)
Hail, O favored one, the Lord is with you (*RSV*)
Hail, full of grace, the Lord is with thee:
    blessed art thou among women (*Douay*, from the Vulgate)
Rejoice, O highly favored daughter! The Lord is with you.
    Blessed are you among women. (*NAB*, from the Greek)

The last two translations, which have official status among
Roman Catholics, point to some traditional and modern debates
in interpretation.

Several of these points are minor. The final clause, "Blessed
are you among women," although found in some Greek
witnesses[277] and the Vulgate, is almost certainly a later addition
to Luke's text by a scribe who anticipated here the identical
words found in the greeting of Elizabeth to Mary in Luke 1:42.
"The Lord . . . with you" (the Greek has no verb[278]) is a usual

---

[276]So Räisänen, *Mutter*, 104-6. He agrees with F. Mussner in com-
paring Mary's faith with that of Abraham as presented in Romans 4.
Many also see Mary's acceptance as a contrast to Zechariah's not believing (1:20).

[277]Codices A, C, D, Theta; the Byzantine text tradition; also some
versions besides the Latin. It is not peculiar to Roman Catholic translations, for it appeared in the *KJV*; but it would be defended by few scholars today. See Metzger, *TCGNT*, 129.

[278]An optative can be added ("May the Lord be with you"), but here
the force is more likely declarative: "The Lord is with you." See W. C.

enough greeting, e.g., Judg 6:12. It has been claimed that such a greeting is unusual for a *woman* in Israel or Judaism;[279] however, Mary's being troubled at "what sort of greeting this might be" (1:29) may come more from being greeted by an angel than from the greeting itself. In any case, it is not to be taken literally in the sense of a conception that has already occurred, i.e., the Lord (Jesus) is within you. The difference in the translation of *chaire* as "Hail" or "Rejoice" is of importance but will be treated below.

Our chief concern here is the translation of *kecharitōmenē*. Although its use involves a play on the similar-sounding *chaire*, this word is the perfect passive participle of *charitoun*, a denominative verb related to *charis* ("favor, grace") which means "to bestow favor on, highly favor, bless"—see Eph 1:6).[280] It concerns Mary as one who has been "graciously favored (by God)"[281] and is explained by Luke in v. 30: "You have found favor with God," i.e., Mary has been elected by God to conceive the Messiah (31-33) and to give birth to the Son of God (35).

Even though a denominative verb is usually instrumental or factitive (*charitoun* means to constitute someone in *charis*), occasionally it carries a sense of plenitude,[282] whence the translation "graciously or highly favored." This is reflected in the Latin Vulgate rendition "(Ave) *gratia plena*," which appears in the famous "Hail Mary" prayer.[283] This translation, *"full of* grace," which is

---

van Unnik, "Dominus vobiscum: The Background of a Liturgical Formula," in *New Testament Essays: Studies in Memory of Thomas Walter Manson* (ed. A. J. B. Higgins; Manchester: University Press, 1959), 270-305, esp. 288-89.

[279]Grundmann, *Lukas*, 55-56. However, in Ruth 2:4 it is addressed to a mixed audience of men and women.

[280]H. Conzelmann, "*charis*...," *TDNT*, 9. 392-393, nn. 148, 168. Also M. Cambe, "La *charis* chez saint Luc: Remarques sur quelques textes, notamment le *kecharitōmenē*," *RB* 70 (1963), 193-207.

[281]To see a reference also to Hannah, the mother of Samuel (1 Samuel 1-2), since that name stems from the Hebrew root *hnn*, "favor," is convincing only to those already convinced that a Hebrew source underlies this section of Luke, e.g., Laurentin (above, n. 225).

[282]Discussed by Moulton, *GNTG*, 2, 393-97.

[283]A portion of that prayer, combining the Vulgate text of 1:28 with 1:42 ("Hail Mary, full of grace, the Lord is with thee; blessed are thou

not literal and is gradually being replaced among Roman Catholic translators,[284] has created difficulty, not on the level of Luke's intention, but in terms of later theology. Luke does convey an exuberance and plentitude in this "favor" of the begetting of God's Son; for that begetting, described in 1:32-33, 35, involves, as we have seen, an anticipation of the christological gospel proclaimed by post-Easter Christianity. However, later mariology took the plentitude literally in terms of Mary's personal possession of graces and privileges, as illustrated in the principle *Numquam satis*, "One can *never* say *enough* about Mary, for she is 'full of grace.' " Objection has also been raised when the "grace" has been interpreted to mean not only a grace or divine favor bestowed on Mary, but also grace which she has to bestow on others.[285] Debates on these points are not within the scope of our study, although we agree that such interpretations clearly go beyond the meaning of Luke's text.[286]

(d) Mary as "Daughter of Zion" and Related Symbolism? (1:28, 35, 43)

The problem of whether to translate the *chaire* of 1:28 as "Hail" or "Rejoice" (esp. *NAB*: *"Rejoice*, O highly favored *daughter")* leads us to an immense literature centered on a proposed Lucan symbolism for Mary as the Daughter of Zion,[287] the

---

among women and blessed is the fruit of thy womb") dates at least from the *Liber Antiphonianus*, attributed to Pope Gregory the Great (died 604). It was authorized as a formula to be taught along with the Creed and the Lord's Prayer ca. A.D. 1198. The second part of the prayer, which adapts the wording of Luke 1:43 ("mother of my Lord"), was added in the fifteenth century: "Holy Mary, Mother of God, pray for us sinners now and [at] the hour of our death."

[284]E.g., *NAB*; McHugh, *Mother*, 48, "favoured with divine grace": Schürmann, *Lukasevangelium*, 41, "begnadete" (graced).

[285]See Plummer, *Luke*, 22: "The *gratia plena* of the Vulg. is too indefinite. It is right, if it means 'full of grace, *which thou hast received*'; wrong, if it means 'full of grace, *which thou hast to bestow*.' "

[286]In Chap. 2, C4, we reflected on the thin line between eisegesis and a perceptive more-than-literal exegesis of the Scriptures in later Christian theology.

[287]Zion was a name for a part of Jerusalem or for one of the hills of the city; it came to serve as a name for Jerusalem itself. With relation to a

female personification of God's people (Israel and the Church), and the Ark of the Covenant. Although much of this writing is in French by Roman Catholics[288] (with little acceptance, however, by their German co-religionists), such symbolism has found strong adherents among non-Romans as well, particularly in the 1940s and 1950s.[289] Drawing heavily on a concordance to the LXX, the proponents of this symbolism often contend that since a term used by Luke is found in a certain OT passage, Luke intended to invoke that passage, its context, and other related passages. Now, it is neither impossible nor unlikely that through vocabulary Luke may refer implicitly to a certain OT passage or that in the infancy narrative he may describe Mary against an OT symbolic background—Luke's infancy narrative abounds in echoes of Abraham and Sarah, of Daniel's description of Gabriel, of the Samuel story, of the promise to David, of annunciation-of-birth patterns. However, the more subtle the proposed OT influence upon Luke, the greater the need for proof, especially if the symbolism is not well attested elsewhere in first-century Christianity.

---

geographical entity, "daughter" designates a subdivision, e.g., a city, town, or village. The OT speaks of a "daughter" of Egypt, Babylon, Edom, Dibon, etc. H. Cazelles, "Fille de Sion et théologie mariale dans la Bible," *BSFEM* 21 (1964), 51-71, has argued that "Daughter of Zion" originally referred to a new suburb of Jerusalem inhabited by poor refugees from the North after the fall of Samaria in 721 (see Micah 4:8, 10, 13). However, it came to stand for all Jerusalem, and even Judah or Israel. See McHugh, *Mother*, 438-44.

[288]Laurentin, *Structure*, 64-81, 148-61, provides a résumé of much of the argumentation.

[289]A. G. Hebert, "The Virgin Mary as the Daughter of Zion," *Theology* 53 (1950), 403-10; G. A. F. Knight, "The Virgin and the Old Testament," *The Reformed Theological Review* (Australia) 12 (1953), 1-13; and "The Protestant World and Mariology," *SJT* 19 (1966), 55-73; M. Thurian, *Mary*, 13-65. Most detailed is H. Sahlin, *Messias*; but the value of his comments depends in part on his theory (pp. 9-10, 56-69) of a Semitic Proto-Luke written ca. A.D. 50 by a Jew from Antioch, and translated into Greek with additions ca. 60-65 probably by Luke. The OT symbolism was more apparent in Proto-Luke, as Sahlin imaginatively reconstructs it, e.g., *Zechariah* spoke the Magnificat about *Zion* the handmaid of the Lord. For Sahlin, Mary was a *literary* symbol of Israel, while some Roman Catholics have thought of Mary as a historical person embodying the "corporate personality" of Israel.

Some methodological considerations are in order here. If the Greek term in question is not uncommon, one cannot assume that Luke borrowed it from the LXX; if it is common in the LXX, one must prove that Luke had one passage in mind rather than others; and one cannot assume that Luke had a concordance enabling him to relate all the passages containing the same term. And finally, even if a certain *possibility* is established of a subtle reference to the OT, one must still ask whether an audience would ever have understood such subtleties without clear indications by Luke. Otherwise, the possible symbolism would not be really helpful for determining early Christian thought about Mary. The task force was not convinced by much of the proposed symbolism, even if we have elected to discuss it briefly.

CHAIRE, "REJOICE." The verb *chairein* (in the sg. or pl. imperative or infinitive) was used for the normal secular Greek greeting in hailing someone (Matt 26:49; 28:9) or in beginning and ending a letter (Jas 1:1; Phil 3:1; 4:4), whence the tendency to translate it in Luke 1:28 by Latin *"Ave"* and English "Hail" or "Hello." This translation agrees with the reference in 1:29 to "this greeting." However, S. Lyonnet[290] has argued that *chaire* should be translated literally as "Rejoice," for in scenes with a Semitic background Luke uses *eirēnē*, "Peace" (Hebrew *shālôm*), not *chaire*, as the ordinary greeting (10:5; 24:36). Of some eighty uses of *chairein* in the LXX, about twenty refer to a joy that greets a divine saving act (e.g., Exod 4:31; 1 Kgs 5:21; Isa 66:7); and it is to this kind of rejoicing that Lyonnet thinks Luke refers. The specific form *chaire* is used in the LXX four times, three of them addressed to the Daughter of Zion. Two are particularly important:

Zech 9:9 (cited in Matt 21:5 and John 12:15):
Rejoice [*chaire*] greatly, O Daughter of Zion!
Shout aloud, O daughter of Jerusalem!
Lo, your king comes to you;
triumphant and victorious is he,
humble and riding on an ass,
on a colt, the foal of an ass.

---

[290]See the articles *"Chaire kecharitōmenē"* and "Le récit"; also Laurentin, *Structure*, 64-71; McHugh, *Mother*, 38-47. The Greek writers from Origen to the Byzantine period took Luke's *chaire* as "Rejoice."

Zeph 3:14-17 (LXX)[291]
Rejoice [*chaire*], O Daughter of Zion, . . .
The King of Israel, the Lord, is in your midst [*en mesō sou*] . . .
Take heart, Zion . . .
The Lord your God is in you [*en soi*]
the Mighty One will save you.

The thesis that Luke had such passages in mind is sometimes
enhanced by pointing out that in 1:27 he twice calls Mary a virgin,
and that the OT speaks of the virgin Daughter of Zion or virgin
Israel; and also by claiming a parallelism between Luke's "The
Lord is with you [*meta sou*]" and Zephaniah's "The Lord is in
your midst . . . in you."[292]

Let us just list some of the difficulties this thesis faces:[293] (a)
Chaire was as common a greeting among Greek-speakers as
"Goodbye" is among English-speakers; without clear warning,
would the readers of Luke guess that what normally meant
"Hello" should be taken literally as "Rejoice," any more than
without warning an English audience would guess that "Goodbye" should be taken literally as "God be with you"? (b) Purely
hypothetical is the contention that Luke would use *eirēnē*,[294] not
chaire, if he meant a normal greeting, because the background

---

[291]We are citing Zechariah according to the Hebrew and Zephaniah
according to the LXX to illustrate that the proponents of the theory
appeal to both languages and even heighten resemblances by shifting
back and forth from Hebrew to Greek within the same passage. We have
not the slightest proof that the author of Luke knew Hebrew.

[292]The motif of humility in a Daughter of Zion passage, such as Zech
9:9, is seen as related to the description of Mary the handmaid in 1:38 and
1:48. Also Mary in 1:45, "Blessed is she who believed that there would
be a fulfillment of what was spoken to her from the Lord," is seen to
evoke the Daughter of Zion who must believe the Lord's promises; see
Leaney, *Luke*, 86.

[293]It is rejected with arguments by A. Strobel, "Der Gruss," and by
Räisänen, *Mutter*, 86-92; see also Schürmann, *Lukasevangelium*, 43-44.

[294]The thesis that a writer *in Greek* would use *eirēnē* as a greeting
when he is imagining a Semitic setting, and *chaire* when he is imagining a
Greek setting, rests in part on the thesis that the LXX uses *chaire* as a
greeting only in books originally composed in Greek; so McHugh,
Mother, 39. This is incorrect since both 1 Maccabees and Tobit had
Semitic originals.

here is Semitic. Luke uses *chairein* as a normal greeting in Acts
15:23 and 23:26. (c) The connection of Mary as "virgin" to Mary
as "Daughter of Zion" is dubious, since almost all the OT references to the virgin Zion or virgin Israel are uncomplimentary,
portraying her in a state of oppression, waywardness, and lust.
(d) The fourth LXX *chaire* passage, the one not addressed to the
Daughter of Zion, is Lam 4:21: "Rejoice . . . O Daughter of Edom
. . . you shall become drunk and strip yourself bare." On what
grounds does one assume that Luke has Zeph 9:9 in mind, when
he uses *chaire*, rather than Lam 4:21? (e) As we have seen, "The
Lord is with you" is a common greeting that normally has no
relation to the idea that the Lord is in your midst or in you. (f)
When *chairein* does refer to the rejoicing of the people of God in
the LXX, it is normally accompanied by a clarifying or
strengthening verb, e.g., "Rejoice and be glad" (Joel 2:23; Lam
4:21; Isa 66:10; Tob 13:13: *euphrainein* or *agallian*). Luke is
aware of this combination (see 15:32); if he wanted *chaire* to mean
"Rejoice" in 1:28, he could have used the combination, rather
than offering his readers a word that they would almost certainly
misunderstand as a normal greeting. We cannot deny the possibility of the Lyonnet thesis, but these arguments mean that nothing
certain or probable can be built upon it.

THE ARK OF THE COVENANT. Closely related to the thesis we
have been discussing is another imagery which sees the Lucan
Mary as the Ark of the Covenant, or the Tabernacle.[295] In 1:35
Mary is told, "The power of the Most High will overshadow
[*episkiazein*] you." The same verb is used when the cloud of
God's glory overshadows the Tabernacle in the desert (Exod
40:35; Num 9:18, 22), and when the winged cherubim overshadow
the Ark of the Covenant (Exod 25:20; 1 Chr 28:18). In Luke 1:43,
as Elizabeth greets Mary, she says: "How is it that the mother of
my Lord should come to me?" In 2 Sam 6:9 David asks, "How

---

[295]Laurentin, *Structure*, 73-81, 159-61; McHugh, *Mother*, 56-63.
McHugh admits that we cannot be certain that this symbolism was in-
tended by Luke; yet he suggests that Luke may have "adapted an early
Christian midrash about the Ark of the Covenant."

can the Ark of the Lord come to me?"[296] At the visitation Mary
remains with Elizabeth about three months (Luke 1:56); the Ark
of the Covenant remained three months in the house of Obede-
dom (2 Sam 6:11). If one combines Luke 1:31 and John 1:14, one
has the Word of God becoming flesh and "tabernacling" among
us (*skēnoun*, from *skēnē*, "tent, tabernacle"), in the womb of the
virgin Mary.

Once again all these observations cloak real problems. We
saw that the language of Luke 1:35 is a retrojection of a christological language once attached to the resurrection and/or to the
baptism of Jesus. If the angel's word to Mary, "The Holy Spirit
will come upon you, . . . therefore the child to be born will be
called holy, Son of God," has resemblances to the descent of the
Holy Spirit at the baptism when God said, "You are my Son,"[297]
the angel's word, "The power of the Most High will overshadow
you," has resemblances to the transfiguration in Luke 9:34-35
where a cloud comes and overshadows Jesus and a voice says out
of the cloud, "This is my Son." Obviously the transfiguration
scene has been affected by OT accounts of God's glory overshadowing the Tabernacle and the Temple, but a relationship between Luke 1:34 and the transfiguration makes it quite uncertain
that the use of the verb "overshadow" would necessarily invoke
the imagery of Mary as the Tabernacle or the Ark of the Covenant.[298] If Elizabeth's question to Mary resembles David's ques-

---

[296]This parallelism approaches fantasy when David's dancing before
the Ark (2 Sam 6:14) is compared to the baby's leaping in Elizabeth's
womb as she greets Mary (Luke 1:41, 44).

[297]See above, n. 253, for the Western text of Luke 3:22: "You are my
Son; today I have begotten you."

[298]In the OT there are other overshadowings, e.g., of Mount Zion
(Isa 4:50), of the Israelites (Num 10:34[36]), of God's chosen ones (Deut
33:12; Ps 91:4). We note that the symbolism of Mary as the Tabernacle
runs into a particular difficulty, depending on how one interprets Luke's
attitude toward Stephen's speech in Acts 7:44-49. Stephen says that the
Most High does not dwell in houses made with hands; Haenchen, *Acts*,
284, n. 3, argues that this included the "Tabernacle of the desert" as well
as the Temple built by Solomon. If that is Luke's theology, a comparison
between Mary and the Tabernacle might not be favorable to her.

tion about the Ark, it also resembles Araunah's question about
David in 2 Sam 24:21, "What is this, that my lord the king has
come to his servant?" Mary's three-month stay with Elizabeth
need have no recondite symbolism; Elizabeth is six months pregnant (1:36) when Mary arrives, and a longer stay would have
Mary present for the birth of John, thus "upstaging" Elizabeth. A
facile combination of Luke 1:32-33, 35 and John 1:14 involves two
different christologies which in the NT are quite independent of
each other. And so, once more, nothing certain or probable can
be built upon this imagery applied to Mary.

   Luke describes most of the adult figures of the infancy narrative against an OT background; it would be surprising if he did not
place Mary against this background as well. (When we discuss
the Magnificat, we shall raise the question of Mary as a spokeswoman for the Anawim or poor ones of Israel.) However, in our
judgment there is no convincing evidence that Luke specifically
identified Mary with the symbolism of the Daughter of Zion or the
Ark of the Covenant. As formerly to the mothers of the great
figures of the OT, an angel announced to Mary the forthcoming
birth of a child who would have a unique place in salvation history. Her obedient response to that annunciation reflects not only
the sanctity of her predecessors but also the anticipated characteristics of a disciple of Jesus.

2. Mary's Visitation to Elizabeth (1:39-56)

   In the annunciation (1:36), by way of a sign, the angel informed Mary of the advanced pregnancy of Elizabeth, her relative.[299] Luke continues the portrait of Mary as the obedient

---

   [299]Luke 1:36 is the only passage in the NT that establishes a family
relationship between Mary and Elizabeth, and thus implicitly between
Jesus and John the Baptist. None of the descriptions of the relations
between these two men in the public ministry would lead us to suspect a
family relationship; and a passage like John 1:33, where the Baptist says,
"I did not know him," casts doubt on the historicity of the Lucan information. See Brown, *Birth*, 282-85. The supposed relationship between
Mary and Elizabeth has contributed to the theory that Mary was of
levitical descent, as was Elizabeth (Luke 1:5; see below, n. 345).

handmaid of the Lord (1:38) by having her respond *with haste*, going to the house of Zechariah to greet Elizabeth (1:39-40). This visitation, which brings together protagonists from each of the two annunciation scenes (see outline above, p. 108), is the occasion both of revelation and of hymnic exaltation. As Elizabeth hears Mary's greeting, the babe in her womb leaps and she is filled with the Holy Spirit; and the oracle or hymn (1:42b-45)[300] that she immediately proclaims hails Mary as "the mother of my Lord"—Elizabeth now knows the secret of Gabriel's annunciation to Mary. If Elizabeth praises Mary, Mary in turn praises God in the Magnificat hymn (1:46-55).[301] Clearly Luke has placed Mary front-stage and center in this scene.

(a) Elizabeth's Words to Mary (1:42b-45)

Since these words constitute the less familiar of the two hymns in the scene—if indeed the designation "hymn" is appropriate—it may be useful to the reader to have a literal translation:

42b *Blessed* [eulogēmenē] *are you among women,*
   and blessed [eulogēmenos] *is the fruit of your womb.*
43 *Whence to me this (gift)*
   that the mother of my Lord should come to me?
44 *For behold, when the voice of your greeting came in my ears,*
   the babe in my womb leaped for joy [agalliasei]
45 *And happy* [makaria] *is she who believed*
   that there would be a fulfillment of the things spoken to her by
   the Lord.[302]

---

[300]Plummer, *Luke*, 27, divides these lines into two strophes of four lines each. Some of the verses, however, are dubiously poetic; only 1:42b is marked by parallelism which is the hallmark of Hebrew poetry. Favorable to the claim that the verses should be treated as a hymn is the fact that *anaphōnein* ("Elizabeth *proclaimed*") is consistently used in the LXX for liturgical music. However, McHugh, *Mother*, 71-72, goes considerably beyond the evidence when he argues for a *pre*-Lucan hymn to Mary. Much more likely we have a Lucan composition that may mark the beginning of Christian hymns praising Mary.

[301]We shall discuss below whether the original Lucan text of 1:46 did have Mary as the speaker of the Magnificat.

[302]Another possible translation for the last line would be: "for there

The opening line has been addressed in the OT to women famous in Israelite history who have helped to deliver God's people from peril: in Judg 5:24, "Blessed be Jael among women"; in Jdt 13:18, "O daughter [Judith], you are blessed by the Most High God above all women on earth" (also Gen 14:19-20). On the one hand, such a blessing invoked upon Mary recognizes that God has employed her in His plan of salvation;[303] on the other hand, the fact that such a blessing has been invoked upon others prevents us from taking it too absolutely, as if it meant that Mary was the most blessed woman who had ever lived. Later mariology will place Mary above all angels and saints in holiness, but that cannot be inferred from this verse. The second line of 1:42b also has an OT echo in the promise of Moses to Israel for being obedient to the voice of God: "Blessed be the fruit [LXX: offspring] of your womb" (Deut. 28:1, 4). If this background was in Luke's mind, the blessing upon Mary is quite appropriate, for she has shown herself obedient to the word of God in 1:38.

We discussed above the dubious contention that 1:43 confirms the symbolism of Mary as the Ark of the Covenant. However, similar expressions of awe in 2 Sam 6:9 and 24:21 confirm the attitude already present in the twofold blessing of 1:42b—awe and respect because of Mary's relationship as mother to the child who is "called holy, Son of God" (1:35). But 1:45 makes it clear that physical motherhood is not the only ground of Mary's blessedness. Later in the Gospel (6:20-22) the Lucan Jesus will pronounce *on his disciples* beatitudes or macarisms such as: "Happy [*makarios*] are you poor, for yours is the kingdom of

---

will be a fulfillment. . . ." Although many translations have "Blessed" in both vv. 42b and 45, there is a distinction between *eulogēmenos* (equivalent to Hebrew *bārûk*) and *makarios* (Hebrew *'ašrē*). The latter, which is used in beatitudes or macarisms, does not normally confer a blessing but recognizes an existing state of happiness. The former generally implies a wish in praise of someone.

[303]We are arguing only from the general OT usage, without committing ourselves to whether the Judith passage was the model for Luke (see discussion in Laurentin, *Structure*, 81-82; McHugh, *Mother*, 69-72; Räisänen, *Mutter*, 108). Judith, who is thus praised, sings a canticle to God (Jdt 16:1-17), even as Mary recites the Magnificat.

God." It is fitting that, if in 1:38 Mary is the first to show the reaction of the Christian disciple, the first macarism of the Gospel is pronounced on her because of her belief in the things spoken to her by the Lord. The culmination of Elizabeth's words of praise stresses that God has chosen Mary and that she has responded in faith.

The task force was particularly struck by how consonant this picture of Mary as "she who believed" is with the picture of her in the Lucan account of the ministry. We have already called attention to the similarity that 1:38 has to 8:19-21 (above p. 125). One may also compare 1:42, 45 to 11:27-28, the scene where a woman in the crowd raises her voice to say to Jesus: "Happy [*makaria*] the womb that bore you, and the breasts you sucked"; but Jesus responds, "Happy rather those who hear the word of God and keep it." In both instances there is a blessing or beatitude in reference to physical motherhood; and then a greater emphasis on the one who believes the things spoken to her or the one who hears the word of God and keeps it. Mary, the handmaid of the Lord (1:38), meets the criterion and gains the beatitude of the Christian believers whom Acts 2:18 calls the servants and *handmaids* of the Lord.[304]

(b) Mary's Magnificat (1:46-55)

The Magnificat is much more clearly poetry than Elizabeth's words to Mary.[305] There is, nevertheless, considerable disagreement about the classification of the poem (a hymn of praise?); the number of strophes (two, four, five, nine); the meter; whether or not there was a Semitic original. Details and bibliography may be found in the various commentaries on Luke; but these disputes are of no direct concern to this study. Three questions do concern us: *First*, did Luke intend that Mary be the speaker of the Magnificat? *Second*, if so, did Mary really compose it? *Third*, what

---

[304]See above, n. 224, for the similarities in atmosphere between the infancy narrative and the first days of the church in Acts 1-2.

[305]See above, n. 300. Verses 1:46b-47 and 1:53 are cited in manuals as perfect examples, respectively, of synonymous and antithetic parallelism, characteristic of Hebrew poetry.

does the Magnificat tell us about Luke's overall picture of Mary?

FIRST, in Luke's text who was the original speaker of the Magnificat? Although almost all Greek MSS and ancient versions assign it to Mary, there is some evidence ascribing it to Elizabeth.[306] Since the end of the last century some prominent scholars have supported an attribution to Elizabeth;[307] yet they remain in the minority. The textual basis for such an attribution, largely Latin, is so weak that it could be forgotten were it not for the principle of favoring the more difficult reading, i.e., one can understand how later scribes might change Elizabeth to Mary but not vice versa. (It has even been proposed, without any textual support, that the original read: "And she said," and that scribes replaced the "she" by either "Mary" or "Elizabeth.") Yet, the awkwardness of two actions attributed successively to Mary (1:46, "And Mary said"; 1:56, "Now Mary remained") may have caused a scribe to change the attribution of the first action to Elizabeth.[308]

Arguments as to whether the content of the Magnificat fits one woman better than the other are inconclusive (in part, because some verses, like 51a, 51b, 52a, fit neither woman). For

---

[306]Three Latin MSS ranging in date from the fourth to the eighth centuries read, "And Elisabet (Elisabel, Elisabeth) said." This reading is supported by dubious passages in translations of Irenaeus and Origen, and by the Yugoslavian bishop Nicetas of Remesiana (ca. A.D. 400). See Brown, *Birth*, 334-36.

[307]Included are Burkitt, Creed, J. G. Davies, Easton, Goguel, J. R. Harris, Harnack, Klostermann, Loisy, and Winter. See S. Benko, "The Magnificat: A History of the Controversy," *JBL* 86 (1967), 263-75. The arguments are discussed by R. Laurentin, *Bib* 38 (1957), 15-23.

[308]In fact, however, the sequence is not at all improved by the Elizabeth reading, for now she has two consecutive speeches: 1:41, "Elizabeth proclaimed"; 1:46, "And Elizabeth said." The whole sequence-argument is relativized if one agrees with Brown (*Birth*, 346-69) and others that the canticles are a secondary insertion into the Lucan infancy narrative. A pre-Gospel sequence would thus have had Elizabeth's proclamation in 1:42-45 followed immediately by 1:56: "And Mary remained." In this hypothesis, the secondary insertion of the canticle, prefaced by "And Mary said," created tension with 1:56, "And Mary remained"; and a late scribe sought to solve this tension by changing the speaker to Elizabeth.

instance, in 1:48 the expressions "handmaid" and "all generations will call me happy [*makariousin*]" fit Mary well (1:38, 42,
45), while the expression "low estate" fits Elizabeth better (1:25).
This hymn is parallel to the hymn of Hannah, the mother of
Samuel (1 Sam 2:1-10)—in 1:5-7, 24-25 Elizabeth, yearning in her
barrenness for a child, resembles Hannah closely; in 2:22-40
Mary, presenting the child in the Temple and encountering Simeon, resembles Hannah closely (1 Sam 1:21-28; 2:19-20). The
argument that it would be appropriate to have both canticles in
chap. 1 uttered by the parents of the Baptist, Elizabeth giving
voice to the Magnificat, Zechariah to the Benedictus, is coun-
tered by the argument that it would be even more appropriate to
have them uttered by the two recipients of angelic annunciations,
Mary and Zechariah. Because of such unconvincing arguments,[309] the task force was inclined to let the enormous
weight of the textual evidence in favor of Mary decide the issue.

SECOND, if "And Mary said" was the original reading, did
Mary herself compose the Magnificat? It may surprise some
readers to learn that today one would be hardpressed to find any
critical biblical scholar who would answer in the affirmative. In
the OT there was already a technique of placing canticles on the
lips of well-known personages in order to have them voice appropriate sentiments of praise at a particular manifestation of God's
goodness, e.g., Jonah's hymn of thanksgiving in 2:2-9. The fact
that such canticles were not originally composed for the situations in which we now find them helps us to be aware of this
technique. In particular, the canticle attributed to Hannah in 1
Sam 2:1-10 offers poetic praise to God in thanks for His gift of a
child to the barren woman; but the warlike character of the last
lines of the canticle makes scholars judge that a more general
psalm has been brought into service here. Similarly, the carefully
hewn poetic lines of the Magnificat are scarcely an on-the-spot

---

[309]An even less convincing argument, based on the supposition of a
Hebrew original, argues for the attribution to Mary: "And Mary
[*Miryām*] said, "Magnifies [*Měrîmāh*] my soul the Lord." But both the
underlying supposition and the reconstructed Hebrew of the wordplay
are far from certain.

poetic utterance, and the past tenses that dominate the canticle suggest that this hymn originally dealt with salvation in retrospect (after the resurrection) rather than the inauguration of salvation. Lines like "He has shown strength with His arm; He has scattered the proud in the imaginings of their hearts; He has put down the mighty from their thrones and has exalted those of low degree" are not really the appropriate sentiments of a maiden who has not yet given birth to the Messiah; they are much more appropriate if composed by those who know that through the resurrection God had reversed the crucifixion.

If Mary did not compose the Magnificat, who did? Scholars are divided[310] as to whether the Magnificat (along with the Benedictus, the Gloria in Excelsis, the Nunc Dimittis) was an original Lucan composition or was adopted by Luke (with adaptation, e.g., by supplying 1:48) from a collection of Jewish Christian hymns.[311] There are good arguments for both views; but the

---

[310]For various theories, see R. A. Aytoun, "The Ten Lucan Hymns of the Nativity in Their Original Language," *JTS* 18 (1917), 274-88; D. R. Jones, "The Background and Character of the Lucan Psalms," *JTS* (n.s.) 19 (1968), 19-50; F. Gryglewicz, "Die Herkunft der Hymnen des Kindheitsevangeliums des Lukas," *NTS* 21 (1974-75), 265-73; also the summary discussion in Brown, *Birth*, 346-55.

[311]The task force was not inclined to accept the thesis that the hymns were non-Christian in origin, e.g., that the Magnificat had been a hymn about John the Baptist (associated with the reading, "And Elizabeth said," in 1:45) or that both Magnificat and Benedictus had been Jewish hymns or, more specifically, Maccabean battle hymns (Bornhäuser, Gunkel, Klostermann, Mowinckel, Spitta)—see P. Winter, *BJRL* 37 (1954-55), 328-47. The clear OT allusions in both canticles leave open the question of whether the author(s) was (were) Jewish or Jewish Christian(s), but the past tenses referring to *accomplished* salvation "in the House of David His Servant" (1:69) favor Jewish Christian authorship: the Davidic Messiah has come. The "christology" of the canticles is relatively simple: God has fulfilled His promises to Abraham and to David—there is no echo of the conception of God's Son through the Holy Spirit of the virgin Mary (1:34-35). The failure to take account of such differences in the christology of chap. 1 invalidates Miguens' attempt (*Virgin Birth*, 148; see 140, 147) to claim that the virginal conception story comes from Mary and contains "a very *primitive* christology," consonant with Mary's Jewish background.

above-mentioned signs that the Magnificat is not totally appropriate on Mary's lips favor Lucan adoption over Lucan original composition, on the principle that Luke would have made an original composition fit the speaker more smoothly. But we did not judge that we had to decide this issue, since, in either case, Luke placed the canticle on Mary's lips because he saw its sentiments as generally compatible with his view of Mary.

THIRD, what does the Magnificat contribute to the Lucan picture of Mary? There are many parallels between the themes of the Magnificat and themes found in the body of Luke's Gospel. Thus, even if Luke did not compose the canticle himself, he adopted it because he found its theology compatible with his own.[312] For instance, the theme of joy in the opening couplet (1:47: "My *spirit rejoices* [*agallian*] in God my Savior") not only continues the words that Elizabeth spoke when filled with the Holy *Spirit* (1:41, 44: "The babe in my womb leaped for joy [*agalliasis*])," but also anticipates a statement about Jesus unique to Luke (10:21: "He rejoiced [*agallian*] in the Holy Spirit").[313]

The core of the Magnificat contrasts the different fates of the proud/mighty/rich and the lowly/hungry: the former are scattered, put down, and sent away hungry, while the latter are exalted and filled (1:51-53). In all the Synoptic Gospels Jesus addresses himself to the outcasts; but Luke places a special emphasis on those who are "on the periphery," the downtrodden, sinners, women, widows, Samaritans (7:11-17, 36-50; 10:29-37; 17:11-19). In particular, Luke dramatizes a theme of reversal where the rich and powerful are frustrated, while the poor and lowly become truly wealthy and exalted (e.g., the parables of the

---

[312]This compatibility has led to the suggestion that Luke adopted the canticles from a collection that had its origins among the early Jewish Christian community described in Acts 2:41-47 (Benoit, Gryglewicz; see Brown, *Birth*, 354-55).

[313]Such inner-Lucan connections do not resolve the problem of the composition of the Magnificat in favor of Luke's authorship; for both Luke 10:21 and the Magnificat may echo the OT, e.g., Hab 3:18, "I shall rejoice [*agallian*] in the Lord; I shall take joy in God my Savior"; Ps 35:9: "Then my soul will rejoice [*agallian*] in the Lord; it will delight in His salvation."

rich barnbuilder [12:16-21], those invited to the banquet [14:7-11], Lazarus and the rich man [16:19-31]). This reversal is most dramatically phrased in the Beatitudes which open Luke's form of the Sermon on the Mount (6:20-26): "Happy [*makarios*] are you poor . . . you that hunger now . . . you that weep now. . . . But woe to you that are rich . . . that are full now . . . that laugh now." By placing the Magnificat on the lips of Mary who has already been declared *makarios* (1:45: "Happy is she who believed"), Luke is making her the spokeswoman of a theme of reversal that will be a vital part of the Gospel message. If by her acceptance of the word of God about Jesus (1:38, 45) Mary is the first Christian disciple and the first one to measure up to the standards of what constitutes Jesus' eschatological family (8:21), she now proclaims the gospel by anticipation.

But if the Lucan Mary becomes the spokeswoman for Christian disciples, she does this as a representative of the pious among Israel. (Mary is not alone in this role in the Lucan infancy narrative, since Zechariah, Elizabeth, the shepherds, Simeon, and Anna share a common piety.) In particular, it has been suggested that Mary is a representative of the piety of the Anawim, the "Poor Ones."[314] This term may have originally designated the economically poor (and frequently still included them), but it came to refer more widely to those who could not trust in their own strength: the downtrodden, the poor, the lowly, the afflicted, the widows and orphans. The opposite of the Anawim were not simply the rich, but the proud and self-sufficient who trusted in their own strength and showed no need of God. There is much scholarly debate about the pre-exilic origins of the Anawim in Israel, and the extent to which they constituted a class or a community. In Ps 149:4 they are equated with the people of God:

---

[314]The word represents a plural from the Hebrew 'ānāw which, along with its cognate 'ānî, is a term for "poor, humble, afflicted." English treatments of the Anawim are found in A. Gelin, *The Poor of Yahweh* (Collegeville, MN: Liturgical Press, 1964); L. Sabourin, *The Psalms* (Staten Island: Alba, 1969), 1. 98-102; and M. Dibelius, *James* (Hermeneia; Philadelphia: Fortress, 1976; German orig. 1920, 1964), 39-45.

"The Lord takes pleasure in His people; He adorns the Poor Ones with victory."[315] It has been suggested that the Qumran community was a sectarian group of Anawim, and certainly the author of the *Hodayoth* (Thanksgiving Psalms) portrays himself as a "poor one."[316] The Jerusalem Christian community described in Acts 2:43-47; 4:32-37 has some resemblances to the Anawim, combining an esteem for poverty with Temple piety which is, at times, also a mark of the "Poor Ones."[317] The task force, without committing itself to the disputed features in the theory of a clearly designated group of Anawim, did agree that the Magnificat continues the theme of the "Poor Ones" exhibited in the Psalms. As spokeswoman of this theme, Mary continues a certain style of Israelite piety and anticipates the spirit of the early Christians whom Luke will later describe in the aftermath of Pentecost. If, as we have seen (n. 220 above), Luke's view of salvation history involves a sequence of Israel, Jesus, and the church, the theme of God's defense of the poor and lowly runs through those three stages. By associating Mary with this theme, Luke gives her an important role in that salvation history, a representative role that will continue from the infancy narrative into the ministry of Jesus, and finally into the early church.

3. Mary and the Birth at Bethlehem (2:1-20)

After the visitation, Luke tells us that Mary returned home (1:56); and he gives her no further role in chap. 1, which concen-

---

[315]In the Psalms God is said to protect, defend, save and rescue the Anawim, either as individuals or as a group. The Anawim implore God and praise His name. See A. Rahlfs, *'Anî und 'Anāw in den Psalmen* (Leipzig: Dieterich, 1892); H. Birkeland, *'Anî und 'Anāw in den Psalmen* (Oslo: Dybwad, 1933); P. Van den Berge, " 'Ani et 'Anaw dans les psaumes," in *Le Psautier* (ed. R. De Langhe; Louvain University, 1962), 273-95.

[316]1QH ii 34-35. References to the whole Qumran group as Anawim and as the Community of the Poor (*'ebyônîm*) are found in 1QH 18:14; 1QM 11:9; 4QpPs[a] 1-2 ii 9; iii 10.

[317]The Hasidean movement (a branch of which is sometimes said to have produced the Qumran community) was deeply concerned about the

trates on the birth, naming, and circumcision of John the Baptist (1:57-80). However, in the parallel scene of the birth, circumcision, and naming of Jesus (2:1-21), Mary reappears in a significant way. Despite the fact that this parallelism between the Baptist and Jesus continues a pattern established by the annunciations of chap. 1 (see above, p. 108), scholars have noted that in many ways chap. 2 is independent of chap. 1.[318] It is not only that the Baptist is never mentioned in chap. 2,[319] but also that no single fact of chap. 1 is clearly presupposed by chap. 2. For instance, in 2:4 the reader is told again that Joseph was of the house of David, and in 2:5 Mary is reintroduced as the betrothed of Joseph, as if those facts had not been mentioned in 1:27. There is no reference to the virginal conception; and if we had just chap. 2, there would be no way of knowing that Jesus had not been conceived by Joseph and Mary in the normal way.[320] Joseph, who was only named in chap. 1, emerges almost as an equal partner with Mary in the narrative of chap. 2.[321]

These differences have led to the suggestion that, in composing chap. 2, Luke drew upon sources other than those used in chap. 1. A common thesis, for instance, is that Luke supplied the preface in 2:1-5 to a pre-Lucan story underlying 2:6-20.[322] (As we saw above, n. 231, the census of 2:1-5 is most likely an incorrect

---

purity of cult, Temple, and priesthood. Although Luke stresses the community of goods among the Jerusalem Christians, L. E. Keck, *ZNW* 56 (1965), 100-29; 57 (1966), 54-78, has argued convincingly against the thesis that "the Poor" was a designation of the early church.

[318]This theory is held by both Bultmann (*History*, 294) and Dibelius (see McHugh, *Mother*, 311-21). It is remarkable that Matthew 2 can also be read independently of Matthew 1. At least this suggests that there is no necessary connection between the virginal conception (Matthew 1; Luke 1) and birth at Bethlehem (Matthew 2; Luke 2).

[319]In 3:20, as in 1:80, Luke narrates the Baptist's future history before he leaves him to concentrate on Jesus.

[320]Luke 2:27, 41, 43 speak of the *parents* of Jesus; Joseph is called the *father* of Jesus in 2:33, 48.

[321]Luke 2:4, 16, 22 ("their purification"), 27, 33, 39, 41-51.

[322]This view is held with variations by scholars like Dibelius, K. L. Schmidt, and F. Hahn. Vögtle, "Offene Frage," 54-56, would attribute to Luke vv. 6-7 as well.

setting for the birth of Jesus; this theory would attribute the mistake to Luke rather than to his sources.) The task force gave no firm adherence to the theory of pre-Lucan sources for the narrative of chap. 1; and it was not convinced that such a theory need be invoked for the narrative of chap. 2 either (or, at least, for 2:1-40). Many OT themes have been suggested as background for 2:1-20;[323] and any or all of them could have been elaborated into a narrative by Luke as well as by putative pre-Lucan sources. Fortunately, once again, the resolution of the question of pre-Lucan source vs. original Lucan composition need not be resolved for a discussion of Mary's importance in the scene, although it has implications for two verses that we shall have to discuss.

(a) "With Mary his betrothed" (2:5)

The overwhelming majority of Greek MSS and the versions support a reading in v. 5 that has Joseph going to Bethlehem to have himself enrolled in the census together with Mary *tē emnēsteumenē autō* ("the one engaged to him," "his betrothed"). The verb is *mnēsteuein* used in Matt 1:18 ("His mother Mary had been betrothed to Joseph") and Luke 1:27 ("A virgin betrothed to a man of the house of David whose name was Joseph"). In both the previous instances Mary had already been married to Joseph but had not yet been taken to live with him (pp. 83-84 above.) Now, however, Mary is traveling with Joseph and is far advanced in pregnancy; and so one might assume that the second stage in the marriage had taken place, namely, that Joseph had taken Mary to his home as *wife* (Matt 1:24: *paralambanein tēn gynaika*). It is somewhat surprising, then, to find Luke still speaking of Mary as

---

[323]As background for the themes of the census, the manger, and the shepherds' flock, passages like the following have been proposed: (a) the Quinta Greek version of Ps 87:6 known by Origen: "In the *census* of the peoples this one will be born there"; (b) Isa 1:3: "The donkey has known the *manger* of its lord, but Israel has not known me"; (c) an exegesis identifying Bethlehem of Micah 5:1(2) and Migdal Eder, the "Tower of the *Flock*" of Micah 4:5, especially if one may invoke the admittedly later *Targum Pseudo-Jonathan* on Gen 35:21 identifying the "Tower of the Flock" as "the place from which the King Messiah will be revealed." For discussion and bibliography, see Brown, *Birth*, 417-24.

Joseph's "betrothed," instead of his "wife" (*gynē*). Did Luke know that the Jewish marriage customs involved two steps (see above, n. 241)? Without great reflection or significance did he simply repeat the description of the relationship between Mary and Joseph that he had given in 1:27? Or was he hinting in 2:5 at the virginal conception which he had previously described in 1:26-35, perhaps with the additional information that, after having conceived, Mary was still a virgin?

The situation is complicated by a poorly attested but important variant reading in the Sinaitic Syriac and some Old Latin MSS: "with Mary his *wife*" (*gynaiki autou*).[324] A number of scholars have argued that this was the original reading of 2:5,[325] sometimes proposing that it came from a source (or even from a stage of Lucan composition) in which there was no knowledge of the virginal conception—in other words before the material now found in 1:27, 34-35 had been prefixed to the material in chap. 2. One could argue another way, however, if "wife" was the original reading, namely, that Luke was being faithful to the *two* steps of Jewish marriage customs (calling Mary "betrothed" before she came to live with Joseph and "wife" afterwards), all the while assuming a virginal conception, even as does Matthew, who uses first the term "betrothed" and then the term "wife" to cover the two stages in the marriage. In that case, a scribe who did not know the customs may have regarded "wife" as a term that did not do justice to Mary's virginity and have substituted "betrothed."

In fact, however, the task force accepted the best attested reading ("betrothed") as the more likely original Lucan wording in 2:5. We doubted that a scribal substitution of "wife" represented a denial of the virginal conception. If the scribe did not know Jewish marriage customs, he may have thought that the idea of Joseph traveling with his betrothed was a bit scandalous

---

[324]A third reading refers to Mary as "his betrothed wife" (*tē memnēsteumenē autō gynaiki*). While this is almost certainly a conflation of the other readings, the scribe who composed it knew of the reading "wife."

[325]Blass, Häcker, Schmiedel, Usener (cited by Taylor, *Virgin Birth*, 32-33), Dibelius, Klostermann, Sahlin. See Schmithals. "Weihnachtsgeschichte," 281-97.

and have substituted "wife." If he did know Jewish marriage customs and was influenced by Matthew, he may have judged Luke's "betrothed" inaccurate and have preferred "wife" as more technically correct. Only if one opts for a theory of sources and posits "wife" as the original reading in the pre-Lucan source is this verse of major significance in the genesis of mariology.

(b) "Mary kept all these things in her heart" (2:19, 51)

At the very beginning of our treatment of Luke/Acts (p. 109), we cautioned the reader not to *assume* that Luke had eyewitness tradition for the infancy narrative. In treating the annunciation in 1:26-38, we argued that in all probability we were not hearing the *ipsissima verba* of Mary, but a distillation of later christology (1:32-33, 35) combined with a formulation about discipleship reflecting the gospel tradition of the ministry (1:38). In n. 231 above, we called attention to evidence that makes the census described in 2:1-5 an unlikely chronological setting for the birth of Jesus. The number of OT motifs that scholars have detected woven into 2:6-20 (n. 323) suggests that the story of the shepherds may involve imaginative or midrashic interpretation. None of these observations denies the possibility (and even the likelihood) that the Lucan infancy narrative preserves items of historical tradition. But they do challenge the thesis that Mary supplied Luke (directly or indirectly) with an eyewitness memory of the events surrounding the conception and birth of Jesus.

Now, however, we turn to two texts that have been taken by many authors to support the thesis of Mary's memoirs.[326] (These texts need to be discussed even if scholars judge that *de facto* Luke did not draw upon Mary as an eyewitness; for it is important to know if Luke's readers would have interpreted them as a *claim* to eyewitness tradition.)

> *Mary kept all these things (*panta syntērei ta rēmata),
> *   pondering (*symballousa) them in her heart (2:19).
> *His mother retained all these things (*dietērei panta ta rēmata)
> *   in her heart (2:51).

---

[326]Bornhäuser, E. Meyer, Miguens, Zahn; see Laurentin, *Structure*, 97; C. Gore, *A New Commentary on Holy Scripture* (London: SPCK, 1928), 316-17.

The fact that Luke would virtually repeat himself within a few verses is striking,[327] and has led some scholars to wonder whether one of the statements belonged to a source (or an earlier stage of Lucan composition) and served as the model for the other.[328] Be that as it may, the impact of the repetition is one of solemnity, especially since the second statement comes at the very end of the infancy narrative and thus is the final description of Mary's reaction.

As a start in interpreting these statements, we may reflect on the scope of "all these things."[329] If Luke were interested in underlining either eyewitness tradition or historicity, such a statement would have been very appropriate after the annunciation which involved the virginal conception. In 2:19 "all these things" involve what the shepherds have told about the angelic revelation; but in 2:51 nothing patently miraculous is involved—there "all these things" refer to the finding of Jesus and his rebuff to his parents, when he placed primacy on his duty toward his Father. What the two scenes have in common is a revelation, explicit or implicit, about the future of the child. The emphasis is not on facts, but on significance.

The synonymous *syntērein* and *diatērein* ("keep, retain") are the main verbs respectively in 2:19 and 2:51. The context of the

---

[327]Note, however, the similar repetition of the statement pertinent to Jesus' growth in 2:40, 52. The fact that in each case the second statement occurs in 2:41-52 may lend support to the thesis that this scene, involving Jesus at age twelve, was a secondary addition to the infancy narrative. See below, nn. 356-59.

[328]For the thesis that 2:51 served as a model for 2:19 (and thus the opposite of what is implied in the preceding footnote), see Räisänen, *Mutter*, 119. Sahlin, *Messias*, 67, 69, 236-38, argues that 2:19 is a Lucan composition inserted into a narrative drawn from Proto-Luke (see above, n. 289). The Greek form of "Mary" in 2:19 is *Maria* (best MSS) as contrasted with *Mariam* in the context (2:15, 16, 34); also the absence of a reference to Joseph in 2:19 is surprising, in his judgment.

[329]The Greek *rēma* means "word," but in the Semitized Greek of Luke's infancy narrative it takes on the double connotation of Hebrew *dābār* (which it renders in the LXX): "word, thing." In 2:15 the shepherds urge one another, "Let us go over to Bethlehem and see this *rēma* ["thing"] that has happened which the Lord has made known to us."

second statement suggests that more than mere memory-retention is meant; and that is made specific in the first statement by the presence of a participle from *symballein*, indicating that in her heart Mary did something with what she retained. However, the exact significance of *symballein*, usually rendered "ponder," is not easy to determine.[330]

Since it is composed of *syn*, "with," and *ballein*, "throw," literally it could mean that Mary *combined* the various things that she had heard, seen, and remembered. Rengstorf,[331] developing this idea psychologically, interprets Luke to mean that Mary put together the details about the census, the trip to Bethlehem, the manger, and the sign of which the shepherds spoke (2:12, 16), showing that in His destiny God had "a well-considered plan for her and her child." In this interpretation Mary is responsible for the consecutive narrative in 2:1-20. A further step in taking *symballein* literally moves beyond Mary the narrator to Mary the theologian, for it has her putting together the events and their interpretation against the background of OT motifs.[332] Quite apart from the methodological difficulties inherent in such a use of etymology,[333] alternative translations based on the usage of key words offer a more plausible understanding of Mary's role.

Drawing on a study of the use of *symballein* in Hellenistic literature from passages assembled by Wettstein over two hundred years ago, W. C. van Unnik[334] understands *symballein* to refer to an interpretation of dark or difficult matters, the right meaning of which is often ascertained only by means of divine

---

[330]In the NT the verb occurs only in Luke/Acts; but its meaning is different here from that found elsewhere: "to speak together, converse" (Acts 4:15; 17:18), or "to come together, meet" (Luke 14:31; Acts 18:27).

[331]"Weihnachtserzählung," 15, 27; also Grundmann, *Lukas*, 86.

[332]Laurentin, *Structure*, 97, 100, 116-19, attributes to Mary the midrashic reflection that many scholars detect in the Lucan infancy narrative.

[333]On the use/misuse of etymology in biblical theology, see J. Barr, *The Semantics of Biblical Language* (Oxford: University Press, 1961), 107-60.

[334]"Die rechte Bedeutung des Wortes treffen, Lukas 2,19," in *Verbum: Essays on Some Aspects of the Religious Function of Words: Festschrift for H. W. Obbink* (ed. T. P. van Baaren, et al.; Utrecht: Kemink, 1964), 129-47.

help (sometimes given in oracles, dreams, or signs). Thus, Josephus[335] describes Joseph as "having interpreted by reflection [*syllabōn tō logismō*]" the dream of the baker in prison (Gen 40:16). Van Unnik may go too far in claiming that Mary, in thus "interpreting," functions like a prophet "in the line of those who can interpret the word of God"; for, as Räisänen objects,[336] a prophet should proclaim and not keep these things in the heart.

A balance is preserved if one complements van Unnik's observations, gleaned from Hellenistic literature, with instances of the LXX background for the various expressions used by Luke in 2:19, 51. The expression *syntērein to rēma* occurs in Gen 37:10-11: after Joseph incurred the jealousy of his brothers by telling of his dream about the wheat sheaves, "his father *kept the saying* in mind." The sense would seem to be: "continued to puzzle over" or "kept with concern." In the LXX of Dan 4:28, we are told that, after King Nebuchadnezzar heard Daniel's interpretation of the dream about the tree, he "kept the words in his heart [*tous logous en tē kardia syntērēse*]," presumably concerned over what had been revealed and puzzled about what it meant.[337] When Luke combines the idea of keeping the words in the heart with *symballein*, the idea may be that Mary has preserved in her heart the mysterious words and events that surrounded Jesus' birth (or his finding in the Temple) *trying to interpret them.*[338] This would mean that Mary did not grasp immediately all that she had heard but listened willingly, letting the events sink into her memory and

---

[335]*Ant.* 2.5.3 §72.

[336]*Mutter*, 121-22, n. 6.

[337]See also the use of *syntērein* in Sir 39:2: the wise scribe who studies the Law and the wisdom of the ancients "will be concerned with prophecies, will *keep* the discourse of notable men." In *T. Levi* 6:2, after Levi has been shown around heaven and been guided to find a mysterious shield, he says, "I kept these words in my heart."

[338]Räisänen, *Mutter*, 118-22, combines the biblical evidence, including the apocalyptic passages in Daniel and *T. Levi*, with the Hellenistic usage; also Brown, *Birth*, 429-31. More emphatic on the apocalyptic element in the appearance of the angels to the shepherds and on Mary's preserving its message in her heart until fulfillment is F. Neirynck, *Luc*, 51-57; also his article in Dutch on 2:19, 51 in *Collationes brugenses et gandavenses* 5 (1959), 433-66.

seeking to work out their meaning.[339]

Such an interpretation of Mary's attitude in 2:19 is buttressed when we realize that her reaction is part of a series of reactions (2:17-20). *The shepherds* begin the reactions by making known the *rēma* which had been told them concerning the child (2:17); and they conclude the reactions by returning (to their flock), glorifying and praising God for all they had heard and seen (2:20). After the shepherds have spoken, we are told "*All who heard it* wondered at what the shepherds told them" (2:18). The third reaction is that of *Mary* who "kept all these things, pondering them in her heart" (2:19). We may have here a series of different reactions to the word of God somewhat like the various reactions mentioned in the explanation of the parable of the seed, which is the word of God (Luke 8:11-15). In the latter series, ultimate approval is given to those "who, hearing the word, hold it fast in an honest and good heart, and bring forth fruit with patience" (8:15 — in 8:21 Jesus says: "My mother and my brothers are those who hear the word of God and do it"). Similarly here, in 2:19, Luke may be strengthening his picture of Mary as a disciple.[340] "All who heard" the shepherds' report wondered; but while this is a good reaction, we never hear of them again. On the other hand, Mary held on to the word and puzzled over its deeper meaning. This suggestion of her growth as a believer would also fit 2:51 where she keeps in her heart difficult words of Jesus that have rebuked her, words that she and Joseph had not understood (2:49-50), and where the next verse (52) stresses that Jesus himself grows "in wisdom, stature, and favor with God and man."

Perhaps this also explains why Mary and not Joseph is featured in 2:19, 51. Joseph is never mentioned as being alive during the Lucan account of the ministry of Jesus; Mary is the only adult among the dramatis personae of the infancy narrative who will reappear in that ministry. Luke is not interested in her

---

[339]Cf. Luke 9:43-44: while just as in 2:18 "all" others are astonished, the disciples are told, "Let these words sink into your ears." See also 21:14-15.

[340]Räisänen, *Mutter*, 122-24; he suggests that Luke is holding up Mary as a paradigmatic figure for a reader like Theophilus (Acts 1:1).

primarily as an eyewitness or the composer of memoirs; he is interested in her as a model of Christian discipleship. Her reaction in the infancy narrative as described in 1:38, 45; 2:19, 51 is one of humility, acceptance, and obedience. But complete discipleship is not possible till the word of God has been proclaimed in its fullness, not only in the ministry of Jesus, but also on the cross and through the resurrection. As Luke will tell us, some of Jesus' own followers who heard the word in the ministry were not able to hold it fast in face of diabolic opposition in the passion without divine help and strengthening (22:31-32). Mary will be told in 2:25 that a sword must pierce her soul also; she is not to be spared the test of discipleship. But Luke shows her initial attitude of keeping "these things and pondering them in her heart" to be one that will lead her into the believing post-Easter community. If this is what Luke implies in 2:19, 51, it tells us something more significant (and more Christian) about his view of Mary than the claim that he drew upon her memoirs.

4. Mary and the Presentation of Jesus in the Temple (2:21-40)

After the birth of Jesus, Luke narrates two consecutive events in Jesus' infancy, both of which illustrate the obedience of the parents. The first, mentioned only in passing (2:21), involves the circumcision and naming of the child "at the end of eight days"—the naming fulfills the command that the angel gave to Mary.[341] The second involves the presentation of Jesus in the Temple at the time of the purification of the parents—actions according to the Law of Moses, as Luke tells us four times (vv. 22, 23, 24, 39).

(a) Marian Issues in 2:22-24

The Lucan description of the details of the presentation and purification reflects confusion about Jewish customs, a confusion

---

[341]Yet, while the angel directed *Mary* to call the child Jesus (1:32), Luke uses a passive in 2:21 ("His name was called Jesus") and so never identifies the parent who did the naming. In Matt 1:21, 25 Joseph names Jesus.

that is another objection to the thesis that he is reporting eyewitness-tradition from Mary.[342] Brief as the description is, it contains four points that have been seen to be of Marian interest.

First, Luke describes Jesus as being presented in Jerusalem according to the Law of Moses, i.e., the law affecting the first-born male narrated in Exod 13:1, 11-16. This is in harmony with Luke's preparatory statement in 2:7: "She gave birth to her *first-born* son"; and this child was to have the privileges and obligations given by the law to the first-born. There is no evidence that in using the term "first-born" Luke was at all concerned with the question of whether or not Mary had other children after Jesus, and no logically deduced answer to that question is possible from his terminology.[343]

Second, in quoting the law of the first-born, Luke describes Jesus in graphic biblical imagery as "a male who opens the womb" (2:22). Although this phrase has created a problem in the discussion of the later Christian idea that Mary gave *birth* to Jesus miraculously (*virginitas in partu*), without rupture of the hymen, Luke may be employing standard OT language (see Exod 13:2, 12, 15 in the LXX) and telling us nothing specific about the manner of Jesus' birth.[344]

Third, no mention is made of the parents paying five shekels to buy back the child Jesus from Temple service after he had been consecrated to the Lord—the payment specified in Num 18:15-16 for non-Levites. This has led to the question of whether Luke thought that Jesus was a Levite who would remain in the service of the Lord. Does not Luke describe Mary as a relative of

---

[342]See above, n. 232. Brown, *Messiah*, 436, 447-51, points out the elements of confusion and the ingenious attempts to explain them away.

[343]The Greek text of the grave inscription of a Jewish woman found near Leontopolis in Egypt and dated to 5 B.C. reads: "In the pains of giving birth to a first-born child, Fate brought me to the end of my life." Obviously, there were no more children after that first-born! See R. F. Stoll, "Her Firstborn Son," *AER* 108 (1943), 1-13; J.-B. Frey, "La signification du terme prōtotokos d'après une inscription juive," *Bib* 11 (1930), 373-90.

[344]It is unlikely, however, that if Luke knew of the tradition of the non-ruptured hymen, he would have used such an expression (J. Galot, *NRT* 82 [1960], 453). See below, pp. 275-78.

Elizabeth (1:36) who was of levitical descent (1:5)? However, Luke clearly thinks of Jesus as a Davidid (1:32; 3:23, 31; 18:38); and he never tells us anything specific about Mary's origin.[345]

Fourth, in fulfilling the ritual for presentation and purification the two parents are shown to be obedient to the Law. In 2:41 we shall be told that they went up every year to Jerusalem for the feast of Passover. We have already seen (above, p. 142) that Luke portrays Mary as a representative of the pious among Israel, and the two Temple scenes at the end of the infancy narrative reinforce that view.

(b) Simeon's Words to Mary (2:34-35)

Luke has Simeon pronounce two blessings when he encounters the child Jesus during the presentation ceremony in the Temple: the first, the Nunc Dimittis, is a blessing upon God (2:28); the second is a blessing upon the parents and is addressed to Mary (2:34). A literal translation of this second oracle will be helpful in our discussion:

> 34c *Behold, this [child] is set for the fall and rise of many in Israel*
> 34d *and for a sign that is [or will be] spoken against.*
> 35a *And a sword will pass through your own soul*
> 35b *so that thoughts* [dialogismoi] *from many hearts will be revealed.*

The "poetry" of these lines is more irregular than that found in the Magnificat, Benedictus, or Nunc Dimittis. Furthermore, those Lucan canticles tend to speak of God's deliverance or salvation as something already accomplished; this oracle speaks more specifically of the future of the child and his mother. These differ-

---

[345]There are levitical names in Jesus' ancestry (Luke 3:23-38), e.g., Eli, Mattathias, Levi—also Zadok in Matt 1:14. See above, n. 299. While Hippolytus and Ephraem knew traditions which attributed partly levitical origins to Jesus (through Mary), Augustine, *Contra Faustum Manichaeum* 33.9, denied that Mary was a priest's daughter. Much more common is the thesis that Mary was of Davidic origin (perhaps already Ignatius, *Eph.* 18.2), sometimes based on reading the phrase "of the house of David" in 1:27 as referring to the virgin rather than to Joseph. See J. Fischer, "Die davidische Abkunft der Mutter Jesu: Biblisch-patristische Untersuchung," *Weidenauerstudien* 4 (1911), 1-115.

ences have led some scholars to attribute 2:34-35 in whole or in part to a pre-Lucan source[346] or to an earlier Lucan stage of composition (before the addition of the Nunc Dimittis).[347] It is unfortunate that no certainty can be reached on this question; for our knowledge of the antiquity of the development of early Christian interest in Mary would be increased if v. 35a were pre-Lucan.

Even if we confine ourselves to Luke's level of intention, it is not clear whether 35a, in which Mary is addressed in the second person singular, is parenthetical, so that 35b should be read as continuing 34cd. In any case, the immediate context of 35a concerns the negative results of the judgment occasioned by Jesus: he is set first for the *fall* of many in Israel; he is a sign to be spoken against; either he or Mary will be the occasion of the unveiling of the *hostile thoughts* of many, if *dialogismos* of 35b has its usual pejorative connotation.[348] How does the sword passing through Mary's soul fit into this context? The symbolic language of a sword passing through occurs in Ezek 14:17: "Let a sword pass through the land so that I may cut off man and beast." The expression recurs in the *Sibylline Oracles* (3. 316) as a description for the invasion of Egypt by Antiochus IV Epiphanes (ca. 170 B.C.): "For a sword shall pass through the midst of you."[349] Thus, Luke may be thinking of a sword of discerning judgment separat-

---

[346]Sahlin, *Messias*, 272-76, attributes 34-35 to Proto-Luke. Räisä-nen, *Mutter*, 129, however, lists Bartsch, Dibelius, Grundmann, Hirsch, and Kraeling as holding that Luke added the poetic oracle (34cd-35ab) to pre-Lucan material, and Krafft would judge 34-35 as Lucan.

[347]See Brown, *Birth*, 454-56: "The Problem of the Two Oracles."

[348]Creed, Knabenbauer, Lagrange, Plummer, and Zahn are among those who take "thoughts" of 35b as both good and bad thoughts, in line with the "fall and rise" of 34c. However, the sequence may stress the more negative tone of 34d ("a sign spoken against"), for all thirteen other uses of *dialogismos* in the NT are pejorative, involving hostility, doubt, and vanity. The five other instances in Luke (5:22; 6:8; 9:46-47; 24:38) refer to thoughts hostile to Jesus or questioning him. G. Schrenk, *TDNT*, 2. 97, takes 2:35 to refer to "evil thoughts" to be revealed "in the divine judgment."

[349]W. Michaelis, *TDNT*, 6. 995-96, argues against the relationship between Luke and these two passages; he thinks Ps 37:15 has influenced Luke: "The sword of them [the wicked] shall pass into their own heart." However, the verb in the psalm (*eiserchesthai*) differs from the verb (*dierchesthai*) shared by Luke, Ezekiel, and the *Sibylline Oracles*.

ing the good from the bad (the "fall and rise" of 34c) to which
Mary too must be subject, in order that it be revealed whether her
thoughts are those of a believer or the hostile thoughts (*dialogis-
moi*) of those who speak against the sign offered in Jesus? But
then, we may ask, where is it fulfilled that such a sword passes
through Mary's soul?

Church writers have made many suggestions in response to
the latter question: Mary lived to see the rejection of her son by
Israel or the tragedy of the fall of Jerusalem; Mary herself suffered by beholding the death of Jesus or even met a martyr's
death by sword; Mary was maligned through the charges of illegitimacy directed against Jesus; Mary came to doubt Jesus,
especially in the passion, etc.[350] Our task force rejected all of
these explanations on the grounds that one finds no support for
them in Luke/Acts, and that 2:35a should not require for its interpretation information that Luke does not supply and which his
readers may never have known. The same principle led us to
reject the most common interpretation of the sword, namely,
Mary's anguish at the foot of the cross as she saw Jesus die.[351]
Only John 19:25-27 depicts the mother of Jesus as present at
Calvary. In the context of the death and burial of Jesus, Luke
mentions women (23:49: "The women who had followed him
from Galilee stood at a distance and saw these things"; 23:55) and
supplies a list of their names (24:10); but Mary, the mother of
Jesus, is not among them. And so Luke can scarcely have expected the reader of 2:35a to think of Mary at the foot of the
cross.[352]

---

[350]See Feuillet, "L'Épreuve," 248-49; Brown, *Birth*, 462-63.

[351]See McHugh, *Mother*, 110-11. He himself follows Benoit (" 'Et
toi-même' ") in seeing Mary here to be a personification of Israel: "Thou
thyself, O *Israel*, shall feel a sword pass through thy soul." McHugh
maintains that, as the Daughter of Zion, Mary would be more aware than
anyone else of the destiny of her child—an evaluation that slips over
from symbolism to historicity. Räisänen, *Mutter*, 133, refers to Mary
here as the *mater dolorosa*, although he acknowledges that Luke makes no
express reference to Mary's sorrow at the death of Jesus.

[352]It is widely recognized that there are parallels between Luke and
John, most often in the sense that common underlying tradition has been
expressed in different ways in the two Gospels. (See J. A. Bailey, *The*

If the meaning of 2:35a is to be deduced from references to Mary within Luke/Acts, then the sense is that she, as part of Israel, must be judged by her ultimate reaction to the child who is set for the fall and rise of many in Israel. Although a woman from the crowd will bless her as physically related to Jesus, he will insist that the criterion of blessing which applies to others applies to her also: "Happy [*makarios*], rather, those who hear the word of God and keep it" (11:27-28). If Mary will be ultimately brought into the eschatological family of those who respond to God's word (Acts 1:14), that will be because of the judgment uttered by Jesus: "My mother and my brothers are those who hear the word of God and do it" (8:21). Presumably, by the imagery of a sword passing through Mary's soul, Luke describes the difficult process of learning that obedience to the word of God transcends family ties.[353] If thus far he has shown Mary as passing the test of obedience (1:38, 45), he has also hinted that the learning process is an ongoing one (2:19); here he insists that it is a process that is not without its perils and its suffering.

5. Mary and the Finding of Jesus in the Temple (2:41-52)

In the final scene of chaps. 1-2 Luke brings the reader back once more to the Temple where the infancy story began with Gabriel speaking to Zechariah over twelve years before. This scene is introduced by verses (2:41-42) similar in tone to those which introduced the previous Temple scene (2:22-24)[354]— despite the interlude which separates the two occasions on which the parents and child come to the Temple, the atmosphere of piety

---

Traditions Common to the Gospels of Luke and John [NovTSup 7; Leiden: Brill, 1963].) But that does not justify interpreting an obscure Lucan saying by a scene from John of which Luke shows no knowledge.

[353]See Luke 12:51-53, noting that the latter part of Luke's "Do you think that I have come to bring peace on earth? No, I tell you, but rather division" appears in Matt 10:34 thus: "I have not come to bring peace, but a sword" ("sword" in Matthew is *machaira*, not the *romphaia* of Luke 2:35a).

[354]Those who argue for a pre-Lucan source for the Finding-in-the-Temple story admit Lucan redaction in the framework, e.g., in vv. 39-40, 41, 51c-52.

is the same. The parents obey the cultic practice by going up to Jerusalem for the Feast of Passover; only now Jesus is old enough to join them on his own. His remaining behind when they return home supplies the occasion for a dramatic reunion after they have searched for him frantically, a reunion which is centered on a confrontation between the parents and the child, and which contains the first recorded words of Jesus in Luke's gospel (2:48-49). Since Luke has surrounded the scene with references to Jesus' wisdom (2:40, 52), it is not surprising that these first words show Jesus' self-understanding of his relationship to God as Father.[355] What is surprising is that his parents do not understand his words (v. 50), despite the preceding revelations of Jesus' identity on which Mary has had twelve years to reflect (1:32-35; 2:11, 17, 19).

This lack of smooth harmony with what precedes,[356] some evidence of a different Greek style,[357] and the fact that the story comes from another stage of Jesus' life different from both the infancy and the ministry have combined to persuade many scholars that the story underlying 2:41-52 had an independent history. Related to such a theory is the suggestion that the original story came to Luke as a unit,[358] that he appended it to an infancy narrative that had previously ended with 2:40,[359] that in adapting the story Luke added a new ending (2:52, imitative of 2:40) so that

---

[355]This holds true no matter which translation one gives to the ambiguous *en tois tou patros mou* of 2:49: "in the house of my Father"; "about the business of my Father"; "among the relatives of my Father" (i.e., the teachers of the Law).

[356]Another possible sign of a lack of harmony is the reference to Joseph as the father of Jesus in 2:48, as if there had been no virginal conception. Luke is capable of being more careful, as we see from 3:23, where he speaks of Jesus as the "supposed" son of Joseph. See nn. 320 above and 365 below.

[357]The Greek style of 2:41-52 is thought to be less marked by the Semitisms so apparent elsewhere in the infancy narrative; see Laurentin, *Structure*, 142; Schlatter, *Lukas*, 205.

[358]The most thorough treatment of this question is Van Iersel, "Finding"; he finds the basic story in vv. 41-43, 45-46, 48-50 with internal additions by Luke in vv. 44, 47. Räisänen, *Mutter*, 134, follows Van Iersel but seems to think that v. 46 is also Lucan as part of a "Wunderkind" motif.

[359]Brown, *Birth*, 479-84.

the story might now serve as a transition to the ministry. Presumably this original story would have belonged to a category of pre-ministry stories (known to us in apocryphal gospels[360]) when as a boy or young man Jesus lived, spoke, and performed miracles in the bosom of his family. The christology of such stories is an anticipation of the christology of the ministry accounts. When we discussed the christology of the two infancy accounts (pp. 89-91, 117-19 above), we saw that the revelation that Jesus was God's Son, once associated with the resurrection and then with the beginning of the ministry (the baptism), was now being associated with a point farther back in time, namely, with the conception of Jesus as interpreted to the father and mother by an angel. However, it is conceivable that in other circles an intermediary stage[361] may have involved an association of this christology with Jesus' youth, so that when he begins to speak, he himself reveals to his parents for the first time his identity and the priority of his heavenly Father. In this theory the original form of 2:41-52 would not have presupposed the virginal conception of Jesus or any previous revelation about him as God's Son, so that, in the traditions upon which Luke drew, some contained knowledge of the virginal conception (as reflected in 1:26-38) and some did not.

The importance of this theory for the history of christology and for the lines of development in the Christian understanding of Mary is obvious, but there is no way to verify it.[362] Faced by such

---

[360]The best example is the *Infancy Gospel of Thomas* where there are stories of what Jesus did at age five, six, eight, and twelve, the last being an apocryphal version of Luke 2:41-52. In Chap. 7, A2, we shall discuss the possibility that on a pre-Gospel level the story of the miracle worked by Jesus at Cana (John 2:1-12) in the presence of his mother and brothers was another example of this type of story. The Cana story has parallels to Luke 2:48-49 in the mother's request and in Jesus' seeming rebuff to her.

[361]For the childhood narrative as filling a lacuna between the infancy narrative and the ministry, see Bundy, *Jesus*, 23, who makes references to Loisy and Guignebert.

[362]A more convincing case can be made, however, for a pre-Lucan source in 2:41-52 than for any other *narrative* section in chaps. 1-2. Brown, *Birth*, 239-53, argues against the general theory of pre-Lucan sources for the infancy narrative, with the exception of the canticles and 2:41-52.

uncertainty, the task force once more chose not to commit itself on the pre-Lucan origins of the material and to concentrate on the Marian import of the scene as it appears in its present sequence in the Gospel. The key to this lies in vv. 48-50. Already those who saw Jesus listening to the teachers in the Temple and heard him asking questions were astounded at his understanding and his answers (46-47). Then Luke (48) adds: "When they saw him, they were amazed." He does not identify the "they," but the sequence from v. 46 seems to require that the "they" be the parents,[363] so that Luke is preparing us for their lack of understanding which he will make specific in v. 50. In what follows the mother serves as the spokeswoman for the parents. This may reflect the beginning of the "eclipse of Joseph," who, though present throughout the chapter and specifically mentioned at 2:4, 16, will not appear again in Luke/Acts (except as mentioned in the genealogy of 3:23). The same phenomenon occurs in John 2:1-11 where Mary is the only parent present and therefore begins the conversation with Jesus.[364]

Mary's complaining question in v. 48 seems to be a reproach to Jesus:[365] "Son, why have you treated us so? Behold, your father and I have looked for you anxiously." How are we to interpret Jesus' answer to his parents in 49: "Why is it that you [plural] were looking for me? Did you not know that it was necessary for me to be in my Father's house [about my Father's business]?"[366]

---

[363]The difficulty is explained if Van Iersel is right (see above, n. 358) that v. 47 was a later insertion, and v. 48 originally followed upon v. 46.

[364]As we saw in Chap. 4, B1d, the most probable explanation is that Joseph had died before Jesus' ministry began, whence his total absence (even by name) from Mark's account of the ministry.

[365]Such a reproach shows a lack of harmony with the reverence toward Jesus that previous revelations should have demanded. Evidently later scribes found the reference to Joseph as Jesus' "father" difficult to accept, for the Curetonian Syriac and Old Latin versions have "we have looked" in place of "your father and I have looked."

[366]See above, n. 355. The presence in this statement of *dei*, "it is necessary," is significant; it is a term redolent of Jesus' destiny, and it will appear in his predictions of his passion and resurrection (Luke 9:22; 13:33; 17:25; 22:37). However, that does *not* mean that Jesus is speaking of his passion in 2:49—a farfetched explanation of why his parents cannot understand.

It is not a sharp rebuff, for the tone is more one of grief that the parents have known him so poorly; it anticipates the statement in v. 50 that they did not understand. Nevertheless, it establishes a distance between Jesus and his earthly parents in favor of his relationship to his heavenly Father.[367] When we treat Luke 8:19-21, we shall see that it treats the mother and brothers of Jesus in a much more benevolent way than does Mark 3:31-35. The tone of 2:48 (which may be pre-Lucan) is somewhat closer to Mark. As one commentator phrases it, this story "is a sort of compensation for some of the traditions on Jesus' relations with his family which Luke found in his sources and which he suppresses or treats in a delicate manner."[368] In the present Lucan sequence, Mary is discovering the meaning of Simeon's prophecy uttered twelve years before: "A sword will pass through your own soul" (2:35); she is learning that Jesus puts his relation to his Father over family ties.

In 2:50-51 Luke continues the theme that he began in 2:19: it will take time for Mary to understand all of this. He says in 2:50: "They did not understand the word [$rēma$] which he spoke to them";[369] and in 2:51: "His mother retained all these things in her heart." As we have already seen (above, p. 152), Luke's idea is that complete acceptance of the word of God, complete under-

---

[367]Räisänen, *Mutter*, 134. Notice how Mary speaks of "your father [Joseph]," while Jesus answers in terms of "my Father [God]." This, plus the fact that Jesus answers Mary in the plural and thus speaks to both parents, lessens the possible element of reproach *to Mary*.

[368]Bundy, *Jesus*, 24, citing Holtzmann among others.

[369]On *rēma* see above, n. 329. As we saw, the "they" of v. 48 probably means the parents of Jesus; and since Mary in that verse refers to "your father and I," there is little real doubt that the "they" in v. 51 refers to the parents. Nevertheless, interpreters have been scandalized that Mary, in particular, does not understand Jesus' reference to his heavenly Father. (Sometimes this is another reflection of the dubious theory that Mary knew Jesus' divinity from the time of the annunciation; see above, n. 258.) Accordingly, they have argued that the "they" refers to the bystanders or to Joseph alone; or else they suppose that Jesus had given an explanation to his parents that he was going to stay behind in the Temple (an explanation not recorded by Luke) and that Luke means that the parents *had* not understood this word. See the articles tending in this direction by M. A. Power, *ITQ* 7 (1912), 261-81, 444-59; J. B. Cortés and F. M. Gatti, *Marianum* 32 (1970), 404-18. This whole effort borders on eisegesis.

standing of who Jesus is, and complete discipleship is not yet possible. This will come through the ministry of Jesus and particularly through the cross and resurrection. It is no accident that the final reaction of the parents of Jesus in the infancy narrative is very much like that of the disciples of Jesus after the third passion prediction: "They did not understand any of these things, and this word [rēma] was hidden from them" (18:34).[370] But Luke does not leave Mary on the negative note of misunderstanding. Rather, in 2:51b he stresses her retention of what she has not yet understood and (implicitly—see 2:19) her continuing search to understand. Thus he prepares the reader for those scenes in the public ministry, which we shall now discuss where Mary will be evaluated according to the criterion of discipleship, and for the final scene in Acts 1:13-14 where she will join the once equally puzzled disciples in the post-resurrectional community—a community to whom the risen Jesus has interpreted the passion (24:25-27, 44-46).

B. Mary in the Public Ministry

Mary is never mentioned by name in the Lucan account of Jesus' ministry, death, and resurrection (chaps. 3-24), although there are two references to Jesus' mother (8:19-21; 11:27-28). Thus what we hear of Mary during this period is not significantly increased over what was reported in Mark. The relative Lucan silence is startling, granted the great interest Luke has shown in Mary in the infancy narrative. However, once we realize that such an interest was not primarily in Mary as a person but in Mary as a symbol of discipleship, Luke's shift of attention becomes more intelligible. When Jesus was an infant, the mother was really the only appropriate figure to illustrate discipleship, since according to tradition she was still on the scene during the ministry and even came into the beginnings of the church. But in the narrative of Jesus' ministry, there is a wider range of figures

---

[370]Räisänen, *Mutter*, 136. See above, n. 366, on *dei*, although that word does not occur in the prediction of 18:34.

who can illustrate discipleship, especially the Twelve. The mother is mentioned only in two scenes that underline a continuity of her discipleship; yet that very continuity makes Luke's references to her more positive and more irenic than those in Mark or even those in Matthew.

1. The Genealogy of the "Supposed" Son of Joseph (3:23)

The genealogy of Jesus in 3:23-38 is of indirect Marian import. Matthew placed his genealogy at the beginning of the Gospel (1:1-17), before the story of Jesus' conception. By tracing Jesus from Abraham through David, Matthew used the genealogy, in part, to explain why he called Jesus "son of David, son of Abraham" (1:1), and in part to affirm that Jesus was descended from David even though Joseph the Davidid did not beget him (1:16—see above, Chap. 5, A1). Luke places his genealogy after the baptism of Jesus when the voice from heaven has identified him as God's beloved Son (3:22). It is not surprising, then, that Luke traces Jesus' ancestry back through Adam to God (3:38).[371] Matthew's localization of the genealogy had a biblical antecedent, e.g., in Genesis 5-9 where a genealogy prefaces the story of Noah. But Luke's localization of the genealogy between the baptism of Jesus and his taking up his ministry also has a biblical antecedent: Moses' genealogy is given in Exod 6:14-25, after the call of Moses and just before he begins his mission of leading the tribes out of Egypt. Nevertheless, scholars have used the Lucan localization as an argument for the theory that Luke began his writing with 3:1 and only after he had finished the Gospel (and Acts), did he prefix the infancy narrative. They contend that the genealogy antedated the composition of the infancy narrative (above, p. 106), for it

---

[371]Although both Luke and Matthew give genealogies of Jesus through Joseph, the genealogies differ in more than length (42 generations from Abraham to Jesus in Matthew [3 × 14]; approximately 77 names from Jesus to God in Luke, with textual variations). The names in the two genealogies between Joseph and David differ almost totally; Matthew's list descends from Abraham to Jesus, while Luke's list ascends from Jesus to God; Matthew uses the formula, "A begot [was the father of] B," while Luke uses the formula, "A [being the son] of B."

betrays no awareness of the virginal conception of Jesus. The key to this theory is in 3:23-25:[372]

> *Now Jesus himself, when he began [his ministry], was*
> *about thirty years of age,*
> *being the son, as was supposed, of Joseph,*
> *the son of Eli [Heli],*
> *the son of Matthat . . .*

Did the genealogy, when it was first composed, indicate that Jesus was the son of Joseph, and was the phrase "as was supposed" inserted by Luke[373] to allow for the virginal conception which had now been introduced in 1:26-38? Or did the genealogy from the beginning have that phrase, and was the story in 1:26-38 Luke's elaboration of the hint in that phrase? There is obviously no way to settle such questions, but the phrase in 3:23 is a rare instance of an agreement in detail between the narratives of the infancy and of the public ministry (above, Chap. 2, n. 18).

2. The Rejection of Jesus at Nazareth (4:16-30)

We have seen that Mark 6:1-6a and Matt 13:53-58 narrate a scene where Jesus comes to "his own country"; and when he begins to teach in a synagogue, the hearers are astonished at his wisdom and his works and wonder how they may be explained, in light of what they know about his family (the carpenter, Mary, James, Joses/Joseph, Simon, Judas, sisters). Consequently they take offense at him; and he cannot or does not do any mighty works there because of their unbelief. In Mark this scene occurs

---

[372]Matthew 1:15-16 reads: "Matthan was the father of Jacob; Jacob was the father of Joseph, the husband of Mary of whom was begotten Jesus." The conflict of the Matthean list of the immediate ancestors of Jesus (Matthan-Jacob-Joseph) with the Lucan list (Matthat-Eli-Joseph) is obvious and has led to ingenious attempts to read one of the genealogies as the ancestry of Mary. See Brown, *Birth*, 88-90, 497-99. The task force accepted the clear mention of Joseph by each evangelist and therefore found no evidence about Mary's ancestry in either genealogy; see above, n. 345.

[373]There is no textual reason to attribute it to a later scribe.

after several chapters describing Jesus' proclamation of the kingdom; in Matthew there precedes an even lengthier proclamation.

At the very beginning of the Lucan account of the ministry, immediately after Jesus has returned from the Jordan valley to Galilee (4:1, 14), there is a scene (4:16-30), lengthier than that of Mark/Matthew, where Jesus comes to Nazareth and teaches in a synagogue. We are told that the hearers "wondered at the gracious words that came from his mouth" in light of his family origins as they knew them. In fact, Jesus' remarks angered them to the point that they put him out of the city and tried to throw him headlong off a hill. "But passing through the midst of them, he went away" (4:30).

There are enough similarities to Mark/Matthew to make it improbable that we are dealing with a totally different scene. Yet what special Lucan theological emphasis accounts for the Lucan localization and form of the scene, or should that question be asked of the Marcan/Matthean narrative with the presumption that the Lucan form is more intelligible as the primitive account? Is Luke boldly rewriting Mark, or did Luke draw upon another source (see above, Chap. 2, n. 27)? Fortunately, we do not have to answer such questions for the purpose of this book.[374] There are only two minor points of Marian interest in the scene.

First, the question about Jesus' family. In Luke 4:22 the wondering hearers ask, "Is not this the son of Joseph?" There is no reference to the carpenter, Mary, the brothers, or the sisters, as in Mark/Matthew, although in all three Gospels the objection that is based on physical-family origin betrays an ignorance of Jesus' real status and what he valued.[375] If Luke is editing Mark,

---

[374]For substantial discussion about the main points in this scene, see the articles of H. Anderson, *Int* 18 (1964), 259-75; D. Hill, *NovT* 13 (1971), 161-80. Also J. Jeremias, *Jesus' Promise to the Nations* (SBT 24; London: SCM, 1948), 44-46.

[375]This is very apparent to the Lucan reader who knows that Jesus is only the "supposed" son of Joseph (3:22) and is really the Son of God (1:35). Quite improbable is the psychologizing of Kraeling, *Four Gospels*, 208, who thinks that the question, "Is not this the son of Joseph?", may be a happy recognition of Jesus who has been gone so long from Nazareth that people hardly know him.

his omission of the mother and brothers may reflect an unwillingness to have them mentioned in a disbelieving question; for as we shall see in both 8:21 and Acts 1:14, Luke thinks approvingly of the mother and brothers. The reference to Jesus as "the son of Joseph" would simply be a standard and, hence, neutral designation,[376] casting no slur on Joseph. However, as we saw in discussing Mark 6:3 (pp. 61, 101-102), the first part of John 6:42 ("Is not this Jesus the son of Joseph?") is quite similar to Luke's question, and so the Lucan form may not be a correction of Mark but the preservation of another tradition that appears in John as well. In either case the scene has lost all possible Marian import in Luke.

Second, the statement about the prophet. In Mark 6:4 Jesus says, "A prophet is not without honor, except in his own country, *and among his own relatives, and in his own house.*" In discussing this, we raised the possibility that Mark had added the italicized phrases in harmony with the picture in 3:20-35 where Jesus' own (i.e., his mother and brothers) thought he was beside himself and went out to seize him, only to have Jesus reject the claims of his physical family in favor of an eschatological family constituted by obedience to the will of God. In Matt 13:57 Jesus says, "A prophet is not without honor, except in his own country, *and in his own house.*" The first of the italicized Marcan phrases, the one offensive to the relatives of Jesus, has been omitted. As we saw (Chap. 5, B2), Matthew's omission here agrees with his previous omission of Mark's unfavorable reference to Jesus' "own" and with Matthew's presentation of Mary's conception of Jesus through the Holy Spirit in 1:20. In Luke 4:24 Jesus says, "Amen, I say to you, no prophet is acceptable in his own country."[377] Not only (as in Matthew) is there no unfavorable reference to Jesus' relatives, but also no unfavorable reference to "his own house." In general, Luke is kinder to those who surround

---

[376]The question tells us nothing about whether Joseph is alive or not.

[377]For the solemnity of Lucan "Amen" sayings, see J. C. O'Neill, *JTS* ns 10 (1959), 1-9. For possible meanings of this saying, see R. C. Tannehill, "The Mission of Jesus according to Luke IV 16-30," in *Jesus in Nazareth* (ed. E. Grässer; BZNW 40; Berlin: de Gruyter, 1972), 57.

Jesus than is either Mark or Matthew;[378] but his sensitivity toward Jesus' relatives and household may be more than an example of general benevolence. The mother who has been praised in 1:38, 42, 45 and 2:19, 51 as one who heard the word of God and did it and as one who kept and retained the mysterious things about Jesus that she heard could scarcely fit into the category of those who did not accept Jesus. Neither could the brothers of Jesus whom, along with the mother, Luke will present as following Jesus (Acts 1:14). Thus, once again, the scene adds no Marian import to the picture of Jesus' ministry; but neither does it detract from Luke's positive picture of Jesus' mother.

3. The Mother and the Brothers and the Family of Jesus (8:19-21)

Like the other Synoptic gospels, Luke has a statement of Jesus about the members of his eschatological family which is constituted by a relationship to God. The passage reads as follows:

> [19]*Now there came to him his mother and his brothers, but they were not able to reach him on account of the crowd.* [20]*It was announced to him, "Your mother and your brothers are standing outside, wishing to see you."* [21]*But he replied and said to them, "My mother and my brothers are those who hear the word of God and do it."*

In Mark 3:20-35 both the context and form of the saying itself betray a negative attitude toward the physical family of Jesus; Matt 12:46-50 has no negative context but preserves the Marcan form of the saying.[379] Luke has a positive context and a positive form of the saying itself as regards the physical family. Let us begin with the saying.

---

[378]For example, Jesus says to the apostles at the Last Supper, "You are those who have continued with me in my trials" (22:14, 28) and he assures Simon Peter that his faith will not fail and that he will "turn again" (22:32). The other Gospels depict Jesus more consistently as pessimistic toward his followers at the Last Supper.

[379]If the textually dubious Matt 12:47 is considered, Luke is closer to Matthew than to Mark (see above, Chap. 5, n. 208).

THE SAYING OF JESUS. Mark and Matthew report that the
mother and brothers stood outside, without explaining why they
did not come into Jesus' presence; indeed, the contrast between
the physical family outside and the family of disciples inside is
dramatic. Luke removes any element of hostility from the fact
that the mother and brothers are outside: "They were not able to
reach him on account of the crowd." In Mark/Matthew when the
news is given to Jesus about the presence of his mother and
brothers outside, he replies with a question which challenges their
status as his true family: "Who are my mother and my brothers?"
No such question is asked in Luke. In Mark/Matthew Jesus answers his own question by pointing to his disciples who sit around
him and identifying them as his family: "Behold [here are] my
mother and my brothers." Neither the gesture of pointing to those
around him nor Jesus' statement appears in Luke. In the
Marcan/Matthean sequence Jesus' final statement ("Whoever
does the will of God [my Father in heaven] is my brother, and
sister, and mother") designates as an eschatological family those
disciples who are inside *in contrast to* the physical family which is
outside. The Lucan sequence implies no contrast: having heard
that his mother and brothers are outside, Jesus comments in
praise of them: "My mother and my brothers are those who hear
the word of God and do it."[380] The last two verbs are present
participles and suggest that they "continue to hear and keep on
doing"—a point in harmony with the Lucan emphasis on daily
discipleship.[381] Luke's notion of what constitutes discipleship and
makes one a member of Jesus' eschatological family is not much
different from the notion found in Mark and Matthew: namely,
obedience to God. Luke, however, is much clearer than Mark and
Matthew in insisting that Jesus' mother and brothers meet that
criterion.

---

[380]This could be read resumptively: "My mother and my
brothers—these are the ones who hear the word of God and do it." The
phraseology of this saying accords with Lucan theology, e.g., the "word
of God" is a favorite Lucan phrase (Luke 5:1; 8:11; Acts 4:31; 6:2, 7; see
Luke 3:2).

[381]See Acts 2:46; 3:2; 17:11; compare Luke 9:23 and Mark 8:34.

THE CONTEXT. The negative thrust of the saying in Mark 3:35 is underlined by the context in which Mark has placed this scene. It follows 3:21 where "his own" hear of his activity and set out to seize him because they think he is beside himself—this explains why the mother and brothers have come asking for Jesus in 3:31-35. The intervening scene (3:22-30) contains the hostile charge of the scribes that Jesus is possessed by Beelzebul, a charge which Jesus answers. In that context, Jesus' statement, "Whoever does the will of God is my brother, and sister, and mother," is almost a response to the charge of "his own" that he is beside himself. Even the immediately following parable of the sower and seed with its explanation (4:1-20) may reflect on the contrasting parties in 3:20-35: the physical family, the hostile scribes, and obedient disciples—they anticipate the different fates of the seed (word) sown by the sower, with the disciples who do the will of God (3:35) being comparable to those who hear the word and accept it (4:20).

The parallel in Matt 12:46-50 has only partially preserved the Marcan context; for Matthew has omitted altogether the reference to "his own" who think he is beside himself and has separated the Beelzebul charge (12:22-32) from the scene about the mother and brothers, so that there is no obvious connection between them. The parable of the sower and seed still follows (13:1-23), but one would now be hard pressed to relate the different episodes in Matthew 12 to the different fates of the seed in Matthew 13.

Luke has drastically changed the context. Not only is there no reference to the Marcan "his own" passage, but the Beelzebul controversy does not occur until three chapters later (11:14-21). Now the parable of the sower and the seed (8:4-15) comes *before* the passage involving the mother and the brothers (8:19-21). In 8:15 the last line of the explanation of the parable refers to the seed that fell into good soil and yielded a hundredfold (8:8): "As for that [seed] in good soil, they are *those* who, *hearing the word*, hold it fast in an honest and good heart, and bring forth fruit with patience." When a few verses later, Jesus says (8:21): "My mother and my brothers are those who hear the word of God and do it," the connection is obvious; indeed the latter saying has probably been rephrased by Luke in light of the former.[382] The Lucan context underlines the fact that the mother and brothers are examples of the fate of the seed that has fallen in good soil. This is totally harmonious with Luke's picture of Mary's first response to the word of God in 1:38: "Behold the handmaid of the Lord. Let it be to me according to your word." This first and only mention of the brothers of Jesus in 8:21 and the association of them with the mother in terms of discipleship anticipates Acts 1:14 and the presence of "Mary the mother of Jesus . . . with his brothers" in the believing community.

4. A Beatitude on Jesus' Mother (11:27-28)

The last reference to the mother of Jesus in the Lucan Gospel involves an exchange of beatitudes or macarisms:[383]

> [27]And it happened while he was saying these things that a woman from the crowd, raising her voice, said to him, "Happy [makaria] the womb that bore you, and the breasts you sucked." [28]But he said, "Happy, rather, those who hear the word of God and keep it."

This passage is unique to Luke; but Jesus' saying sounds almost as if it were a variant of his final saying in the preceding scene: in both sayings value is placed, not on physical relationship, but on

---

[382]Contrast the position of Conzelmann, *Theology*, 35, 47-48, who thinks that Luke does not "soften" Mark's picture of the mother and the brothers, a position followed by Braumann and Flender (see Räisänen, *Mutter*, 138). Conzelmann holds that the arrival of the mother and brothers in 8:19 illustrates 8:18: "To him who has, more will be given, and from him who has not, even what he thinks he has will be taken away." He contends that in wishing to *see* Jesus (8:20), the relatives want to see some miracles performed by him (even as Herod wishes to see Jesus in 9:9; 23:8). All of this is forced, since Luke hints at no sinister reason for the wish of the relatives to see Jesus; and certainly there is no hint to anything being "taken away" in the favorable statement about the relatives in 8:21. Conzelmann misses completely the exact word parallel between 8:15 and 8:21; and he reconstructs his theology of Luke without recourse to the picture of Mary in the infancy narratives.

[383]See above, n. 302, on macarisms.

hearing the word of God and doing or keeping it. The possibility of a variant preserved in a different tradition increases when we note that the Lucan context consists of "Q" material and that the saying follows the Lucan account of the Beelzebul controversy (11:14-23, from Mark and "Q"), even as the Marcan parallel to Luke 8:19-21 follows the Beelzebul controversy. Thus, 8:21 might be a saying that has come to Luke through Mark, and 11:28 a saying that has come to Luke through "Q."[384] However, 11:27-28 may have come from a special Lucan source,[385] or even be a Lucan reworking or redaction of 8:19-21.[386]

On first reading, 11:27-28 seems to be a bit more negative toward the mother of Jesus than 8:19-21.[387] In part, this depends on the contrasting force given to the two beatitudes by the particle *menoun* which we have translated "rather." In an answer this particle can correct what was said previously: "No, rather"; or it can modify what was said previously: "Yes, but even more."[388] This ambiguity forces us to a closer examination of the two beatitudes. On the surface the beatitude uttered by the woman is a praise of Mary.[389] Nevertheless, literally, the praise is for the womb "that bore you" and the breasts "you sucked." The combination "womb and breasts" is a Jewish circumlocution (see 23:29),[390] and the beatitude of the mother may lie in the son she

---

[384]This would then be our sole evidence about the role or estimation of Mary in "Q."

[385]See Chap. 2, n. 27. Räisänen, *Mutter*, 139, opts for this derivation of the material, as does Kraeling, *Gospels*, 227.

[386]Creed, *Luke*, 162, and Bundy, *Jesus*, 349, opt for this derivation.

[387]The context is not particularly helpful, for the relationship between the incidents in chap. 11 is loose. What immediately precedes might indicate that Jesus' words about exorcisms led to the woman's outburst, but that seems far-fetched. What follows is a negative estimation of an evil generation.

[388]BDF §450, 4. See Rom 9:20; 10:18 for the former; Phil 3:8 for the latter. See further M. E. Thrall, *Greek Particles in the New Testament* (NTTS 3; Leiden: Brill, 1962), 35; she supports the corrective sense.

[389]Bundy, *Jesus*, 349: "One of the rare suggestions in the Synoptic tradition of a religious disposition which later found full form and expression in Mariolatry [sic]."

[390]Str-B, 1. 161, 188. The late midrash *Genesis Rabbah* 98:20 on Gen 49:25 takes the blessing on Joseph ("blessing of the breasts and of the womb") to be a blessing of his mother Rachel.

has produced; so that the primary object of the macarism is the son not the mother. In that case, the contrasting beatitude uttered by Jesus in v. 28 would mean that one should not judge God's blessings by marvelous words or by exorcisms (11:24-26) but by obedient retention of God's word.

However, such an interpretation separates too sharply the mother from the son. When we discussed 1:42b, we saw a similar blessing (*eulogēmenos*, however, not *makarios*) addressed directly by Elizabeth to Mary: "Blessed are you among women and blessed is the fruit of your womb." This implies that Mary is blessed because she has conceived a son like Jesus; yet she herself is truly the object of praise. In 1:45 Elizabeth makes it clear that Mary's share in the praise is not purely physical: "Happy is she who believed that there would be a fulfillment of the things spoken to her by the Lord." The same contrast may be at work here: the woman praises the mother because she has given birth to a son like Jesus; but Jesus stresses that real beatitude comes from hearing the word of God and keeping it.[391] The second beatitude, which is a generalizing plural ("those who hear"), is not a contrast with the first in the sense of contrasting those who are "happy" and those who are not. Rather it contrasts the reasons for happiness. Just as Luke 1:45 does not negate the blessing in 1:42b, 11:28 does not negate the macarism in 11:27; but it makes clear Jesus' priorities. In the overall Lucan picture of Mary, 11:28 stresses that Jesus' mother is worthy of a beatitude, yet not simply because she has given birth to a child. Her beatitude must be based on the fact that she has heard, believed, obeyed, kept, and pondered the word, and continued to do it (Acts 1:14). Implicitly, 11:28 is a more positive way of expressing that, like all others, Mary too must meet a criterion of discipleship (see 2:35a: "A sword will pass through your own soul"). She herself predicted: "Behold, henceforth all generations will call me happy" (1:48— *makarioun*), but now we have come to understand why.[392]

---

[391] As in 8:21, Luke uses participles which connote repeated action: "continue to hear and continue to keep." For this usage of the verb "to keep" (*phylassein*), see Luke 18:21 and Acts 7:53.

[392] Räisänen, *Mutter*, 141, speaks of Mary's relation to believers as *prima inter pares* (first among equals).

C. Mary in the Jerusalem Community of Acts 1:14

Like Mark/Matthew (see above, Chap. 4C), Luke mentions the presence of women followers of Jesus at the crucifixion and burial, and at the finding of the empty tomb; and he supplies some of their names. But he is in agreement with the other Synoptics and in disagreement with John 19:25-27, in not mentioning the presence of the mother of Jesus.[393] Consequently, it is somewhat unexpected to find a reference to her presence in Acts 1:14 after the ascension of Jesus and before Pentecost. Luke tells us that the apostles whom Jesus had chosen (1:2) had returned from Mount Olivet to the upper room in Jerusalem where they were staying (1:12-13). He then stops to list the Eleven by name, following up his list with this comment:[394]

> *These all were devoting themselves with one accord to prayer, together with women, and Mary, the mother of Jesus, and together with his brothers.*

This verse is usually considered to be one of the summary statements by means of which Luke links the action of the various scenes in Acts.[395] The connection of these statements with their

---

[393]In 24:10 he mentions Mary Magdalene, Joanna, and Mary of James (presumably the mother of James). Of course, Mary, the mother of Jesus, could have been among the "women" of 23:49, or "the women who had come with him from Galilee" (23:55), or "the other women" of 24:10, or even among "his acquaintances" [*gnōstoi*] of 23:49. (Bundy, *Jesus,* 549, argues that the latter [which is masculine] includes members of Jesus' family, and sees Luke as intermediary between Mark/Matthew, who mention no family presence, and John, who mentions the mother and the beloved disciple.) But certainly Luke's failure to mention her by name means that a reader would have no way to know of her presence at the crucifixion and that her presence there could have been of no importance for Luke (see above, n. 352).

[394]The grammar is awkward, and the second "together with" (*syn*) is omitted by Codices A, D, and S and many minuscules. The omission may be a scribal improvement; but Metzger, *TCGNT,* 284-85, thinks of the phrase as a possible scribal addition to separate Mary from the brothers, reflecting sensitivity about her perpetual virginity and the conviction that the "brothers" were not her children.

[395]See *JBC* art. 45, §4 and the literature on summaries cited there. Lucan composition of 1:14 is suggested by some of the vocabulary, e.g.,

context is more literary and theological than historical, and that must make us cautious about whether in 1:14 Luke is giving us a precise historical memory of a particular scene. On the other hand, since Mary is never mentioned in any of the other summary statements (or anywhere else in Acts) there is a certain deliberateness to his mention of her here.[396] Of what historical value is the general Lucan picture that Mary and the brothers of Jesus were members of the believing Christian community after the resurrection? In answering this question, we must be careful not to confuse the evidence of different NT works and not to confuse what is said about the brothers with what is said about Mary.

First, as regards Mary, nowhere in the NT is she ever described by name as an unbeliever. We have seen that Mark 3:20-35 associates a statement that "his own" thought Jesus was beside himself with a scene where the mother and brothers of Jesus arrive asking for him; and so, for Mark, the mother apparently thought that Jesus was beside himself. But it is important that the actual statement in 3:21 does not mention the mother of Jesus; and so Mark may be giving us his own interpretation of the tradition. A more common Gospel picture of Mary is that she was *not a disciple* of Jesus during his ministry, i.e., an active follower. In Mark/Matthew she (with the brothers) makes only one appearance during the ministry, and in that appearance she is clearly distinguished from the eschatological family of disciples of Jesus. In John 2:1-12 the mother is shown as not understanding Jesus, and she (with the brothers) is listed separately from Jesus' disciples. Thus, when in Acts 1:14 she appears in the company of the disciples after the resurrection and the ascension, it may legitimately be wondered when and for what reason did she join the company of the disciples.[397] That is not a question, however, which one need pose to Luke; for (unlike the other Gospels) Luke has portrayed Mary as a disciple from the time of Jesus' concep-

---

"with one accord" (*homothymadon*, ten times in Acts), "devote to" (*proskarterein* in Acts 2:42, 46; 6:4).

[396]The same holds true for the mention of Jesus' "brothers."

[397]This has sometimes been answered by supposing that the risen Jesus appeared to his mother, an appearance never mentioned in the NT (see below, Chap. 7, n. 484; Chap. 9, nn. 598-600).

tion, and in 8:19-21 has shown that she (with the brothers) met the criterion of members of the eschatological family of Jesus. It is interesting that, despite a more negative initial scene at Cana, John also depicts Mary as a believing disciple at the crucifixion, joining her in a family relationship to the disciple par excellence, the beloved disciple (19:25-27). The agreement of John and Luke on this point,[398] together with the favorable view of the mother of Jesus in later Christianity, led the task force to a firm rejection of Goguel's skepticism that Mary never belonged to the church.[399] Luke may have known little of how Mary became a public disciple, and his silence about her in the rest of Acts may mean that he knew little about the details of her subsequent career, but the basic affirmation in Acts 1:14 is scarcely the product of his wishful thinking.

Second, as regards the brothers, we can speak more briefly since Mark, Matthew, and Luke make no distinction between Mary and the brothers in their portrait of Jesus' ministry. The problem is John 7:5 which describes Jesus' brothers as unbelievers, and that is the final judgment on the brothers in the Johannine literature. However, here we may be hearing John's negative judgment on the low christology of Jewish Christians, rather than a historical affirmation that no one of the brothers ever became a Christian[400]—an affirmation refuted by a mass of NT and Jewish evidence about James, the brother of the Lord.[401] As to when the brothers shifted from non-discipleship to discipleship, 1 Cor 15:7

---

[398]See below, Chap. 7B. The parallel to Luke is enhanced if we realize that the Johannine crucifixion scene is virtually an ascension or lifting up of Jesus (John 12:32-33), so that both Gospels picture Mary as present, together with one or more model disciples, after the lifting up of Jesus.

[399]M. Goguel, *La naissance du christianisme* (Paris: Bibliothèque historique, 1946), 141.

[400]One may always contend that John 7:5 refers only to the ministry of Jesus, and that John and his readers took it for granted that the brothers became believers after Jesus' ministry. Such speculation, however, about what was presupposed by the Fourth Gospel is always dangerous. See below, Chap. 7, A5.

[401]1 Cor 15:7; Gal 1:19; 2:9, 12; James 1:1; Jude 1; see below, Chap. 7, n. 442.

may be of assistance, since it mentions an appearance of the risen Christ to James. What is strange is that Luke, who mentions Jesus' "brothers" in Acts 1:14, never refers to the brothers again in the history he narrates in Acts and never makes it clear that James, the leader of the Jerusalem community (12:17; 15:13; 21:18), is a brother of Jesus! (Contrast Gal 1:19.)

Turning now from the question of historicity to that of Luke's intent in Acts 1:14, we note first the dramatis personae: the Eleven, together with "women," Mary, and the brothers. Presumably "women" means the women mentioned at the crucifixion, burial, and empty tomb (Luke 23:49, 55; 24:10; see also 8:2-3).[402] Thus Luke has brought over into Acts some main witnesses of the Gospel-story. The company of the Eleven includes, in the words of Peter (Acts 1:21-22), "the men who have accompanied us during all the time that the Lord Jesus went in and out among us, beginning from the baptism of John until the day Jesus was taken up from us." Yet they are not mentioned as present for the crucial scene of the crucifixion and burial, nor did they discover the empty tomb (Luke 24:10); the witnesses for those events were the women. And Mary was the one who kept in her heart and pondered all the events surrounding Jesus' birth and childhood (2:19, 51). Clearly there is continuity between the various disciples of the Jesus story and the believing community of the church story.

The Eleven are presented in "the upper room" (1:13) devoting themselves to prayer.[403] When Luke begins the Pentecost story in 2:1, he will say, having just mentioned Matthias and the Eleven, "They were all together in the same place," when the sound came from heaven and the wind filled the house. Since the women, Mary, and the brothers were associated with the Eleven

---

[402]The absence of the definite article creates some doubt, as seen in the reading of Codex Bezae: "the women and children" (cf. Acts 21:5)—a reading that suggests a reference to the wives and children of the Eleven.

[403]The presence of the definite article before "prayer" makes theoretically possible a reference to "the prayer" of the Temple (Acts 3:1) or to prayer in a synagogue or a place of teaching. (See *The Beginnings of Christianity*, 4. 10-11.) The more obvious meaning, however, is prayer in the upper room.

in 1:14, most have assumed that they were also together with the Twelve on Pentecost, even though Luke does not say that specifically. He is content in his last mention of Mary to show her of one accord with those who would constitute the nascent church at Pentecost, engaged in prayer that would so mark the life of that church (Acts 2:42; 6:4; 12:5). He may not have known much about her subsequent life,[404] but he has taken care to give a consistent picture of her from the first annunciation of the good news to the eve of the coming of the Spirit who would empower the spread of that good news from Jerusalem to the end of the earth (Acts 1:8). Mary's first response to the good news was: "Behold the handmaid of the Lord. Let it be to me according to your word." The real import of Acts 1:14 is to remind the reader that she had not changed her mind.

---

[404]Conzelmann, *Theology*, 172, thinks that Luke knew little concrete about Mary and regards Acts 1:14 as an interpolation. By systematically ignoring the infancy narrative, he can make the extraordinary statement: "Mary disappears to a greater extent in Luke than in Mark and Matthew."

CHAPTER SEVEN:
THE MOTHER OF JESUS
IN THE GOSPEL OF JOHN*

In this Gospel we may distinguish two kinds of passages relevant to a study of Mary: first, two scenes in which the "mother of Jesus"[405] makes an appearance, namely, at the wedding feast of Cana (2:1-11, 12) and at the foot of the cross (19:25-27); second, some verses that may or may not have a pertinence to Marian questions, e.g., the virginal conception (1:13; 6:42; 7:41-43; 8:41) and the brothers of Jesus (2:12; 7:1-10). We shall treat these passages in the order in which they appear in the Gospel, grouping those that are found in the narrative of the public ministry (chaps. 1-12), and then discussing the reappearance of the mother of Jesus in the account of "the hour" (chaps. 13-21).

As a preliminary, let us note some common scholarly approaches to the composition of the Gospel.[406] Although Johan-

---

*The discussion for this chapter was led by G. Krodel, and the first draft was composed by K. P. Donfried. Three sessions of the task force (March, April, and Oct., 1976) were devoted in whole or in part to the evidence of John.

[405]The personal name (Mary) of the mother of Jesus never occurs in the Fourth Gospel, a striking omission since the author is not loath to mention women by name and refers to Marys some fifteen times (Mary the sister of Martha, Mary Magdalene, Mary the wife of Clopas).

[406]The scholars who hold the views we shall mention and the arguments pro and con can be easily found in the introduction to a number

nine studies have not produced unanimity, there is a large agreement on three stages of composition: (1) A pre-Gospel body of
material about Jesus. Some would speak of traditions, others
would speak of written sources, especially in reference to the
"signs" of Jesus. The majority of scholars would think that this
material took shape within the Johannine community (or parts of
the community), over against a theory that the evangelist adopted
material completely shaped by circles outside the community.
But probably no single judgment about provenance is true of all
Johannine material. (2) The work of the evangelist. By
"evangelist" we mean the person who composed the main part of
the Fourth Gospel, taking over previous traditions, making his
own contributions, and weaving the results into a consecutive
whole. We found no need in this book to make a decision about
the identity of the evangelist, although in fact none of us identifies
him as John, son of Zebedee. (3) The work of the redactor. Most
scholars posit a figure who edited the gospel left behind by the
evangelist and added to it. (Chap. 21 is his most agreed-upon
addition.) There is less agreement on whether he was a disciple of
the evangelist, chiefly working to complete the gospel (albeit with
a slightly different tone), or a censor-like corrector of the
evangelist, giving the gospel a very different orientation (in the
direction of conformity with the institutional church). The most
often cited date for the final Gospel is after A.D. 85, but that date
becomes of less significance if stages 1 through 3 reflect several
decades of continuity.

A. Passages of Marian Import in Chaps. 1–12

The solemn judgment on the public ministry of Jesus in
12:41-43 and the emphasis on the "hour" of Jesus in the opening
of the Last Supper (13:1) have led most scholars to divide the
Gospel into chaps. 1-12 and 13-21 (with the understanding that 21

---

of commentaries on John, e.g., Brown, *Gospel*, 1. XXIV-XL. A thorough
survey of contemporary scholarship is supplied by Kysar, *Fourth
Evangelist*.

is an addition)—chaps. 1-12 cover the public ministry; chaps. 13-21 cover the "hour" of Jesus' return to his Father.

1. Begotten of God (1:13)

In the Prologue of the Gospel there is a contrast between Jesus' own people who did not accept him (1:11), and those who did accept him:

> [12]*But to all those who accepted him, who believed in his name, he gave power to become children of God—*[13]*those who were begotten, not of blood, nor of the will of the flesh, nor of the will of man, but of God.*

Every Greek MS of the Gospel supports the plural reading in v. 13 which then refers to the begetting (or birth) of Christian believers.[407] However, the singular "he who was begotten" is read by one Old Latin MS[408] and is supported by Tertullian, Ambrose, and Augustine (and by the Latin versions of Irenaeus and Origen). A number of modern scholars, particularly French-speaking Roman Catholics, have argued for the singular as original.[409] When so read, the verse becomes a possible reference to the virginal conception of Jesus.

We have agreed with the overwhelming majority of textual critics and translations that the plural is the original reading. Not only is it a dubious procedure to give credence to a reading for which we have not a single Greek textual witness, but also the

---

[407]The aorist passive of *gennan* (*egennēthēsan*) can refer to *birth* from a female or *begetting* by a male (see above, Chap. 5, n. 152). The mention of "the will of man" (*anēr*, male) makes it more likely that begetting is meant. Begetting by God rather than birth from God is clearly a Johannine idea in 1 John 3:9, which refers to the seed of God.

[408]The evidence of the Curetonian Syriac and of six Peshitta MSS is ambiguous, for they read the plural "those who" with what appears to be a singular verb "was begotten [born]," but this may be an alternate plural form.

[409]For example, Boismard, F.-M. Braun, Dupont, and Mollat. The most complete defense of the singular is J. Galot, *Etre Né de Dieu: Jean 1, 13* (AnBib 37; Rome: PBI, 1969). Other supporters of the singular include Büchsel, Blass, Burney, Loisy, Resch, Seeberg, and Zahn.

context favors an explanation of the nature of the believers as contrasted with the "his own" who did not accept him. Moreover, it is dubious that a Johannine writer would describe Jesus as "begotten,"[410] while that is a common Johannine designation of believers (John 3:3-8; 1 John 3:9; 4:7; 5:1-4; 5:18a).

Even were the singular original, it is far from clear that this would constitute a Johannine reference to the virginal conception, an idea that is never mentioned elsewhere in John. If John 3:1-5 is seen as parallel to 1:12-13, the contrast between being begotten of the flesh and being begotten by God (or of the Spirit) has nothing to do with the absence of a male parent—it refers to two spheres, namely, from below or of the earth, and from above or of heaven. Nor could 1:13 have been understood by Greek scribes as a reference to the virginal conception of Jesus, for how then would they have dared to change the (allegedly) original singular to a plural which apparently eliminated such a reference? The movement of exegesis was almost certainly in the opposite direction: some Latin writers, encountering the pronoun *qui* which could mean either "those who" or "he who," saw the opportunity of reinterpreting the general Johannine statement about Christians so that it would become a reference to Jesus; and from their knowledge of the Matthean and Lucan infancy narrative they read into 1:13 a reference to the virginal conception.

Sir Edwyn Hoskyns[411] maintained that the plural was the original reading but thought that the language was so phrased as to recall the virgin birth of Jesus. One of the members of our study group found Hoskyns persuasive, but the rest of us found no convincing reason to see even an indirect reference to the conception of Jesus by Mary in John 1:13.

2. The Scene at Cana (2:1-11)

This episode occurs in the Fourth Gospel after the first disci-

---

[410]The only possible Johannine instance of *gennan* applied to Jesus is 1 John 5:18bc. In that verse commentators like Westcott, Plummer, Brooke, Dodd, and Bultmann think that "the one begotten by God" is Jesus, while Beyer and Schnackenburg refer that phrase to the Christian.

[411]*Fourth Gospel.* 164-65.

ples have joined Jesus (1:35-51) and before he goes to Jerusalem where he cleanses the Temple (2:13-22). The opening time reference ("on the third day") connects the Cana scene to what precedes; the transitional v. 12 connects it to what follows.

> ¹*Now on the third day there was a wedding at Cana in Galilee, and the mother of Jesus was there.* ²*Jesus himself was invited to the wedding, along with his disciples.* ³*When the wine ran short, the mother of Jesus said to him, "They have no wine."* ⁴*But Jesus said to her, "Woman, what have you to do with me? My hour has not yet come."* ⁵*His mother said to the waiters, "Do whatever he tells you."* ⁶*Now six stone water jars were there for the Jewish rites of purification, each holding twenty to thirty gallons.* ⁷*Jesus said to them, "Fill those jars with water." And they filled them to the brim.* ⁸*"Now draw some out," he said to them, "and take it to the steward of the feast." So they took it.* ⁹*As soon as the steward tasted the water made wine (he did not know where it came from; only the waiters who had drawn the water knew), the steward called the bridegroom* ¹⁰*and said to him, "Everyone serves the good wine first; then, when the guests have been drinking a while, the poor wine. But you have kept the good wine until now."* ¹¹*This, the first of his signs, Jesus did at Cana in Galilee, and manifested his glory; and his disciples believed in him.*

Working with the methodology of Johannine scholarship described above, we shall discuss first the possible pre-Gospel history of this story; but then, and with far more attention, concentrate on the meaning the scene has within the Gospel.[412]

THE PRE-GOSPEL TRADITION. Appealing to the Gospel's own reference to many signs worked by Jesus (20:30) and using the tools of source analysis, many scholars have posited that the Fourth Evangelist drew upon a sign-source in writing the Gospel—a collection of Jesus' miracles.[413] Some posit a long written source which involved a passion account; others favor a

---

[412]There has been no major effort to attribute this story or large parts of it to the redactor, so the post-evangelist period of Gospel composition need not concern us here.

[413]For recent discussions of source theories of composition, see Kysar, *Fourth Evangelist*, 13-37. John does not use the term "miracle"; and even though most of the sign-narratives involve miracles, scholars are not clear whether in Johannine thought a sign would have to involve a

more restricted source of sign-tradition. But if any form of the theory is accepted, it usually involves the two Cana signs of 2:1-11 and 4:46-54, because of John's counting these signs: "This, the first of his signs, Jesus did at Cana in Galilee" (2:11); "This was now the second sign that Jesus did on coming from Judea to Galilee" (4:54).[414]

If we take seriously, then, the possibility of a pre-Gospel form of the Cana wedding story, what might this have consisted of? The most elaborate attempt to reconstruct the signs-material underlying the Gospel is that of R. T. Fortna who offers the following form of the Cana story:[415]

Now there was a wedding at Cana in Galilee, and the mother of Jesus was there. Jesus himself was invited to the wedding along with his disciples. But they had no wine, for the wine provided for the wedding had been used up. The mother of Jesus said to the waiters, "Do whatever he tells you." Now six stone water jars were there, each holding twenty to thirty gallons. Jesus said to the waiters, "Fill those jars with water." And they filled them to the brim. "Now draw some out," he said to them, "and take it to the steward of the feast." So they took it. As soon as the steward tasted the water made wine, the steward called the bridegroom and said to him, "Everyone

---

miraculous action, e.g., is the cleansing of the Temple a sign? We have decided that it is not germane to our purpose to spend time discussing Bultmann's thesis (*Gospel*, 118-19) that the Cana story was taken over from a pagan legend of the Dionysus wine-festival. This thesis has had little acceptance; see H. Noetzel, *Christus und Dionysos* (Stuttgart: Calwer, 1960), but also E. Linnemann, "Die Hochzeit zu Kana und Dionysos," *NTS* 20 (1973-74), 408-18.

[414]Brown, *Gospel*, 1. 195: "[I] have not accepted a source theory in the composition of John, at least in the Bultmannian sense. However, it is reasonable to suppose that there were collections of miracles in the corpus of Johannine material that was edited to give us the Gospel. In one of the stages of editing, two closely related [Cana] miracles may have been split up to form the beginning and the end for Part Two . . . 'From Cana to Cana,' in the Gospel."

[415]Fortna, *Gospel*, 38 gives the pre-Gospel Greek text of 2:1-11 with many sigla indicating omissions or doubts about reconstruction. The English translation given above has been conformed to the English translation of the Gospel text given earlier. Fortna's various sigla of uncertainty are omitted.

serves the good wine first; then, when the guests have been drinking
a while, the poor wine. But you have kept the good wine until now."
This first sign Jesus did, and his disciples believed in him.

As Fortna reconstructs the pre-Gospel story, it is a rather simply
narrated miracle which Jesus does at the indirect request of his
mother. For our purposes, it is particularly significant that the
reconstruction lacks the dialogue between Jesus and his mother,
wherein he seems to correct and even refuse her. Indeed, the
awkwardness of that Gospel dialogue, which has a refusal followed by the granting of what was refused, is one of the reasons
for seeing layers of composition in the story, especially since
features characteristic of the Fourth Evangelist appear at least in
part of the dialogue.[416] If one accepts the hypothesis of a pre-
Gospel story without the full dialogue of 2:3-4 (at least without
the reference to "hour"), the significance of the sign seems to
have resided in the marvelous changing of water to wine. Jesus'
mother expected him to be able to work marvels; and the marvel
was granted through family intervention without hesitation on
Jesus' part. Thus Mary emerges as a believer in Jesus, even if the
Jesus in whom she believes is primarily a wonder-worker (a view
not surprising in a collection of miracles or signs).

Indeed, Lindars and Brown have thought that a plausible
case can be made for considering the original Cana story to have
been a "pre-ministry" story[417]—a story where Jesus has not yet
begun his public ministry, but is younger, still with his family

---

[416]Among the Johannine characteristics may be mentioned: the use
of "Woman" by Jesus for his mother; the use of "*oupō*, not yet" in
relation to time or hour; the theological use of "hour." See McHugh,
Mother, 462-66, for arguments that John added 2:3-4 to a pre-Johannine
narrative; he gives a survey of different views. However, the Sign Source
posited by Bultmann would attribute the dialogue of 2:3-4 to the pre-
Gospel stage (Smith, *Composition*, 39); and Nicol, *Sēmeia*, 30, sees
Johannine characteristics only in the last half of v. 4: "My hour has not
yet come."

[417]B. Lindars, *NTS* 16 (1969-70), 318-24; Brown, "Roles," 695-99.
This background would explain peculiar features in the Cana story: Jesus
is still up in the highlands of Galilee (where he does not work miracles in
the Synoptic tradition); he has not yet left his home and moved to Caper-

("His mother and his brothers" in vs. 12—see below, section A3), and behaves in a marvelous manner at their request or for their convenience. Many pre-ministry, "hidden-life" stories are reported in a fantastic form in apocryphal gospels, especially in *The Infancy Gospel of Thomas*, but we have a canonical example in Luke 2:41-51 where Jesus at age twelve astonishes his parents through his wisdom (2:48).[418] Such a pre-Gospel tendency to anticipate within the context of the family circle the later wisdom and the power of the ministry of Jesus would run strongly against the attitude we saw in Mark where a sharp delineation is made between the natural family and the disciples of Jesus. Since the Johannine pre-Gospel tradition may have been contemporary with the composition of Mark's Gospel, we get another example of very different views of Mary and the family in circulation at the same time.

THE GOSPEL-LEVEL INTERPRETATION. We have discussed the possibility of a pre-Gospel form of the Cana wedding story precisely because, in one way or another, it is posited in much of current scholarship. Speculations, however, about a pre-Gospel tradition cannot be proved and cannot constitute the main focus of our interest. We are chiefly interested in how the Fourth Gospel itself presents the mother of Jesus, and it is to that we now turn.

We acknowledge the common agreement of scholars that the Cana scene was intended by the evangelist to carry a primary christological message,[419] not a mariological one. (There is also the possibility of a secondary sacramental or eucharistic meaning of the scene, but that is not of concern here; for we are not

---

naum (2:12) which will be the center of his public ministry; he is in the family circle of his mother and brothers; the miracle that he performs at his mother's request for the sake of family friends is exuberant (approximately 100 gallons of wine). None of these features are found in the ministry miracles of Jesus, but all of them are typical of the apocryphal accounts of Jesus' boyhood miracles.

[418]See above p. 159.

[419]Still very effective on this score, and serving as a rejection of exaggerated Marian interpretation, is the work of the German Roman Catholic scholar R. Schnackenburg, *Das erste Wunder Jesu* (Freiburg: Herder, 1951). For various interpretations of the scene in reference to Jesus and his disciples, see Brown, *Gospel*, 1. 104-7.

attempting a complete exegesis.) The story pertains in some way to the "hour" of Jesus; the water intended for the Jewish rites of purification has been replaced by a wine that is better than any hitherto offered—a wine that by its quality and perhaps even by its abundance reveals to Jesus' disciples in a wedding setting the *glory* of Jesus.[420] The disciples have already in the preceding section acknowledged Jesus as the Messiah, the one foretold by Moses and the prophets, the King of Israel, and the Son of God. But there Jesus replied, "You shall see greater things than these" (1:50). Now the disciples have begun to have that promise realized—the glory manifested at Cana through the first of Jesus' signs is the "glory as of the only Son from the Father" (1:14).[421]

Nevertheless, even though the dominant motif at Cana is christological, the mother of Jesus does have an important role in the events that lead up to the sign. (If one posits a pre-Gospel story without some of the dialogue in 2:3-4, the role of the mother of Jesus may have become more prominent in the Gospel form of the story, although we shall have to discuss what new tone has been added.) The very fact that the mother of Jesus is mentioned in the first verse, which supplies the setting for the scene, and that she raises the question concerning the wine, clearly directs the reader's attention to her and her expectations. Let us now proceed point by point to deal with factors in the scene that have been seen by commentators as significant for John's view of the mother of Jesus.

(a) "They have no wine" (2:3)

Is the mother of Jesus asking for a miracle to meet the deficiency? This would imply at least a faith in Jesus as a wonder-

---

[420]Calculating that six full water jars of wine would yield some 120 gallons, commentators have pointed to texts promising an abundance of wine in the last days: Amos 9:13-14; Hos 14:7; Jer 31:12; and *2 Baruch* 29:5. Others have stressed the motif of the good or choice wine as contrasted with inferior wine, and have compared the saying in 2:11 to the Synoptic saying where Jesus speaks of his work in terms of new wine versus old (Mark 2:22 and par.). Still others have called attention to the wedding and banquet motifs in the Synoptic tradition (Matt 8:11; 22:1-14; Luke 22:16-18).

[421]Some scholars think that the Prologue was added by the final redactor of John (Brown, *Gospel*, 1. 21-23); nevertheless, it is quite proper to comment on the Gospel as it now stands.

worker—perhaps also a greater faith, but at least that much faith. Such a faith is understandable if one posits a pre-Gospel collection of miracles of Jesus done in a family circle, as mentioned above; but it is more surprising on the level of the Fourth Gospel itself where to this moment Jesus has done nothing marvelous. Accordingly, some scholars have refused to posit any expectation of a miracle on Mary's part. Perhaps, they speculate, she was simply informing Jesus of a difficult situation that seems to have no solution. (Her remark, then, would resemble the despairing complaint of the disciples in Mark 8:2, "How can one feed these men with bread here in the desert?") And, on a pedestrian level, her words have been read as a suggestion that Jesus should leave. Yet the rather sharp response of Jesus indicates clearly that she has placed some burden on him, and so we should recognize on Mary's part some expectation that Jesus can meet the need. If there is no logical preparation for such an estimation of Jesus, neither is there logical preparation for John the Baptist's recognition of Jesus in John 1:29 or Nathanael's confession of him in 1:49. The Johannine Jesus has an air of mystery about him which causes some people to react with at least a glimmering of the heavenly reality that they are encountering. This glimmering does not necessarily prevent misunderstanding (and in Mary's case, the dialogue will show that there is misunderstanding); but her inaugural recognition is not to be negated by the practical question, "How could Mary have known that Jesus would be able to do anything about such a problem?" Such a question does not do justice to the literary genre or to the atmosphere of the Johannine narrative.

(b) "Woman" (2:4)

There is no precedent in Hebrew or, to the best of our knowledge, in Greek, for a son to address his mother thus; and so most scholars have detected a special significance in the term. It is not an impolite address, and the various Gospels attest that it is Jesus' normal way of speaking to women.[422] Since it is repeated

---

[422]Matt 15:28; Luke 13:12; John 4:21; 8:10; 22:13.

for Mary as she stands at the foot of the cross when Jesus con-
signs her to the beloved disciple, one can scarcely interpret the
address as a sign of lack of affection. However, for Jesus to
address his mother in the same way as he addresses the Samaritan
woman (4:21) and Mary Magdalene (20:13) may mean that he
places no special emphasis on her physical motherhood. This
interpretation, to which we shall return below, would bring John
into agreement with the Synoptic Gospels where, as we saw, a
family of disciples takes precedence over the natural family and
its claims. If it is objected that John cannot mean to play down
physical motherhood since he calls Mary the "mother of Jesus"
four times in 2:1-12, it may be answered that the final scene in
which she appears (19:25-27) will make clear why for John she is
truly "mother" —she met the criterion of discipleship.

Either in addition to the interpretation just offered or, indeed, as opposed to it, the address "Woman" has been seen as a
symbolic evocation of the role of Eve in chap. 3 of Genesis.[423] In
order to see the full argument for this thesis, the reader must be
aware of suggestions that have been made for interpreting John
19:25-27 and Revelation 12, passages yet to be discussed. But at
least the following similarities may be pointed out here: (1) Eve is
called the woman in the Genesis story, and at her instigation
Adam disobeys the command of God. Mary, addressed as
"Woman," may be seen as asking Jesus to misuse his power here
to become a wonder worker, but he rejects her request and performs a sign that reflects his true glory. (2) In Gen 3:15 the woman
is not left without hope; rather it is predicted that there will be
enmity between the serpent and the woman, and that her seed will
bruise the head of the serpent. The passion and death of Jesus is
seen in the Fourth Gospel as the triumph of Jesus over the Prince
of this World (12:31; 14:30); and at the very moment of his
triumph Mary is brought back on the scene, addressed as

---

[423]The works of F.-M. Braun and Feuillet are (from somewhat different perspectives) the most complete discussion of this symbolism. For a
summary see Brown, *Gospel,* 1. 107-9; 2. 925-26; McHugh, *Mother,*
373-87.

"Woman," and brought within the family of discipleship. In other words, the two Johannine scenes in which Mary is addressed as "Woman" may be seen as a reenactment of the Eve motif with a happier ending.[424]

Certainly many of the church Fathers related Mary to the New Eve motif,[425] but is that a *later* symbolic application rather than an interpretation of John's own intentions? Why, many have asked, should "Woman" be symbolically more important in John when addressed to the mother of Jesus than when addressed to the Samaritan woman or to Mary Magdalene? One may reply that the two scenes in which the mother of Jesus appears are more strategically placed in the Gospel, one at the beginning and one at the end of the public life of Jesus; and so the reader's attention would be focused on their symbolism. Moreover, the Gospel began with the opening words of the Book of Genesis ("In the beginning"), and many detect further Genesis echoes in the Prologue and in the counting of (seven) days in 1:29 and 2:1.[426] Thus, it has been argued that the reader would be psychologically prepared for recognizing an Eve motif in 2:1-11. Most of the members of the task force were not inclined to accept an Eve symbolism on the level of the evangelist's intention; but the fact that some scholars do accept this symbolism, including at least one of our members, betrays the difficulty of setting limits to symbolism in a Gospel that tends toward symbolism and signs.

---

[424]Obviously this would involve a Christian interpretation of Gen 3:15; but most of those who hold this theory do not suggest that the author of Gen 3:15 foresaw Christ or Mary. Moreover, the possible Johannine reference to Gen 3:15 in no way involves the Vulgate (mis)translation where the woman crushes the head of the serpent. See above, Chap. 2, n. 40.

[425]For references, see H. de Lubac, *The Splendour of the Church* (New York: Sheed and Ward, 1956), chap. IX. Also below, Chap. 9, pp. 255-56, 279-80.

[426]See examples in Brown, *Gospel*, 1. 26-27, 105-6. Genesis motifs have been found in the context of the second Mary scene of John as well, e.g., a second set of seven days at the end of the Gospel (20:26). Feuillet, "L'heure," argues that 16:21, "For joy that a man is born into the world," echoes Gen 4:1 where upon giving birth Eve exclaims, "I have got a man (child) with the help of the Lord"—her joy reversing the sorrow of 3:16, even as joy replaces sorrow in John 16:19-22.

(c) "What have you to do with me?" (2:4)

The Semitism, "What to me and to you?", has at least two shades of meaning in the Hebrew OT: (1) When one party is unjustly bothering another, the injured party may use this phrase, meaning, "What have I done to you that you should do this to me?" Examples are Judg 11:12; 2 Chr 35:21; 1 Kgs 17:18. (2) When someone is asked to get involved in something which he feels is no business of his, he may use this phrase, meaning: "That is your business; how am I involved?" Examples are 2 Kgs 3:13; Hos 14:8. Although, even in antiquity, some have seen a rebuke to Mary along the lines of meaning (1), most have read the passage along the lines of meaning (2) and have spoken of a dissociation of Jesus from Mary. Thus, at least what Mary is asking for, or the aspect under which she is speaking to Jesus, does not belong to Jesus' understanding of the work his Father has given him to do.

(d) "My hour has not yet come" (2:4)

The Greek *oupō hēkei hē hōra mou* can also be read as a question, "Has not my hour come?" In deciding whether the statement or the question is to be preferred, much depends on what "my hour" means. Is it the hour of the public ministry? In that case the question may be preferable. In first asking, "What have you to do with me?", Jesus has dissociated his mother's interest from his own. When he asks "Has not my hour come?", Jesus is offering a reason for the dissociation, namely, he has now begun his ministry by gathering disciples and has passed from a situation where family interests can direct his life.[427] The great difficulty with this interpretation is that on several occasions during the ministry (7:30; 8:20) John says unambiguously that Jesus' hour had not yet come. Only as the passion and death approach, do we hear that Jesus' hour had come, namely, the hour for Jesus to be glorified (12:23). If one takes "hour" in this sense of hour for ultimate glorification, then it is best to read 2:4 as a statement,

----

[427] A. Vanhoye, *Bib* 55 (1974), 157-67, argues strongly for the question-translation, and argues that the relationship on a family level which had hitherto existed between Jesus and his mother is now giving place to the hour in which the Father's call must be given primacy.

"My hour has not yet come." However, such a statement, when applied to Jesus' dissociation of himself from his mother, might mean that when the hour for glorification has come, his mother will have a role. Then he will no longer say to her, "Woman, what have you to do with me?" Thus, many would see 2:4 as preparing for the reappearance of Jesus' mother at the foot of the cross when Jesus will say, "Woman, behold your son." Be that as it may, the contention that the "hour" of Jesus is the hour for him to pass from this world to the Father (13:1) means that the dissociation of Jesus from his earthly mother has something to do with the purposes of his heavenly Father; and thus in John 2:3-4 we are very close to the Synoptic tradition wherein Jesus contrasted the claims of an earthly family with the will of God (Mark 3:31-35 and par.). Indeed, there is a particularly close parallel to Jesus' reaction to his mother in the story in Luke 2:41-52. There when his mother puts a family demand on him ("Why have you treated us so? Behold, your father and I have been looking for you anxiously"), Jesus answers, "Why is it that you were looking for me? Did you not know that it was necessary for me to be in my Father's house?"[428] If one interprets 2:4 in whole or in part as a Johannine addition to a pre-Gospel miracle story, then the evangelist has inserted a theme of the primacy of God over the natural family which makes the story conform with a general Gospel theme. This story can now serve as a vehicle for a christology that sees Jesus as more than a wonder-worker.

(e) His mother said to the waiters, "Do whatever he tells you" (2:5)

This line and its sequence are most difficult for the logic of the Johannine narrative. After Jesus has rebuffed his mother, why does she go ahead with her plan to have him take care of the need

---

[428]The parallel is even closer if we follow the question-translation of 2:4, for then Luke and John have Jesus respond to his mother with two consecutive questions, the second of which places emphasis on his Father's sphere of interest. We saw above that the Johannine Cana story and the Lucan boy-in-the-Temple story may be two canonical examples of pre-ministry stories involving Jesus *en famille*.

for wine?[429] (The very fact that she does indicates that she did expect Jesus to do something when she reported in 2:3, "They have no wine.") And why does Jesus grant her request when he has told her that this concern of hers is not his concern? A whole spectrum of interpretations concerning the role of Mary has been offered to explain this inconsistency.[430]

On one extreme of the spectrum is an exegesis once popular among Roman Catholics (but scarcely held by any scholar today) that the story is an example of Mary's power of intercession: the first miracle worked by Jesus was at the behest of his mother, and this is meant to teach us to pray to Jesus through Mary. On the other extreme, it has been argued that.by persisting in her demand after Jesus' refusal, Mary showed that she really did not believe in Jesus.[431] Most commentators want to take a position somewhere between such extremes. There is a good Synoptic example of persistence by a woman in the face of a seeming refusal by Jesus, an example where the woman's faith was praised rather than decried (Matt 15:21-28). Moreover, the second sign at Cana in John 4:46-54, which has many parallels with the first sign, also involves a rebuff of the petitioner and a persistence which brings the granting of the requested favor. Thus, we should not exaggerate the negative side of the picture of the mother of Jesus in 2:3-5. The very fact that Jesus finally *does* supply the wine requested makes it virtually impossible to maintain that the scene contains a harsh polemic against his mother. Rather she falls into a general category of those who, despite their good intentions, misunderstand Jesus (e.g., Nicodemus in chap. 3, and the Samaritan woman in chap. 4). The fact that her misunderstanding involves a

---

[429]Indeed, she does so in a phraseology that recalls the Gen 41:55 where Pharaoh tells the Egyptians, "Go to Joseph; do whatever he tells you"—a statement made with the assurance that Joseph could do something to allay the lack of food.

[430]If one postulates a pre-Johannine form of the story without some of the dialogue in 2:3-4, the inconsistency has been introduced by the evangelist's addition.

[431]Rissi, "Hochzeit," 88: Mary's final words show misunderstanding—"Whoever does not understand, does not believe (7:5); so Mary is the representative of unbelief."

miraculous action is not surprising, for signs in John have an ambivalent function.[432] Sometimes the request for a sign betrays a hostile lack of faith (2:18); at other times enthusiasm for signs represents a faith in which Jesus has no confidence (2:23-24); and still other times a request for a sign shows both naive trust and a lack of comprehension, leading ultimately to solid faith (4:47, 48, 53; 20:30-31). The fact that the mother of Jesus remains with him after he has changed the water to wine (2:12) and ultimately appears at the foot of the cross (19:25-27) makes it likely that it is the last mentioned category which most suits her in the Johannine spectrum.[433] But until she appears at the foot of the cross, she is not yet a model for believers and indeed is kept distinct from the disciples who at Cana saw his glory and believed in him (2:11 — notice the continued distinction between the mother and disciples in 2:12).

3. The Transition to Capernaum (2:12)

The last appearance of the mother of Jesus in the public ministry before the passion is in the verse which follows the Cana story and serves as a transition to the next scene to take place in Jerusalem:

> [12]*After this Jesus went down to Capernaum, along with his mother and his brothers and his disciples; and there they stayed only a few days.*

There are textual difficulties about this verse that may reflect problems in its origin and interpretation. Many of the later MSS have the reading "his brothers," but the two second-century

---

[432]See the survey of reactions to signs in Brown, *Gospel*, 1. 530-31.

[433]If one accepts the thesis of a pre-Gospel miracle story, some of Mary's faith in Jesus has been carried over from that story into the Gospel narrative, even though faith in a wonder-worker is now set over against a faith that relates to the real value of signs. If John does not spell out the transformation of Mary's faith, it is because at Cana he is satisfied to lead *the reader* through such a transformation by appealing to the example of the disciples in 2:11.

Bodmer papyri of John favor the omission of the possessive. Codex Sinaiticus and some of the early versions omit "and his disciples." As we shall see, this reflects the problem of the relationship of the brothers and the disciples. Finally, Codex Alexandrinus favors the singular "he stayed," probably a scribal correction meant to stress that it was Jesus who stayed only a few days in Capernaum (since he goes to Jerusalem in the next verse)— presumably therefore the mother and brothers could have stayed at Capernaum longer.

The brothers of Jesus have not been mentioned before this verse, for the Cana scene involved only the mother and the disciples. Were the brothers originally a part of the Cana scene on a pre-Gospel level (especially if we accept the hypothesis of a miracle worked *en famille*) and were they replaced by the disciples as part of the Gospel adaptation of the miracle story?[434] Is that history reflected by a scribal addition of "and his disciples" in 2:12, so that Codex Sinaiticus which speaks only of the mother and the brothers has a more original text? Or was the history the other way around—only Mary and the disciples were involved and the "brothers" of 2:12 were originally the disciples, as in the use of "brothers" for disciples in 20:17-18?

It is impossible to resolve these questions of pre-Gospel history. But if we accept the best attested text, involving all three dramatis personae (Mary, brothers, disciples), as the final intention of the evangelist, we note several interesting details. First, John joins the Synoptic tradition in associating Mary with the brothers of Jesus, so that the question of her being their mother is not foreign to this Gospel either (see above, pp. 65-72). The absence of Jesus' father, Joseph, in these family scenes is noteworthy in both traditions, once more suggesting that Joseph was dead (above, p. 64). Second, John also joins the Synoptic tradition in

---

[434]In the form of the Cana story which appears in the *Epistula Apostolorum* (early second century?), we find: "Then there was a wedding in Cana of Galilee, and he was invited with *his mother and his brothers*" (chap. 5; *HSNTA* 1. 193); also Chrysostom and Epiphanius. Boismard, *Synopse*, 3. 100, argues that the original text of John 2:1 read "brothers," not "disciples."

not confusing Mary and the brothers of Jesus with the disciples.
There is no reason in the Fourth Gospel, any more than in the
Synoptic Gospels, to think that Mary was a disciple of Jesus
during his ministry. (In the light of 7:5 it is clear that the brothers
were *not* disciples during the ministry.) Third, John joins Mark in
particular in having Mary's appearance during the public ministry
occur early in the narrative and in connection with Capernaum.
The only Marcan appearance of the mother and brothers of Jesus
(3:21, 31-35) occurs shortly after Jesus has returned to Galilee
from the Jordan (1:14) and has moved his headquarters to Capernaum (1:21; 2:1). It is seemingly to that "home" (3:20) that "his
own" come down from Nazareth to seize him (3:21), only to find
that he is surrounded by disciples to whom he gives priority
(3:31-35). One could put Mark and John together and postulate an
early tradition that at the beginning of Jesus' ministry his separation from his family was a deliberate action on his part, that they
came to Capernaum to try to hold onto him, but recognized eventually that his calling had separated him from them, and that
henceforth they remained in Nazareth while he traversed Galilee
and Judea.

4. The Son of Joseph (6:42)

In the midst of the bread-of-life discourse, "the Jews" mur-
mured in disbelief at Jesus' words, "I am the bread which came
down from heaven." By way of objection they said,[435]

> [42]"*Is not this Jesus the son of Joseph? Do we not know his father
> and his mother? How does he now say, 'I have come down from
> heaven?' "*

We have already discussed this passage in relation to Mark 6:1-6a
(see above, p. 61), and we shall not repeat here what has already
been said about the possible pre-Gospel history of the saying. Our

---

[435]We chose to follow the vast majority of textual witnesses in including "and his mother" in this verse. The omission of those words by
the original scribe of Codex Sinaiticus and in the Old Syriac is probably a
scribal omission. See Metzger, *TCGNT*, 213.

main concern now is what the Fourth Evangelist intended to convey by his use of the saying.

Clearly it is an example of the Johannine technique of misunderstanding, where Jesus is speaking on one level and his dialogue partner is thinking on another level.[436] In John 3:3-5, when Jesus speaks of being begotten (born) from above or again, Nicodemus poses what he thinks is an insuperable obstacle, namely, a person cannot get back into the mother's womb and be born all over again. His statement is quite true but has nothing to do with the type of birth Jesus is talking about. So also here, the Johannine reader will recognize that the objection about Jesus' human parents really has nothing to do with his origins from above—the pre-existent Son of God has been with the Father in heaven before the Word became flesh.

Why is this example of Jewish misunderstanding of concern in a study of Mary? In the history of exegesis, it has been used both as proof that John believed in the virginal conception and proof that John denied the virginal conception. Those who opt for John's belief in the virginal conception think that the Jewish misunderstanding concerned Jesus' being the son of Joseph. Theoretically, it is possible that Johannine misunderstanding be based on a wrong statement of the dialogue partner as well as on a wrong understanding of the implications of that statement for what Jesus is claiming. However, as the Nicodemus example shows, most often the statement of the dialogue partner is quite true for the level on which that partner is thinking (see 2:20; 4:11; 8:57). Therefore, the contention that John wants the reader to recognize that "the Jews" are wrong in claiming that Jesus is the son of Joseph is not defensible unless there are clear indications elsewhere in John which would enable the reader to know that. In fact, however, John nowhere mentions the virginal conception; and his christology is one of pre-existence which allows for divine sonship independently of virginal conception.

On the other hand, it is equally objectionable methodologi-

---

[436]For a brief explanation of this Johannine stylistic feature, see Brown, *Gospel*, 1. CXXXV-CXXXVI; also Wead, *Literary Devices*; and H. Leroy, *Rätsel und Missverständnis* (BBB 30; Bonn: Hanstein, 1968).

cally to posit that in 6:42 John is explicitly denying the virginal conception and affirming that Jesus is the son of Joseph *over against* the theory of virginal conception. First of all, a reference to Jesus as "the son of Joseph" does not in itself disprove the virginal conception, since the Luke who wrote the infancy narrative and accepted the virginal conception (the majority interpretation of Luke 1:26-35) has no difficulty in 4:22 with the affirmation that Jesus is "the son of Joseph." Second, there is no indication that John even knew of the thesis of a virginal conception, knowledge of which is attested for only Matthew and Luke. True, John gives us no reason to think that he did not regard Jesus as the physical son of Joseph, for he does nothing to correct the Jewish assumption on that score. But it is unwarranted to move from that silence to explicit denial of virginal conception. All that we can be sure of from 6:42 is that human parentage is no obstacle to divine origins.

Another point of Marian interest flows from the second question in 6:42: "Do we not know his father and mother?" This question seems to imply that Jesus' father was still alive. Perhaps we should distinguish between historical fact and Johannine knowledge. Since in the Fourth Gospel (or in any other Gospel) Joseph does not appear in the ministry of Jesus, even in scenes where we might expect him (e.g., alongside the mother at Cana or at the foot of the cross), the better historical surmise is that Joseph was dead. But we cannot be sure that the Fourth Evangelist knew this—especially since with the vast majority of modern scholars we are not positing that the evangelist himself was an eyewitness of the ministry of Jesus. "Son of Joseph" is his normal designation for Jesus (1:45 also). When trying to use that designation as a basis for a Jewish objection to Jesus' heavenly origins, the evangelist may have thought it quite natural to mention both father and mother, without ever speculating on whether Joseph was still alive during Jesus' ministry or indeed whether the question was so phrased as to raise that suspicion in the reader.[437]

---

[437]The setting, after all, is not the same as in Mark 6:1-6a, where Jesus is in Nazareth, and the people are pointing out his relatives who are "here with us."

Once again then we must be cautious about developing Marian conclusions from passages that do not have as their interest Mary or her family situation.

5. The Unbelieving Brothers of Jesus (7:1-10)

The multiplication of the loaves and the discourse on the bread of life (chap. 6) took place in Galilee. The next chapter begins with the possibility of Jesus' leaving Galilee for Judea:

> ¹Now after this Jesus went about in Galilee because, with the Jews seeking to kill him, he could not go about in Judea. ²However, the Jewish feast of Tabernacles was at hand; ³so his brothers said to him, "Leave here and go to Judea, that your disciples may see the works you are doing; ⁴for no one works in secret if he seeks to be known publicly. If you are going to do these things, show yourself to the world." (⁵For even his brothers did not believe in him.) ⁶Jesus said to them, "My time has not yet come, but your time is always here. ⁷The world cannot hate you, but it hates me because I testify against it that its works are evil. ⁸Go to the feast yourselves; I am not going up to the feast, for my time has not yet fully come." ⁹Having said this, he remained in Galilee. ¹⁰But after his brothers had gone up to the feast, then he also went up, not openly but in private.

In the latter part of the previous chapter there were different reactions to Jesus: "the Jews" did not believe in him (6:41, 52); many of his disciples characterized his bread-of-life discourse as a hard saying and drew back, no longer accompanying him (6:60-66); speaking for the Twelve, Simon Peter refused to abandon his Lord, for he recognized that Jesus had the words of eternal life (6:67-69); but within the very Twelve Judas was a devil who would betray Jesus (6:70-71). This series of reactions is continued by the reference to the unbelieving brothers of Jesus.

In 2:12 the mother and the brothers of Jesus were mentioned together and yet kept distinct from the disciples of Jesus. Clearly here too the brothers are not disciples; indeed, in v. 3 they seem to refer to the disciples of Jesus as another group. There are definite parallels to the Cana scene involving the mother. In 2:3, 5 Mary implicitly expected Jesus to meet the need for wine, presumably by a miracle; in 7:3-4 the brothers ask Jesus to perform miraculous works.[438] Jesus answered his mother by pointing out that his hour had not yet come (2:4); he answers his brothers by twice stating that his time had not yet come (7:6, 8). Although Jesus seemingly refuses both his mother and his brothers, ultimately he does what each has requested; he turns water to wine; he goes up to Judea. It was because of this parallelism that Rissi appealed to 7:5, "His brothers did not believe in him," as a judgment that Mary at Cana was also an example of unbelief.[439] However, no such judgment was passed by the evangelist on Mary at Cana as is expressly passed on the brothers here—she was not declared an unbeliever and associated with "the world" (7:4, 7). And so one can argue exactly to the opposite of Rissi: after 2:12, respectively once each, the brothers and the mother are brought back on the scene; the brothers are specifically cited as unbelievers; the mother is favorably associated with the beloved disciple and brought within the believing family of Jesus (19:25-27).[440]

The harshness of John's judgment on the brothers is heightened when we realize that this is the last mention of them in the Johannine writings. In Acts 1:14 Luke portrays the brothers as part of the believing community before Pentecost; and Acts, Paul, and the Letters of James and Jude[441] show that one brother, James, achieved a prominence in the Christian community. Indeed, James had died as a martyr in Jerusalem.[442] But there is no

---

[438]Since this scene follows that of the multiplication of the loaves, there can be little doubt that it is *miraculous* works that the brothers of Jesus are asking Jesus to do in Judea so that his disciples may see them. "Works" (*erga*) is a term that is often interchangeable in John for "signs" (*sēmeia*); see Brown, *Gospel*, 1. 525-32.

[439]See above, n. 431.

[440]In discussing Mark 3:21 and 3:31-35, we saw that, even though Mark associates Jesus' *own* with Jesus' mother and brothers, what he says about Jesus' own (they charge that Jesus is beside himself) is harsher than what he says specifically about Jesus' mother and brothers. Nowhere is Mary ever presented as hostile to Jesus, although there is evidence of hostility toward him in his family.

[441]See above, Chap. 6, n. 401. It is almost universally assumed that the "James" mentioned in the Letters of James and Jude is meant to be "the brother of the Lord."

[442]See Josephus, *Ant.* 20.9,1 §200; Hegesippus, as cited in Eusebius, *History* 2.23,3-25.

such redeeming note in the Fourth Gospel's picture of the brothers. It may be that John is describing only the public ministry of Jesus and thus a period in which the brothers had not yet been converted. More likely, some scholars feel,[443] the evangelist may be reflecting divisions at the end of the century when the Johannine community was not in harmony with Jewish Christian communities which revered the memory of the brothers of the Lord but which had not developed sufficiently (according to Johannine standards) in their christology. Be that as it may, the hostile picture of the brothers makes all the more remarkable the favorable picture of the mother at the end of the Gospel.

6. Is Not the Messiah to Come from Bethlehem? (7:41-43)

When Jesus does go to Judea and Jerusalem for the feast of Tabernacles in chap. 7, his very presence produces discussion about him and division among "the Jews" (7:10-13; 25-36). On the last day in response to his words, John tells us that some of the people said, "This is really the prophet."

> [41]*Others said, "This is the Messiah." But some objected, "The Messiah is not to come from Galilee, is he? Has not the Scripture said that the Messiah comes from the seed of David and from Bethlehem the village where David was?"* [43]*So there was a division in the crowd over him.*

How are we to understand John's attitude toward the objection of those in the crowd who doubted that Jesus was the Messiah[444] on the grounds that the Messiah should have been born in Bethlehem?

It is possible that John 7:42 is an example of Johannine mis-

---

[443]J. L. Martyn, *History and Theology in the Fourth Gospel* (New York: Harper & Row, 1968; rev. ed., Nashville: Abingdon, 1979), gave emphasis to the insight that the discussions between Jesus and his opponents in John often reflect the church-situation at the end of the century. R. E. Brown, " 'Other Sheep Not of This Fold,' " *JBL* 97 (1978), 5-22, has applied this to the discussion between Jesus and the brothers of the Lord.

[444]The Greek term in 7:41-42 is *Christos*. Admittedly, this term on Christian lips frequently means more than Messiah, but here as a Jewish objection against Jesus, "Messiah" seems an appropriate translation.

understanding not unlike that in 6:42 discussed above. The faction in the crowd who raised the question would be thinking on the level of "below" or "of this earth"; and their objection against Jesus as the Messiah would be no more valid than the earlier objection of "the Jews" who protested that they knew Jesus' father and mother. Jesus would be the Messiah (in John's understanding) whether or not he was of Davidic descent and no matter where he was born, because his true descent is from God and from heaven. In this interpretation (which thus far certainly reflects a correct reading of Johannine christology) the objection proposed in 7:42 may well be factually true on the level of "below." When we discussed 6:42, we found no Johannine protest that the Jews were wrong because Joseph was not the father of Jesus; and so we concluded that it is perfectly possible that John thought that Joseph begot Jesus. Similarly here we find no protest that Jesus really was descended from David and really was born in Bethlehem; and so John may have thought that Jesus was not a Davidid and was born in Nazareth. Indeed, there may even be a Johannine polemic against Jesus' Davidic descent and his birth at Bethlehem as those ideas were being proposed by other first-century Christians, either on the grounds that such christology was false (since Jesus was not a Davidid and was not born at Bethlehem) or that it gave emphasis to the wrong things (What difference did it make where Jesus was born or to which family he belonged?). The major difficulty with this theory is that, on the question of Davidic descent, it pits John against most of the NT. It is one thing to suggest that John did not know of Jesus' birth at Bethlehem or even denied it, for the Bethlehem localization of Jesus' birth is mentioned only in Matthew 2 and Luke 2. It is quite another thing to say that John did not know or even denied Jesus' Davidic descent; for that is affirmed by Paul, Mark, Matthew, Luke, the Pastorals, and Revelation (often with christological implications).

It is also possible to read 7:42 in a totally different way. It might be an example of that Johannine figure of speech called irony,[445] according to which opponents are portrayed as making

---

[445]See Brown, *Gospel*, 1. CXXXVI; H. Clavier, "L'Ironie dans le quatrième évangile," *SE* 1. 261-76; Wead, *Literary Devices*.

statements about Jesus which are derogatory or incredulous, but which are true in a way they do not perceive. The Samaritan woman, for instance, exemplifies irony when she asks Jesus, "You are not greater, are you, than our father Jacob who gave us this well?" (4:12). Her negative question reflects for the perceptive reader the truth that Jesus *is* greater than Jacob, despite her ignorance of this fact. Consequently, we must ask whether here too the negative question raised by some among the crowd does not reflect for the perceptive reader the truth that Jesus is descended from David and was born at Bethlehem, despite the ignorance of those in the crowd about such a past history.

Perhaps the best conclusion is that we have no way of discovering John's ignorance or knowledge of Jesus' Davidic descent and birth at Bethlehem or John's attempt to refute such ideas. All we do know is that in John's christology such historical details[446] would not have had much theological importance. Our chief reason for going into the intricacies of this question is the conclusion of some scholars from 7:42 that John knew that Jesus was born at Bethlehem and hence that Jesus was virginally conceived.[447] Their methodology is doubly faulty. First, there are several ways to interpret 7:42 and only one of them favors knowledge of birth at Bethlehem.[448] Second, birth at Bethlehem has no necessary connection with the virginal conception of Jesus. It is true that both ideas appear in the Matthean and Lucan infancy narratives—but not in the same part of the narratives. In both Gospels birth at Bethlehem occurs in chap. 2 (never being mentioned in chap. 1), and in neither Gospel is there a necessary

---

[446]Of course these were not simply historical details for the NT authors who mention them; often they had christological significance.

[447]See the chain of affirmations in McHugh, *Mother*, 273: John presupposes that the reader knows that Jesus was born in Bethlehem (for the irony is evident); the readers could only have learned of this from Matthew and Luke; those infancy narratives contain the story of the virginal conception. He concludes: "If this passage in Jn 7 is considered along with Jn 1:13, it is surely not improbable that John's readers, who are presumed to have known of the birth in Bethlehem, are presumed to have heard also of Jesus' virginal conception." In our judgment McHugh is combining the unprovable and the unlikely, and this yields no probability at all.

[448]See Stendahl, "Quis et Unde," 97-98.

reference to virginal conception in chap. 2 (above, p. 144.) The
two ideas have separate histories and knowledge of one need not
presuppose knowledge of the other.

7. "Born of Fornication" (8:41)

In the bitter debate with Jews who believed in Jesus which
begins in 8:31,[449] the question of their status as Abraham's children is quickly raised (8:33, 37, 39). This question comes to a
head in the dialogue of 8:40-41, as Jesus challenges his opponents:

> [40]"Now you seek to kill me, a man who has told you the truth which
> I heard from God. This is not what Abraham did. [41]You are doing
> what your father did." They said to him, "We were not born of
> fornication. We have one father, God himself."

It is not totally clear whether, in telling these "Jews" that they
were doing what their father did by seeking to kill him, Jesus is
already hinting that the devil is their father, a murderer from the
beginning (see 8:44). In any case his words are looked upon by
"the Jews" as a challenge to their religious legitimacy, and they
respond vigorously.

How are we to understand the claim, "We were not born of
fornication"? Is it simply an affirmation of the legitimacy of "the
Jews who believed in him" as children of Abraham and/or children of God? Or does the presence of the Greek personal pronoun
(first person plural: *hēmeis*, "we") also have the tone of a contrast: "*We* are not the ones who were born of fornication" (as you
are or are reported to have been). Indeed, John 8:41 is one of the

---

[449]It is difficult to be certain who are in mind on the Gospel-level of
meaning and in the evangelist's own view of Christianity. It may be
Jewish Christians within the synagogue who, in John's mind, are not
really different from "the Jews" who do not believe in Jesus. See B.
Schein, *Our Father Abraham* (Yale Univ. Dissertation; Ann Arbor, MI:
microfilm, 1972). In any case, they are soon referred to simply as "Jews"
(8:48) and are described as seeking to stone Jesus (8:59). In that case, the
debate of these opponents with the Johannine Christians would more
likely concern monotheism vs. ditheism (Jesus the pre-existent is equivalent to a second God) than the question of the legitimacy of Jesus' conception in Mary's womb.

NT passages cited as evidence for a Jewish charge that Jesus' birth was illegitimate.[450] As such the verse has been invoked in reference to the virginal conception, for Matt 1:18-20 associates a suspicion about how Mary became pregnant with the angel's answer that it was through the Holy Spirit.

We would make two comments. First, any suggestion of illegitimacy in 8:41 would be extremely subtle, especially since previously (6:41) John has had "the Jews" say that Jesus is the son of Joseph and that they know his father and mother.[451] Could a reader, who had already read such a reference to Jesus' parents, be expected to catch simply through an emphatic *"we"* a totally different charge by opponents that Jesus was illegitimate? Second, even if one grants a slight possibility to a hint of a charge of illegitimacy in 8:41, it would be an extraordinary leap from that to a Johannine affirmation of the virginal conception. The more logical conclusion would be that by hinting at illegitimacy Jesus' opponents were rejecting his references to God as Father; for his divine origins are the subject of the debate which continues through the rest of the chapter. Not his human parentage but his divine parentage would be under attack.

Since this is the last of the texts we shall be considering in the public ministry of Jesus, we might note by way of summary that we have found implausible the tenuous references to the virginal conception which various investigators would find in 1:13; 6:42; 7:42; and 8:41.[452] This means that in the first half of the Gospel the only real attention given to Mary involves the appearance of the mother of Jesus in the Cana scene and the transitional verse which follows it (2:1-12) and the reference to the father and mother of Jesus in 6:42. John is quite unlike Matthew and, *a fortiori*, unlike Luke in speculation about Mary's role in the conception and birth of Jesus, where she is associated with christology from the beginning. John is closest to Mark in having only

---

[450] For other passages, see Brown, *Birth*, 534-42.

[451] If 8:41 contains pre-Gospel tradition, this argument based on the Johannine context would not be applicable on that hypothetical earlier level.

[452] As noted above, one of our group agreed with Hoskyns' evaluation of 1:13 as reflecting knowledge of the virgin birth.

one appearance of Mary and then a subsequent dialogue where others refer to her as a parent of Jesus. John may present her intervention at Cana somewhat more positively than Mark presents her intervention at Capernaum (Mark 3:21, 31-35), but both Gospels show Jesus rejecting any peculiar claim that she might have on him because of her status as his physical mother. Yet John is quite unlike Mark in bringing the mother of Jesus back in a positive setting at the end of the Gospel—a scene to which we now turn.

B. The Mother at the Foot of the Cross (19:25-27)

The fact that there is one clear Marian passage in the last half of the Gospel is significant, for this is the section of John which deals with Jesus' "own" in "the hour" in which he was departing from this world to the Father. There is less here by way of controversy with opponents (whether synagogue Jews or inadequate Christians) and more by way of instruction and care for those whom Jesus would consider his disciples. To introduce the mother of Jesus into this atmosphere is to bring her into the context of discipleship.

The Johannine account of the crucifixion (19:16-42) consists of a series of short episodes with symbolic theological importance. Almost precisely in the middle of the account[453] there occurs a scene picturing Mary at the foot of the cross of Jesus. It is preceded (19:23-24) by the story of how four soldiers divided among themselves Jesus' clothes and cast lots for his seamless tunic. It is followed by the offering of wine to slake Jesus' thirst and Jesus' death statement: "It is completed."

> [25]*Meanwhile, standing by the cross of Jesus were his mother, and his mother's sister, Mary the wife of Clopas, and Mary Magdalene.* [26]*When Jesus saw his mother with the disciple whom he loved, he said to his mother, "Woman, behold your son!"* [27]*Then he said to the disciple, "Behold your mother!" And from that hour the disciple took her to his own.*

---

[453]For a discussion of the structure of this account in John, including the possibility that there are seven episodes in chiastic arrangement (with the Mary episode as the fourth), see Brown, *Gospel*, 2. 910-12.

As with the Cana scene we must raise the question of possible pre-Gospel tradition before we concentrate on the meaning intended by the evangelist.

THE PRE-GOSPEL TRADITION. In discussing the women at the crucifixion as listed in Mark 15:40 (above, Chap. 4C), we made some observations that may summarily be called to mind here. We agreed that most probably John refers to four women.[454] We agreed that, leaving aside for the moment the mother of Jesus, John 19:15 names three women who may be compared to the three named women[455] of Mark 15:40 and Matt 27:56 with the following results: Mary Magdalene is clearly the same in the three lists; possibly John's "Mary the wife of Clopas" may be the same as the Marcan/Matthean "Mary the mother of James (the younger) and Joses/Joseph"; but it would be a sheer guess to identify John's "his mother's sister" with Mark's "Salome" and Matthew's "mother of the sons of Zebedee." The very differences make it unlikely that John borrowed the names of the three women from Mark and Matthew;[456] yet the presence of three named women (besides the mother of Jesus) in John as well as in the Synoptics makes it possible that a tradition of three women was fixed early in Christian tradition.

These observations cause a problem in analyzing the present form of the Johannine list in 19:25. If the verse is scarcely a total creation of the evangelist's imagination, what combination of pre-Gospel tradition and evangelist's creativity gave us the present form? Did the evangelist find a tradition that mentioned three

---

[454]See above, Chap. 4, n. 128; also Brown, *Gospel*, 2. 904-6. The four women may be meant as a contrast with the four soldiers who also are present at the cross.

[455]To be precise, both Mark and Matthew speak of many women "among whom" three are named. Luke 23:49 gives no names but speaks of the women who had followed Jesus from Galilee; yet it is likely that Luke 24:10 is referring to these same women when at the tomb he mentions "Mary Magdalene, and Joanna, and Mary the mother of James and the other women with them."

[456]Nor is John directly dependent on the tradition of names gained by combining Luke 23:49 and 24:10 despite the fact that John 19:25 and Luke 23:49 share the Greek verbal form *heistēkeisan*, "they were standing."

women to which he added Jesus' mother in order to prepare for
the scene in 19:26-27 which would focus on her? Or was Mary
(i.e., the mother of Jesus) already part of the pre-Gospel tradition?[457] The three Synoptic Gospels (Mark 15:40; Matt 27:55-56;
Luke 23:49) mention the presence of the women only after they
describe the death of Jesus. Is John's situating the scene while
Jesus is alive an original datum from the pre-Gospel tradition, or
has the evangelist moved a post-mortem scene to its present loca-
tion to serve as an introduction to 19:26-27?[458] Finally, the three
Synoptists place the women at a distance, all using the same
Greek expression *apo makrothen*. Was that setting also in the
Johannine tradition and did the evangelist replace it with *para tō
staurō* ("by the cross")?[459] These questions are virtually impossible to answer with surety, but many of the scholarly suggestions
about what was in the pre-Gospel tradition and what the
evangelist added would mean that the evangelist heightened the
dramatic importance of the scene and gave Mary a greater role.

Thus far we have been discussing the role of the women in
the hypothetical tradition underlying 19:25. In the two verses
which follow only one of those women is mentioned, the mother
of Jesus; and she is associated with the beloved disciple. Very
few scholars would posit a pre-Gospel written tradition behind
19:26-27; for the role of the beloved disciple is so peculiar to the
Fourth Gospel that virtually all source analyses attribute to the
evangelist the scenes in which he appears.[460]

Here it is not inappropriate to press beyond the pre-Gospel

---

[457]Bultmann, *Gospel*, 672 offers still another possibility: "No answer can be given to the question whether the enumeration of the four
women is cited from the source, or whether the Evangelist has replaced
one of the four names in the tradition by the Mother of Jesus."

[458]Bultmann, Fortna, and Dauer all opt for the original post-mortem
position in the Johannine source.

[459]Bultmann, *Gospel*, 671 suggests that he has done this, but Fortna,
Gospel, 130, n. 1, thinks that *in the source* the women already stood by
the cross.

[460]There are distinct Johannine stylistic features in 19:26-27, e.g.,
Jesus' addressing his mother as "Woman"; the "Behold" formula (see
below, n. 470). If one attributes chap. 21 to a redactor, the beloved
disciple would also appear in his work; and the parenthetical 19:35 has
also frequently been attributed to the redactor.

source and ask a question of historicity. John alone posits the presence of the mother of Jesus and the beloved disciple at the cross. Is this historical information? Even if neither appeared in the Johannine pre-Gospel tradition, that would not preclude historicity;[461] for one could suppose that the evangelist (who was not the beloved disciple) supplemented the pre-Gospel written material by information about the beloved disciple, perhaps information so well known in the community that hitherto there was no need to put it into writing. Objections against historicity include: (a) No mention of Mary, the mother of Jesus, in Jerusalem during the passion in any other NT work.[462] (b) The stress in Mark 14:50; Matt 26:56; and John 16:32 that the male disciples of Jesus had fled or been scattered—a stress that leaves little room for the continued presence of one believing disciple. (c) The fact that in other scenes involving the beloved disciple his presence seems to be in conflict with the Synoptic picture.[463] (d) The presence of the

---

[461]Nor would the presence of either figure in the pre-Gospel tradition insure historicity. All hypothetical pre-Gospel sources are separated in time from the actual career of Jesus, and one must discern the historicity of sources even as one must discern the historicity of the Gospels themselves. See above for the discussion of *Stage One* in Gospel formation (Chap. 2, B2a).

[462]In discussing Mark 15:40 and Matt 27:56 we saw the probability that "Mary mother of James and Joses/Joseph" was not Mary the mother of Jesus. Mary the mother of Jesus appears on the scene shortly after the resurrection of Jesus in Acts 1:14; yet that very Lucan reference makes it unlikely that Luke would have failed to mention Mary at the crucifixion and burial if he knew a tradition that she was there.

[463]For instance, Schnackenburg, "Origin," 240, discusses the Synoptic and Johannine accounts of the Last Supper: "Considered from the historical view, he [the beloved disciple] was certainly not present there (cf. Mk 14:17 parr.)." As for 20:2-10, while John has the beloved disciple accompany Peter to the tomb, Luke 24:12 mentions only Peter (yet see Luke 24:24: "*Some* of those who were with us went to the tomb"). Of course, disagreement between John and the Synoptics is not to be solved on some overall principle that the Synoptic Gospels are more historical. Moreover, a problem is raised if we discount the historicity of all the Johannine appearances of the beloved disciple—he is the human witness par excellence for the Johannine community (19:35; 21:24), and how do we explain this emphasis if the evangelist knew that the beloved disciple really was not present at any of the events he is supposed to have witnessed?

women at the foot of the cross instead of at a distance (as in the Synoptic Gospels) serves Johannine theological convenience.[464] Once again there is no way of deciding the issue with certainty. Paradoxically, if the scene is not historical and the presence of the mother of Jesus and the beloved disciple reflects Johannine theological inventiveness, that may enhance the importance of Mary for the Johannine community—the evangelist would scarcely have created a central crucifixion scene if it did not have significance.

THE GOSPEL-LEVEL INTERPRETATION. Let us now turn to the meaning that the evangelist gave to the scene no matter what its pre-Gospel or historical origins. The first question we must ask concerns the relative importance of the beloved disciple and the mother of Jesus in 19:26-27. Although this is often numbered among "beloved disciple scenes," a reading of these verses on their own merits would incline us to judge that neither figure is clearly more important than the other. While the scene ends with a statement concerning the future care of the mother, rather than of the beloved disciple, the logic of the scene requires this. To make the account plausible, the dying Jesus should be presented as more concerned about the care of his mother than about a male disciple who would be able to care for himself. However, this should not lead us to conclude that the evangelist's *primary* interest is biographical, i.e., to report simply that after Jesus died his mother went to live in the home of a favorite disciple.[465] To inter-

---

[464]Yet, as we pointed out in Chap. 4, n. 127, the *apo makrothen* of the Synoptic Gospels may be just as theological, as an echo of the Psalms.

[465]This simplistic approach has been responsible for much Marian legend, e.g., that when the beloved disciple, identified as John the son of Zebedee, went to live at Ephesus (a domicile determined in part by the attribution of the Book of Revelation to John the son of Zebedee; see Rev 1:1; 2:1), Mary went along—hence the Christian tradition of the house of Mary in the Ephesus region (Panaya Kapulu), commemorated by a church on the site. Supposedly, either in Palestine or at Ephesus, Luke (while traveling with Paul) is presumed to have met Mary or John or both and received from her, from him, or from them the story of Jesus' conception and birth narrated in Luke 1-2. Many similarities between the Lucan and Johannine Gospel have been explained by this supposed

pret John thus would be to misinterpret the way the evangelist
uses symbols, as well as the significance he attributes to the beloved disciple. Moreover, all the other Johannine crucifixion
episodes have clear symbolic and theological significance, and by
analogy that should be true of 19:25-27 as well.

Before we discuss the symbolic value of the mother of Jesus
in this scene, we should comment briefly on the beloved disciple,
a mysterious figure who has been the subject of an immense
literature.[466] We accept (as we did also in *Peter in the New Testament*) the working hypothesis that the beloved disciple was a
real person, even if now no longer identifiable, who was thought
to have been a companion of Jesus. Whether or not he was the
founder of the Johannine community, he had at least a twofold
significance for that community. First, he is presented as the ideal
or model disciple of Jesus, the object of Jesus' special love. He
never deserted Jesus and was particularly attuned to him, so that
after the resurrection he came to believe more quickly than anyone else (20:8; 21:7). The peculiar privileges of the beloved disciple are described most frequently through contrast with Peter, the
spokesman of the Twelve (6:67-68).[467] Second, he is the witness
par excellence (19:35; 21:24), guaranteeing the validity of the
Johannine community's understanding of Jesus and thus giving it
a status that is in no way inferior to that of other churches who

---

encounter. The scene has also been used to prove that Mary had no other
children besides Jesus, or else she would have been left in the care of her
sons, Jesus' brothers. This argument ignores the fact that in John 7:1-10
Jesus' brothers are described as hostile non-believers.

[466]For details, theories, and bibliography, see Brown, *Gospel*, 1.
XCII-XCVIII, CIV.

[467]Many scholars today argue that the beloved disciple was not one
of the Twelve. It is significant that both Schnackenburg and Brown who
originally identified the beloved disciple (but not the evangelist) as John
the son of Zebedee have changed their minds and agree that most plausibly he was not a member of the Twelve who (especially in the person of
Peter) are contrasted to him. See Schnackenburg, "On the Origin," 239:
"In the beloved disciple we have to do with the authority behind the
Johannine circle, a historical personage, a disciple of the Lord, who,
however, was not one of the Twelve." Similarly, Brown, *Int* 31 (1977),
386-88. For the relation of the beloved disciple to Peter, see *Peter in the
New Testament*, 133-47.

claimed Peter or the Twelve as founders or foundation stones.

Granted all this, what does it mean when Jesus says to his mother in reference to the beloved disciple, "Woman, behold your son!" Initially, it is significant that the scene brings together two figures for whom John never gives us personal names. That may mean that the significance of both figures lay in their respective roles.[468] Nevertheless, the mother's primary role would not be her physical motherhood, since here, in a scene more benevolent than Cana, Jesus once more calls her "Woman," the title which we saw that he uses for all women. Her motherly role is rather in relation to the beloved disciple and hence not a physical one. Since it is a role that she receives only as Jesus dies and goes to his Father—a role received in "the hour" of Jesus (13:1)—it is a role that does not pertain to the earthly ministry of Jesus but to subsequent Christian history, the era of the community after Jesus' glorification. It has often been remarked that for John the elevation of Jesus on the cross is already part of his return to his Father and that Pentecost is anticipated on the cross in symbolic references to the Spirit.[469] Accordingly the crucified Jesus does not die alone but leaves behind him at the foot of the cross a small community of believing disciples—the kind of community that in other NT works is called into being in the post-resurrectional or pentecostal period. This may be the reason why after the scene involving Jesus' mother and the beloved disciple, John says that Jesus knew that all was now completed (telein in 19:28)—the completion of his work involves the bringing into existence of the Christian community.

In light of this thought pattern, it has been suggested that the

---

[468]See above, n. 405. The Johannine community surely knew the personal name of the mother of Jesus, just as they probably knew the personal name of the beloved disciple. We may remember that the Qumran community never mentions the name of the figure whom they honor as the Righteous Teacher (the possible founder and the great teacher of the group), although again they surely knew his identity.

[469]Possible references are in John 19:30: "He bowed his head and handed over his spirit"; and in 19:34: "At once there came out [from Jesus' pierced side] blood and water" (when that is interpreted in light of 7:38-39: "From within him shall flow rivers of living water. Now this he said about the Spirit which those who believed in him were to receive").

new mother-son relationship proclaimed by Jesus[470] in John 19:26-27 reflects the replacement of his natural family by a new family of disciples, the eschatological family we spoke of in reference to Mark 3:31-35. We saw that in Mark's view the physical family members were not among those whom Jesus pointed to as his eschatological family of disciples, i.e., those of whom he says, "Behold my mother and my brothers!" Luke 8:19-21, however, changed the import of the scene by including the physical family in the family of disciples: "My mother and my brothers are those who hear the word of God and do it." In the same direction as Luke, John also seems to modify the Marcan view, whether or not he knew the Marcan scene. The rebuff of Jesus' mother at Cana and the careful distinction between the mother/brothers and his disciples in John 2:12 are in harmony with the Marcan theme; but at the foot of the cross Jesus gives his physical mother a spiritual role as mother of the disciple par excellence, and the disciple a role as her son. Thus there emerges a familial relationship in terms of discipleship. Jesus' physical mother, just as in Luke, meets the criterion of the eschatological family; but his physical brothers do not (7:1-10—and here John disagrees with Luke). They are replaced by the beloved disciple, no natural relative, but someone especially loved. This interpretation is not without its difficulties. There is no mention of "brother" in 19:26-27,[471] and so brotherhood is only a logical deduction from

---

[470]There is no agreement among scholars on the exact import of the formula "Behold your son . . . Behold your mother." Barrett, *Gospel*, 459 and Dauer, "Das Wort," 81 interpret it as an adoption-formula. But the adoption-formulas we find in Scripture generally have a "you are" pattern, e.g., Ps 2:7, "You are my son; today I have begotten you" (also 1 Sam 18:21; Tobit 7:12); and there is no precise parallel where the mother is addressed first. Another possibility is to find in John's formula an example of a revelation pattern isolated by M. de Goedt, *NTS* 8 (1961-62), 142-50, namely, when a messenger of God says about a person whom he sees, "Behold [*ide*]," he follows this by a description penetrating the mystery of the person's mission. Examples in John are 1:29,36, "Behold the Lamb of God"; and 1:47, "Behold, one who is truly an Israelite."

[471]This makes dubious Dauer's contention that the main purpose of the scene is to emphasize the importance of the beloved disciple as seen in the fact that Jesus raised him to the rank of his own brother.

the mother of Jesus having a new son. Moreover, the idea that Mary was to have a continuing role in terms of discipleship does not do full justice to John's statement, "And from that hour the disciple took her to his own."[472] Nevertheless, the discipleship interpretation of the scene may well be more plausible than some of the others we shall now mention (symbolisms that need not contradict the primary symbolism based on the family of discipleship, but which may be secondary or supplementary).

* * *

As the first of what we are considering as suggestions for supplementary symbolism, we turn to an interpretation that Bultmann[473] has made famous: "The mother of Jesus, who tarries by the cross, represents Jewish Christianity that overcomes the offense of the cross. The beloved disciple represents Gentile Christianity, which is charged to honor the former as its mother from whom it has come, even as Jewish Christianity is charged to recognize itself 'at home' within Gentile Christianity." Attractive as this is, it faces almost insurmountable difficulties. Scholars increasingly agree that Johannine Christianity is not in its origins a Gentile Christianity but a Jewish Christianity.[474] Thus there is little to recommend Bultmann's thesis that the beloved disciple represents Gentile Christianity, and that weakness calls in doubt

---

[472]This formula should not be taken too literally. It need not mean "from that very moment," as if the beloved disciple left Calvary immediately before Jesus died. (He seems to be present after Jesus' death in 19:35.) It can mean "from the general time," or even from "the hour" of Jesus' glorification. The "to his own" probably means "to his own home" as in Esther 5:10; 3 Macc 6:27; Acts 21:6. Once again, however, we need not be too literal in thinking that the beloved disciple had a house in Jerusalem where he could take Mary. The phrase has a connotation of care.

[473]Bultmann, *Gospel*, 673.

[474]See J. L. Martyn, in *L'Évangile de Jean: Sources, rédaction, théologie* (ed. M. de Jonge; BETL 44; Gembloux: Duculot, 1977), 149-75—reprinted in *The Gospel of John in Christian History* (New York: Paulist, 1979); G. Richter as summarized by A. J. Mattill, *TS* 38 (1977), 294-315; R. E. Brown, *Int* 31 (1977), 379-93.

his thesis that the mother of Jesus represents Jewish Christianity. Perhaps something could be salvaged if we postulated that the mother represents Israel and that John is telling us that what was truly valid in Israel has come over to Christianity and found a home there, as opposed to the synagogue of "the Jews."[475] Alternatively, John may be claiming that what was most authentic in the family background of Jesus has come over to Johannine Christianity, not to the Christianity represented by the brothers of Jesus (especially James?) who never believed in him. This significance would have been facilitated if Mary's career as a Christian was lived out in the kind of Christianity that John appreciated, rather than in the Christianity associated with Jerusalem and James.[476] But such a theory is little more than a guess.

The symbolism just discussed tries to cope with the emphasis in the last line of 19:25-27: "From that hour the beloved disciple took her to his own," i.e., an emphasis on the sheltering or care of the mother by the disciple-son. Another metaphorical interpretation shifts the emphasis to what is not mentioned in John: the care of the mother for the son. In later church writing and continuing into modern Roman Catholicism this scene has been invoked as a basis for the spiritual motherhood of Mary or for the picture of Mary as the mother of Christians.[477] At Cana Mary was denied a salvific role in the ministry; but now in the hour of Jesus' glorification she is given her place in salvation history. This interpretation faces the added difficulty that it requires the mother of Jesus

---

[475]So R. H. Strachan, *Fourth Gospel*, 319. John seems to use the term "Israel" favorably (1:31, 50; 3:10; 12:13) even as he generally uses "the Jews" unfavorably. He speaks of Nathanael as one who is truly an Israelite (1:47).

[476]See above, n. 443. The emphasis that Mary's role does not depend on her physical motherhood may be part of a Johannine polemic against importance given to the brothers who claimed physical relationship to Jesus. (For the precise physical relationship of these "brothers" to Jesus and to Mary, see the discussion of the brothers and sisters in Chap. 4, B2.)

[477]See, for instance, D. Unger, "The Meaning of John 19,26-27 in the Light of Papal Documents," *Marianum* 21 (1959), 186-221. Today, Roman Catholics would make a greater distinction between the church teaching on this question and the teaching of Scripture. They may accept the spiritual motherhood of Mary without claiming that it is taught by the Scriptures.

in 19:25-27 to be treated as an individual (Mary) while the beloved disciple is treated as a general symbol of every Christian. An ordinary symbolic pattern would treat both as individuals or both as general. A better variant of this approach (and one with much older attestation, beginning with Origen) is to treat the mother of Jesus as a general symbol for the church, so that Jesus is leaving the church to the Christians as their mother.[478] While this interpretation does some justice to "Behold your son . . . Behold your mother," one is still left with the problem of why the last line stresses the care of the Christians for the church rather than vice versa.

A synthesis of the best points proposed in these various symbolisms may be fashioned as follows. We know that early Christians read some of the prophetic passages pertaining to the birth of a Davidic king (e.g., Isa 7:14) as a reference to the birth or advent of Jesus. There are other OT passages[479] in which Israel or Zion is a woman whose childbirth brings forth a new people (Isa 49:20-22; 54:1; 66:7-8). Now John was not interested in the mother of Jesus as the mother of the messiah king with a natural claim on him, since the Johannine Jesus is the messianic Son of God not because of his earthly birth from Mary but because of his heavenly pre-existence with the father. This would mean that the evangelist would not be interested in the symbolic possibilities of Mary as Israel giving birth *to Jesus*; yet he might be interested in the symbolism of Israel giving birth *to the Christian community*[480] through discipleship and acceptance of Jesus. If the beloved disciple was the special model for the Johannine Christians and they were of Jewish Christian origin, then John would see Israel as the true mother of (Johannine) Jewish Christianity; and it would be among such Jewish Christians that the genuine heritage

---

[478]The history of this exegesis is well documented by T. Koehler, "Les principales interprétations traditionnelles de Jn. 19,25-27 pendant les douzes premiers siècles," *Études mariales* 16 (1959), 119-55. See below, Chap. 9, p. 281.

[479]See A. Kerrigan, "Jn 19, 25-27 in the Light of Johannine Theology and the Old Testament," *Antonianum* 35 (1960), 396-416. Some of Kerrigan's method would border on the allegorical, but the article covers in detail passages that enter various discussions of Johannine symbolism.

[480]Frequently brought into the picture to complement John 19:25-27 is John 16:17-22 where Jesus, speaking to his disciples, compares his

of Israel would find a home. As a support for this symbolism, Rev 12:1-5, 17 has been invoked. There a "Woman" in the apparel of the sun, moon, and twelve stars (similar to the symbolism in Gen 37:9 for Jacob/Israel and the twelve sons who founded the tribes of Israel) gives birth to a messianic child; she then survives the snatching off of that child "to God and to His throne" and continues life on earth with her offspring (seed) consisting of Christian disciples ("those who keep the commandments of God and bear testimony to Jesus"). Revelation 12, then, seems to employ the symbolism of a woman described like Israel who is the mother of the messiah and the mother of Christian disciples (see below, Chap. 8, B4).

Related to this is the possibility of Mary/Eve symbolism in John 19:25-27 as already mentioned when we discussed the Cana scene,[481] especially since the woman in Revelation 12 is in conflict with a dragon who in 12:9 is specifically identified with the ancient serpent of the Genesis story. According to Gen 3:15 there would be enmity between the serpent and the "woman," between the serpent's seed (offspring) and the woman's seed (offspring). If the mother of Jesus whom he addresses as "Woman" has an Eve symbolism, this would be the moment when she would become a mother with seed (offspring), the Christian disciple; and then in the language of Rev 12:17 there would be war between the dragon/serpent on the one side and the woman and her offspring on the other.

* * *

One cannot prove any of these symbolic suggestions; possibility is the *most* that one can accord to them. The majority of the

---

departure in death and his return after the resurrection to a "woman" who has sorrow while she is in birth pangs but rejoices once the child is born. See above, n. 426.

[481] The scenes at Cana and at the foot of the cross are the only two appearances of the mother of Jesus in John; in both she is addressed as "Woman"; at Cana the hour has not yet come, while at the cross the hour has come (13:1). For a discussion of F.-M. Braun's attempt to relate the two scenes through the Eve motif, see McHugh, *Mother*, 361-87.

task force was willing to settle for a primary symbolism in 19:25-27 based on a new eschatological family relationship to Jesus stemming from discipleship, without any clear commitment toward a secondary symbolism for the mother of Jesus as Israel, or Zion, or the New Eve.[482] The invocation of Revelation 12 (to be discussed in the next chapter) caused uneasiness for many in our group because the meaning of that chapter and its relation to Mary are far from clear. Even if they were clear, one could not be sure that the audience of the Fourth Gospel would have been familiar with Revelation, a work that has a disputed relationship to Johannine thought.[483] Yet we recognized that some major scholars do see in 19:25-27 one or other of these supplementary symbolisms, and also that it is very difficult to be certain of the limits of Johannine symbolism. In the early post-NT period a great deal of symbolism did attach itself to Mary, including some of the symbols we have discussed, e.g., the church, or Eve. Whether or not these were explicitly in the mind of the Fourth Evangelist, his own symbolic treatment of Mary is the beginning of a process that will continue.[484]

---

[482]It has been mentioned that one of our members thinks the evangelist may have intended such a secondary symbolism. Another member supported the symbolic interpretation of Mary/Israel/Eve on the canonical level, i.e., not as explicitly intended by the evangelist, but as a potentiality realized when John was joined in the NT to Luke 1 and Revelation 12. See above, pp. 30-31.

[483]See below, Chap. 8, nn. 515, 519.

[484]For the sake of completeness it may be mentioned that in some later traditions Mary the mother of Jesus was thought to have been present during the visit to the tomb described in John 20:1-18. The correct Greek text of John 20:1 speaks of "Mary Magdalene," but the Sinaiticus Old Syriac version omits "Magdalene" in 20:1 and 18, and speaks simply of "Mary." From the time of Tatian's *Diatessaron* (2d century) some Church Fathers, especially those writing in Syriac, identified this Mary as the mother of Jesus, e.g., Ephraem, *On the Diatessaron*, 21.27; CSCO 145 (Armenian 2), 235-36. Loisy thought that this interpretation might be original, but it has no following today. Its importance in antiquity was as part of a larger tradition that the risen Jesus appeared first to his mother—a tradition with no biblical foundation whatsoever.

CHAPTER EIGHT:
THE WOMAN
IN REVELATION 12*

The term "revelation" in the title of this book translates the Greek word *apokalypsis* (whence the other English title "Apocalypse"), meaning "unveiling"; and from that word has come the designation of a whole genre of biblical literature.[485] Before we begin our discussion of the passage in Revelation that may refer to Mary, it is important that we set the book in the general context of other works of the same nature, and also that we review the very different interpretations that have been offered for the book as a whole. A review of these points will help to explain our cautiousness about any proposal definitively interpreting Revelation 12.

A. General Remarks on Apocalyptic and Revelation

1. The Genre Called "Apocalyptic"

Several biblical books more or less resemble aspects of Revelation, e.g., Isaiah 24-27, 34-35 and Daniel, as do also some non-

---

*The discussion for this chapter was led by J. A. Fitzmyer, and the first draft was composed by R. H. Fuller. One half-session of the task force (Nov. 1976) was devoted to the material in Revelation 12.

[485] A genre covers a group of writings, marked by distinctive recurring characteristics, which constitute a recognizable and coherent type of literature. See J. J. Collins, "Apocalypse," 359.

canonical works (*1 Enoch, 2 Baruch, 4 Ezra*)—a body of literature that belongs to the last centuries before Christ and the first
centuries of the Christian era. Among the literary features prominent in these works, we may list two. *First*, there is usually a
setting where a seer receives a revelation through a dream, a
vision, or angelic guidance. This revelation generally involves a
transcendent reality, e.g., what is happening in heaven or in various heavens, along with what will happen in the future or at the
end of times. Often the seer will see simultaneously events both in
heaven and on earth, both present and future; and there will be a
correspondence between the two sets of events, so that the narrative may move back and forth from one to the other in bewilder-
ing fashion. *Second*, characteristically there is an exuberant use
of symbolic images (women, animals, monsters, trumpets, ves-
sels) and numbers (four, seven, twelve, etc.). The same set of
events or characters may be described over again or recapitulated
under a succession of different images. This warns us against
assuming logical sequences from one scene to another and too
quickly assigning unique significance when we turn to the symbolism of Revelation 12.

Also there are often common patterns of thought in
apocalyptic. The general atmosphere of apocalyptic is, for instance, one of hard times and persecution, and so apocalyptic
revelation tends to center on a deliverance by God that is soon to
come. The element of persecution presupposes a world divided
dualistically under forces of good and evil, with the evil forces
receiving help from otherworldly diabolic figures. Hope is gained
from a determinism wherein God is thought to have laid out the
whole course of history in a fixed pattern (often numerically
fixed, and already written down in a book). At the end of that
predetermined pattern is the terminus of history, the final de-
struction of the evil forces, and the eternal reward of the good.

Although the distinctive literary features and the distinctive
patterns of thought generally go together, scholars are divided as
to which element is more important in diagnosing the presence of
"apocalyptic," with a resultant lack of agreement about whether
this designation can be applied to literature that has one element
without the other. There is also disagreement about whether

apocalyptic has a closer relationship to and descent from the prophetic books of the Bible[486] or the wisdom literature.[487] Indeed, some would detect a strong influence upon apocalyptic from outside Israel, e.g., from Persian determinism, dualism, and demonology, from Babylonian astrology, and from Greek mythology. Tied in with this question is a debate about whether some works of the fifth century B.C. (Ezekiel, Zechariah) may be designated "apocalyptic," or at least "proto-apocalyptic." Many of these debates[488] will not affect our discussion of Revelation 12, although they alert us to the danger of studying that chapter in isolation from other and even earlier forms of apocalyptic.

2. *Various Interpretations of the Book of Revelation*

Besides the general complexities of apocalyptic literature, we must deal with the obscurity of the whole Book of Revelation, an obscurity so pronounced that it has led to totally different interpretations of the book throughout Christian history. A brief survey[489] may be informative to the reader. (1) The oldest attested interpretation, found in patristic writers of the second century (Justin Martyr, Irenaeus, et al.) is chiliastic or millenarian, the key to which is the hope of the glorious thousand-year reign of Christ on earth (Rev 20:1-6). (2) Later, in the fourth century (e.g., Victorinus of Pettau), the recapitulative interpretation emerged. This interpretation saw similar visions (seven seals, seven trumpets, seven bowls) not as a sequence of events in a progressive course of history, but as repeated descriptions of the same events

---

[486]Like the apocalyptic seer, the prophet has been introduced to the mysteries of the heavenly court. However, unlike apocalyptic literature, prophetic literature is often written as a corrective in good times ("good" from the secular or naturalistic viewpoint) rather than in times of persecution; and generally the prophet sees punishment and reward in the context of continuing history rather than outside history.

[487]Some of the features of apocalyptic (numerical patterns, catalogues of known things) occur in the wisdom tradition.

[488]See the discussion of these points in Hanson, *Dawn*, 1-31.

[489]The main interpretations are mentioned but there is no attempt to be exhaustive. See further Goppelt, *Theologie,* 2. 511-14; Feuillet, *Apocalypse*, 11-21.

under different images. The recapitulative interpretation lasted
into the early Middle Ages, and elements of it still appear in
modern commentaries.[490] (3) At the end of the twelfth century,
especially with Joachim of Flora, Revelation was interpreted as a
description of seven periods of the history of the church in the
world, e.g., the first three chapters referred to the struggle of the
apostles against the Jews; chaps. 4-7 referred to the struggle of
the martyrs against the Romans; and chaps. 15-17 referred to
Joachim's own time, while the last chapters of the book referred
to the future.[491] This mode of interpretation has been steadily
revised over the centuries, and is still popular in some Christian
circles today. (4) As a product of the Reformation, Protestant
theologians tended to identify the Roman Church with the woman
and the beast of Rev 17:9, continuing some strands of medieval
anti-papal exegesis. (5) During the sixteenth (e.g., F. Ribeira) and
seventeenth centuries and in part as a Roman Catholic reaction,
the whole Book of Revelation was interpreted eschatologically,
i.e., as a prediction of the end of the world and of the signs that
would precede it. Elements of this interpretation still persist in
many commentaries. (6) In the eighteenth century, with the advent of biblical criticism, there emerged an interpretation of Revelation in terms of the contemporary history of the man who wrote
it. His visions were thought to refer to the first-century persecution of Christians by Jews or Romans or both. This mode of
interpretation, which has come to dominate today, is often combined with the view that Revelation offers insights of permanent
value for Christians, especially in times of persecution. (7) Toward the end of the nineteenth century (Gunkel, Bousset) there
emerged an interpretation of Revelation that was heavily dependent on the comparative study of religions, wherein the origin of
the various images in Revelation was sought in the folklore, myth,
or astrology of other peoples. Certain elements of this mode of
interpretation are accepted as background by almost all modern

---

[490]A. Y. Collins, *Combat*, 32-44 argues strongly for recapitulation as
a key to Revelation.

[491]In this interpretation chap. 12 belonged to the struggle of the
religious orders against the Moslems at the time of the crusades.

commentators, but it is scarcely a key to the meaning of the book as a whole.

In general it is the sixth manner of interpretation that will govern our interpretation of Revelation 12: behind the narrative with its imagery and action there lies a reference to something that had happened in the recent first-century history of Israel and Christianity. Most commentators would clearly agree on that general approach; but its relatively late appearance in the hermeneutical history of the book means that the meaning originally intended by its author may have had little influence on interpreters until the eighteenth century. Indeed, it is only now becoming a dominant force in exegesis.

B. The Interpretation of Revelation 12

Before turning to chap. 12 itself, we shall try to set that chapter in the overall outline of the book.

1. Its Place in the Plan of the Book

There is no unanimity among scholars on the plan that the author followed in composing the book; some would even propose that the book consists of two independent apocalypses glued together. Nevertheless, an intelligent case can be made for the thesis that chap. 12 belongs to the second half of the book. If the first three chapters, consisting of the inaugural vision and the seven letters to the seven churches, are considered as an *Introduction*, then many would see chaps. 4-11 as *Part One* of Revelation, and chaps. 12-20 as *Part Two*, followed by a *Conclusion* (21-22).[492] So that the reader may be familiar with what has preceded chap. 12, the contents of chaps. 4-11 (Part One) may be schematized thus:

---

[492]The Conclusion would then structurally match the Introduction in chaps. 1-3. However, in content the Conclusion refers to the Almighty and the Lamb and thus matches the Preface to Part One (chaps. 4-5).

chaps. 4-5:   Preface in heaven involving the Enthroned
and the Lamb, and the Scroll with
Seven Seals.

chaps. 6-11:   The Scroll with Seven Seals.
Six *seals* are opened (chap. 6).
   Interlude (chap. 7).
   Seventh Seal is opened (8:1) and it in-
   volves seven trumpets.
Six *trumpets* are blown (chaps. 8-9).
   Interlude (10:1-11:14).
   Seventh trumpet is blown (rest of chap.
   11), involving the triumph of the king-
   dom of Christ who shall rule forever.

If chap. 12 is seen as the opening of Part Two, how does it
relate to what precedes? It may be intended as part of the Preface
to Part Two, parallel to the Preface (chaps. 4-5) in Part One—a
Preface in heaven and on earth corresponding to the previous
Preface in heaven. It would be followed, then, by a series of
angels in chap. 14 (seven angels, but not counted as such by the
author[493]), by seven bowls in chaps. 15-16, and by a final triumph
of Christ in chaps. 19-20—in other words, by a sequence not
unlike that of Part One. To enhance the parallelism between
chaps. 4-5 and chap. 12, one may note the theory that, just as the
scroll with seven seals marked chap. 5, so chap. 12 should be
understood as the delayed opening of the little scroll first mentioned in 10:8-10.[494]

But even if all of this parallelism has some plausibility, it is
not clear whether Part Two in general and chap. 12 in particular is
recapitulative of what happened in Part One (i.e., the same events
under new imagery), or really presents some new events in historical sequence to the events narrated in Part One. A common
analysis flowing from the *recapitulative* theory of the book is that
the whole of chaps. 4-20 deals with the events of the author's life,
i.e., church life under Roman rule in the reign of Domitian (A.D.

---

[493]In any schema of Revelation it must be recognized that the numerical patterns in Part Two are less precise than in Part One.

[494]See A. Y. Collins, *Combat*, 21-28.

81-96)[495]—events described three times over by the seven seals, the seven trumpets, and the seven bowls. On behalf of the recapitulative theory one may mention the commonness of this feature in apocalyptic, and the similarity of the seven bowls (15-16) to the seven trumpets (8-9). Yet those who argue for a *sequence* involving new events point to the presence in Part Two of the dragon and of the two beasts (chap. 13) representing Rome, as contrasted with their absence from Part One. A common analysis of the sequence is that Part One involves God's past judgment *upon the Jews* who rejected Jesus and persecuted Christians (particularly during the Revolt in the period before A.D. 70), culminating in handing over the Temple court to the Gentiles (11:2); and that Part Two involves God's contemporary and future judgment *upon Rome* and emperor worship, culminating in the end of the world.

The very fact that scholars do not agree on such a fundamental issue as that of recapitulation over against sequence warns us how difficult it is to argue from the context to the meaning of Revelation 12.

2. The Structure of Revelation 12

Let us begin with a translation of the passage:

> [1]*And a great sign appeared in heaven, a woman clothed with the sun, with the moon under her feet, and on her head a crown of twelve stars.* [2]*She was with child; and she cried out in her pangs of*

---

[495]Irenaeus, *Adv. Haer.* 5.30,3, quotes a statement (from Papias?) that "the Revelation was seen not long ago, but almost in our generation, at the end of Domitian's reign." Most commentators follow this dating in the 90s, although from time to time an earlier date in Nero's reign (54-68) is proposed; see J. A. T. Robinson, *Redating*, 221-53. A minor variant of the Domitian dating is that, while the author wrote in that reign, he pretends to be writing earlier, e.g., in Vespasian's reign—a frequent phenomenon in apocalyptic. A key to this thesis is a proposed interpretation of the seven kings of 17:10-11. The five who have fallen are Augustus, Tiberius, Caligula, Claudius, and Nero; the one who is is Vespasian (69-79), the one who is to come but remain only a little while is Titus (79-81), while the eighth who belongs to the seven is Domitian who was *Nero Redivivus.* For a fuller discussion of dating, see Kümmel, *Introduction*, 466-69.

birth, in anguish for delivery. ³And another sign appeared in heaven; behold, a great red dragon, with seven heads and ten horns, and seven diadems upon his heads. ⁴His tail swept down a third of the stars of heaven, and cast them to the earth. And the dragon stood before the woman who was about to bear a child, that he might devour her child when she brought it forth. ⁵She brought forth a male child, one who is to rule over all the nations with a rod of iron, but her child was snatched off to God and to His throne. ⁶And the woman fled into the wilderness, where she has a place prepared by God, in which to be nourished for one thousand two hundred and sixty days.

⁷Now war arose in heaven, Michael and his angels fighting against the dragon; and the dragon and his angels fought, ⁸but they were defeated and there was no longer any place for them in heaven. ⁹And the great dragon was expelled, that ancient serpent, who is called the Devil and Satan, the deceiver of the whole world—he was expelled to earth, and his angels were expelled with him. ¹⁰And I heard a loud voice in heaven saying,

"Now the salvation and the power
and the kingdom of our God
and the authority of his Christ have come,
for the accuser of our brethren has been cast down,
who accuses them day and night before our God.
¹¹And they have conquered him by the blood of the Lamb
and by the word of their testimony,
for they loved not their lives even unto death.
¹²Rejoice then, O heaven
and you that dwell therein!
But woe to you, O earth and sea,
for the devil has come down to you in great wrath,
because he knows that his time is short!"

¹³And when the dragon saw that he had been expelled to earth, he persecuted the woman who had borne the male child. ¹⁴But the woman was given the two wings of the great eagle that she might fly from the serpent into the wilderness, to the place where she is to be nourished for a time, and times, and half a time. ¹⁵The serpent poured water like a river out of his mouth after the woman, in order to sweep her away with the flood. ¹⁶But the earth came to the help of the woman, and the earth opened its mouth and swallowed the river which the dragon had poured from its mouth. ¹⁷Then the dragon was angry with the woman, and went off to make war on the rest of her offspring, on those who keep the commandments of God and bear testimony to Jesus. And he stood on the sand of the sea.

As the paragraphing of the translation hints, there are three discrete sections in the narrative:

Vv. 1-6:   Scene One in heaven, involving the woman, the dragon, and the woman's child.

Vv. 7-12:   Scene Two beginning in heaven but coming down to earth, involving Michael and the dragon.

Vv. 13-17:   Scene Three on earth, involving the dragon, the woman, and her offspring.

The interrelation of the scenes is not easy to discern, and much of the difficulty centers around Scene Two. Since Scene One portrays the birth of the child who is protected from the dragon and snatched off to God, we might have expected this child, when he grew up, to have been the adversary who (in Scene Two) would expel the dragon from heaven. Instead Michael appears suddenly to accomplish the feat. This has led to the common suggestion that two once-separate stories have been melded together, and that Scene Two is an intrusion in a story that once consisted of Scenes One and Three. If one regards vv. 6 and 13a as editorial additions designed to smooth over this intrusion, one can establish a relatively smooth sequence from 1-5 to 13b-17.[496]

Be that as it may, the present narrative involving the three scenes leaves us with a difficulty similar to that of the narrative of the whole Book of Revelation—is there a real sequence of new events from scene to scene, or are we dealing with recapitulation, so that we are hearing the same events recited over again under new imagery? For instance, is Scene Two another version of what happens in Scene One? This might be easier to answer if the localization of the scenes was clearer. Certainly in Scene Three both the dragon and the woman are on earth. In Scene Two we are told how the dragon who began in heaven was expelled to earth, but nowhere are we told how the woman who began in heaven got down to earth. Most interpreters have assumed that she was already on earth in Scene One when she gave birth to the

---

[496] Verse 13b would then read: "The dragon persecuted the woman who had borne the male child."

child.[497] This would mean that Scene One and Scene Two both began in heaven and ended on earth and would raise the possibility of seeing Scene Two as recapitulative of Scene One. Yet one could still argue that while the two scenes are parallel, they are not really recapitulative: Scene One tells how the woman came down from heaven to earth to bear her child; Scene Two tells how the dragon came down from heaven to earth; and Scene Three tells what happened on earth. The obscurity here is a real problem for our purposes, since if the birth takes place in heaven, the likelihood of a reference to Mary is considerably lessened.

3. Possible Sources of the Imagery and the Narrative

Before turning to what the author of Revelation meant by his narrative, let us consider briefly the possible background of the author's material. Whether or not there were originally two stories behind chap. 12, the material in Scene Two may have an origin or background that is different from the rest of the material in the chapter. If we focus on the heavenly battle between Michael and his angels vs. the dragon in vv. 7-9,[498] the background is surely the Jewish myth of the fall of the evil angels from heaven, a myth told in various forms in Gen 6:1-4; *1 Enoch* 6-19, *Jubilees* 5; *Adam and Eve* 12-17. In particular there may be influence upon Revelation of the struggle between Michael (the angel guardian of Israel) and the angel guardian of Persia, Israel's enemy, in Dan 10:13, 20; 12:1-2.

More important for our purposes is the struggle between the dragon and the woman who gives birth to the ruler in Scenes One and Three. Quite plausibly this may be related to the ancient myth

---

[497]The case is strengthened by v. 6 with its mention of the wilderness, for clearly in v. 14 the wilderness is on earth. We may not dismiss the evidence of v. 6 on the grounds that it is an editorial attempt to connect Scene One with Scene Three, for then the connective would have been supplied by the author of the book; and we are interested in whether *he* intended Scene One to involve earth as well as heaven.

[498]The hymn of vv. 10-12 may be of different provenance from the rest of Scene Two, for it refers to the victory over the "Accuser of our brethren" through the blood of the Lamb. This is quite different from Michael's victory over the serpent.

of the combat with the serpent monster attested in the Bible and in the cultures surrounding Israel.[499] The common features of the myth in its full form involve an evil power, represented by a dragon or serpent, which attacks a young god and defeats him, thus establishing an evil reign. However, through the help of a woman who undoes the work of the dragon, the god is revived to enter a final battle with the dragon and establish the victory over evil.[500] Those who think that the story in Revelation reflects even distantly this combat myth suspect that the parallels were clearer before the Michael section in Scene Two was introduced, for then the expulsion of the dragon from heaven would have been accomplished by the woman's child who was taken away to heaven. But even in the present form of Revelation it is clearly Christ who accomplishes the ultimate defeat of the dragon in 21:7-10

Though such a myth may have supplied the combat motif in Revelation 12, we are interested in more precise background for the details and symbols in the chapter. The most important may be listed as follows:

(a) The dragon with seven heads and ten horns, and seven diadems upon the horns (12:3) is evocative of Daniel's description of the beast with ten horns (Dan 7:8, 20, 24). In Daniel this beast was the fourth and worst of the world empires that persecuted the Jews, the Syrian or Seleucid Kingdom descended from the Greek general of Alexander the Great. This is not unlike Revelation's relation of the dragon to two beasts who represent Roman authority and religion in chap. 13.

(b) The dragon is identified as the ancient serpent (of

---

[499]See, for instance, Isa 27:1. The possible parallels are discussed at length by A. Y. Collins, *Combat*, 61-71. She finds the closest parallel in the Greek story of the victory of Apollo over Python with the help of Leto. Others who posit the influence of non-Jewish myth include Vögtle, "Mythos," 399-400; Lohse, *Offenbarung*, 68; Caird, *Revelation*, 147-48.

[500]The Nag Hammadi *Apocalypse of Adam* seems to be a first- or second-century Gnostic work of Jewish background. In V 78-80 there is a series of myths about the illuminator: he was nourished in the heavens, he came to the bosom of his mother and the water (see Rev 12:15-16), he was cast out of the city with his mother and brought to a desert place and nourished there; demons sought him out there and even dragons.

Genesis 3) in Rev 12:9.[501] This means that the dragon's struggle
with the woman and her offspring may be meant to evoke the
words addressed to the serpent in Gen 3:15: "I will put enmity
between you and the woman, and between your seed and her
seed; it [the seed] shall bruise your head and you shall bruise its
heel."[502] We see in 2 Cor 11:3 (and possibly in Rom 16:20) Christian awareness of the Eve/serpent struggle.

(c) The male child of Rev 12:5 who "is to rule over all the
nations with a rod of iron" echoes the description of the Davidic
king of Ps 2:9; and we know that Psalm 2 (especially v. 7) was
frequently used in the NT with reference to the Messiah (Luke
3:22; Acts 13:33, etc.). The reuse of this same description and its
application to "The Word of God," in Rev 19:15, assure us of the
author's intention to refer to Christ here.

(d) The woman who appears "clothed with the sun, with the
moon under her feet, and on her head a crown of twelve stars"
(Rev 12:1) evokes the description in Gen 37:9, in the dream of
Joseph where the sun stands for Jacob/Israel, the moon for
Rachel, and the twelve stars for the twelve sons of Jacob who
would be the founders of the tribes of Israel.[503]

(e) The woman crying out in her pangs of birth, in anguish
for delivery (Rev 12:2), may be meant to evoke the figurative
descriptions of the people of Israel or Zion as a woman in labor
(Isa 26:17; 54:1; 66:7-9; Micah 4:19). The birth pangs are the
troubled times that introduce the messianic age. In particular,
attention has been called to a passage in a Qumran scroll which

---

[501]If one posits a source behind this chapter, it would seem more
likely that the identification of the dragon as "the ancient serpent who is
called the Devil and Satan" in 12:9 is the work of the author of Revelation, for the same designation occurs in 20:2 (which could scarcely represent the same source that hypothetically underlies chap. 12). This would
mean that the author himself wanted to underline the Genesis reference.

[502]See above, Chap. 2, n. 40.

[503]McHugh, *Mother*, 421-29, following Gollinger, prefers Cant 6:10
as the background; but while that passage mentions one as "fair as the
moon, bright as the sun, majestic as the marching stars," it does not
mention *twelve* stars. McHugh accepts an allegorical reference of the
Canticle to Israel.

describes a woman in birth pains who gives birth to a wonderful counselor (the term for the Davidic prince in Isa 9:6), and conjoined to this is a reference to a woman pregnant with an asp or viper (1QH 3:7-10, 12). But there is no reference to opposition between this viper and the woman, and so it is impossible to know whether this Qumran symbolism served as background for Revelation.[504]

(f) The woman-in-the-wilderness motif of Rev 12:6, 14 is probably meant to recall Israel in the Exodus. Certainly the story of the Exodus shows how God protected Israel in the wilderness, and even "nourished" her there (cf. Rev 12:14 and Exod 16:4-17); and the transportation of the woman by "the two wings of the great eagle" (Rev 12:14) echoes God's words to the house of Jacob/Israel in Exod 19:4: "I bore you on eagle's wings" (also Deut 32:11-12).

(g) The "time, and times, and half a time" of Rev 12:14 echoes Dan 7:25 which says that the Saints of the Most High (Israel) will be given into the hand of the fourth beast for that period.

4. The Primary Meaning of Revelation 12

The overall purpose of the author of Revelation is to assure his readers of ultimate victory in times of persecution. This story of how the dragon failed to destroy the child of the woman, and of how God continues to protect the woman and her offspring in the wilderness when the dragon pursues her surely fits into the overall purpose. But what does the author mean by the symbol of the woman? Since very few interpreters today would see a primary or exclusive reference to Mary, let us postpone that question for a moment to investigate what most authors regard as the primary

---

[504]The *Hodayoth* (Hymn) passage is fragmentary and unclear, and commentators are in disagreement as to its meaning. Although there was a tendency among pioneer translators to interpret the hymn messianically, this has generally been abandoned for an eschatological interpretation. See the translation, discussion, and bibliography in the article of S. Brown, *NTS* 14 (1967-68), 247-59; and A. Y. Collins, *Combat*, 92.

reference, namely, to the people of God (whether Israel or the Church or both).[505]

Adela Collins, who opts for Jewish sources behind Revelation 12, argues that only on a Jewish level does the whole story make sense. The narrative is concerned with the birth, not with the death, of the Messiah; there is no detail about the life and deeds of the Messiah; indeed his messianic function is seemingly projected into the future when implicitly he will grow up—none of which makes Christian origin plausible.[506] Nevertheless, she admits that, whether or not it was originally framed by Christians, this narrative, as it appears in Revelation, has now to be seen in a Christian context.

What her theory makes clear is something already suggested strongly by the background as surveyed in the previous section (especially points d through f), namely, it is most likely that the woman is a personification of Israel, the people of God of the OT, and that the Christian adaptation of the symbolism involves having the woman, after the birth of the messianic child, become the Church, the people of God of the NT.[507] The main difficulty with

---

[505]For a review of recent interpretations of the woman of Revelation 12, see J. Michl, "Deutung," 309. Among the many recent authors who interpret the figure of the woman in a collective sense, we may list Féret (1943), Sickenberger (1945), Wikenhauser (1949), Bratsiotis (1950), Bonsirven (1951), Ketter (1953), Meinertz (1955), Stefaniak (1957), Giet (1957), and Kassing (1958). See also nn. 510 and 512 below. An unusual view, not followed by any other scholar, is that of Lohmeyer (1953), who identified the woman with Sophia, the personified Wisdom of God; she is giving birth to the divine logos. His theory really failed to explain anything in the narrative except the birth.

[506]A. Y. Collins, *Combat*, 104-7. She deals with Christian reinterpretation on pp. 130-45.

[507]One can accept such a general interpretation of the symbolism without turning Revelation 12 into an allegory in which each detail corresponds to some historical event, e.g., the snatching off of the child is the ascension; the flight into the wilderness is the escape of the Jerusalem church to Pella before the fall of the city; the flood of water represents heresies at the end of the century. Such an allegorical interpretation was popular among earlier commentators, e.g., Swete, *Apocalypse*, 148-49; but it is still maintained by S. Giet, *L'Apocalypse et l'histoire* (Paris: Presses Universitaires, 1957), 110-11.

this theory is that the woman is described *in heaven* (12:1), for neither Israel nor the Church is in heaven.[508] But the difficulty is not insuperable. According to a theory of sources, that element may have originally belonged not to the narrative of the woman vs. the dragon but to the narrative of Michael vs. Satan (12:7-9). Yet, as it is now attached to the woman, the phrase "in heaven" may be explained as a reflection of the apocalyptic sense of simultaneity, i.e., heavenly and earthly reality depicted at the same time. Such an outlook is suggested already in the OT, e.g., in Hosea where the relationship between the prophet and his unfaithful wife represents the relationship between Yahweh and Israel. In Isaiah 54 God calls Israel or Jerusalem, the barren one, to Himself as His wife and adorns her in a way that suggests that she is now looked on as a heavenly being.

Our previous discussion as to whether the author intended to situate the birth of the messianic child in heaven or on earth is probably also best decided in this way—it has heavenly and earthly facets. The birth pangs and the birth itself are described in OT terms (as we have seen in point e above) because, even though the Christian author and his community understood this to refer to Jesus, the story has not been reshaped to correspond with the details of Jesus' life. Here the birth of the Messiah means the emergence of messianic salvation. Neither is the snatching off of the child to God and his throne rewritten to refer precisely to Christ's resurrection or ascension; rather it describes in a general way the protection of the Messiah and promises that ultimately God will not let evil triumph over His people.

We should probably understand what follows in Scene Two in terms of a Christian reshaping of Jewish imagery. As already remarked, we would have expected the Messiah immediately to destroy the dragon. But in Christian experience, although the Messiah has come, his victory is not apparent to all, and there is a future expectation of an ultimate victory. Therefore the author first assures the reader that as a consequence of the birth of the

---

[508]Yet the idea of a spiritual church "created before the sun and moon" is found in *2 Clem.* 14.1. See K. P. Donfried, *The Setting of Second Clement in Early Christianity* (NovTSup 38; Leiden: Brill, 1974), 160-66.

Messiah, the dragon already has been defeated in heaven. The fall of Satan, which in Jewish thought was associated with the primordial times, is reassociated with the snatching off of the Messiah to God and his throne. We see traces of this in the Fourth Gospel where the Johannine Jesus sees the hour of his own glorification as the time of the expulsion of the ruler of this world (John 12:27-31).[509] But such a victory in heaven does not destroy the dragon; rather it leads to a continued struggle on earth—an insight that came from the Christian experience of ongoing combat with satanic forces (Eph 6:12; 2 Thess 2:9).

This ongoing struggle means that the Church, consisting of those who keep the commandments of God and bear testimony to Jesus (Rev 12:17), undergoes the wilderness experience of the Israel of the OT. The idea that the woman represents both Israel and the Church is less troublesome if we see that in the author's mind the Church is reliving aspects of Israel's career. Indeed, the Church's hostile experience with Roman emperor worship (which the author will describe in the next chapter) reminds him of Israel's struggle with the Seleucid emperor Antiochus IV Epiphanes who tried to introduce false worship, whence the reference to Daniel's "time, and times, and a half time"—the period of God's tolerance of evil under such persecution by a world power. The notion that the woman (Israel) who gave birth to the Messiah could also be the Church who has other offspring (Rev 12:17) may well reflect the Christian concept that Christians have been born or begotten as children of God in the image of Christ. The imagery of many offspring may also be an aspect of the struggle in Gen 3:15 between the serpent and the woman, between the serpent's seed and the woman's seed (point b in the previous section).

One may have qualifications about one or the other aspect of this interpretation of Revelation 12, but in its broad outlines it would represent where most contemporary scholarship would stand in regard to the primary significance of the woman.

---

[509]See also Col 2:15. A Synoptic parallel (Luke 10:18) has "Satan fall like lightning from heaven" during the ministry of Jesus, as part of the mission of the seventy.

5. A Reference to Mary in Revelation 12?

Granted that the woman described in Revelation 12 refers primarily to the people of God, Israel and the Church, is there a possibility of a secondary reference to Mary?[510] The plasticity of apocalyptic symbolism makes a double reference for the one symbol a possibility, and the biblical conception of corporate personality makes it possible for an individual to represent a collectivity.[511] The main argument for a reference to Mary is that the narrative refers to the woman as the mother of the Messiah, and one may ask whether any Christian of the late first century could refer to the mother of the Messiah without thinking of Jesus' mother Mary.

Let us mention some of the difficulties that the suggestion of a reference to Mary faces. A primary objection is that early Church writers did not interpret Revelation 12 in a mariological sense; indeed our first known mariological interpretation dates to the fourth century.[512] However, we have seen that by modern

---

[510]In recent scholarship the following interpret the woman primarily in a collective sense but allow for a secondary application to Mary: Boismard (1950), A. Müller (1951), Kosnetter (1952), P. Häring (1955), McHugh (1975). The following interpret the woman as primarily a reference to Mary but find a secondary reference to the Church: Le Frois (1952), F.-M. Braun (1954), Cerfaux and Cambier (1955).

[511]Le Frois makes this suggestion, and it would make more sense if the Marian references were primary. It is more difficult to invoke corporate personality if the primary reference of the woman is to the collectivity.

[512]Epiphanius (*Panarion* 78.11) and Andrew of Crete (*In Apoc.* 33) state that some individuals (unnamed) were identifying the woman with Mary. The first known writers to make this identification were Oecumenius and Pseudo-Epiphanius (sixth century), and these were followed by Ambrosius Autpertus (died 784) and Alcuin (died 804). It was by no means the majority opinion. McHugh, *Mother*, 470-71, following Le Frois, lists these patristic writers who equated the woman with the Church: Hippolytus, Methodius, Pseudo-Cyprian, Tyconius, Victorinus of Pettau, Pseudo-Augustine, Primasius, Andrew of Crete, and Bede. A. Trabucco (1957) investigated the history of Roman Catholic interpretation from 1563 to 1954 and found only two interpreters who equated the woman exclusively with Mary (Michl, "Deutung," 305-6).

standards the whole Book of Revelation was misinterpreted for over sixteen centuries, and in most of that time very little light was thrown on what we today would consider the author's real intention. Nevertheless, even if the ancient exegesis of Revelation is an uncertain guide to what the author meant by the woman of chap. 12, the fact that the mariological emphasis on Revelation 12 is relatively recent raises the question of whether it represents an exegesis of the text itself or simply an imaginative theological application as part of a search for biblical support for Marian doctrine.[513]

A second objection is that the author does not explicitly identify the woman as Mary, while he does not hesitate to supply a secondary identification of the dragon as "the ancient serpent who is called the Devil and Satan" (12:9). Obviously, his silence on this score weakens the case for Marian identification, but it does not really foreclose it. After all "the ancient serpent" was not a reference immediately suggested by the mention of a dragon. The author may have thought that the mother of the Messiah would have been recognizable as Mary without such assistance.

A third objection is that the description of the birth really does not fit what happened at Bethlehem—it is not clear in Revelation 12 that the birth takes place on earth, and the birth is immediately followed by the snatching off of the child, without even a nod toward the public ministry of Jesus. (This difficulty is aggravated if the snatching off is taken as the resurrection or ascension—Jesus did not ascend into heaven immediately after his birth at Bethlehem.) However, the presupposition behind this objection, namely, that the birth of the Messiah should be compared to the Bethlehem scene, has its own difficulties.[514] The idea that Jesus was born of Mary at Bethlehem appears in only two

---

[513]The idea that the woman is portrayed in heaven in Rev 12:1 has been used to support the thesis of Mary's assumption. The text is mentioned in the papal bull on the assumption (*Munificentissimus Deus*, 1950), but only as an example of symbolic interpretation by medieval theologians. See *AAS* 42 (1950), 763; *Catholic Mind* 49 (1951), 72.

[514]The difficulties increase if one moves beyond the canonical literature: from the *Protevangelium of James* (17-20) onward there was a thesis that the birth of Jesus occurred without pain on Mary's part.

places in the NT (Matthew 2 and Luke 2), and so we are far from certain that for most Christians the birth of the Messiah would necessarily evoke Bethlehem. Rather, in Acts 13:33 the begetting or birth of God's Son refers to the resurrection, and in the Western text of Luke 3:22 it refers to the baptism of Jesus. Therefore, if we wish to deal perceptively with a possible reference to Mary in the woman of Revelation 12, we have to ask if there is some other birth scene where Mary could be involved which would fit the imagery of Revelation 12.

The following thesis has been proposed on the supposition that Revelation is in some way related to the Fourth Gospel.[515] That Gospel reports nothing about birth at Bethlehem; rather its use of birth imagery in relation to Jesus occurs at the Last Supper. In 16:20-21 Jesus compares the present sorrow and future joy of the disciples to that of a woman in birth pangs, who forgets her sorrow once the child has been born into the world. The birth pangs would seemingly refer to the pain surrounding Jesus' departure and death; the birth itself would refer to his return after victory.[516] At the foot of the cross, and therefore at the death of Jesus, attention is called to the presence of the *mother* of Jesus who is addressed as "Woman" (John 19:25-27). This death and subsequent victory, which constitute Jesus' hour, are seen as the moment of the expulsion of Satan (John 12:27-31). Thus, one has in John many of the elements that are found in Revelation 12. And if the birth of the Messiah is a reference to Jesus' going to his

---

Understood as part of her *virginity in birth*, a painless delivery has been looked upon as a dogma of the faith by many Roman Catholics. Against such a background the depiction in Revelation 12 of the mother of the Messiah as suffering in labor caused real difficulty for some Roman Catholics who thought that Mary was meant. See Michl, "Deutung," 309.

[515]The best known form of the thesis is that the Gospel, the three Johannine Epistles, and Revelation were all written by John, son of Zebedee. J. A. T. Robinson, *Redating*, 255, lists modern scholars who still maintain this position. A mediating view is that the evangelist and the seer of Revelation were different members of the same school (J. Weiss, Bousset, Moffatt, Barrett, R. E. Brown, K.P. Donfried). See the discussion by Charles, *Revelation*, 1. xxix-xlv.

[516]The Nag Hammadi *Apocryphon of Paul*, V 18, describes the risen Christ as a little child.

father after his death, then it becomes intelligible that Rev 12:5 associates the birth of the child with his being snatched off to God and to his throne.[517] The possibility of the woman/Eve motif in John[518] may also be brought into the discussion as a parallel to Rev 12:9 where the dragon is identified as the ancient serpent (of Genesis 3).

Nevertheless, there are objections to this method of finding a reference to Mary in Revelation 12. *First*, the relationship between Revelation and the Fourth Gospel has been questioned;[519] and even though some relationship is commonly admitted, that relationship must be acknowledged to have dissimilarities as well as similarities. *Second*, even though in the Fourth Gospel the mother of Jesus, addressed as "Woman," is present at a death scene which earlier has been symbolically depicted in terms of birth pains, Mary does *not* give birth to Jesus in that scene. Rather through the death scene she becomes the mother of the beloved disciple. It may be responded that this motif also occurs in Revelation 12, for there the woman is the mother of other offspring who are Christian believers (12:17). However, one must recognize that in Revelation 12 the woman primarily gives birth to the Messiah and is only mentioned incidentally as having other offspring, while in John 19:25-27 the emphasis is just the opposite: the one who is mentioned as the mother of Jesus becomes the mother of the Beloved Disciple. *Third*, if there is a reference to the woman as Eve in Revelation 12 and to the mother of Jesus as Eve in John 2:1-11; 19:25-27 (note: the majority of this task force

---

[517]See above, pp. 216-17, for our treatment of the Johannine passages in question here. Many of the elements of this thesis are borrowed from Feuillet, "The Messiah."

[518]See above, pp. 189-90. The Anglican scholar A. Richardson (*Introduction to the Theology of the New Testament* [New York: Harper & Row, 1958] 176) thought that Rev 12:17 might imply a double symbolism in which the woman represented both the Jewish Church and Eve/Mary, but he recognized that the latter symbolism was not beyond doubt and that it was hinted at rather than asserted.

[519]Particularly by E. S. Fiorenza, "The Quest for the Johannine School: The Apocalypse and the Fourth Gospel," *NTS* 23 (1976-77), 402-27: "The Apoc is the work of a member of an early Christian prophetic-apocalyptic rather than of the Johannine school" (424).

denied a reference to Eve in the Fourth Gospel), there is no proof that the second-century Church writers who proposed the Eve/Mary antithesis recognized this reference. They turned rather to the infancy narrative of Luke, contrasting the obedience of the virgin Mary in Luke 1:38 with the disobedience of Eve who was still a virgin in the Garden scene.[520]

A secondary reference, then, to Mary in Revelation 12 remains possible but uncertain, so far as the intention of the seer himself is concerned. What is more certain is that his symbol of the woman who is the mother of the Messiah might well lend itself to Marian interpretation, once Marian interest developed in the later Christian community. And eventually when Revelation was placed in the same canon[521] of Scripture with the Gospel of Luke and the Fourth Gospel, the various images of the virgin, the woman at the cross, and the woman who gave birth to the Messiah would reinforce each other (see above, Chap. 2, C4).

---

[520]See Justin, *Dialogue*, 100; Irenaeus, *Adv. Haer.* 3.22,4; and below, Chap. 9D.

[521]Yet the picture remains nuanced here as well, for Revelation was a relatively late comer into the canon of some sections of the Eastern churches (see Kümmel, *Introduction*, 501-3), so that this "canonical" Marian symbolism would not be equally ancient in all areas.

CHAPTER NINE:
MARY IN THE LITERATURE
OF THE SECOND CENTURY*

The preceding chapters have shown how difficult it is in an investigation like ours to arrive at a clear picture of the "Mary of history" (*Stage One* of our Gospel inquiry).[522] Most of our discussion, therefore, was concentrated on subsequent stages of Christian thought about Mary, i.e., in the traditions that preceded the writing of the Gospels (*Stage Two*), and in the final Gospels (*Stage Three*) and other NT works. Thus, we have had to admit from the outset that we were more certain about theology than about history. Of course, the theology of the NT writers is itself a part of history, namely, the developing history of the church. This history included a growing doctrinal interest in mariology (Mary's role in the plan of salvation) and an ever-expanding devotion to the Mother of the Lord. It is now time for us to pursue some Marian themes in their post-biblical unfolding and to trace the emergence of new lines of argument which blossomed into an impressive body of patristic Marian thought and doctrine.

In this book we restrict our post-biblical investigation to the

---

*The discussion for this chapter was led by E. Pagels and K. Froehlich. The latter composed the first draft. One-half session of the task force (Nov. 1976) was devoted to the second-century Marian evidence, as well as part of the plenary session of April 1978.

[522]See above, Chap. 2, B2a.

second century; the inclusion of further developments would go beyond the scope of the book and the competence of this particular task force. The literature of the second century is an important link between the emerging canon of NT writings and the broader life situation of the church of the Fathers. Of course, we do not find in this period a fully developed system of theological reflection on Mary: she appears only at the fringe of more central christological discussion, and an independent interest in her person and role cannot be documented before the latter part of the century (and even then, more in works of popular piety). Nevertheless, major Marian themes began to gain form and importance during this century.

The investigation we are undertaking faces two major difficulties with regard to the available material. *First*, much of the extracanonical Christian literature of the second century is preserved only in fragmentary form. We do not have the text of many works that we know were written in this century; and even existing texts are often incomplete, uncertain in their exact wording, or preserved only in later translations.[523] Obviously, in reconstructing Marian lines of development in this period, we must be aware of the real limitations imposed by the source material. *Second*, even in the available literature, Marian references are extremely rare before A.D. 150, and are often difficult to interpret in works written between A.D. 150 and 200. Understandably, mariologists have examined every scrap of evidence in the hope of finding early traces of doctrinal positions that are part of their church's devotional and theological heritage. As a group of biblical and historical scholars from diverse backgrounds, we understand our task differently. Rather than discussing every possible allusion to later Marian themes, we shall survey the more important texts identified by modern scholars.[524] Then we shall try to interpret them in their historical context, giving attention to the

---

[523]The Nag Hammadi collection, largely Gnostic, has many complete texts; but they are preserved in Coptic rather than in their original Greek.

[524]Most of the relevant texts are conveniently available in the two recent Marian collections by D. Casagrande and S. Alvarez Campos. A good selection according to the best critical editions may be found in Delius, *Texte*.

lines of Marian development insofar as they can be reconstructed for this period—particularly the continuation of lines detected in the previous chapters of this study.

A. Survey of the Texts[525]

Marian texts in the second century come from two major groups of writings: the apocrypha (gospels, epistles, apocalypses), and the patristic writings.

1. New Testament Apocrypha

Most of these apocrypha[526] appear under the name of an apostolic authority or as anonymous imitations of writings of the apostolic age. They were not accorded canonical authority, and many were recognized and rejected as products of heretical groups. But others were used for centuries as if they had been written during the early days of the church and have exercised a tremendous influence on doctrine and popular piety. As we shall see, there is a chance that some preserve tradition independent of the canonical Gospels[527] and can be of help in our investigation of the early levels of the tradition. However, in many cases their actual composition has to be assigned to a period much later than the second century. Thus, a number of apocryphal gospels or acts with important Marian material such as the *Latin Pseudo-Matthew*,[528] the *Infancy Gospel of Thomas*,[529] and the *Acts of*

---

[525]The English translation of the texts given here is at times simplified in grammatical structure, style, and diacritical marks.

[526]There are excellent English collections by Hennecke-Schneemelcher *(HSNTA)* and by James *(JANT)*.

[527]Scholarly opinion varies widely on many early apocrypha; important disagreements are reported in the footnotes.

[528]*HSNTA*, 1. 410-13 (extracts); *JANT*, 73-79. J. Gijsel, the editor of the new critical edition (see *RSPT* 60 [1976], 318), dates the compilation ca. A.D. 550.

[529]*HSNTA*, 1. 388-99; *JANT*, 49-65. Gero, "Infancy," concludes that the present form does not antedate the fifth century, although individual pieces may have been written earlier.

Pilate (Gospel of Nicodemus)[530] fall outside the purview of our study.

PREVIOUSLY KNOWN GOSPELS. Among the apocryphal gospels of a Synoptic type,[531] the Jewish Christian gospels have been thought to reflect possibly old, independent traditions. They exist under a variety of designations: *Gospel According to the Hebrews, Gospel of the Ebionites, Gospel of the Nazaraeans* (or *Nazorites*), *Hebrew Gospel According to Matthew, Gospel of the Twelve* (Apostles).[532] It is unclear how many actual writings these designations cover, but the following four fragments are relevant for our investigation.

One speaks about Mary's role in the coming of Christ in terms of a cosmic myth:[533]

> *When Christ wished to come upon the earth to men, the good Father summoned a mighty heavenly power, called Michael, and entrusted Christ to its care. And the power came into the world, and it was called Mary; and Christ was in her womb seven months.*

From the same gospel probably comes a saying in which Jesus designates the Holy Spirit as his mother:[534]

> *Even so did my mother, the Holy Spirit, take me by one of my hairs and carry me away onto the great mountain Tabor.*

To another gospel belongs a dialogue not recorded in the canonical Gospels between "the mother of the Lord and his brothers" and Jesus:[535]

---

[530]*HSNTA*, 1. 444-84; *JANT*, 94-146. There is a possibility that an early form of this writing was available to Justin. However, the composition of even the oldest parts of the *present* text is generally attributed to the fifth century; see *HSNTA*, 1. 447-48.

[531]For the distinctions made here, see *HSNTA*, 1. 80-84: "Types of Apocryphal Gospels."

[532]*HSNTA*, 1. 118-65.

[533]*Gos. Heb.* 1; *HSNTA*, 1. 163; *JANT*, 8.

[534]*Gos. Heb.* 3; *HSNTA*, 1. 164; *JANT*, 2. This idea is found in the Gnostic *Gospel of Philip* (see below, n. 538).

[535]*Gos. Nazareans* 2; *HSNTA*, 1. 146-47; *JANT* 6.

> *Behold, the mother of the Lord and his brothers said to him: "John the Baptist baptizes unto the remission of sins, let us go and be baptized by him." But he said to them: "Wherein have I sinned that I should go and be baptized by him? Unless what I have said is ignorance."*

A final fragment parallels the Synoptic episode about Jesus' true family (Mark 3:13-35 and par.) in a somewhat abbreviated form:[536]

> *Moreover they deny that he was a man, evidently on the ground of the word which the Savior spoke when it was reported to him: "Behold, your mother and your brethren stand outside," namely: "Who is my mother and who are my brothers?" And he stretched forth his hand towards his disciples and said: "These are my brothers and mother and sisters, who do the will of my Father."*

NAG HAMMADI APOCRYPHA. The study of early gospels of a Gnostic type has received new impetus through the spectacular find of a Coptic Gnostic library in the vicinity of Nag Hammadi (near ancient Chenoboskion) on the Nile *ca.* 1945. This find yielded original texts hitherto unknown or known only by title. Since many of them are mentioned by the Fathers of the late second and early third centuries, the find has great significance for our knowledge of the Gnostic literature before A.D. 200.[537] Two "gospels" contained in the thirteen codices of the Nag Hammadi find deserve special attention.

The *Gospel of Philip*, a collection of Gnostic meditations which seem to go back to the second century, contains among other references an unusual variant to the Matthean and Lucan versions of the virginal conception, advocating a symbolic understanding of the human persons of the gospels. While Mary and Joseph are called Jesus' mother and father, the Virgin Mother is also interpreted as a heavenly power, i.e., the Holy Spirit; and the

---

[536]*Gos. Eb.*, 5; *HSNTA*, 1. 158.

[537]A good orientation is given by J. M. Robinson, "The Coptic Gnostic Library Today," *NTS* 14 (1968), 356-401. A full English translation of all the writings is available in Robinson, *Nag Hammadi*.

Father-in-heaven is interpreted as Jesus' true Father. We quote the relevant passages:[538]

> *(55:23) Some said: "Mary conceived by the Holy Spirit." They are in error. They do not know what they are saying. When did a woman ever conceive by a woman?[539] Mary is the virgin whom no power defiled. She is a great anathema to the Hebrews, who are the apostles and (the) apostolic men. This virgin whom no power defiled (. . .) the powers defile themselves. And the Lord (would) not have said, "My (Father who is in) heaven," unless (he) had had another father; but he would have said simply, "My Father."*

> *(59:6) There were three who always walked with the Lord: Mary his mother and her sister and Magdalene, the one who was called his companion. His sister and his mother and his companion were each a Mary.*

> *"The Father" and "the Son" are single names; "the Holy Spirit" is a double name. For they are everywhere: they are above, they are below; they are in the concealed, they are in the revealed. The Holy Spirit is in the revealed: it is below. It is in the concealed: it is above.*
> *The saints are served by evil powers, for they are blinded by the Holy Spirit into thinking that they are serving an (ordinary) man whenever they do (something) for the saints. Because of this a disciple asked the Lord one day for something of this world. He said to him: "Ask your mother and she will give you of the things which are another's."*

> *(71:3) Is it permitted to utter a mystery? The Father of everything united with the virgin who came down, and a fire shone for him on that day. . . . (71:16) Adam came into being from two virgins, from the Spirit and from the virgin earth. Christ, therefore, was born from a virgin to rectify the fall which occurred in the beginning.*

> *(73:8) Philip, the apostle said, "Joseph the carpenter planted a garden because he needed wood for his trade. It was he who made the cross from the trees which he planted. His own offspring hung on that which he planted. His offspring was Jesus, and the planting was the cross. . . ."*

---

[538]Robinson, *Nag Hammadi*, 134, 135-36, 143, 144; R. McL. Wilson, *The Gospel of Philip* (New York: Harper & Row, 1962), 31, 35, 47, 49.

[539]The writer draws upon the feminine gender of "Spirit" (*rûaḥ*) in Hebrew.

The *Gospel of Thomas*[540] has been the subject of much controversy. Mentioned already by Hippolytus and Origen in the early third century, it must have had its origin no later than the second century. This gospel consists of a series of sayings of Jesus which are quoted without a connecting narrative and with only minimal situational remarks. In its present Coptic form the collection as a whole has clear Gnostic overtones, but several indications point to a pre-history in an earlier tradition possibly of a Synoptic type.[541] Scholars are still divided over the question whether or not this tradition was dependent upon the canonical Gospels. It contains, however, several texts of interest for us. Logion 31 is a version of Mark 6:4 and par.[542] Logion 79 combines Luke 11:27-28 and 23:29. The Logia 99, 101, and 105 resemble in part the Synoptic words about Jesus' eschatological family, hinting, however, at a true or heavenly Mother as well as Father:[543]

(99) The disciples said to him: "Your brothers and your mother are standing outside." He said to them: "Those here who do the will of my Father, they are my brothers and my mother; these are they who shall enter the kingdom of my Father."

(101) [Jesus said]: "Whoever does not hate his father and his mother as I do cannot become my disciple. And whoever does [not] love his father and his mother as I do cannot become my disciple, for my mother [gave me falsehood] but [my] true [mother] gave me life."

(105) Jesus said, "Whoever knows father and mother shall be called the son of a harlot."

PROTEVANGELIUM OF JAMES. While the category of birth and infancy narratives multiplied in later times, only the so-called

---

[540]A. Guillaumont et al., *The Gospel According to Thomas* (New York: Harper & Row, 1959). See the survey by H. Quecke, "L'Évangile de Thomas. État de recherches," in *La venue du Messie* (ed. E. Massaux; RechBib 6; Bruges: Desclée, 1962), 217-41.

[541]Among these indications the following may be mentioned: The parallels in three Greek papyri from Oxyrhynchus; the presence of non-Gnostic sayings; the occurrence of doublets. See H. Montefiore and H. E. W. Turner, *Thomas and the Evangelists* (London: SCM, 1962).

[542]See above, Chap. 4, n. 105.

[543]Guillaumont, *Thomas*, 51-53; Robinson, *Nag Hammadi*, 128-29.

Protevangelium of James[544] had its origin in the second century. Probably written as an expansion of Jesus' birth story, the book was apparently the first Christian writing to exhibit an independent interest in the person of Mary. In the West, the so-called Gelasian Decree (ca. A.D. 500), which listed it under the title, "Book about the Birth of the Redeemer and about Mary or the Midwife," evaluated it as an apocryphon which "the catholic and apostolic Roman Church does not in any way receive."[545] In the East, the book remained in general use, and its stories were well known everywhere through numerous secondary apocrypha based on its material. A recent discovery has provided us with a reliable Greek text from as early as the third or fourth century. However, the book was already known to Clement of Alexandria and Origen and may have influenced Justin Martyr.[546] In this case a composition-date not much later than A.D. 150 must be assumed.

The author poses as "James," presumably James, the brother of the Lord, and recounts in legendary fashion the background and life-story of Mary. He gives details about her family, her birth, her childhood in the Temple, her betrothal to Joseph (who is portrayed as an aged widower with children), the annunciation, Joseph's doubt, Mary's vindication before the High Priest, the birth of Jesus in a cave outside of Bethlehem, the adoration of the magi, and finally the massacre of the innocents with the death of Zechariah, the father of John the Baptist. De Strycker, a Belgian Jesuit scholar and the most recent editor, judges the *Protevangelium* to be a piece of "inventive hagiography." Despite its condemnation in official documents, it has dominated the development of the Marian legend, providing much of the basic mate-

---

[544]*HSNTA*, 1. 370-88; *JANT*, 38-49. The title in the oldest MS is "Birth of Mary: Revelation of James." The name, "Protevangelium" goes back to a 16th-century editor, G. Postel.

[545]*HSNTA*, 1. 47.

[546]This possibility is still considered by Delius, *Geschichte*, p. 4. Most scholars today assume the reverse, i.e., dependence of the *Protevangelium* on Justin, e.g., Cothenet, "Protévangile," 1382; de Aldama, *Maria*, 97, n. 80. Van Stempvoort, "Protevangelium," gives a date between A.D. 180 and 204. For the witness of Clement and Origen, see de Strycker, *La forme*, 412-13.

rial for Mary's biography. We shall have to ask to what extent this book preserves independent traditions and what is the direction of its Marian implications.

APOCRYPHAL ACTS OF THE APOSTLES. Two of these contain important references to Mary. Tertullian (died ca. 220) tells us of a presbyter in Asia Minor who, out of love for the Apostle, confessed to having forged *Acts of Paul*, presumably during the last two decades of the second century.[547] Papyrus-finds have enabled scholars to establish a firmer textual basis for the parts of this writing that are still extant. One passage is drawn from a sermon of Paul at Puteoli:[548]

For in these last times God, for our sake, has sent down a spirit of power into the flesh, that is, into Mary the Galilean, according to the prophetic word, who was conceived and borne by her as the fruit of her womb, until she was delivered and gave birth to [Jesus] the Christ, our King, of Bethlehem in Judea.

The author also filled a gap in the Pauline correspondence adding a letter of the Corinthians to Paul and Paul's answer *(3 Corinthians)*. The Corinthians ask advice about two heretics who, among other things, hold: "That the Lord is not come in the flesh, nor was he born of Mary."[549] Paul's answer emphasizes the true apostolic tradition:[550]

Our Lord Jesus Christ was born of Mary of the seed of David, when the Holy Spirit was sent from heaven by the Father into her, that he might come into this world and redeem all flesh through his own flesh.

Another sentence explains it more fully:[551]

God . . . sent the [Holy] Spirit [through fire] into Mary the Galilean, who believed with all her heart; and she received the Holy Spirit in her womb that Jesus might enter into the world.

---

[547]Tertullian, *De Baptismo*, 17; *HSNTA*, 2. 323.
[548]*HSNTA*, 2. 382.
[549]*Ibid.*, 374 (1:14).
[550]*Ibid.*, 375 (3:5-6).
[551]*Ibid.*, 376 (3:12-14).

The Old Latin translation of a section of the *Acts of Peter* (*Actus Vercellenses*), written ca. A.D. 180/190, has a polemic against a scornful remark of Simon the Magician about "Jesus the Nazarene, the son of a carpenter and a carpenter himself, whose family comes from Judea." Simon is refuted in an interesting series of proof texts, biblical and apocryphal, which support Jesus' virginal conception and miraculous birth:[552]

> *But Peter said: "A curse on your words against Christ! Did you presume to speak in these terms while the prophet says of him: 'His generation, who shall declare it?' And another prophet says: 'And we saw him and he had no grace nor beauty.' And: 'In the last times a boy is born of the Holy Spirit; his mother knows not a man, nor does anyone claim to be his father.' And again he says: 'She has given birth and has not given birth.' And again: 'Is it a small thing for you to make trouble . . . ?' (And again:) 'Behold a virgin shall conceive in her womb.' And another prophet says in the Father's honor: 'We have neither heard her voice, nor is a midwife come in.' Another prophet says: 'He was not born from the womb of a woman but came down from a heavenly place.' "*

CHRISTIAN REVISIONS OF JEWISH APOCALYPTIC WRITINGS. Among these the *Ascension of Isaiah* occupies an important place because of its early date. Probably in the second century Christians added a vision of the prophet (chaps. 6-11). The following section on the miraculous appearance (rather than birth) of the Christ child is an additional interpolation of uncertain date:[553]

> *And I saw a woman of the family of David the prophet. This woman named Mary, who was a virgin, was betrothed to a man called Joseph, a carpenter; and he too was of the seed and family of the righteous David, of Bethlehem in Judah. And he came to his portion. And when she was betrothed, it was found that she was with child; so Joseph, the carpenter, wished to put her away. But the angel of the Spirit appeared in this world; and after that, Joseph did not put Mary away. He kept her but did not reveal the matter to*

---

[552]*Ibid.*, 306-7 (23-24); for the date, see p. 275.

[553]*Ibid.*, 661 (11:2-14). For the textual problems, see the introduction, p. 643. Differences in dating the piece are discussed by de Aldama, *Maria*, 94, n. 66. Zahn, *Brüder*, 312, assumed dependence on the *Protevangelium*.

anyone. And he did not approach Mary but kept her as a holy virgin, although she was with child. And he did not [yet] live with her for two months.

After two months, Joseph was in his house, with his wife Mary, the two of them alone. It came to pass, while they were alone, that Mary suddenly beheld with her eyes and saw a small child; and she was amazed. When her amazement wore off, her womb was found as it was before she was with child. And when her husband Joseph said to her, "What amazed you?", his eyes were opened; and he saw the child and praised God that the Lord had come to his portion. And a voice came to them: "Tell this vision to no one." But the report concerning the child was noised abroad in Bethlehem. Some said, "The virgin Mary has given birth before she was married two months"; and many said: "She has not given birth; the midwife has not gone up to her, and we have heard no cries of pain."

In Book Eight of the *Sibylline Oracles* there are late second-century Christian additions to a Jewish-Hellenistic source, and several poetic sections refer to the "holy virgin" or the "virgin Mary." A long section seems to paraphrase the Lucan annunciation and birth stories, adding such features as the virgin's laughter, which is echoed after the birth by the laughter of the heavenly throne:[554]

From heaven he came, and put on mortal form.
First, then, the holy, mighty form of Gabriel was displayed.
And second the archangel addressed the maiden in speech:
"In your immaculate bosom, virgin, you receive God."
Thus speaking, God breathed grace into the sweet maiden.
But then she was seized with both alarm and wonder as she listened,
and stood trembling—her mind was in turmoil,
her heart leaping at such unheard-of tidings.
But again she rejoiced and her heart was warmed by the saying.
And the maiden laughed, her cheeks flushed scarlet,
gladly rejoicing and touched in her heart with shame;
then she took courage. The Word flew into her body,
was made flesh in time and brought forth to life in her womb,
was molded to mortal form and became a boy
by virgin birth-pangs. This, a great wonder to mortals,
is no great wonder to God the Father and to God the Son.

---

[554]*HSNTA*, 2. 740 (8:458-76). For the date, see pp. 707-8; and Altaner, *Patrologie*, 120-21.

When the child was born, delight came upon the earth,
the heavenly throne laughed, and the world rejoiced;
a new-shining star, God-appointed, was revered by the Magi.

To the end of Book One (323) probably belong several lines which have been recovered from the so-called Sibylline Theosophy. Their date, however, is uncertain:[555]

When the maid [damalis] shall give birth to the Logos of God Most High,
but as wedded wife [alochos] shall give to the Logos a name,
then from the East shall a star shine forth in the midst of the day.

Scholars are still puzzled by the *Epistula Apostolorum*, of which an Ethiopic version was discovered in 1895. It can be compared with a fourth- or fifth-century fragmentary Coptic papyrus text and some later Latin fragments. Because of its anti-Gnostic polemics and its archaic eschatology some scholars date the *Epistula* in the second century. Others, however, are more hesitant since no mention of this writing is known from early Christian literature.[556] In the beginning of the *Epistula*, addressed to the "churches of the East and West, towards North and South," we find a creedal passage which mentions the incarnation of the Logos of the "holy virgin Mary" and the apocryphal story of the boy Jesus challenging his teacher:[557]

We believe that the word that became flesh through the holy virgin Mary, was carried [conceived] in her womb by the Holy Spirit, was born not by the lust of the flesh but by the will of God, was wrapped [in swaddling clothes], made known at Bethlehem; and that he was reared and grew up, as we saw.

The dependence of this text on the Lucan and Johannine materials is obvious, yet they cannot have been the only source as the

---

[555]*HSNTA*, 2. 709, with n. 1.

[556]An early date has been convincingly defended by M. Hornschuh, *Studien zur Epistula Apostolorum* (Berlin: De Gruyter, 1965), 116-17, against C. Schmidt and H. Duensing. See also de Aldama, *Maria*, 19, n. 36.

[557]*HSNTA*, 1. 192-93.

following story of the teacher shows.[558]

Our survey has covered a wide variety of apocryphal texts in which Mary is mentioned. However, apart from the *Protevangelium*, she is nowhere the center of attention, and even a coherent reflection on her place in the Christian story seems to be missing.

2. Patristic Writings

The picture is similar when we turn to the church writers of the second century. Most of the earliest patristic writings do not even mention Mary. Among the "Apostolic Fathers" we find no reference to her in *1 Clement*, *Didache*, *Papias*, *Barnabas*, *Hermas*, the *Epistle of Polycarp*, or the *Epistle to Diognetus*. The so-called *Second Epistle of Clement*, an early Christian homily (before A.D. 150) alludes to Christ's coming in the flesh and to the Synoptic logion about Jesus' true relatives (*2 Clem.* 9.5,11) but does not mention Mary in this context.

The only exception is in the letters of Ignatius, bishop of Antioch (A.D. 110-115).[559] His five references to Mary provide not only an early witness to the belief in Jesus' virginal conception but allow some inferences about a polemical situation in which this theme must have played a role. The human reality of Jesus' birth from the virgin Mary is stressed at the beginning of *Smyrnaeans* (1.1):

> You are fully persuaded concerning our Lord, that he is in truth of the family of David according to the flesh, Son of God by the will and power of God, truly born of a virgin.

---

[558] "This is what our Lord Jesus Christ did, who was delivered by Joseph and Mary to where he might learn letters. And he who taught him said to him as he taught him: 'Say Alpha.' He answered and said to him: 'First you tell me what Beta is' " (*HSNTA*, 1. 193). The same logion appears in the *Infancy Gospel of Thomas* (6:3; 14:2) and elsewhere. It must represent an earlier tradition. See Gero, "Infancy," 71-73; W. Bauer, *Leben*, 92-93.

[559] Seven letters are generally regarded as authentic; see M. P. Brown, *The Authentic Writings of Ignatius: A Study of Linguistic Criteria* (Durham: Duke University, 1963). The date of Ignatius' execution in Rome falls in the reign of Trajan (died A.D. 117).

The same point is made in *Trallians* (9.1):

> Be deaf therefore when anyone speaks to you apart from Jesus
> Christ, of David's lineage, of Mary, who was truly born and ate and
> drank. . . .

Jesus' double descent is a central theme in *Ephesians*:

> There is only one physician, both of flesh and of spirit, born and
> unborn, God in man, true life in death, sprung from Mary and from
> God (7.2).

> For our God, Jesus the Christ, according to God's dispensation,
> was conceived in the womb by Mary, from the seed of David and
> from the Holy Spirit (18.2).

Ephesians 19.1 explicitly points to the "mystery" of Jesus' birth:

> And hidden from the prince of this world were the virginity of Mary,
> and her giving birth, and likewise the death of the Lord: three
> mysteries crying out to be told, but wrought in the silence of God.

The apologist Aristides of Athens (ca. A.D. 145) mentions the
"virgin" once in what approaches a creedal formula. The text
may contain later interpolations:[560]

> He is confessed as the Son of the highest God, descending from
> heaven [on account of the salvation of men] through the Holy
> Spirit; and [born] of a [holy] virgin [without seed and in purity], he
> took flesh. . . .

But it was only with Justin Martyr, the apologist and philos-
opher (died ca. A.D. 165), that Marian themes and particularly
Jesus' virginal conception, gained some prominence in theological argument.[561] It is possible, as we have mentioned, that Justin
knew the *Protevangelium* and used it. However, his interest in

---

[560]*Apology* 15.1; see E. Goodspeed, *Die ältesten christlichen
Apologeten* (Göttingen: Vandenhoeck & Ruprecht, 1914), 19. For the
textual problems, see von Campenhausen, *Virgin Birth*, 19-20, n. 4; de
Aldama, *Maria*, 18-19 and 330-31.

[561]*Apology*, 1.21,1; 22,5; 31,7; 46,5; 54,8; 63,16. The fullest passage
is 32,9–35,1. For a discussion of Justin, see von Campenhausen, *Virgin
Birth*, 23-26, 31-32; Delius, *Geschichte*, 52-58; and the appropriate sections in de Aldama, *Maria*.

Mary basically serves a christological and soteriological purpose: Jesus' birth of the virgin is, on the one hand, proof of his messiahship and, on the other, the sign of a new time. While Justin's *Apology* concentrates at several points on a defense of the tradition of a virginal conception (which is a miracle but not incredible in the light of pagan parallels and prophetic predictions[562]), his *Dialogue with Trypho* the Jew adds a new dimension. We find here, perhaps for the first time, the typological parallel between the virgin Eve and the virgin Mary:[563] Eve believed and obeyed the serpent, Mary believed and obeyed the angel. Thus Eve through her disobedience became the mother of sin and death, but Mary through her obedience the mother of the one who destroyed the works of the serpent.

Justin was followed by Irenaeus in this symbolic expansion of Mary's significance; and it was Irenaeus (writing ca. A.D. 180) who spelled out the basis of this typology in the Pauline analogy of Adam and Christ:[564]

> *He [Christ] recapitulated in himself what was shaped of old. As through one man's disobedience sin had gained entrance, and death had obtained power as a result of sin, so through the obedience of one man righteousness was introduced and has caused life to flourish in men previously dead. And as Adam was first made from untilled soil and received his being from virgin earth (since God had not yet sent rain and man had not yet cultivated the ground) and was fashioned by the hand of God (that is, by the Word of God "by whom all things were made" . . .), so he who existed as the Word, recapitulating in himself Adam, received from Mary, who was still a virgin, a birth befitting this recapitulation of Adam.*

For Irenaeus, mariological themes are linked not only to christological concerns in the narrow sense but, as the Eve-Mary

---

[562]Prominent passages among the latter are Isa 11:1; 51:5; 7:14; Mic 5:2; Isa 9:6. See below, nn. 643-44.

[563]*Dialogue*, 100. A reference in the *Epistle to Diognetus* 12.7 is sometimes thought to be the first instance: "Then Eve is not seduced, and the virgin is trusted"; see de Aldama, *Maria*, 265, n. 9. However, the date of the epistle is very uncertain (Altaner, *Patrologie*, 77-78).

[564]*Adversus Haereses* 3.21,10; see 3.22,4; 5.19,1. On Irenaeus in this context, see the studies by Plagnieux, "La doctrine," and Jouassard, "La théologie." Also the sections in de Aldama, *Maria*; Delius, *Geschichte*, 58-63; and von Campenhausen, *Virgin Birth*, 34-44.

typology and the above quotation show, to his total view of salvation history and his theory of "recapitulation." In this context Mary could be seen both as the new Eve and as the person at the threshold of the new humanity, the mother of the new humanity in whom God made a new beginning.

The chords struck in Justin and Irenaeus were soon orchestrated, very likely under the additional influence of the *Protevangelium* whose popularity must have already peaked before the end of the second century. The fathers of the early third century (Clement of Alexandria, Hippolytus, Origen, and Tertullian) carry on the traditions of the preceding century. They already manifest a considerable awareness both of Marian traditions of the kind we found in the *Protevangelium* and of the controversies connected with them. Even the unfriendly references to Mary by the second-century pagan polemicist Celsus, known through Origen's refutation, may well rest (apart from Celsus' possible use of earlier Jewish polemics) on the late second-century expansion of fragmentary NT tradition about Mary. Here are some quotations from Origen's book *Against Celsus*:[565]

> *After this he represents the Jew as having a conversation with Jesus himself and refuting him on many charges, as he thinks: first because he fabricated the story of his birth from a virgin; and he reproaches him because he came from a Jewish village and from a poor country woman who earned her living by spinning. He says that she was driven out by her husband who was a carpenter by trade, as she was convicted of adultery. Then he says that after she had been driven out by her husband and while she was wandering about in a disgraceful way she secretly gave birth to Jesus.*

> *Let us return, however, to the words put into the mouth of the Jew, where the mother of Jesus is described as having been turned out by the carpenter who was betrothed to her, as she had been convicted of adultery and had a child by a certain soldier named Panthera. Let us consider whether those who fabricated the myth that the virgin and Panthera committed adultery and that the carpenter turned her out, were not blind when they concocted all this to get rid of the miraculous conception by the Holy Spirit.*

---

[565]1.28,32,39. English translation (italics omitted) by H. Chadwick, *Origen: Contra Celsum* (Cambridge: University Press, 1953), 28, 31-32, 37-38.

I do not think it worthwhile to combat an argument which he does not put forward seriously, but only as mockery: Then was the mother of Jesus beautiful? And because she was beautiful, did God have intercourse with her, although by nature he cannot love a corruptible body? It is not likely that God would have fallen in love with her since she was neither wealthy nor of royal birth; for nobody knew her, not even her neighbors. It is just ridicule also when he says: When she was hated by the carpenter and turned out, neither divine power nor the gift of persuasion saved her.

In the framework of this chapter we cannot discuss these patristic Marian developments in detail. However, in analyzing the growth of Marian symbolism in the second century, we shall have to come back to the patristic writers. They are important witnesses for the state of the tradition in the late second century, if not earlier.

B. The Question of Independent Traditions about Mary

If we approach the Marian texts of the second century with the hope that they reflect additional independent sources for our quest of Mary, the result is disappointing. The noncanonical literature, including the apocrypha, furnishes very little information about Mary which is not paralleled in the NT. Furthermore, as was the case in the NT, Jesus' mother appears almost exclusively in connection with christological discussions and concerns. Even if there was an interest in Mary's person, no substantial, independent memories of her life and of her role in the early church seem to have been available. The few details we learn from sources outside the NT seem to rest on hearsay, oral tradition, or theological speculation and were beyond verification even for the early generations.

On the other hand, in the second century, the canonical texts themselves proved open to interpretive developments under the impact of new emphases in Christianity, of polemical arguments of one group against another (docetists, Gnostics, Judaizers), and finally of the influence of allegory and typology on biblical texts.

The growing ascetic and encratitic[566] tendencies in the churches everywhere prepared the way for a new, independent Marian emphasis.[567] The virginal mother of Jesus became here the idealized model of the holy and perfect life of purity. But even in circles which embraced the new direction we do not yet find a consistent, developed mariology. In addition, much of the development took place outside the mainstream of Christianity, for many of the writings discussed in the preceding section had their origin or use in groups which the church rejected. Some writings, declared heretical by one group, were valued highly by another. They all reflected in one way or another the interests of a special group at a particular time, and it should not surprise us to find conflicting interpretations and rival traditions.

1. Mary's Background and Status

The most recent research on the *Protevangelium of James*[568] has confirmed the view that this writing is no exception in giving us no new information about the "Mary of history." While its author probably wrote from within the church, it is easy to detect an apologetic interest which he shares with other writers of the period. Mary for him is the honored model of the pure virginal life which he extols as the will of God for his hearers. Thus, Mary's biography becomes the vehicle for a specific emphasis in the author's theology. The story is based upon the canonical Gospels, especially the Matthean and Lucan birth narratives. The additions and changes have the character of hagiographic amplification. The author freely supplies dramatic detail as a means of

---

[566]This movement stressed celibacy over against sexual relations and marriage.

[567]Together with a pre-theological interest in a mother figure, P. Rusch stresses asceticism as the second important root of the mariological development: "Mariologische Wertungen." For the importance of Syria in this context, see A. Hamman, "Le *Sitz im Leben* des actes apocryphes du Nouveau Testament" (Studia patristica, 8; TU 93; Berlin: Akademie, 1966), 62-69.

[568]See above, n. 546; also in the bibliography the works on the *Protevangelium* by Cothenet, de Aldama, de Strycker, Smid, and van Stempvoort.

enlivening the story, drawing "not upon new historical research but solely on his vivid imagination."[569] This does not mean that individual traits in the *Protevangelium* could not reflect independent traditions, particularly when they are at variance with the biblical evidence. However, at closer scrutiny the chances are slim, as we see when we study two major Marian references which have been thought to preserve older tradition.

1. The names of Mary's parents: Joachim and Anne/Anna (1-5). These names passed without rival into all later references to Mary's family. Both names have a background in the LXX and may well have been borrowed from there: Joachim from Susanna 4; Anna (Hannah) from 1 Sam 1-2; Tob 1:9, 20. If one considers the laws of hagiography where the naming of the nameless is a common feature, the historical reliability of the information remains doubtful, especially when Luke 2 already draws a parallel between Mary and Hannah.

2. The birth of Jesus in a cave near Bethlehem (18:1; 19:1-3; 20:3; 21:3).[570] Since this localization differs from the "manger" of Luke 2:7, 12, 16, it could represent an old rival tradition. The same tradition appears in Justin's *Dialogue* (78.5—perhaps dependent on our text) and later in Origen. However, the manger is mentioned later in the *Protevangelium* (22:2), as the place where Mary hid the baby from Herod's soldiers. The "cave" may have been imagined as a shelter for the flock of the shepherds (Luke 2:8), where the animals were fed at a manger.[571]

Not even the minor instances in which the author deviates from the Synoptic tradition have to be read as reflecting independent sources. For example, when he locates the annunciation in Jerusalem (11:1), he is simply consistent with his general geographical framework which connects all of Mary's early life with that city. One can detect in the *Protevangelium* the traces of numerous popular literary motives which are found in other writings of this genre, e.g., the cosmic silence at the moment of the

---

[569]De Strycker, "Protévangile," 356. See also the methodological remarks in Laurentin, *Court traité*, 169.

[570]For this motif cited from the *Protevangelium*, see Benz, "Die heilige Höhle."

[571]Brown, *Birth*, 401. He mentions the passage in Isa 33:16 (LXX): "He will dwell in a high cave of strong rock."

birth of the savior in 18:2, which appears as an "I-Report" of Joseph. This is reminiscent of the birth of Alexander, the birth of the Bodhisattva, and of Vergil's Fourth Ecologue.[572] In summary, one thing seems clear: The author of the *Protevangelium* betrays no use of significant, independent sources for the life of Mary; seemingly, his principal source was the canonical Gospels.

Besides the "story" of the *Protevangelium*, second-century tradition contains some specific details about Mary's background which must be discussed here. That Mary was a "Galilean" is mentioned in the *Acts of Paul*. This information is surely an inference from the setting of the Lucan annunciation and from the general Gospel information that Jesus came from Nazareth in Galilee.

Even stronger in the second-century literature is the claim that Mary was a Davidid. This seems to be already implied in Ignatius (especially *Eph.* 18.2);[573] and it is clear in the *Protevangelium* 10:1, in Justin, Irenaeus, the *Ascension of Isaiah*, and *3 Corinthians*. Of course, the NT indicates that Jesus himself was a Davidid,[574] and "relatives of the Lord" were reportedly accused as Davidic royal pretenders before the Emperor Domitian.[575] Most likely, however, any historical claim to Davidic descent came through Joseph (Matt 1:20; Luke 1:27). Tatian's *Diatessaron*, in reference to Luke 2:4, seems to have claimed that both Joseph and Mary were of Davidic descent.[576] The NT never specifies that Mary is a Davidid,[577] and the second-century attribution of Davidic ancestry to Mary is generally connected with the title "virgin" (and thus perhaps with the Davidic passage in

---

[572]See Smid, *Protevangelium*, 127-28. On the other hand, van Stempvoort and Cothenet stress the Jewish haggadic material here and elsewhere. The reference to cosmic silence is often regarded as an interpolation, for the early papyrus text, Bodmer V, does not contain it.

[573]See above, p. 254; also de Aldama, *Maria*, 78-80; W. Bauer, *Leben*, 13-15.

[574]Brown, *Birth*, 505-12.

[575]The story from Hegesippus is found in Eusebius, *History*, 3.19-20.

[576]See *Ephrèm: Commentaire de l'évangile concordant* (ed. J. Leloir; SC 121; Paris: Cerf, 1966), 58-60.

[577]See above, Chap. 6, n. 345.

Isa 7:13-14). In this attribution we may have a theological deduction intended to reconcile Jesus as "David's Son" (Rom 1:3; see above, Chap. 3, A2) with the belief in Jesus' virginal conception. Still another tradition, attested by Origen and Ephraem the Syrian (died A.D. 375), attributes Levitic origin to Mary.[578] It seems obvious that certain christological assumptions about the provenance of the Messiah[579] have shaped these particular genealogical assertions about his mother, and they can claim only theological significance.

The situation is less clear with regard to the details which Celsus, the pagan critic, cites in his anti-Christian polemic, as reported by Origen. Celsus appealed to "a Jew" as his source, and his information could go back in substance before the middle of the second century. For instance, Celsus describes Panthera as the father of Jesus,[580] and "Ben Panthera" (Son of Panthera) appears later as a designation for Jesus in the Talmud.[581] The general charge of an illegitimate birth is repeatedly attested;[582] e.g., the *Acts of Pilate* (2:3) refers to it as a Jewish accusation before Pilate, although we cannot be sure of the date of this section of the *Acts*.[583] Tertullian mentions that Jesus is called "the son of a carpenter or of a prostitute" in pagan polemics,

---

[578]Origen, *Commentary on Romans* 1:5 (*PG*, 14. 850C); *Ephrèm*, 58-60—both authors reject this tradition. See above Chap. 6, nn. 299, 345.

[579]*T. Sim.* 7; *T. Levi* 2:11; *T. Dan* 5:10; *T. Gad* 8:1; and *T. Jos.* 19:11 combine the lines of David (Judah) and Levi to describe Jesus as king and priest. It is not clear whether these passages are Christian interpolations in the *Testaments* or repeat Jewish expectations of two anointed figures (messiahs)—see *JBC* art. 68 §104, and D. Slingerland, *The Testaments of the Twelve Patriarchs: A Critical History of Research* (SBLMS 21; Missoula: Scholars Press, 1977), esp. 45-49.

[580]See above, n. 565; Vagaggini, *Maria*, 47-65. For an interpretation of the tradition of Mary's "poverty," see Vogt, "Ecce Ancilla," 251-56.

[581]*b. Sabb.* 104b; *b. Sanh.* 67a. See Str-B, 1. 36-38; M. Goldstein, *Jesus in the Jewish Tradition* (New York: Macmillan, 1950), 35-39; 118-22 (on Mary).

[582]Brown, *Birth*, 534-42, raises the question of whether it goes back to the NT itself; see above, Chap. 7, A7.

[583]*HSNTA*, 1. 453-54; see above, n. 530.

perhaps referring to Celsus.[584] However, it is likely that such anti-Christian polemics presuppose the Christian claim of a virginal conception to which they oppose a more natural explanation. The very name of Jesus' alleged father, Panthera, has been explained by some scholars as a distortion of the title "parthenos" (virgin).[585] Others derive it from the Greek word for "panther." The name was not uncommon among Roman soldiers at the period;[586] however, to attempt to find behind the Panthera story the "true" circumstances of Jesus' birth is fanciful. It is possible to read the details of Celsus' materials as tendentious distortions of known Christian traditions rather than as reflections of independent sources. His notion of Mary as a poor country woman may rest on the obvious misunderstanding of Nazareth as an unknown Jewish "village." The dismissal of Mary by the carpenter husband because of adultery could reflect the Matthean tradition about the doubt of Joseph. Her wandering about and giving birth to Jesus in a corner recalls the journey to Bethlehem, the cave, and the manger. Thus, while Celsus' report might indeed acquaint us with some themes of early Jewish polemics against Jesus, these polemics may contain little history.

2. Mary during Jesus' Ministry

Little interest seems to be attached in this literature to Mary's role during Jesus' ministry. However, references to the major episodes known from the canonical Gospels are present and yield a certain measure of interpretation and commentary.

One new story appears in the above-quoted fragment (n. 535) of the *Gospel of the Nazareans*.[587] The scope of the brief

---

[584]*De spectaculis* 30.6.

[585]See L. Patterson, "Origin of the Name Panthera," *JTS* 19 (1917-18), 79-80; J. Klausner, *Jesus of Nazareth* (New York: Macmillan, 1953), 24.

[586]See A. Deissmann, "Der Name Panthera," in *Orientalische Studien für Theodor Nöldeke* (ed. C. Bezold; Giessen: Töpelmann, 1906), 871-75.

[587]See above, p. 245. Cf. A. Resch, *Agrapha: Aussercanonische Schriftfragmente* (2d ed.; Leipzig: Hinrichs, 1906), 233-34; J. Jeremias, *Unknown Sayings of Jesus* (2d Eng. ed.; London: SPCK, 1964), 28.

dialogue appears to be the assertion of Jesus' sinlessness, so that he has no need of John's baptism for the forgiveness of sins.[588] As in the Synoptic Gospels, his mother and his brothers appear together. Like the mother in John 2:1-11 and the brothers in John 7:1-9, they urge Jesus to take a step to which he objects. It seems that mother and brothers misunderstand Jesus' true nature,[589] but it is not clear whether a criticism of Mary is intended. The apologetic tendency focused on Christ stands out, and Mary remains a secondary figure. Resch, Jeremias, and others regard the logion as a "tendentious invention"; however, the possibility of an older, independent tradition cannot be totally excluded.

The Wedding at Cana is mentioned in the *Epistula Apostolorum* 5:[590]

> *Then there was a wedding in Cana of Galilee, and he was invited with his mother and his brothers. And he made water into wine.*

The mother and brothers appear here as a group, as hinted in John 2:12.[591] One cannot tell whether they are regarded as among those who do not understand Jesus or as disciples. Irenaeus implies a criticism of Mary and her rashness as found in John 2:4:[592]

> *When Mary pressed on toward the admirable sign of the wine and wanted prematurely to participate in the anticipated cup, the Lord said, repelling her untimely haste: "Woman, what have I to do with you?"*

---

[588]A parallel passage in the pseudo-Cyprian treatise *On Rebaptism* (17) attributes the scene to an apocryphal and otherwise unknown *Praedicatio Pauli*: "You will find [there] Christ, who alone did not in any way sin, and who is said to have been compelled to accept John's baptism almost against his will by his mother Mary. Likewise it is said that, when he was baptized, fire was seen above the water."

[589]The parallel in the preceding footnote makes Mary alone responsible for the pressure inappropriately exerted on Jesus.

[590]*HSNTA*, 1. 193.

[591]See above, Chap. 7, n. 434.

[592]*Adversus Haereses* 3.16,7. A "certain reproach" is admitted by Jouassard, "La théologie," 276. For a milder interpretation in line with other attempts at safeguarding Mary's blamelessness, see de Aldama, *Maria*, 320-24.

Obviously, Irenaeus saw no contradiction between this rebuke and his exalted image of Mary in other passages.

The logion about Jesus' true family (Mark 3:31-35 and par.) had a somewhat surprising and unusual history. Epiphanius of Salamis tells us that some "Ebionites" denied Jesus' humanity on the basis of this text.[593] Indeed, Tertullian already cited such a reading as a "most pervasive argument" of Docetists like Marcion and Apelles who claimed that Jesus denied his carnal birth in this logion. Their logic was that Jesus' rejection of his "mother and brothers" standing outside in favor of a family of disciples inside was a denial that he had a human mother and brothers and thus that he was "born." Tertullian replied:[594]

One could not have announced to him that his mother and brothers were standing outside seeking to see him if there were no mother and brothers.

He stressed in this context that Jesus' mother and his brothers (whom he regards as younger sons of Mary) were not among Jesus' followers, but stand outside as types of unbelief:[595]

There is a figure of the Synagogue in the separated mother, and of the Jews in the unbelieving brothers. In them Israel was outside.

---

[593]*Panarion* 30.14,5: "Again they deny that he is a man, apparently on the basis of the word which the Savior said when he was told: 'Behold, your mother and your brothers are standing outside,' namely, 'Who is my mother and my brothers?' And stretching out his hand toward his disciples, he said: 'These who do the will of my father are my brothers and mother and sisters.' "

[594]*Adversus Marcionem* 4.19,7; cf. *De carne Christi* 7.1.

[595]*De carne Christi* 7.13. Cf. 7.9: "The brothers of the Lord did not believe in him, as it is stated in the gospel issued before Marcion's time. Likewise the mother is not shown to have adhered to him, while Martha and Mary and other (women) enjoyed his close company. In this passage their unbelief finally appears: While Jesus teaches the way of life to those outside who cling to him, those so close were missing. . . ." In 7.13 Tertullian adds a reference to Luke 11:27 as having the same meaning: "In the same manner he replied to that exclamation, not denying the womb and the breasts of the mother but calling those more blessed who hear the word of God."

The *Gospel of Thomas*, Logion 99, has a form of this tradition.[596] Jesus' disciples are now the ones that tell him about his brothers and his mother standing outside. The disciples are addressed in Jesus' logion about his true family and hear the promise that "these are they who shall enter the kingdom of my Father." It seems that the context is Jesus' teaching about discipleship. Logion 101 comes back to the requirements for true disciples by contrasting the hatred of natural parents with the love for the true heavenly parents. The conclusion of this logion suggests that Jesus does reject his earthly mother for his true mother, presumably the Holy Spirit. (As we have seen, the notion of a feminine Holy Spirit as Jesus' mother is found elsewhere.) The rejection of human parents seems underscored once more by Logion 105. Here the one who knows father and mother is called "son of a harlot." One may speculate that this term reflects Jewish or pagan polemics against the birth from a virgin, giving it an interpretation which clarifies why it does not apply to Jesus: Jesus can be the "son of a harlot" only for those who are interested in his natural origins, not for those who know his (and their) true heavenly parents. The Gnostic tone of these interpretations cannot be denied. However, if the *Gospel of Thomas*, Logion 99, reflects older tradition at this point, we may have a trace of an early interpretation which reinforces the more negative tone of Mark 3:31-35 in contrast to Luke 8:19-21.

The presence of Jesus' mother at the cross (cf. John 19:25-27) is not mentioned in the second century except by Tatian in his *Diatessaron*.[597] Nor do we find any reference to a post-resurrectional appearance of Jesus to Mary. Later, Ephraem's commentary on the *Diatessaron* attributes Jesus' appearance to Mary Magdalene at the tomb, as well as the dialogue between her

---

[596]See above, p. 247; Logia 99, 101, 105. For commentary, see J.-E. Ménard, *L'Évangile selon Thomas* (NHS 5; Leiden: Brill, 1975), 198-200. W. Schrage, *Das Verhältnis des Thomas-Evangeliums zur synoptischen Tradition und zu den koptischen Evangelienübersetzungen* (BZNW 29; Berlin: Töpelmann, 1964), 122, 185-89; B. Gärtner, *The Theology of the Gospel of Thomas* (London: Collins, 1961), 137-38; R. McL. Wilson, *Studies in the Gospel of Thomas* (London: Mowbray, 1960), 115-16.

[597]See *Ephrèm* (see above, n. 576), 382.

and Jesus (John 20:15-16), to Jesus' mother.[598] While we have no indication that his correction goes back to Tatian, it is also presupposed in other texts of a later date.[599] In a further development, the Greek *Acts of Thaddaeus*[600] (sixth century) claims Mary's absolute priority in regard to the Easter appearances: "And he appeared first to his mother and the other women."

The second-century sources are equally silent about Mary's residence in Ephesus, which may be an inference drawn from John 19:27 under the assumption that the beloved disciple was John of Ephesus.[601] Even if such a tradition existed later in the fifth century at the time of the Council of Ephesus (A.D. 431), it did not enjoy wide acceptance. Its development belongs in the Middle Ages.[602]

Furthermore, the notion of Mary's assumption into heaven has left no trace in the literature of the third, much less of the second century. M. Jugie, the foremost authority on this question, concluded in his monumental study: "The patristic tradition prior to the Council of Nicea does not furnish us with any witness about the Assumption."[603] The actual development of this tradition must be linked to the expansion of Marian devotion and piety in later centuries. The historical root of this expansion probably lies in the development of Mary's role as the virgin mother of Jesus—a theme of great importance for early christology, and most fruitful for the pursuit of an independent interest in the person of the Mary and its symbolic potential.

---

[598]*Ibid.*, 386-91. See above, Chap. 7, n. 484.

[599]See W. Bauer, *Leben*, 263; and Gianelli, "Témoignages."

[600]*Acta Thaddaei* 6 (*Acta apostolorum apocrypha* [ed. Lipsius-Bonnet; Leipzig: Mendelssohn, 1891], 1. 277).

[601]See Brown, *Gospel*, 2. 923; also above, Chap. 7, n. 465.

[602]See M. Jugie, *La mort et l'assomption de la Sainte Vierge: Etude historico-doctrinale* (Studi e Testi, 114; Vatican City: Bibliotheca Apostolica, 1946), 96-98.

[603]*Ibid.*, 56. For other recent work on the question, see W. Burghardt, *Testimony*; and A. Wenger, *L'Assomption de la Très Sainte Vierge dans la tradition byzantine du VIe au Xe siècle* (Paris: Institut des études byzantines, 1955).

C. The Theme of Mary's Virginity

In contrast to the lack of interest in Mary's role during Jesus' ministry, considerable interest during the second century centers around her conception of Jesus and her giving birth to him. Again, almost all these Marian references seem to have their basis in the canonical material, i.e., the Matthean and Lucan birth narratives. True, there is some evidence in the second century, even in Christian circles, for a belief in the normal generation of Jesus by a human father and a human mother. However, the overwhelming witness is clearly on the side of a virginal conception.

Concerning Jesus' actual *birth*, one line of Christian thought stressed its miraculous aspects: absence of labor pains, or an undefined "appearing" of the child. Another line, reacting to the apparent docetism involved in such miracles, insisted on the reality of Jesus' birth, while stressing at the same time its uniqueness in terms of a preceding virginal conception.

1. Among Jewish Christians and Gnostics

Advocacy of a normal human conception was not restricted to a specific segment of the Christian movement or a specific heresy, as if the virginal conception were a major dividing point in the history of the early church. We mentioned already the Jewish polemical tradition that Mary's child was illegitimate. The motif of Joseph's doubt (Matt 1:19-20) was often interpreted in terms of this possibility.[604] A number of Christians in different camps, however, clearly regarded Joseph as Jesus' natural father. For Irenaeus it was one of the signs of Ebionite heresy to hold to a human generation of Jesus, when God had given a new sign to mankind in his virginal conception.[605] Irenaeus apparently presupposed the polemical character of this Jewish Christian position,

---

[604]See *Protevangelium* 13:1 (*HSNTA*, 1. 381); Justin, *Dialogue* 78.3; *Acts of Pilate* 2:3 (see above nn. 530, 583).

[605]*Adversus Haereses* 5.1,3.

assuming that it had been formulated in antithesis to the tradition of the virginal conception. Some confirmation for this reading may be found in Irenaeus' knowledge that, in Isa 7:14, these Jewish Christians read *neanis* (young woman) rather than *parthenos* (virgin), as did the Jews against whom Justin argued,[606] and that they tried in this way to invalidate the proof from prophecy. However, it is also possible that their position simply reflected the defense of an older tradition against the "new" claims connected with the virginal conception, which they were not ready to accept. The later heresiological tradition indicates a split among the Ebionites: some continued to reject the virginal conception, others accepted it.[607] At the beginning of the third century, Origen still knows of Gentile Christians, though admittedly few, who did not believe that Jesus was conceived by a virgin;[608] and the Sinaitic Syriac New Testament contains textual corrections in Matt 1:16, 21, 25; Luke 2:4, 5, which some would read to imply Joseph's natural fatherhood.[609]

Most Gnostic speculations about Jesus' heavenly descent apparently assume his physical generation from Joseph and Mary. Origen mentions not only Ebionites but also Valentinians as asserting that "Jesus was born of Joseph and Mary."[610] The same position is attributed to Cerinthus, a Gnostic named Justin, and Carpocrates. The manner in which they combined the savior's natural conception with his supernatural origin is illustrated by Irenaeus' report about a group of unnamed Gnostics who "say that Jesus was born of Joseph and Mary and that into him Christ descended, who was from the higher realms, being without flesh and impassible."[611] On the basis of a concept of two

---

[606]*Adversus Haereses* 3.21,1; cf. Justin, *Dialogue* 43.7-8; 67.1; 84.3. For the meaning of the original Hebrew of Isa 7:14, see above, Chap. 5, nn. 193, 194.

[607]Origen, *Contra Celsum* 5.61; Eusebius, *History* 3.27,2-3; Epiphanius, *Panarion* 30.2-3,14,16. See the material in W. Bauer, *Leben*, 30-31.

[608]Origen, *Commentary on Matthew* 16.12 (Matt 20:29-34).

[609]See above, Chap. 5, n. 152; Chap. 6, n. 324; Brown, *Birth*, 62-64, 130, 132, 396-97.

[610]Origen, *Commentary on Titus* (Latin fragment, *PG*, 17. 1304).

[611]Irenaeus, *Adversus Haereses* 3.11,3.

natures, one human, the other divine, the Valentinians established a link between a natural generation and a divine intervention.

While some Gnostics posit a totally human conception and birth of Jesus, others could deny the human birth of Jesus, in agreement with Marcion who held that Christ simply "appeared" as an adult.[612] The latter idea was shared by Cerdo, Saturninus, Basilides, Apelles, and Monoimus.[613] The apocryphal *3 Corinthians* refers to the heterodox opinion that "the Lord is not come in the flesh, nor was he born of Mary."[614] It seems that for such docetists the very thought of the divine Christ being subjected to a human birth was inappropriate. In the third century, the prophet Mani expressed it succinctly:[615]

Far be it from me that I should confess our Lord Jesus Christ to have come down through the natural reproductive organs of a woman. For he himself gives witness that he descended from the bosom of the Father.

The *Gospel of Thomas* uses the logion about Jesus' true family to emphasize Jesus' descent from his heavenly Father and Mother, but it is not possible to decide whether *Thomas* presupposes the Synoptic tradition of Jesus' virginal conception (even if it would reject that tradition as regards Mary). Although the *Gospel of Philip* (above, pp. 245-46)[616] clearly uses the Matthean and Lucan birth accounts, it can speak of Jesus as the offspring of Joseph (73:8) and of Mary (59:6). It denies that Mary conceived without a husband by the Holy Spirit, because the Holy Spirit is

---

[612]See Tertullian, *Adversus Marcionem* 1.15,19; 3.11; 4.7,21.

[613]See the references in von Campenhausen, *Virgin Birth*, 23, n. 3.

[614]See above, p. 249.

[615]Quoted in the *Acta Archelai* 54 (47; GCS 16.80). Cf. Epiphanius on the Manicheans: *Panarion* 66.6,9: "Now their vain labor went so far that they did not admit that the Only-Begotten, the Christ who had come down from the bosom of the Father, was the son of a certain woman named Mary, born of flesh and blood and the other uncleanness of women."

[616]For a commentary, see Wilson, *Gospel of Philip* (above, n. 538), 81-82; J.-E. Ménard, *L'Évangile selon Philippe* (Paris: Letouzey, 1967), 136-37; 150-51; 201-3.

feminine (55:23). It affirms that Jesus was born of a virgin, just as Adam came into being from two virgins, "from the Spirit and the virgin earth" (71:16). However, the Virgin Mother is no longer a human person but a symbol for a heavenly power. (We found a similar idea in one of the fragments from the *Gospel according to the Hebrews*.) Her name is the symbol of the Holy Spirit—Christ's "sister, mother, and companion" (59:6).

If the *Gospel of Philip* is Valentinian, it appears to confirm Origen's report that "Valentinians" regarded Joseph as Jesus' natural father. (It is not clear from Origen whether this group knew of the virginal conception, or, if so, whether they argued against it or interpreted it symbolically.) Irenaeus mentioned Valentinians who maintained that Jesus "passed through Mary as water runs through a tube."[617] There can be little doubt that the formula was intended to interpret the virgin birth. Tertullian characterized one Valentinian position by the formula: *per virginem, non ex virgine* (through the virgin, not from her).[618] Perhaps the Valentinians who accepted the four canonical Gospels also accepted the tradition of the virginal conception, and used such interpretations to explain how the divine Christ was not tainted by the admixture of any human element. We have, in fact, ample patristic evidence for the Valentinian image of "water running through a tube," sometimes enriched by others such as "light passing through a crevice."[619] It seems to have been used elsewhere, too, for instance by the Bardesanites.[620] Irenaeus had already recognized and rejected it as docetic. Yet it must have had a certain appeal in circles interested in the glorification of Mary as the pure virgin, as we shall see.

2. *Among the Patristic Writings*

The vast majority of Christian writers of the later second century seemingly accepted the virginal conception as part of

---

[617]*Adversus Haereses* 1.7,2; cf. 3.11,3.

[618]Tertullian, *De carne Christi* 20.1; cf. 20.2; *De resurrectione carnis* 1; *Adversus Valentinianos* 27. Cf. Pseudo-Tertullian, *Adversus omnes haereses* 4.5 (CCL, 2. 1407).

[619]See W. Bauer, *Leben*, 37-38.

[620]See Adamantius, *De recta in deum fide* 5.9 (GCS 4. 1901), where it is put in the mouth of the Bardesanite Marinus.

their acknowledgment of the Matthean and Lucan Gospels. The fact of this shared belief is attested by the pervasive designation of Mary as "virgin" which reflects Isa 7:14, as quoted in Matt 1:23 (Luke 1:32?). *Epistula Apostolorum 3* explains the title by reference to John 1:13-14: "We believe that *the Word*, which *became flesh* through the (holy) virgin Mary, was carried (conceived) in her womb by the Holy Spirit and was born *not by the lust of flesh but by the will of God*."[621] However, the precise interpretation of the designation "virgin" underwent development during the second century.

VIRGINITAS ANTE PARTUM. The most common emphasis in the references to Mary as "virgin" was her virginity before giving birth, i.e., she conceived Jesus without involvement of a male. This is what the birth narratives in Matthew's and Luke's Gospel imply. However, such a conception need not imply Mary's virginity in giving birth or her perpetual virginity after Jesus' birth. Clarifying this, Tertullian who still rejected any wider interpretation, coined the phrase:[622] *Virgo quantum a viro, non virgo quantum a partu* (virgin in terms of a husband, not virgin in terms of giving birth).

This limited understanding of "virgin" is the only one which can be detected with surety in the early references of the Ignatian letters. In *Eph.* 19.1 Ignatius names "three mysteries of silence" which remained hidden from the ruler of this aeon: Mary's virginity, her giving birth, and the death of the Lord. Since the birth is mentioned separately, the term "virginity" probably refers to the time prior to it.[623] Ignatius clearly turns the idea of birth from a virgin against those who deny Jesus' true humanity, and thus he gives almost more weight to the reality of the birth than to the virginal conception. Compared with a natural generation, the virginal conception could in itself carry docetic overtones, as suggested by the early Jewish and Jewish Christian polemics against

---

[621]*HSNTA*, 1. 192-93.

[622]*De carne Christi* 23.

[623]The term *parthenia* (virginity) in *Eph.* 19.1 has often been read as "a state of virginity." Jerome already quoted Ignatius among the witnesses for Mary's perpetual virginity. However, the context and the biblical use of the term "virginity" in Luke 2:36 for Hannah's virginity before marriage speak against this interpretation. See Aldama, *Maria*, 230-33.

it. But Ignatius saw no contradiction here. For him Jesus' birth from the virgin was already an unquestioned piece of apostolic tradition which he quoted in almost creedal formulations. What he stressed was the paradox of the simultaneous divine and human generation of Jesus the Christ. Both were necessary to fulfill the secret all-embracing plan of God.

The slightly paradoxical anti-docetic use of the virginal conception continued throughout the second century. For this reason Tertullian opposed any extension of Mary's virginity beyond the conception of Jesus. For Tertullian, although the miraculous conception was God's sign to the world that a new spiritual race would be emerging, Jesus' subsequent birth was totally normal. Anything else would be a concession to docetic and Gnostic speculations. It is difficult to detect more than the virginal conception behind the developed use of the titles "chaste virgin" or "holy virgin" found in the poetic passages of the *Sibylline Oracles*.[624] The "holy virgin" may even appear to be nothing less than a mediatrix of grace. But she is a "virgin," as the vessel into whose body the Logos "flew," i.e., virgin before conception. In a similar vein the above-quoted fragment from the end of Book 1 (323), if it is a Marian reference at all, distinguishes between the time when the *damalis* (cow? maid?) will give birth to the Logos

---

[624]See 8:269-70; 357-58. It is not entirely clear that these are Marian references since they may be symbolic allusions to the Church. A similar difficulty surrounds the use of the title in the Abercius inscription (see below, p. 281). For a discussion of these texts, see J. B. Bauer, "Oracula," and de Aldama, "De quibusdam titulis," 130-32. However, most of the development of these titles seems to fall after the second and early third centuries. For instance, the title *theotokos* for Mary, which gained such prominence later, is not clearly attested before the early fourth century—alleged testimonies of Hippolytus and Origen being recognized today as interpolations; see Laurentin, *Court traité*, 170. The idea of Mary's "holiness" which became important in the later discussions about the immaculate conception, is indeed present in the *Protevangelium* in the second century but is spelled out in terms of ritual purity or holiness *for* God. The ethical component remains contested for quite some time; see Jouassard, "Le problème." The title "holy virgin" as such appears first in Hippolytus (*De Christo et antichristo* 4; *Contra haeresim Noeti* 17). Earlier occurrences, including *Epistola Apostolorum* 3, are spurious; cf. de Aldama, "De quibusdam titulis," 132-33.

and the time when the *alochos* (married wife) will give the Logos his name.

VIRGINITAS POST PARTUM, or perpetual virginity. A change occurred with the advance of ascetic and encratitic tendencies.[625] As we have seen already, admiration for the "pure" and "inviolate" virgin Mary prompted the writing of such pieces as the *Protevangelium*, and theological reflection followed suit. A pseudo-Justin treatise from the late second century, *On the Resurrection*,[626] already argued for the necessity of a virginal conception because the son of the virgin was "to destroy the begetting from lawless lust and to prove to· the ruler of this world that God can form a human being without human copulation." In this ascetic climate it is not surprising that the title "virgin" for Mary eventually came to mean more than virgin *ante partum* (virginal conception). For many authors in the third century it included her virginity *post partum*, i.e., perpetual virginity. In the second century, only the *Protevangelium* seems (by implication) to endorse the concept, in line with its overall design. The early creedal statements are still ambiguous on this point. The old Roman creed, e.g., simply says: "Born of the Holy Spirit and the Virgin Mary." But later synods determined *ex Maria semper Virgine* (of Mary Ever-Virgin) as the one and only correct reading of the phrase.[627] When and how the tradition of Mary's perpetual virginity became the dominant corollary of the virgin birth remains difficult to determine. The penetrating analyses of Hugo Koch have shown that it is problematical to read the concept back into Irenaeus, Justin, or Ignatius.[628] A really unambiguous witness is a

---

[625]See above, n. 566.

[626]Frg. 107, lines 89-93; *Fragmente vornicänischer Kirchenväter in den Sacra Parallela* (ed. K. Holl; TU 20/2; Leipzig: Hinrichs, 1899), 39. On this text, see von Campenhausen, *Virgin Birth*, 56-57.

[627]For a discussion of the early creedal formulas, see de Aldama, *Maria*, 7-32, and Carpenter, "The Birth." The first synod in the West that gave a clear rationale for the *semper virgo* interpretation seems to have been Milan in A.D. 391 (see Ambrose, *Epistle* 42.5-7; *PL*, 16. 1125-26; also above, Chap. 4, n. 116).

[628]See his studies, *Adhuc Virgo* and *Virgo Eva*. This does not exclude the possibility that some Irenaeus texts (*Adversus Haereses* 4.55,2; *Demonstratio* 54) can be read as implying her virginity *in* birth, though

(Syriac) pseudo-Justin fragment, attributed today by almost all scholars to a much later period:[629]

> *Justin, one of the authors who were in the days of Augustus and Tiberius and Gaius, wrote in his third discourse: Mary the Galilean, who was the mother of Christ who was crucified in Jerusalem, and not been with a husband; and Joseph did not repudiate her. But Joseph continued in holiness without a wife, he and his five sons by a former wife. And Mary continued without a husband.*

One difficulty facing the assertion of Mary's perpetual virginity is the mention of "brothers" and "sisters" of Jesus in the canonical Gospels and in Paul.[630] In the *Protevangelium*, these brothers and sisters are understood as Joseph's children by a former marriage, i.e., as Jesus' stepbrothers and stepsisters (9:2; 17:1; 18:1). This explanation, which reappears in Clement of Alexandria was soon widely accepted and became *opinio communis* in the Church up to the mid-fourth century. (Jerome replaced it for the West with a different construction based on a reading of "brothers" as "cousins" or other close relatives.) There is, however, no evidence for such an interpretation at an earlier time, and one may doubt the existence of an independent tradition behind the *Protevangelium* at this point, even as we have seen that this work is secondary on most points. Origen, while endorsing the explanation,[631] does not seem to regard it as old. Attributing it to the *Gospel of Peter* and the *Protevangelium*, he admits that the tradition of Jesus' half-brothers is asserted by people eager to preserve Mary's perpetual virginity.

The other difficulty with the concept of Mary's perpetual virginity is the need to assume that Joseph, the "husband" of Mary, never consummated his marriage with her.[632] The litera-

---

the emphasis is christological. Cf. Burghardt, "Western," 121-22; Delius, *Geschichte*, 61.

[629]B. H. Cowper, *Syriac Miscellanies* (London: William & Norgate, 1861), 61.

[630]See above, pp. 41, 65-72; and *HSNTA*, 1. 418-26.

[631]*Commentary on Matthew* 10.17; *Commentary on John* 1.4 (6); *Homily 7 on Luke*.

[632]A Pseudo-Athanasian treatise *De incarnatione contra Apollinarium* 1.4 states it as a generally accepted tradition: "For that they

ture of the second century does not deal with this issue directly, although those who had a docetic or ascetic understanding of Jesus' birth presumably shared this assumption. Origen understood that the assertion of an unconsummated marriage did not have a clear warrant in the canonical writings of the NT, and so he did not argue for it exegetically. He rather considered the argument "appropriate," as the "sane way" of thinking about Mary upon whom the Holy Spirit and the power of the Most High had descended, since it allowed one to say that Mary remained the first fruit of all perpetually chaste women.[633] Tertullian, despite his personal ascetic leanings, uncompromisingly affirmed the contrary: Jesus was virginally conceived, but Joseph and Mary did consummate their marriage, and the "brothers" of Jesus were the fruit of this union.[634] Tertullian probably thought this to be the meaning of the biblical texts. In his anti-docetic and anti-gnostic argument he seems convinced that he is defending the true apostolic tradition against innovation.

We do not know the exact origin of the tradition of Mary's perpetual virginity, although the *Protevangelium* already gives evidence of this idea. This work was influential in the spread of the tradition which was clearly connected with the growing veneration of the virgin, as a prototype of a holy, virginal life of perfection.

VIRGINITAS IN PARTU or a miraculous giving birth to the child. The *Protevangelium* is also the first witness to another amplification of the meaning of the title "virgin" for Mary: the concept of Mary's virginity *in partu*, i.e., her giving birth with her physical organs remaining intact. It is the implication of the

---

remained virgins (*athigeis*) has been witnessed" (*PG*, 26. 1097). The writing belongs at the end of the 4th century. In the West it was Jerome who most fervently advocated an alternative solution in which the "brothers" and "sisters" of Jesus were the children neither of Joseph nor of Mary, thus paving the way for an emphasis on the virginal Joseph. For the patristic development, see the (somewhat apologetic) book by G.-M. Bertrand, *Saint Joseph dans les écrits des pères de saint Justin à saint Pierre Chrysologue* (Paris/Montreal: Fides, 1966).

[633]*Commentary on Matthew* 10.17 (Matt 13:53ff.).

[634]McHugh, *Mother*, 448-50, tries to deny both assertions for Tertullian on the basis of an unconvincing argument from silence.

Salome episode of the *Protevangelium* (19:3-20):[635]

> *The midwife came out of the cave, and Salome met her. And she said to her: "Salome, Salome, I have a new sight to tell you; a virgin has brought forth, a thing which her nature does not allow." And Salome said: "As the Lord my God lives, unless I put (forward) my finger and test her condition, I will not believe that a virgin has brought forth." And Salome went in and made her ready to test her condition. And she cried out saying: "I have tempted the living God. . . ."*

This story, the historical value of which is most uncertain, may have an apologetic purpose. It is quoted at the beginning of the third century by Clement of Alexandria, and often thereafter.[636] Indeed, a number of other sources from the second century may share similar beliefs. These heighten the mystery of Jesus' birth by suggesting a mere "appearance" of the child, without labor pains or an active involvement on the mother's part. The *Protevangelium* itself speaks of a great light which drew back until finally the child appeared (19:2). The account in the *Ascension of Isaiah* is similar.[637] In Joseph's house, with Joseph present, the birth is a painless, mysterious appearance, which leaves the mother "amazed," and outsiders asserting: "She has not given birth; the midwife has not gone up to her, and we have heard no cries of pain." While the story in this form seems to contradict the midwife episode in the *Protevangelium*, it reflects the same tendency to surround the birth itself with mystery and to describe it as a miracle.

One of the most interesting texts in this regard is the passage from the *Acts of Peter* 24 quoted earlier.[638] The context shows

---

[635]*HSNTA*, 1. 385. For a discussion about Ignatius, Irenaeus, and Justin as "witnesses" for Mary's virginity in giving birth, see K. Rahner, "Virginitas in partu," 147-48, n. 39. A good survey of present views of the question may be found in Laurentin, *Court traité*, 177-81.

[636]*Stromata* 7.16 (93.7–94.2); Origen, *Commentary on Matthew* 10.17.

[637]See above, n. 553. For the interpretation, see de Aldama, *Maria*, 204-5; Cothenet, "Marie," 79.

[638]See above, n. 552. On this text, see the extensive commentary by de Aldama, *Maria*, 122-28; also L. Vouaux, *Les actes de Pierre* (Paris: Letouzey, 1922), 367-70.

Simon the magician insisting that Jesus is Joseph's son. Peter's answer consists of a series of prophetic words all of which point to the unique, mysterious character of Jesus' birth. Isaiah 53:8, 53:2; and 7:14 are alluded to; but then follows a more paradoxical saying: "She has given birth and has not given birth." (This particular saying must have had some currency: Clement of Alexandria quotes it in connection with the midwife story from the *Protevangelium*; Tertullian identifies it as an apocryphal word of Ezekiel, which he rejects because of its docetic tendency.[639]) Another prophetic word in the *Acts of Peter* is: "We have neither heard her voice, nor is a midwife come in"—seemingly a quotation from the *Ascension of Isaiah*. However, the absence of a midwife at birth and the absence of labor pains are also part of a description of Mary's giving birth in the 19th *Ode of Solomon* (7-9):[640]

> So the virgin became a mother with great mercies. And she labored and gave birth to a son without pain. . . . She did not require a midwife, since He caused her to give life. She gave birth of her own will as if she were a man.

It is difficult to say under what conditions such a tradition may have started. It belongs clearly in the second century. If the last sentence were meant as a reference to John 1:13, it would support the reading of that verse as a witness to the virginal conception and/or birth. We saw a similar idea in the *Ascension of Isaiah*. The *Acts of Peter* has still another prophecy: "He was not born of the womb of a woman but came down from a heavenly place." In this form, the saying clearly has docetic implications, even though the author may not have understood it this way. If it

---

[639]Clement, *Stromata* 7.16 (95); cf. Epiphanius, *Panarion* 30.30,3; Tertullian, *De carne Christi* 23: "Now we read in Ezekiel about that heifer which 'gave birth and did not give birth.' "

[640]See J. H. Charlesworth, *The Odes of Solomon* (Oxford: Clarendon, 1973), 82. For the date (ca. A.D. 150) see *HSNTA*, 2. 809-10; also Plumpe, "Little-known," 574-77; Charlesworth would date it earlier.

parallels a logion from a (Slavonic) *Baruch* apocryphon[641] ("This is my anointed one, my chosen one; born while the [mother's] womb remained inviolate, he is said to have been born and to have suffered"), the thrust may well be Mary's virginity *in partu*.

Actually, the line between the assertion of a virginity *in partu* and a docetic christology is hard to draw. Some of the sayings just quoted sound very much like the Gnostic and docetic denials of a real birth of Jesus. Even if the expansion of the understanding of Mary as virgin into the concept of her virginity *in partu* arose out of a heightened concern for Mary's honor and purity, as the *Protevangelium* suggests, it could be accepted easily by those who held an unambiguously docetic position. Thus, at the end of the second century, we are confronted with a somewhat paradoxical situation. While the church had tried to refute Docetism for christological reasons, affirming the reality of the virgin birth as a *birth*, it fostered at the same time the glorification of the Virgin Mary for ascetic reasons, allowing an interpretation of the birth in terms of her inviolate virginity and thus introduced a new danger of docetic trends. Tertullian saw the danger. His refusal to endorse Mary's virginity in giving birth and after birth was intended as a continuation of the old battle against those who denied the human nature of the Savior.

D. Other Marian Themes

In the later tradition the expanded understanding of Mary as virgin received new support. We have already mentioned that, with Gregory of Nyssa and Augustine, Luke 1:34 began to be read as indicating a "vow" of perpetual virginity on Mary's part.[642] The idea of perpetual service in the form of a vow by which her mother Anna consecrated Mary to the Lord already underlies Mary's childhood story in *Protevangelium* 4:1. But with the un-

---

[641]Quoted in A. von Harnack, *Geschichte der altchristlichen Literatur bis Eusebius, Teil II: Die Chronologie* (Leipzig: Hinrichs, reprint 1958), 561.

[642]See Chap. 6, n. 242.

folding of Marian piety as a phenomenon which had a momentum of its own, other lines of symbolism developed, as Christians saw Mary's role in the wider context of the divine history of salvation.

Some of these symbolic themes go back to the second century. Justin Martyr's apologetic theology was based to a large extent on the scheme of prophecy and fulfilment. The OT was for him a book of types waiting for their antitypal fulfilment in the story of Jesus. The virginal conception as such was a fact clearly prophesied in Isa 7:14.[643] Beyond this, Jacob's blessing upon Judah (Gen 49:11: "He washes his garment in the blood of the grape") was a prophecy of Jesus' birth of the virgin: He had real blood in his veins, but like the blood of the grape it owed its origin to the power of God alone.[644]

One of Justin's types proved particularly fruitful: the comparison of the "virgin Eve" with the "virgin Mary."[645]

For Eve, being a virgin and incorrupt, conceived the word of the serpent and brought forth disobedience and death. But Mary the virgin, being filled with faith and joy when the angel Gabriel announced to her that the Spirit of the Lord would come upon her . . . answered: "Let it be to me according to your word."

This typology appears only here in Justin; but it may be older, drawing on the Pauline typology of the first and second Adam (Rom 5:12-21). The motif of the second Eve reappears elaborately in Irenaeus in the framework of understanding God's plan of salvation as a precise correspondence between prophecy and fulfilment.[646] Not only is Mary the antitype of Eve, "untying" by her obedience the knot of Eve's disobedience; but Adam, born of the virgin earth, is here paralleled to Christ, born of the Virgin. For Irenaeus such parallels reveal the theological cohesion of God's work of "recapitulation." Mary's role is not exhausted by her

---

[643]*Apology* 1.33; *Dialogue* 68.84.

[644]*Apology* 1.32; *Dialogue* 54.2; 63.2; 76.2.

[645]*Dialogue* 100.5.

[646]*Adversus Haereses* 3.32,1; 22,3-4; cf. 18,7; 21,10; 5.19,1; *Epideixis* 33. For the theme of Eve and Mary, see Koch, *Virgo Eva*; von Campenhausen, *Virgin Birth*, 34-44; Jouassard, "La nouvelle Eve"; Laurentin, *Court traité*, 42-44; de Aldama, *Maria*, 273-93.

giving birth. If Eve cooperated with the devil in bringing death upon mankind, Mary's obedience became the presupposition for the universal redemption and salvation through Christ.

Many other scriptural types which later found a symbolic elaboration in a mariological context cannot be traced in the literature of the second century. For instance, Gen 3:15, the prophecy about the triumph of the "seed of the woman" over the serpent, received an early christological interpretation by Irenaeus: Christ was this seed.[647] But an explicit interpretation of the woman as Mary, or a Marian reading of the second half of the verse as in the Vulgate ("*she* will crush your head") are not attested before the fourth century.[648] Of course, a Marian reference may be implicit in the parallelism between Mary and Eve.

The mariological interpretation of the Song of Songs, in which Mary appears as the bride in conversation with Christ, cannot be traced back to the ancient church. It had its vogue in the Middle Ages, beginning with the twelfth-century commentator, Rupert of Deutz. Even the "bride" title for Mary, which could have been connected with numerous scriptural texts, had a very hesitant early history; and the first clear attestations belong to the fourth century.[649]

We have already discussed the reference to the "woman clothed with the sun" in Revelation 12. Two fourth-century fathers, Epiphanius and Andrew of Caesarea, report that "some" people identified the woman with Mary the mother of Jesus.[650] We do not know to whom they refer, but the reference may not take us back very far behind their own time. Earlier tradition,

---

[647]*Adversus Haereses* 3.23,7; 4.40,3; 5.21,1; cf. Laurentin, "L'Interprétation," 93-97; de Aldama, *Maria*, 295.

[648]See above, Chap. 2, n. 40. For the history of this question, see R. Laurentin, "L'Interprétation." D. J. Unger, *The First-Gospel: Gen. 3:15* (St. Bonaventure, NY: Franciscan Institute, 1954) reads the evidence with an openly admitted apologetic purpose.

[649]See von Campenhausen, *Virgin Birth*, 60, n. 2. The earliest instance seems to be Cyril of Jerusalem, *Catechesis* 12.26. For the various interpretations of the Song of Songs, see F. Ohly, *Hohelied-Studien: Grundzüge einer Geschichte der Hoheliedauslegung des Abendlandes bis um 1200* (Wiesbaden: Steiner, 1958).

[650]See above, Chap. 8, n. 512.

starting with Hippolytus, saw the woman as a figure of the church without making the connection to Mary.[651] Whether, in fact, an ancient tradition existed in which Mary was symbolically identified with the church either in reference to scriptural passages or independently must remain an open question.[652] Several texts from the early third century seem to point in this direction, even though they present no more than a parallelism between Mary and the church. Clement of Alexandria pointed out that each of the two is a virgin and thus undefiled, and each is a mother and thus lovingly affectionate.[653] In a discussion of the creation of Eve, Tertullian explained that God was aware that for Adam, "the sex of Mary and also of the church" would be a blessing; but Tertullian leaves the sequence Eve-Mary-church incomplete.[654] What is meant by the "spotless virgin" in the famous but obscure Abercius inscription from Hierapolis in Phrygia (ca. A.D. 180) is hard to decide:[655]

Having Paul as a companion, everywhere faith led the way and set before me for food the fish from the spring, mighty and pure, whom a spotless virgin caught, and gave this to friends to eat, always having sweet wine and giving the mixed cup with bread.

Both Mary and the church have been suggested, or both together. If the latter interpretation is possible, we would already have a witness for the acceptance of the Mary-church symbolism in the late second century, at least in Asia Minor.

The limits of this book prevent us from pursuing the further growth of these varied traditions. It is already clear that, while the literature of the second century does not show that there had

---

[651]See the texts discussed by Prigent, *Apocalypse*, 3-23.

[652]For a positive answer to this question, see Barré, "Marie"; and the rich book by Müller, *Ecclesia–Maria*. However, note the careful critique in Congar's "Marie." Much more hesitant is von Campenhausen, *Virgin Birth*, 43-44 and nn. 4-6.

[653]*Paidagogos* 1.6 (42.1). However, even here the reference to Mary is not altogether clear.

[654]*Adversus Marcionem* 2.4.

[655]For this English translation and literature, see J. Quasten, *Patrology* (Westminster, Md.: Newman, 1950), 1. 172-73.

been handed down significant Marian traditions independent of the NT accounts, it allows us to trace the origin of many later Marian developments. In the context of a lively, diversified church, the NT texts about Mary, scant as they were, became the starting point of a rich and imaginative unfolding of a new body of doctrine. This doctrine reflected the polemic, devotional, and ethical emphasis of the church of the second century. The history of the mother of Jesus flowed into the history of Marian piety and mariology.

CHAPTER TEN:
CONCLUSIONS
FROM THE STUDY*

At the end of our study of Mary in the NT it is appropriate to state at least the more important conclusions at which we have arrived. The material for our investigation was relatively slight; the mother of Jesus is not frequently mentioned in the NT. And however important the place given to her in some texts (e.g., the Lucan infancy narrative), there are others which speak of her negatively (Mark 3:20-35) or at best neutrally (Gal 4:4). We have refused to find a "high mariology" in the NT by using the argument from silence, i.e., the argument that authors like Mark who do not speak explicitly of the virginal conception are silent about it because they take it for granted. Our assumption throughout has been that the NT portrait of Mary can be derived only from what the texts say or from what they can legitimately be taken to imply.

In estimating the Gospel passages in which Mary appears, we have been aware that later first-century images of Mary, sometimes those favored by a particular evangelist, have been retrojected upon the ministry of Jesus.[656] Although retrojection of this sort is usually positive in tone toward Mary, it need not be.

---

*The first draft of this chapter was composed by M. M. Bourke, and it was discussed in the editorial meeting of March 1978 and in the final plenary session of April 1978.

[656]See above, Chap. 2, B2a, for the problem of relating *Stage Three* of Gospel formation (the view of the evangelist) to *Stage One* (the historical ministry of Jesus).

The negative portrait of Mary in Mark's Gospel does not necessarily show the "true" Mary as opposed to the obedient and
believing Mary of Luke. Mark's preoccupation with emphasizing
the misunderstanding shown towards Jesus by his disciples during the time of his ministry could well have been extended to his
portrayal of Mary.[657] With this *caveat*, we may proceed to a
summary of our conclusions.

(A) The Picture of Mary before the Gospels

Since Mary is mentioned only once in Acts (1:14), it is clear
that Luke was not concerned with exalting her role in the post-
Easter community. Undoubtedly, his placing Mary in that group
of believers is consonant with his portrayal of her in his Gospel;
yet the task force did not regard Acts 1:14 as a Lucan creation but
as a tradition which should be accepted as reliable. Although it is
impossible to establish the time at which Mary's belief began, or
the cause of it, she shared the faith in Jesus of the earliest Christian community. This conclusion has an important bearing on the
way in which Mark's depicting of Mary is to be judged. We have
said that his interest in emphasizing the misunderstanding of
Jesus by his disciples may have extended to his picture of Mary
too. But since she was from the first a member of the post-Easter
community, it is unlikely that her earlier misunderstanding of her
Son is simply a creation of Mark or of the tradition which he
repeats; for it is hard to believe that such a misunderstanding
would have been attributed to the believing mother of the risen
Lord if there had been no basis for such an attribution. The basis
seems to have been that, in fact, she did not follow Jesus about as
a disciple during the ministry.

The only reference to Mary in the earliest NT book which
alludes to her, the letter to the Galatians, is simply to the fact that
the Son of God was "born of a woman" (Gal 4:4). The theological
interest of that statement is christological, pointing to the true
humanity of Jesus. The designation "born of a woman" is found

---

[657]See above, Chap. 4, nn. 97, 101.

in the OT, at Qumran, and in other NT passages simply as the designation of a human being; and we found no other meaning for it in Paul's use. Nor did we find in the other Pauline texts referring to Jesus' origin any indication of an unusual part given to Mary in Jesus' birth, either at the Pauline or the pre-Pauline level.

(B) The Image of Mary in the Infancy Narratives

The infancy narrative of Matthew says little about Mary apart from the virginal conception. In the Gospel of Luke, on the other hand, the evangelist's estimation of Mary is found principally in his infancy narrative. She is hailed by Gabriel as one favored by God (1:28, 30); her response to the angel shows her as the obedient handmaid of the Lord (1:38); Elizabeth calls her "the mother of my Lord" (1:40) and declares her blessed because of what God has done for her (1:42) and because of her faith that the word spoken to her would come to fulfillment (1:45). In the Magnificat Mary acknowledges the greatness of what God has done for her, his lowly handmaid, and predicts that Elizabeth's macarism (beatitude) will be repeated by all generations to come.

The task force did not accept the view that Luke here portrays Mary as the Daughter of Zion or the Ark of the Covenant. But we recognized that he does depict her as the spokeswoman and representative of the Anawim, the poor of Israel, with all the connotations of humble obedience to God and His word implied thereby. Rejecting the view that Luke's narrative was derived from information supplied either directly or indirectly to him by Mary, we saw in his portrait of her the influence of texts from the part of his Gospel dealing with Jesus' ministry, in which the mother of Jesus appears as a faithful hearer of the word of God. The influence of these texts on the infancy narrative was probably reciprocal. Luke's acceptance of the tradition of the virginal conception led him to show Mary as a faithful hearer of the word during Jesus' ministry; conversely, the obedient faith manifested in the ministry texts was retrojected into the infancy narratives where it appears in Luke's editing of his traditions.

This picture of Mary's faith reaching back to the time of

Jesus' conception is importantly supplemented in the birth narrative by Luke's speaking of her pondering the meaning of the things which had taken place (2:19, 51). Her faith does not include clear understanding of all these events, yet because she is the believing handmaid of the Lord, she seeks to penetrate their meaning.

(C) Mary's Role during Jesus' Ministry in the Four Gospels

1. The Synoptics

We have spoken of a "negative portrait" of Mary in the Gospel of Mark. As indicated in Chap. 4A of our study, the principal text which leads to that designation is Mark 3:20-35. We have agreed that the passage is the result of Marcan redaction. By combining into a unit 3:20-21, 22-30, and 31-35, the evangelist has shown that in his estimation Mary at this point stands outside of Jesus' "eschatological family."[658] Although one member of our group felt that Mark had thus blocked later mariological development, the majority opinion was that Mark did not exclude the possibility of Mary's later passing from mere natural relationship with Jesus to membership in his true family. But if Mark did not exclude such a change, he nevertheless gave no indication that it ever took place. His negative view is strengthened in 6:4, where Jesus complains that a prophet is not without honor except in his own country, *among his own relatives*, and in his own house.

The Matthean and Lucan parallels to Mark 3:20-35 (Matt 12:24-50; Luke 8:19-21)[659] give a rather different picture, largely by modification of the Marcan text. Both evangelists have dropped the harsh introduction in Mark 3:20-21. Luke goes further in softening the Marcan picture by eliminating also the

---

[658]One member of the task force suggested that in the pre-Marcan tradition 3:20-21 and 31-35 were already united.

[659]Because of Luke's arrangement of his material, 8:19-21 is parallel only to the latter part of the scene in the other two Gospels (Mark 3:31-35 and Matt 12:46-50).

question of Jesus, "Who are my mother and brothers?" and by transferring the Beelzebul controversy to another place (11:14-23). While both Gospels make clear that a person belongs to the eschatological family of Jesus only if he or she does the will of the heavenly Father (so Matthew) or hears the word of God and does it (so Luke), Mary is not excluded from that family. In fact, when one reads Luke's text in the light of his infancy narrative, it is plain that from the beginning Mary possessed the qualification for entrance into Jesus' family: she was the obedient handmaid of the Lord (1:38). This picture is heightened by a passage peculiar to Luke's Gospel (11:27-28) in which Jesus responds to a woman who declares his mother blessed by saying that those are blessed who hear and keep the word of God. Theoretically, it is possible for that response to be seen as a corrective to the woman's praise of Mary for her motherhood, and some have so interpreted it. However, in light of Luke's positive description of Mary in 8:19-21, it is more likely that Jesus is emphasizing that Mary's chief blessedness lies in her being one who obediently hears the word of God. In line with this, Luke's version of the rejection of Jesus at Nazareth speaks only of a prophet's being unacceptable *in his own country* (4:24), thus eliminating the two negative Marcan phrases that Jesus is without honor *among his own relatives* (omitted also by Matthew), and *in his own house* (retained by Matthew).

Thus, in the Synoptic depiction of Mary during Jesus' ministry, we have a development from the negative estimation of Mark to the positive one of Luke, with Matthew representing the middle term.

2. The Gospel of John

While John sets the Cana story (2:1-11) within the ministry of Jesus, we have entertained the hypothesis that he built upon a story dealing with the pre-ministry period, in which Mary appeared as one who believed in Jesus, at least in him as a wonder-worker. The story as redacted by the evangelist probably retains that belief (cf. 2:3), although for him it is clearly a misunderstanding of Jesus. Jesus dissociates himself from his mother, who does not realize that the work which the Father has given him takes precedence over the claims and interests of his natural family (2:4). But Mary's misunderstanding does not rank her with unbelievers (unlike the case of Jesus' brothers—7:5). She will appear again in the Gospel at the foot of the cross, where she becomes the mother of the beloved disciple, who for the evangelist is the supreme model of Christian faith. Thus the Cana story, both on the traditional and redactional level, places Mary in a less negative light than that in which she appears in the Gospel of Mark, but because of her imperfect faith at Cana she is not comparable to the believing and obedient Mary of Luke's Gospel.

The majority of the task force did not see an Eve-symbolism in Jesus' address to his mother as "Woman," although at least one member accepted it.

(D) Mary's Role at the Foot of the Cross (John 19:25-27)

This episode in John's crucifixion-account is of central importance for the evangelist's view of Mary. This scene which comes after the ministry points to the future, the era of the disciples who will come after Jesus. When we raised the question not only of theological significance but of historicity, we were able to agree only that the latter question cannot be answered with certainty. We recognized the beloved disciple as a historical person who was also the ideal disciple of Jesus, and the witness *par excellence* who guaranteed the validity of the Johannine community's understanding of Jesus. The majority of the task force thought that the primary significance of the scene was that, in giving the beloved disciple to Mary as her son, and Mary to the disciple as his mother, Jesus brought into existence a new community of believing disciples, that same "eschatological family" which appears in the Synoptic Gospels. The brothers of Jesus, as unbelievers, have no part in this family; and John shows no appreciation for the role of James, the "brother of the Lord," in the early church.[660] But Mary, who in the Cana episode had been

---

[660]It is possible that the Gospel's silence on James may indicate an hostility to the type of Christianity with which he was identified.

distinguished from the disciples, now becomes the mother of the disciple *par excellence*, and so becomes herself a model of belief and discipleship.[661] She is thus associated with that Johannine Christianity which in some respects is quite different from the Christianity derived from the witness of Peter and the rest of the Twelve.

Seeing this as the primary symbolism of the episode, most of us did not exclude, but were very hesitant about accepting, a further, secondary symbolism for Mary, whether as the Israel which brings forth Jewish Christianity, Lady Zion, or the new Eve. We were doubtful, to say the least, that any of those symbolisms represents the thought of the evangelist. We did see in John's own symbolic treatment of Jesus' mother an opening made for the process of further Marian symbolizing within the church.

(E) The Virginal Conception

As mentioned above, we rejected the argument from silence in estimating which NT books bear witness to the virginal conception. But outside the infancy narratives of Matthew and Luke, various texts have been proposed as at least implying that Jesus was virginally conceived: Mark 6:3, John 1:13, 6:42, 7:42, and 8:41. Although one member of the task force saw an indirect reference in John 1:13,[662] the majority thought that none of those texts (nor Gal 4:4, as noted above) has anything to do with the virginal conception. We found no reference to this in the NT apart from Matthew and Luke.[663]

1. As Described in the Infancy Narratives

MATTHEW. Not only does Matt 1:18-25 clearly speak of the virginal conception of Jesus, but, in our opinion, this has been

---

[661]Since the beloved disciple is the witness *par excellence* for Johannine Christianity, Mary's being given him as her son may indicate that her faith depends on his witness.

[662]This view accepts the plural reading of the verb, but holds that the evangelist's description of those who have been born of God is dependent upon a pre-gospel tradition of Jesus' being virginally born "of God." See above, Chap. 7, n. 411.

[663]Luke 3:23, though outside the infancy narrative, does indicate virginal conception: Jesus is the son (*as was supposed*) of Joseph.

prepared for by the mention of the four women who appear in the Matthean genealogy of Jesus. Whether the genealogy was composed by Matthew or was part of the tradition which he received, we regard the mention of these four women as Matthew's own work. We think that the most likely reason for his placing them in the genealogy was that each of them had an irregular or extraordinary marital union through which God worked out His purposes. That is the trait which they share in common with Mary. The child Jesus is conceived through the Holy Spirit and thus is the "Son of God." Nevertheless, because of Mary's union with Joseph, the "son of David" who takes the child as his own, Jesus is of the family of David, and so the messianic hopes attached to the house of David are fulfilled. This latter point is of major importance for Matthew, and it is Joseph rather than Mary who is the central figure of Matt 1:18-25. But the virginal conception, which was already in the tradition that Matthew received, is emphasized by the evangelist's addition of the formula citation from Isa 7:14, and by his final redactional touch in 1:25 that Joseph did not "know" Mary until she had borne the child conceived of the Holy Spirit.

The episodes that make up Matthew 2 are composed of traditional and redactional elements which even in their Matthean form can be read so as to suggest nothing unusual about the conception of Jesus. However, it is clear that any such understanding is made impossible by the Matthean narrative in its totality.

LUKE. The task force found in the Lucan narrative an OT annunciation-of-birth pattern which the evangelist followed in his description of the parallel announcements of the births of John the Baptist and of Jesus. Principally because of this pattern, we rejected the view that Luke 1:34-35 is an interpolation into the story of 1:26-38. While Luke is not so clear as Matthew, we considered most probable an interpretation of the Lucan story as the announcement of a virginal conception. We saw in v. 34 no indication of Mary's intention to remain a virgin, or of her understanding that the conception had already taken place when the angel spoke. We took that verse to be rather a literary device for furthering the dialogue, expressed in terms which show Luke's intention to say that the conception was indeed virginal.

While holding that the Matthean narrative may well have been shaped out of existing sources,[664] we found it impossible to assert with confidence that any source was used by Luke, apart from the hymns of the narrative and possibly in his story of the boy Jesus in the temple (2:41-52). Obviously, that does not mean that we think that Luke did not have items of tradition which he used in composing his narrative. We believe that the virginal conception was one such tradition, as indicated by the fact that it is found also in the very dissimilar Matthean narrative.

2. Possible Origins

The task force agreed that both infancy narratives, and especially the Lucan, reflect a christology which finds its earliest expression in such formularies as Rom 1:3-4. Both narratives have moved Jesus' being "constituted" Son of God back from the resurrection, beyond the baptism, to the time of his conception. But such a conclusion does not necessitate a *virginal* conception, and we had to inquire whence that idea was derived.[665] Although one member favored derivation from a putative Hellenistic-Jewish tradition about the virginal conception of Isaac, the majority found that suggestion unconvincing, as well as other proposed derivations from Jewish or pagan sources. Family tradition, coming ultimately from Mary, was also deemed an unsatisfactory explanation. It was suggested that the "catalyst" for the notion might have been that Jesus was born prematurely (i.e., too early after Joseph and Mary came to live together—cf. Matt 1:18), a "fact" which was interpreted by his enemies in terms of his illegitimacy, and by Christians in terms of his having been miraculously conceived. The tenuousness of this hypothesis was acknowledged. The task force agreed that the question of the his-

---

[664]We here use "source" in the technical sense: cf. Brown, *Birth*, 241, n. 9: "An oral or written consecutive narrative or collection of material."

[665]We may note that neither Matthew nor Luke speaks of the pre-existent Son of God who became incarnate, and that John, the only evangelist who does, apparently knows nothing of a virginal conception.

toricity of the virginal conception could not be settled by
historical-critical exegesis, and that one's attitude towards church
tradition on the matter would probably be the decisive force in
determining one's view whether the virginal conception is a
theologoumenon or a literal fact.[666]

In respect to the church tradition of the perpetual virginity of
Mary, we agreed that the intention of Matt 1:25 was to exclude
sexual relations between Joseph and Mary before the birth of
Jesus, so that the verse does not necessarily indicate what took
place afterwards in the marital relationship of Joseph and Mary.
The fact that the NT speaks of the brothers and sisters of Jesus
does not constitute an insuperable barrier to the view that Mary
remained a virgin, but there is no convincing argument from the
NT against the literal meaning of the words "brother" and "sister" when they are used of Jesus' relatives.[667] Here again, as in
the case of the virginal conception, church tradition will be the
determining factor in the view that one takes, with the important
difference that while the tradition of the virginal conception is
based on NT evidence, the doctrine of Mary's perpetual virginity
goes beyond anything said of her in the Scriptures.

(F) The Woman of Revelation 12

With many modern commentators on Revelation, we agreed
that the primary reference of the woman is to the people of
God—both *Israel*, which brings forth the Messiah, and *the
Church*, which relives the experiences of Israel and brings forth
other children in the image of Christ. Whether there is also a
secondary reference to Mary as the mother of the Messiah *in the
intention of the author* is a question the answer to which depends
in large measure on what view one takes of the relation between
the Book of Revelation and the Fourth Gospel. What is certain is

---

[666]Here it may be useful to recall to the attention of the reader the
remarks above in Chap. 2, C1, on pluralism in the NT.

[667]One should keep in mind the problem that Mark 15:40, 47; 16:1
creates for the interpretation of Jesus' "brothers" in Mark 6:3. See
above, Chap. 4C.

that when the former was taken into the canon of Scripture, the possibility was opened of interpreting its imagery of the woman in terms of the mariology of the other canonical books.

(G) After the New Testament

Our investigation of the post-NT literature was confined to that of the second century; the material surveyed was both apocryphal and patristic. We found that in the sources where Mary is mentioned, this is done chiefly in connection with christological questions. Not until the latter part of the century is any independent interest in Mary shown; the principal witness to such interest is the *Protevangelium* of James. In none of the material is there any clear evidence of reliable historical tradition about Mary unrelated to what is said of her in the canonical Gospels. Some of the literature is frankly docetic, and in this connection the Synoptic passage about Jesus' true family (Mark 3:31-35 and parallels) is taken as a denial of his humanity.

The Marian theme with which the second-century literature is mainly concerned is the virginal conception. The vast majority of the references to it are affirmative, although there is a significant amount of dissent. Curiously enough, at times this dissent appears in Gnostic circles: Origen attributes to the Valentinians the view that Jesus was the son of Joseph and Mary, as does Irenaeus. Yet the latter also speaks of Valentinians who maintained the virgin birth in a docetic sense:[668] Jesus "passed through Mary as water runs through a tube," a view against which Tertullian polemicized. Although belief in the virginal conception was widespread, there is no second-century evidence of belief in Mary's remaining a virgin after the birth of Jesus, apart from the implications of the *Protevangelium*. The later development of this doctrine went hand in hand with the ascetic glorification of virginity. The second-century evidence for belief in Mary's virginity *in partu* (miraculous birth), while relatively slight, is more copious than for belief in her perpetual virginity.

---

[668]The *Gospel of Philip* (above, Chap. 9, pp. 245, 270) also combines both views.

Another Marian theme which achieved much popularity in later centuries, the Eve-Mary typology, is already attested in the second century in the writings of Justin Martyr and Irenaeus.

Our study has shown that in the NT and in second-century literature the mother of Jesus was pictured in ways that were not uniform and, in some cases, not harmonious (e.g., Mark's presentation as compared to Luke's; Tertullian's as compared to that in the *Protevangelium*). Nevertheless, we were able to trace some lines of development which were increasingly positive in portraying Mary as a disciple par excellence and as the virgin. In later centuries these positive lines dominated and were greatly enhanced. If the churches today are not in agreement as to how they evaluate Mary, it is not only because they have reached different conclusions about the post-NT developments, but also because they give different emphases to the varied elements in the NT itself. Discussions among the churches may be facilitated by removing confusion about the biblical evidence; and so the task we set for ourselves was to see whether, as a group of scholars from different church backgrounds, we could agree upon a presentation of the NT data about Mary. The reader can judge whether we have achieved our purpose with reasonable accuracy and adequacy.

BIBLIOGRAPHIES

In this volume we have accepted the standard abbreviations used by the *Journal of Biblical Literature* 95 (June 1976), 339-46 and the *Catholic Biblical Quarterly* 38 (July 1976). In addition:

AKG Arbeiten zur Kirchengeschichte

BSFEM *Bulletin de la societé française des études mariales*

GNTG Moulton, J. H., and N. Turner, *Grammar of New Testament Greek* (4 vols.; Edinburgh: Clark, 1908-76).

HSNTA Hennecke, E., and W. Schneemelcher, *New Testament Apocrypha* (2 vols.; Philadelphia: Westminster, 1963-65).

IBNTG Moule, C. F. D., *An Idiom Book of New Testament Greek* (Cambridge: University Press, 1953).

JANT James, M. R., *The Apocryphal New Testament* (rev. ed.; Oxford: Clarendon, 1953).

MS *Marian Studies*

NCB New Century Bible

TCGNT Metzger, B. M., *A Textual Commentary on the Greek New Testament* (New York: United Bible Societies, 1971).

GENERAL BIBLIOGRAPHY

1. General New Testament Works (cited more than once in this volume)

Bultmann, R., *The History of the Synoptic Tradition* (New York: Harper & Row, 1963).

Bultmann, R., *Theology of the New Testament* (2 vols.; New York, Scribners, 1951-55).

Fuller, R. H., *The Foundations of New Testament Christology* (London: Lutterworth, 1965).

Hengel, M., *The Son of God* (Philadelphia: Fortress, 1976).

Jeremias, J., *Jerusalem in the Time of Jesus* (Philadelphia: Fortress, 1969).
Kraeling, E. G. H., *The Four Gospels* (The Clarified New Testament, 1; New York: McGraw-Hill, 1962).
Kümmel, W. G., *Introduction to the New Testament* (rev. ed.; Nashville: Abingdon, 1975).
Robinson, J. A. T., *Redating the New Testament* (Philadelphia: Westminster, 1976).

2. Bibliographies on Mary

Baumeister, E. J., *1949 Booklist of the Marian Library* (Dayton, OH: University of Dayton, 1949).
Besutti, G. M., "Bibliografia mariana 1958-1966," *Marianum* 28 (1966), i*-xx* + 1*-505*.
Besutti, G. M., "Bibliografia mariana 1967-1972," *Marianum* 35 (1973), i*-xvi* + 1*-358*.
Langevin, P.-E., *Bibliographie biblique . . . 1930-1970* (Quebec: Université Laval, 1972), §§ 17556-17759 (pp. 699-706).
Laurentin, R., "Bulletin marial," *RSPT* 46 (1962), 324-75 (and every other year thereafter, sometimes under differing titles; the latest installment appeared in 1976).
Nober, P., "Vita et persona beatae Virginis Mariae," in "Elenchus bibliographicus biblicus," *Bib* 33 (1952), 97*-100*.
Nober, P., "Beata Maria Virgo," in "Elenchus bibliographicus biblicus," *Bib* 34 (1953—).

3. Surveys on Mariology

Benko, S., "An Intellectual History of Changing Protestant Attitudes towards Mariology between 1950 and 1967," *Ephemerides mariologicae* 24 (1974), 211-26.
Carroll, E. A., "A Survey of Recent Mariology," *MS* 18 (1967), 103-21 [and continued in subsequent years].
Carroll, E. A., "Theology on the Virgin Mary: 1966-1975," *TS* 37 (1976), 253-89.
Heath, T. R., "Recent Studies on Our Lady in the New Testament," in St. Thomas Aquinas, *Summa Theologiae* (60 vols.; New York: McGraw-Hill, 1969), 51. 103-10.
Kugelman, R., "Mariology and Recent Biblical Literature," *MS* 18 (1967), 122-34.
Piepkorn, A. C., "Mary's Place within the People of God according to Non-Roman-Catholics," *MS* 18 (1967), 46-83.

4. General Works Pertinent to Mary

Asmussen, H., *Maria, die Mutter Gottes* (Stuttgart: Evangelisches Verlagswerk, 1960).

Balić, C. (ed.), *De mariologia et oecumenismo* (Rome: Academia mariana internationalis, 1962).

Beinert, W., *Heute von Maria reden? Kleine Einführung in die Mariologie* (2d ed.; Freiburg: Herder, 1974).

Benko, S., *Protestants, Catholics and Mary* (Valley Forge, PA: Judson, 1968).

Blinzler, J., *Die Brüder und Schwestern Jesu* (SBS 21; Stuttgart: Katholisches Bibelwerk, 1967).

Boslooper, T., *The Virgin Birth* (Philadelphia: Westminster, 1962).

Brandenburg, A., *Maria in der evangelischen Theologie der Gegenwart* (Paderborn: Bonifacius-Druckerei, 1965).

Brown, R. E., *The Birth of the Messiah: A Commentary on the Infancy Narratives in Matthew and Luke* (Garden City: Doubleday, 1977).

Brown, R. E., "The Meaning of Modern New Testament Studies for an Ecumenical Understanding of Mary," in *Biblical Reflections on Crises Facing the Church* (New York: Paulist, 1975).

Brown, R. E., "The Problem of the Virginal Conception of Jesus," *TS* 33 (1972), 3-34. Cited from the revision in *The Virginal Conception and Bodily Resurrection of Jesus* (New York: Paulist, 1973).

Cole, W. J., "Scripture and the Current Understanding of Mary among American Protestants," *Maria in Sacra Scriptura* (6 vols.; Acta congressus mariologici-mariani in republica Dominicana anno 1965 celebrati; Rome: Academia mariana internationalis, 1967), 6. 95-161.

Craghan, J. F., "The Gospel Witness to Mary's *Ante Partum* Virginity: The Biblical View," *AER* 162 (1970), 361-72.

de Aldama, J. A., *Maria en la patrística de los siglos I y II* (BAC 300; Madrid: Editorial católica, 1970).

Delius, W., *Geschichte der Marienverehrung* (Munich: Reinhardt, 1963).

Dibelius, M., "Jungfrauensohn und Krippenkind: Untersuchungen zur Geburtsgeschichte Jesu im Lukas-Evangelium," in *Botschaft und Geschichte: Gesammelte Aufsätze von Martin Dibelius* (Tübingen: Mohr, 1953; orig., 1932), 1. 1-78.

Edwards, D., *The Virgin Birth in History and Faith* (London: Faber and Faber, 1943).

Fitzmyer, J. A., "The Virginal Conception of Jesus in the New Testament," *TS* 34 (1973), 541-75.

Flanagan, D., "Mary in the Ecumenical Discussion," *ITQ* 40 (1973), 227-49.

Frank, K. S. et al., *Zum Thema Jungfrauengeburt* (Stuttgart: Katholisches Bibelwerk, 1970).

Fuller, R. H., "New Testament Roots to the Theotokos," *MS* 29 (1978), 46-64.

Fuller, R. H., "The Virgin Birth: Historical Fact or Kerygmatic Truth?" *BR* 1 (1956), 1-8.

Graef, H., *Mary: A History of Doctrine and Devotion* (2 vols.; London: Sheed and Ward, 1963).

Greeley, A., *The Mary Myth: On the Femininity of God* (New York: Seabury, 1977).

Jouassard, G., "Marie à travers la patristique: Maternité divine, virginité, sainteté," in *Maria: Etudes sur la Sainte Vierge* (ed. H. du Manoir; Paris: Beauchesne, 1959), 1. 69-157.

Koch, H., *Adhuc Virgo: Mariens Jungfrauschaft und Ehe in der altkirchlichen Überlieferung bis zum Ende des 4. Jahrhunderts* (BHT 1; Tübingen: Mohr [Siebeck], 1929).

Koch, H., *Virgo Eva—Virgo Maria: Neue Untersuchungen über die Lehre von der Jungfrauschaft und der Ehe Mariens in der ältesten Kirche* (AKG 25; Berlin/Leipzig: de Gruyter, 1937).

Langemeyer, B., "Konziliare Mariologie und biblische Typologie: Zum ökumenischen Gespräch über Maria nach dem Konzil," *Catholica* 21 (1967), 295-316.

Laurentin, R., *Court traité sur la Vierge Marie* (5th ed.; Paris: Lethielleux, 1967).

Laurentin, R., "Foi et mythe en théologie mariale," *NRT* 89 (1967), 281-307.

Laurentin, R., *The Question of Mary* (New York: Holt, Rinehart and Winston, 1965).

McHugh, J., *The Mother of Jesus in the New Testament* (Garden City: Doubleday, 1975).

Machen, J. G., *The Virgin Birth of Christ* (New York: Harper, 1930).

Maria in Sacra Scriptura (6 vols.; Acta congressus mariologici-mariani in republica Dominicana anno 1965 celebrati; Rome: Academia mariana internationalis, 1967).

May, E. E., "The Problems of a Biblical Mariology," *MS* 11 (1960), 21-59.

Michl, J., "Die Jungfrauengeburt im Neuen Testament," *Mariologische Studien* 4 (1969), 145-84.

Miegge, G., *The Virgin Mary: The Roman Catholic Doctrine* (Philadelphia: Westminster, 1953).

Miguens, M., *The Virgin Birth: An Evaluation of Scriptural Evidence* (Westminster, MD: Christian Classics, 1975).

Oberman, H. A., *The Virgin Mary in Evangelical Perspective* (Philadelphia: Fortress, 1971).

O'Meara, T. A., *Mary in Protestant and Catholic Theology* (New York: Sheed and Ward, 1966).

Pannenberg, W., "Mary, Redemption and Unity," *US* 24 (1967), 62-68.

Piper, O. A., "The Virgin Birth: The Meaning of the Gospel Accounts," *Int* 18 (1964), 131-48.

Quanbeck, W. A., "Problems of Mariology," *Dialogue on the Way: Protestant Report from Rome on the Vatican Council* (ed. G. A. Lindbeck; Minneapolis: Augsburg, 1965), 175-85.

Räisänen, H., *Die Mutter Jesu im Neuen Testament* (Annales academiae scientiarum fennicae, B/158; Helsinki: Suomalainen Tiedeakatemia, 1969).

Reese, J. M., "The Historical Image of Mary in the New Testament," *MS* 28 (1977), 27-44.

Rusch, P., "Mariologische Wertungen," *ZKT* 85 (1963), 129-61.

Schoonenberg, P., "Ereignis und Geschehen: Einfache Überlegungen zu einigen gegenwärtig diskutierten Fragen," *ZKT* 90 (1968), 1-21.

Söll, G., "Die Anfänge mariologischer Tradition," *Kirche und Überlieferung: Festschrift J. R. Geiselmann* (ed. J. Betz and H. Fries; Freiburg: Herder, 1960), 35-51.

Sträter, P. (ed.), *Katholische Marienkunde* (3d ed.; Paderborn: Schöningh, 1962).

Taylor, V., *The Historical Evidence for the Virgin Birth* (Oxford: Clarendon, 1920).

Thurian, M., *Mary, Mother of All Christians* (New York: Herder and Herder, 1964).

Vallauri, E., "L'esegesi moderna di fronte alla verginità di Maria," *Laurentianum* 14 (1973), 445-80.

von Campenhausen, H., *The Virgin Birth in the Theology of the Ancient Church* (London: SCM, 1964).

Wilkinson, J., "Apologetic Aspects of the Virgin Birth of Jesus Christ," *SJT* 17 (1964), 159-81.

Zahn, T., "Brüder und Vettern Jesu," *Forschungen zur Geschichte des neutestamentlichen Kanons und der altkirchlichen Literatur* (Leipzig: Deichmann, 1900), 6. 225-364.

BIBIBLIOGRAPHY FOR CHAPTERS OF THIS BOOK

Chapter Three: The Birth of Jesus in the Pauline Writings

A. COMMENTARIES, GENERAL WORKS:

Philippians
NCB: R. P. Martin, 1976

Galatians
CNT: P. Bonnard, 1953; HTKNT: F. Mussner, 1974; MeyerK: H. Schlier, 1971.

Romans
HNT: E. Käsemann, 1973; HNTC: C. K. Barrett, 1957; ICC: W. Sanday and A. C. Headlam, 1902; C. E. B. Cranfield, I, 1975; MeyerK: O. Michel, 1963; NICNT: J. Murray, I, II, 1960/65.

O. Kuss, Fascicles 1 and 2, 1957/59 (Ger.).

Fitzmyer, J. A., *Pauline Theology: A Brief Sketch* (Englewood Cliffs, NJ: Prentice Hall, 1967); also in *JBC*, art. 79.

B. SPECIFIC WORKS PERTAINING TO THE BIRTH OF JESUS IN PAUL:

Carman, A. S., "Philo's Doctrine of the Divine Father and the Virgin Mother," *AJT* 9 (1905), 491-518.
Cooke, R. J., *Did Paul Know of the Virgin Birth?* (New York: Macmillan, 1926).
Danell, G. A., "Did St. Paul Know the Tradition about the Virgin Birth?" *ST* 4 (1951), 94-101.
de Roover, E., "La maternité virginale de Marie dans l'interprétation de Gal 4,4," in *Studiorum paulinorum congressus internationalis catholicus 1961* (AnBib 17-18; Rome: Biblical Institute, 1963), 17-37.

Grelot, P., "La naissance d'Isaac et celle de Jésus: Sur une interprétation 'mythologique' de la conception virginale," *NRT* 94 (1972), 462-87, 561-85.

Legault, A., "Saint Paul a-t-il parlé de la maternité virginale?" *ScEccl* 16 (1964), 481-93.

Lightfoot, J. B., "The Brethren of the Lord," *The Epistle of St. Paul to the Galatians with Introduction, Notes, and Dissertations* (Grand Rapids: Zondervan, 1967 reprint; orig., 1865), 252-91.

Robinson, W. C., "A Re-study of the Virgin Birth of Christ," *EvQ* 37 (1965), 198-211, published as a Supplement to the *Columbia Theological Seminary Bulletin* (1966), 1-14.

Robinson, W. C., "The Virgin Birth—A Broader Base," *Christ Today* 17 (1972), 238-40.

Chapter Four: Mary in the Gospel of Mark

A. COMMENTARIES, GENERAL WORKS:

HTKNT: R. Pesch, I, 1976; NTD: E. Schweizer, 1967 [Engl. tr.: *The Good News According to Mark* (Richmond: John Knox, 1970)].

V. Taylor, 1952.

Achtemeier, P. J., *Mark* (Proclamation Commentaries; Philadelphia: Fortress, 1975).

Bundy, W. E., *Jesus and the First Three Gospels: An Introduction to the Synoptic Tradition* (Cambridge: Harvard University, 1955).

Haenchen, E., *Der Weg Jesu: Eine Erklärung des Markus-Evangeliums und der kanonischen Parallelen* (Berlin: Töpelmann, 1966).

B. SPECIFIC WORKS PERTAINING TO MARY OR THE FAMILY OF JESUS IN MARK:

Best, E., "Mark iii.20,21,31-35" *NTS* 22 (1975-76), 309-19.

Crossan, J. D., "Mark and the Relatives of Jesus," *NovT* 15 (1973), 81-113.

Grässer, E., "Jesus in Nazareth," *NTS* 16 (1969-70), 1-23.

Hartmann, G., "Mark 3,20f.," *BZ* 11 (1913), 249-79.

Lambrecht, J., "The Relatives of Jesus in Mark," *NovT* 16 (1974), 241-58.

Lathrop, G. W., *"Who Shall Describe His Origin?" Tradition and Redaction in Mark 6:1-6a* (Dissertation; Nijmegen: Catholic University, 1969).

McArthur, H. K., "Son of Mary," *NovT* 15 (1973), 38-58.

Schroeder, H. H., *Eltern und Kinder in der Verkündigung Jesu: Eine hermeneutische und exegetische Untersuchung* (TF 53; Hamburg: Reich, 1972), esp. 110-24.

Stauffer, E., "Jeschu ben Mirjam: Kontroversgeschichtliche Anmerkungen zu Mk 6:3," in *Neotestamentica et semitica: Studies in Honour of Matthew Black* (ed. E. E. Ellis and M. Wilcox; Edinburgh: Clark, 1969), 119-28.

Wansbrough, H., "Mark iii.21—Was Jesus Out of His Mind?" *NTS* 18 (1971-72), 233-35.

Wenham, D., "The Meaning of Mark iii.21," *NTS* 21 (1974-75), 295-300.

Chapter Five: Mary in the Gospel of Matthew

A. COMMENTARIES, GENERAL WORKS:

AB: W. F. Albright and C. S. Mann, 1971; ICC: W. C. Allen, 1912; NTD: E. Schweizer, 1973 [Engl. tr.: *The Good News According to Matthew* (Atlanta: John Knox, 1975)]; PCB: K. Stendahl, 1962.

Davies, W. D., *The Setting of the Sermon on the Mount* (Cambridge: University Press, 1974).

Didier, M., *L'Evangile selon Matthieu: Rédaction et théologie* (BETL 29; Gembloux: Duculot, 1972).

Kingsbury, J. D., *Matthew: Structure, Christology, Kingdom* (Philadelphia: Fortress, 1975).

Strecker, G., *Der Weg der Gerechtigkeit* (FRLANT 82; 3d ed.; Göttingen: Vandenhoeck & Ruprecht, 1971).

B. SPECIFIC WORKS PERTAINING TO MARY OR THE BIRTH OF JESUS IN MATTHEW:

Bourke, M. M., "The Literary Genus of Matthew 1-2," *CBQ* 22 (1960), 160-75.

Davis, C. T., "The Fulfillment of Creation: A Study of Matthew's Genealogy," *JAAR* 41 (1973), 520-35.

Davis, C. T., "Tradition and Redaction in Matthew 1:18–2:23," *JBL* 90 (1971), 404-21.

Johnson, M. D., *The Purpose of the Biblical Genealogies with Special Reference to the Setting of the Genealogies of Jesus* (SNTSMS 8; Cambridge: University Press, 1969).

Léon-Dufour, X., "L'Annonce à Joseph," *Etudes d'évangile* (Paris: Seuil, 1965), 65-81. From two previous articles: "L'Annonce à Joseph," in *Mélanges bibliques rédigés en l'honneur de André Robert* (Paris: Bloud & Gay, 1957), 39-97; and, "Le juste Joseph," *NRT* 81 (1959), 225-31.

Paul, A., *L'Evangile de l'enfance selon saint Matthieu* (Lire la Bible, 17; Paris: Cerf, 1968).

Soares-Prabhu, G. M., *The Formula Quotations in the Infancy Narrative of Matthew* (AnBib 63; Rome: Biblical Institute, 1976).

Spitta, F., "Die Frauen in der Genealogie des Matthäus," *ZWT* 54 (1912), 1-8.

Stegemann, H., " 'Die des Uria': Zur Bedeutung der Frauennamen in der Genealogie von Matthäus 1, 11-17," in *Tradition und Glaube: Festgabe für K. G. Kuhn* (ed. G. Jeremias et al.; Göttingen: Vandenhoeck & Ruprecht, 1972), 246-76.

Stendahl, K., "*Quis et Unde?* An Analysis of Mt 1-2," in *Judentum, Urchristentum, Kirche: Festschrift für J. Jeremias* (ed. W. Eltester; BZNW 26; Berlin: Töpelmann, 1964), 94-105.

Chapter Six: Mary in the Gospel of Luke and the Acts of the Apostles

A. COMMENTARIES, GENERAL WORKS:

Luke
HNTC: A. R. C. Leaney, 1958; HTKNT: H. Schürmann I, 1969; ICC: A. Plummer, 1922; NCB: E. E. Ellis, 1974, rev. ed.; THKNT: W. Grundmann, 1961.

Danker, F. W., *Jesus and the New Age* (St. Louis: Clayton, 1972).
Schlatter, A., *Das Evangelium des Lukas*, 1931.

Acts
HNT: H. Conzelmann, 1963; MeyerK: E. Haenchen, 1965 (Engl. tr.: 1971).

Conzelmann, H., *The Theology of St. Luke* (New York: Harper & Row, 1960).
Erdmann, G., *Die Vorgeschichten des Lukas- und Matthäus-Evangeliums und Vergils vierte Ekloge* (FRLANT 48; Göttingen: Vandenhoeck & Ruprecht, 1932).

Flender, H., *St Luke: Theologian of Redemptive History* (Philadelphia: Fortress, 1967).

Foakes Jackson, F. J. and K. Lake (eds.), *Beginnings of Christianity* (5 vols.; London: Macmillan, 1920-33).

Marshall, I. H., *Luke: Historian and Theologian* (Grand Rapids: Zondervan, 1970).

Moehring, H. R., "The Census in Luke as an Apologetic Device," in *Studies in the New Testament and Early Christian Literature: Essays in Honor of A. P. Wikgren* (ed. D. E. Aune; NovTSup 33; Leiden: Brill, 1972), 144-60.

Neirynck, F. (ed.), *L'Evangile de Luc: Problèmes littéraires et théologiques* (BETL 32; Gembloux: Duculot, 1973).

Neirynck, F., *L'Evangile de Noël selon S. Luc* (Paris: Pensée catholique, 1960).

Oliver, H. H., "The Lucan Birth Stories and the Purpose of Luke-Acts," *NTS* 10 (1963-64), 202-26.

Sahlin, H., *Der Messias und das Gottesvolk: Studien zur protolukanischen Theologie* (ASNU 12; Uppsala: Almqvist, 1945).

Tatum, W. B., "The Epoch of Israel: Luke i-ii and the Theological Plan of Luke-Acts," *NTS* 13 (1966-67), 184-95.

Taylor, V., "Luke, Gospel of," *IDB*, 3. 180-88.

Turner, N., "The Relation of Luke i and ii to Hebraic Sources and to the Rest of Luke-Acts," *NTS* 2 (1955-56), 100-9.

Winter, P., "The Proto-Source of Luke I," *NovT* 1 (1956), 184-99.

B. SPECIFIC WORKS PERTAINING TO MARY OR THE BIRTH OF JESUS IN LUKE:

Benoit, P., " 'Et toi-même, un glaive te transpercera l'âme!' (Luc 2, 35)," *CBQ* 25 (1963). 251-61. Reprinted in his *Exégèse et théologie* (Paris: Cerf, 1968), 3. 216-27.

Feuillet, A., "L'Épreuve prédite à Marie par le vieillard Siméon (Luc, II 35a)," in *A la Rencontre de Dieu: Mémorial A. Gelin* (Le Puy: Mappus, 1961), 243-63.

Feuillet, A., "Les hommes de bonne volonté ou les hommes que Dieu aime: Note sur la traduction de Luc 2,14b," *Bulletin de l'association Guillaume Budé* 4 (1974), 91-92.

Graystone, G., *Virgin of all Virgins: The Interpretation of Luke 1:34* (Rome: Pio X, 1968).

Krafft, E., "Die Vorgeschichten des Lukas: Eine Frage nach ihrer sachgemässen Interpretation," *Zeit und Geschichte: Dankesgabe an Rudolf Bultmann* (Tübingen: Mohr [Siebeck], 1964), 217-23.

Laurentin, R., *Jésus au Temple: Mystère de Pâques et foi de Marie en Luc 2,48-50* (Paris: Gabalda, 1966).

Laurentin, R., *Structure et théologie de Luc I-II* (Paris: Gabalda, 1957).

Léon-Dufour, X., "L'Annonce," see bibliography for Gospel of Matthew.

Lyonnet, S., "*Chaire kecharitōmenē*," *Bib* 20 (1939), 131-41.

Lyonnet, S., "Le récit de l'annonciation et la maternité divine de la Sainte Vierge," *Ami du Clergé* 66 (1956), 33-48. Partially in English, "St. Luke's Infancy Narrative," in *Word and Mystery* (ed. L. J. O'Donovan; New York: Newman, 1968), 143-54.

Minear, P. S., "Luke's Use of the Birth Stories," in *Studies in Luke-Acts: Essays Presented in Honor of Paul Schubert* (ed. L. E. Keck and J. L. Martyn; Nashville: Abingdon, 1966), 111-30.

Rengstorf, K. H., "Die Weihnachtserzählung des Evangelisten Lukas," in *Stat crux dum volvitur orbis* (ed. G. Hoffmann et al.; Berlin: Lutherisches Verlagshaus, 1959), 15-30.

Schmithals, W., "Die Weihnachtsgeschichte Lukas 2,1-20," in *Festschrift für Ernst Fuchs* (ed. G. Ebeling et al.; Tübingen: Mohr, 1973), 281-97.

Strobel, A., "Der Gruss an Maria (Lc 1,28)," *ZNW* 53 (1962), 86-110.

Van Iersel, B., "The Finding of Jesus in the Temple: Some Observations on the Original Form of Luke ii 41-51a," *NovT* 4 (1960), 161-73.

Vögtle, A., "Offene Fragen zur lukanischen Geburts- und Kindheitsgeschichte," *BibLeb* 11 (1970), 51-67. Reprinted in *Das Evangelium und die Evangelien* (Düsseldorf: Patmos, 1971), 43-56.

Chapter Seven: The Mother of Jesus in the Gospel of John

A. COMMENTARIES, GENERAL WORKS:

AB: R. E. Brown, I, II, 1966/70; HTKNT: R. Schnackenburg, I, II, III, 1965/71/75; MeyerK: R. Bultmann, 1941 [Engl. tr.: *The Gospel of John* (Oxford: Blackwell, 1971)]; NCB: B. Lindars, 1972.

C. K. Barrett, 1956.
E. C. Hoskyns, 1947.
R. H. Strachan (3d ed.), 1941.

Benoit, P. and M.-E. Boismard (eds.), *Synopse des quatre évangiles en français: III. L'Evangile de Jean, Commentaire par M.-E. Boismard et A. Lamouille* (Paris: Cerf, 1977).

Fortna, R. T., *The Gospel of Signs* (SNTSMS 11; Cambridge: University Press, 1970).

Kysar, R., *The Fourth Evangelist and His Gospel* (Minneapolis: Augsburg, 1975).

Nicol, W., *The Sēmeia in the Fourth Gospel* (NovTSup 32; Leiden: Brill, 1972).

Smith, D. M., Jr., *The Composition and Order of the Fourth Gospel: Bultmann's Literary Theory* (New Haven: Yale University, 1965).

Wead, D. W., *The Literary Devices in John's Gospel* (Basel: Reinhardt, 1970).

B. SPECIFIC WORKS PERTAINING TO THE MOTHER OF JESUS IN JOHN:

Braun, F.-M., *The Mother of God's People* (Staten Island: Alba, 1967; French orig., 1954).

Brown, R. E., "Roles of Women in the Fourth Gospel," *TS* 36 (1975), 688-99, esp. 695-99.

Brown, R. E., "The 'Mother of Jesus' in the Fourth Gospel," in *L'Evangile de Jean: Sources, rédaction, théologie* (ed. M. de Jonge; BETL 44; Gembloux: Duculot, 1977), 307-10.

Buck, H. M., "Redactions of the Fourth Gospel and the Mother of Jesus," in *Studies in the New Testament and Early Christian Literature: Essays in Honor of A. P. Wikgren* (ed. D. E. Aune; NovTSup 33; Leiden: Brill, 1972), 17-80.

Collins, R. F., "Mary in the Fourth Gospel: A Decade of Johannine Studies," *Louvain Studies* 3 (1970), 99-142.

Dauer, A., "Das Wort des Gekreuzigten an seine Mutter und den 'Jünger, den er liebte,' " *BZ* 11 (1967), 222-39; 12 (1968), 80-93.

de la Potterie, I., "La parole de Jésus 'Voici ta Mère' et l'accueil du Disciple (Jn 19, 27b)," *Marianum* 36 (1974), 1-39.

Feuillet, A., "The Hour of Jesus and the Sign of Cana," in *Johannine Studies* (Staten Island: Alba, 1964), 17-37; French orig., *ETL* 36 (1960), 5-22.

Feuillet, A., "L'heure de la femme (Jn 16, 21) et l'heure de la Mère de Jésus (Jn 19, 25-27)," *Bib* 47 (1966), 169-84, 361-80, 557-73.

Feuillet, A., "Les adieux de Christ à sa Mère (Jn 19, 25-27) et la maternité spirituelle de Marie," *NRT* 86 (1964), 469-89. Condensed in Engl. tr., *TD* 15 (1967), 37-40.

Rissi, M., "Die Hochzeit in Kana (Joh 2,1-11)," in *Oikonomia: Oscar Cullmann gewidmet* (ed. F. Christ; Hamburg: Reich, 1967), 76-92.

Schnackenburg, R., "On the Origin of the Fourth Gospel," *Jesus and Man's Hope* (2 vols; Pittsburgh: Pittsburgh Theological Seminary; *Perspective 11* [1970]), 1. 223-46, esp. 233-43 (on the beloved disciple).

Zehrer, F., "Das Gespräch Jesu mit seiner Mutter auf der Hochzeit zu Kana (John 2,3f.) im Licht der traditions- und redaktionsgeschichtlichen Forschung," *BLit* 43 (1970), 14-27.

Chapter Eight: The Woman in Revelation 12

A. COMMENTARIES, GENERAL WORKS:

HNTC: G. B. Caird, 1966; HNT: E. Lohmeyer, 1953; H. Kraft, 1974; ICC: R. H. Charles, I, II, 1920; NTD: E. Lohse, 1971.

G. Ladd, 1972.
H. B. Swete, 1907.

Böcher, O., *Die Johannesapokalypse* (Ertäge der Forschung, 41; Darmstadt: Wissenschaftliche Buchgesellschaft, 1975). Excellent bibliography.

Collins, A. Y., *The Combat Myth in the Book of Revelation* (HDR 9; Missoula: Scholars Press, 1976). Excellent bibliography.

Collins, J. J., "Apocalypse: Toward the Morphology of a Genre" (SBLASP 11; Missoula: Scholars Press, 1977), 359-70.

Feuillet, A., *The Apocalypse* (Staten Island, N.Y.: Alba, 1965). A bibliography of older works (112-15).

Frost, S. B., *Old Testament Apocalyptic: Its Origins and Growth* (London: Epworth, 1952).

Goppelt, L., *Theologie des Neuen Testaments* (Göttingen: Vandenhoeck & Ruprecht, 1976), 2. 506-28.

Hanson, P. D., "Apocalypse, Genre," "Apocalypticism," *IDBSup*, 27-34.

Hanson, P. D., *The Dawn of Apocalyptic* (Philadelphia: Fortress, 1975).

Koch, K., *The Rediscovery of Apocalyptic* (SBT 2/22; Naperville: Allenson, 1972).

Minear, P., *I Saw a New Earth: An Introduction to the Visions of the Apocalypse* (Washington: Corpus, 1969).

Rissi, M., *Time and History: A Study on Revelation* (Richmond: John Knox, 1966).

Rowley, H. H., *The Relevance of Apocalyptic* (rev. ed.; New York: Harper & Row, 1946).

Russell, D. S., *The Method and Message of Jewish Apocalyptic* (Philadelphia: Westminster, 1964).

B. SPECIFIC STUDIES PERTAINING TO REVELATION 12:

Bartina, S., "La celeste mujer, enemiga del dragón (Ap. 12)," *Ephemerides mariologicae* 13 (1963), 149-55. (Twelve reasons for a Marian interpretation)

Braun, F.-M., "La femme vêtue de soleil (Apoc XII): État du problème," *Revue thomiste* 55 (1955), 639-69.

Bruns, J. E., "The Contrasted Women of Apocalypse 12 and 17," *CBQ* 26 (1964), 459-63.

Cerfaux, L., "La vision de la femme et du dragon de l'Apocalypse en relation avec le protévangile," *ETL* 31 (1955), 21-33.

Ernst, J., "Die 'himmlische Frau' im 12. Kapitel der Apokalypse," *TGl* 58 (1968), 39-59.

Feuillet, A., "Le Cantique de Cantiques et l'Apocalypse: Etude des deux reminiscences du Cantique dans l'Apocalypse johannique (Apc 3,20 et Cant 5.1-2; Apc 12 et Cant 6,10," *RSR* 49 (1961), 321-53.

Feuillet, A., "The Messiah and His Mother according to Apocalypse XII," in *Johannine Studies* (Staten Island: Alba, 1965), 257-92. French orig., *RB* 66 (1959), 55-86.

Gollinger, H., *Das "Grosse Zeichen" von Apokalypse 12* (SBM 11; Stuttgart: Katholisches Bibelwerk, 1971).

Kassing, A. T., *Die Kirche und Maria: Ihr Verhältnis im 12. Kapitel der Apokalypse* (Düsseldorf: Patmos, 1958).

Le Frois, B., *The Woman Clothed with the Sun (Ap. 12): Individual or Collective?* (Rome: Orbis catholicus, 1954).

Michl, J., "Die Deutung der apokalyptischen Frau in der Gegenwart," *BZ* 3 (1959), 301-9. (Covers the period 1946-57).

Montagnini, F., "Le signe d'Apocalypse 12 à la lumière de la christologie du Nouveau Testament," *NRT* 89 (1967), 401-16.

Prigent, P., *Apocalypse 12: Histoire de l'exégèse* (BGBE 2; Tübingen: Mohr [Siebeck], 1959).

Roets, A., "Een vrouw omkleed met de zon: Maria en kerk in de Apoc. 12," *Collationes brugenses* 8 (1962), 332-60.

Stramare, A., "La donna ravvolta dal sole," *Tabor* 37 (1966), 38-53.

Vögtle, A., "Mythos und Botschaft in Apokalypse 12," in *Tradition und Glaube: Festgabe für K. G. Kuhn* (Göttingen: Vandenhoeck & Ruprecht, 1971), 395-415.

Chapter Nine: Mary in the Literature of the Second Century

A. COLLECTIONS OF TEXTS:

Alvarez Campos, S., *Corpus marianum patristicum* (3 vols.; Burgos: Aldecoa, 1970-74).

Casagrande, D., *Enchiridion marianum biblicum patristicum* (Rome: "Cor Unum," 1974).

Delius, W., *Texte zur Geschichte der Marienverehrung und Marienverkündigung in der Alten Kirche* (KlT 178; 2d ed.; ed. H.-U. Rosenbaum; Berlin: de Gruyter, 1973).

B. NEW TESTAMENT APOCRYPHA:

Bagatti, B., "La verginità di Maria negli apocrifi del II-III secolo," *Marianum* 33 (1971), 281-92.

Bauer, J. B., "Die Messiasmutter in den Oracula Sibyllina," *Marianum* 18 (1956), 118-24.

Bauer, J. B., "Oracula Sibyllina I 323ab," *ZNW* 47 (1956), 284-85.

Bauer, W., *Das Leben Jesu im Zeitalter der neutestamentlichen Apokryphen* (Tübingen: Mohr [Siebeck], 1909).

Benz, E., "Die heilige Höhle in der alten Christenheit und in der östlich-orthodoxen Kirche," *ErJb* 22 (1953), 365-432.

Cothenet, E., "Marie dans les apocryphes," *Maria: Etudes sur la Sainte Vierge* (ed. H. Du Manoir; Paris: Beauchesne, 1961), 6. 71-156.

Cothenet, E., "Protévangile de Jacques," *DBSup* 8 (1972), 1374-83.

de Aldama, J. A., "Il Protevangelio de Santiago y sus problemas," *Ephemerides mariologicae* 12 (1962), 107-30.

de Strycker, E., *La forme la plus ancienne du Protévangile de Jacques* (Subsidia hagiographica, 33; Brussels: Bollandistes, 1961).

de Strycker, E., "Le Protévangile de Jacques: Problèmes critiques et exégétiques," *SE* III/2 (TU 88; Berlin: Akademie, 1964), 343-59.

Gero, S., "The Infancy Gospel of Thomas: A Study of the Textual and Literary Problems," *NovT* 13 (1971), 46-80.

Laurentin, R., "Mythe et dogme dans les apocryphes," *De primordiis cultus mariani: Acta congressus mariologici-mariani in Lusitania anno 1967 celebrati* (Rome: Academia mariana internationalis, 1970), 4. 14-29.

Peretto, L. M., *La mariologia del Protevangelo di Giacomo* (Rome: Angelicum, 1955).

Plumpe, J. C., "Some Little-Known Early Witnesses to Mary's *virginitas in partu*," *TS* 9 (1948), 567-77.

Robinson, J. M. (director), *The Nag Hammadi Library* (New York: Harper & Row, 1978).

Smid, H. R., *Protevangelium Jacobi: A Commentary* (Assen: Van Gorcum, 1975).

van Stempvoort, P. A., "The Protevangelium Jacobi: The Sources of Its Theme and Style and Their Bearing on Its Date," *SE* III/2 (TU 88; Berlin: Akademie, 1964), 410-26.

Vielhauer, P., *Geschichte der urchristlichen Literatur: Einleitung in das Neue Testament, die Apokryphen und die apostolischen Väter* (Berlin: de Gruyter, 1975).

C. PATRISTIC WRITINGS:

Altaner, B., *Patrologie* (7th ed.; Freiburg: Herder, 1966), 120-21.

Barré, H., "Marie et l'Eglise," *BSFEM* 9 (1951), 77-81.

Burghardt, W. J., "Mary in Western Patristic Thought," *Mariology* (ed. J. B. Carol; Milwaukee: Bruce, 1955), 1. 109-55.

Burghardt, W. J., "Mary in Eastern Patristic Thought," *Mariology* (ed. J. B. Carol; Milwaukee: Bruce, 1957), 2. 88-153.

Cignelli, L., *Maria nuova Eva nella patristica greca (sec. II-V)* (Assisi: Porziuncula, 1966).

Congar, Y., "Marie et l'église dans la pensée patristique," *RSPT* 38 (1954), 3-38.

Holstein, H., "Marie et l'église chez les pères anté-nicéens," *BSFEM* 9 (1951), 11-26.

Jouassard, G., "Le problème de la sainteté de Marie chez les pères depuis les origines de la patristique jusqu'au Concile d'Ephèse," *BSFEM* 5 (1947), 13-31.

Jouassard, G., "La nouvelle Eve chez les pères anté-nicéens," *BSFEM* 12 (1954), 35-54.

Jouassard, G., "La théologie mariale de S. Irénée," *L'Immaculée Conception: Actes du VIIe congrès marial national de France: 29 juin—4 juillet 1954: Compte rendu in extenso* (Lyons: Secrétariat du congrès, 1954), 265-76.

Koehler, T., " 'Blessed' from Generation to Generation: Mary in Patristics and the History of the Church," *Seminarium* 27 (1975), 578-606.

Neubert, E., *Marie dans l'église anté-nicéenne* (2d ed.; Paris: Gabalda, 1908).

Ortiz de Urbina, I., "Lo sviluppo della mariologia nella patrologia orientale," *Orientalia christiana periodica* 6 (1940), 40-82.

Plagnieux, J., "La doctrine mariale de S. Irénée," *RevScREl* 44 (1970), 179-89.

Vagaggini, D. C., *Maria nelle opere di Origene* (Orientalia christiana analecta, 131; Rome: Pontificium institutum studiorum orientalium, 1942).

D. SPECIAL MARIAN THEMES:

Burghardt, W. J., *The Testimony of the Patristic Age Concerning Mary's Death* (Westminster, MD: Newman, 1957).

Carpenter, J. J., "The Birth from Holy Spirit and the Virgin in the Old Roman Creed," *JTS* 40 (1939), 31-36.

Clark, A. C., "Born of the Virgin Mary," *The Way* Supp. 25 (1975), 34-45. On *virginitas in partu*.

Craghan, J. F., *Mary: The Virginal Wife and the Married Virgin: The Problematic of Mary's Vow of Virginity* (Rome: Gregorian University, 1967).

de Aldama, J. A., "De quibusdam titulis honorificis Beatae Mariae Virginis collatis in primaeva litteratura christiana," *De primordiis cultus mariani: Acta congressus marilogici-mariani in Lusitania anno 1967 celebrati* (Rome: Academia mariana internationalis, 1970), 2. 125-44.

Gianelli, C., "Témoignages patristiques d'une apparition du Christ résuscité à la Vierge Marie," *Revue des études byzantines* 11 (1933), 106-19.

Laurentin, R., "L'Interprétation de la Genèse 3:15 dans la tradition jusqu'au début du XIIe siècle," *BSFEM* 12 (1954), 77-156.

MacKenzie, J. A. R., "The Theme of Eve and Mary in the Early Church," *The Way* Supp. 25 (1975), 46-57.

Müller, A., *Ecclesia-Maria: Die Einheit Mariens und der Kirche* (Paradosis, 5; 2d ed.; Freiburg: Paulus, 1955).

Rahner, K., "Virginitas in Partu," *Theological Investigations* (Baltimore: Helicon, 1966), 4. 134-62.

Vogt, J., "Ecce ancilla domini: Eine Untersuchung zum sozialen Motiv des antiken Marienbildes," *VC* 23 (1969), 241-63.

INDEX
OF
AUTHORS

This is *not* an index of the discussions of views held by various authors; rather it lists the page on which the reader may find *bibliographical information* about an author's book or article. Where no title follows an author's name, the information on the work cited appears on the indicated page in a footnote. Where an abbreviated title follows an author's name, the information on the work cited appears on the indicated page in the bibliographies which immediately precede this index. Our general policy is to list names containing the prepositions *da, de, van,* and *von* under "d" and "v" respectively.

313

INDEX

OF

MARIAN TOPICS

All the following listings are to be understood *as pertinent to Mary*. It will help to read the entry as if one of the following phrases stood before it: "Mary and the . . .," or "Mary as . . .," or "Mary at . . .," etc. Topics that can be more easily found in the Table of Contents (e.g., Annunciation to Mary, Visitation, Mary in the Book of Revelation) are not included.